Religion and ideology

This reader is one part of an Open University integrated teaching system and the selection is therefore related to other material available to students. It is designed to evoke the critical understanding of students. Opinions expressed in it are not necessarily those of the course team or of the University.

Religion and ideology

A reader edited by
ROBERT BOCOCK *and* KENNETH THOMPSON
at the Open University

Manchester University Press
in association with the Open University

Published by Manchester University Press
Oxford Road, Manchester M13 9PL, UK

British Library cataloguing in publication data

Religion and ideology: a reader.
  1. Religion—Philosophy
  I. Bocock, Robert II. Thompson, Kenneth, *1937*–
  III. Open University
  200'.1   BL51

ISBN 0-7190-1840-4

Printed and bound by Unwin Brothers Ltd.,
The Gresham Press, Old Woking, Surrey GU22 9LH
A Member of the Martins Printing Group

Contents

Preface

This book, along with its companion volumes, Donald J. and Hall S. (eds) *Politics and Ideology*, and Beechey V. and Donald J. (eds) *Subjectivity and Social Relations*, Open University Press, 1985, forms part of the teaching materials for the Open University course, *Beliefs and Ideology*. In preparing this book, we have been greatly helped by the suggestions and assistance of the *Beliefs and Ideology* course team, which included Veronica Beechey, James Donald and Stuart Hall.

Professor John Eldridge, the External Assessor to the course, and Dr Nicholas Abercrombie, Assessor to this part of the course, provided helpful comments. We are also particularly grateful to Tom Hunter and Keith Stribley for their editorial assistance and to Marie Day, Joan Higgs, Carol Johns and Jo Mathieson for their secretarial contribution.

Robert Bocock
Kenneth Thompson   February 1985

Introduction

It is widely appreciated that the study of cultural forms and processes has been greatly stimulated in recent years by a more sophisticated and flexible Marxism than that which existed in the decades of Stalinist orthodoxy. Whereas the older, economistic Marxism relegated religion and other cultural phenomena to the category of mere epiphenomena – part of a superstructure determined by the economic base – recent Marxist-inspired debates about ideology and culture have allowed a higher degree of relative autonomy to such phenomena. The sociology of religion has much to gain from a careful consideration of developments in the analysis of ideology, and in return it has much to offer, particularly by a reappraisal of the light thrown on ideology by the classical sociologists of religion (Durkheim and Weber, featured in Section I(a)) and by some social anthropologists' work on symbolic structures and processes (as exemplified by Evans-Pritchard, Mary Douglas and Clifford Geertz, in Section I(b)).

Classical statements and their development

Durkheim's special contribution to the study of religion as ideology was to show how its symbolic representation corresponds to something socially real (leaving aside any supernatural reference, which cannot be studied sociologically) and yet in an imaginary way. As he puts it, 'if in the midst of these mythologies and theologies we see reality clearly appearing, it is none the less true that it is found there only in an enlarged, transformed and idealized form' (Durkheim, 1915, p. 468). Like Marx, Durkheim made clear that religion and ideology have a social basis, particularly in patterns of social relations and organization, but they also have a degree of autonomy, following certain rules peculiar to culture. In rejecting the crude Marxist historical materialism of his own day, Durkheim had something in common with those present day Marxists who would agree with his statement of the need to avoid producing a theory of religion that was 'a simple restatement of historical materialism' (ibid., p.471).

It was Max Weber, above all, who produced the most sensitive and complex account of the 'elective affinities' between social groups (classes, status groups, occupations, sexes) and sets of beliefs or ideologies (meaning systems, legitimations, theodicies). The contrasts he drew between religious messages that contain theodicies of good fortune for the privileged, and those which contain theodicies that offered compensation to the underprivileged, are still instructive for the sociology of religion. Similarly, his perceptive discussions of the different ideological inclinations of various intellectual strata, provide a link with Marxist insights, such as those of Gramsci on 'organic intellectuals' (the leaders of thought in each class). Like Durkheim, and no doubt Gramsci also, Weber rejected a crudely reductionist explanation of the relation between beliefs/ideologies and material-base/interests. Beliefs and ideologies could not be reduced to a mere function or reflection of material circumstances and interests:

> It is not our thesis that the specific nature of a religion is simply a 'function' of the social situation of the stratum which appears as its characteristic bearer, or that it represents the stratum's 'ideology' or that it is a 'reflection' of the stratum's material or ideal interest situation.
> (Weber, 1969, p.22, and in this volume.)

Nevertheless, Weber was far from falling over into the opposite, idealist, extreme, which would have led to the unsociological conclusion that social relations and social circumstances do not affect beliefs and values. He wanted to arrive at a formulation which would do justice to material circumstances and interests and also to the channelling effects of ideas in determining people's actions:

> Not ideas, but material and ideal interests, directly govern men's conduct. Yet very frequently the 'world images' that have been created by 'ideas' have, like switchmen, determined the tracks along which action has been pushed by the dynamic of interest. 'From what' and 'for what' one wished to be redeemed and, let us not forget, 'could be' redeemed, depended upon one's image of the world.
> (Weber, op. cit., pp.34–4, and in this volume.)

The Marxist tradition for a long time reflected the rather ambiguous and sometimes contradictory accounts of ideology to be found in the various writings of Marx and Engels. In the early writings of the young Marx, which were of a philosophical nature, he considered religion in the context of alienation, a condition giving rise to false consciousness and a systematised pattern of beliefs that he called ideology. In their later historical and political writings, Marx and Engels (especially the latter), tended to explain religious phenomena as directly motivated by class interests. Thus, English religiosity was contrasted, by Engels, with working-class radicalism and bourgeois free-thinking on the Continent, and explained in terms of the greater cunning of the English bourgeoisie in safeguarding their class interests by spreading religion among the workers and pretending to be religious themselves (see the extract from Engels' *Introduction to Socialism: Utopian and Scientific*, on pp. 17–20). This reductionist explanation of ideology as a simple function of class situation and interests is inadequate, as will be made clear in the course of this book, especially in the discussion of 'Religion and social control' in Section II.

Marx's analysis of ideology was potentially much more subtle and suggestive when he avoided the pitfalls of a reductionist class interest theory and focused instead on homologies or parallels between the principles of symbolisation in different ideological spheres (e.g. religion and economics) and related these to principles of structuration in the relevant social formation. However, Marx did not pursue the analysis of symbolisation very far and tended to fall back on the notion of ideas simply being a 'reflection' of the 'real' world. As in the statement in *Capital* that:

The religious world is but the reflex of the real world. And for a society based upon the production of commodities, in which the producers in general enter into social relations with one another by treating their products as commodities and values, whereby they reduce their individual private labour to the standard of homogeneous human labour – for such a society, Christianity with its *cultus* of abstract man, more especially in its bourgeois developments, Protestantism, Deism, etc., is the most fitting form of religion.
(*Capital*, Book 1, quoted in Marx and Engels, *On Religion*, p. 135, and in this volume.)

Recent developments in the analysis of ideology have been concerned with improving explanation of how and why ideology takes a particular form and of how it works. Two important developments are discernible: Firstly, more attention has been given to what Geertz has called 'autonomous process of symbolic formulation', which entails examining ideologies as systems of interacting symbols and the ways in which they provide plausible interpretations of problematic social reality for particular groups (see extracts from Geertz in this book, pp. 76–83). This has led to a greater appreciation of the complexity and variability of symbolic processes, which cannot be differentiated simply in terms of false consciousness versus true consciousness (a subject taken up in Section Ib of this book). Secondly, there is now an awareness of the field of ideology in relation to classes and groups as being one of contestation and a 'lived relationship', not a mechanical process. (This will be evident in Sections II, III and IV.)

Culture, ideology and rationality

Although this book acknowledges that many of the developments in the analysis of ideology have derived from debates within Marxism, it also recognises that many of the classical works on the sociology of religion were implicitly concerned with religion's ideological character and effects. A bridge between these classical studies and recent developments, including the Marxist-inspired debates, is provided by Clifford Geertz's discussions of religion and ideology as cultural systems. Geertz defines culture as 'an historically transmitted pattern of meanings embodied in symbols, a system of inherited conceptions expressed in symbolic forms by means of which men communicate, perpetuate, and develop their knowledge about and attitudes towards life' (C. Geertz, 1966, pp. 3–4; this volume p. 66).

Geertz defines religion as:

... (1) a system of symbols which acts to (2) establish powerful, pervasive, and long-lasting moods and motivations in men by (3) formulating conceptions of a general order of existence and (4) clothing these conceptions with such an aura of factuality that (5) the moods and motivations seem uniquely realistic. (op. cit., p. 4)

Ideology, for its part, refers 'to that part of culture which is actively concerned with the establishment and defence of patterns of belief and value', whilst bearing in mind that 'the patterns of belief and value defended may be, of course, those of a socially subordinate group, as well as those of a socially dominant one, and the "apology" therefore for reform or revolution' (Geertz, this volume, p. 83). The difference between science and ideology as cultural systems is to be sought in the sorts of symbolic strategy for encompassing situations that they respectively represent. 'Where science is the diagnostic, the critical, dimension of culture, ideology is the justificatory, apologetic, one' (Geertz, op. cit.).

Science can itself, however, become part of an ideological system of beliefs and values, as in Comtean positivism, and Stalinist dialectical materialism. In these kinds of belief system science is seen as an alternative set of beliefs and values which can replace those of traditional religions. The notion of 'science' comes to form a central component of such ideologies – that is, science is the measure of all things. On the other hand, some belief systems claim to be sciences, such as astrology, scientology and some forms of meditation. These systems of belief, however, do not welcome critical appraisal of their predictions or techniques, and might be better seen as ideologies rather than sciences. Only complete relativists try to maintain that there is no difference between education into some form of critical rational thinking, and indoctrination, or socialisation into an ideology, such that the notion of an educated public, open to reasoned argument, is virtually meaningless. (See P. Feyerabend, 1975.) Relativists, however, cannot use reasoned arguments to support their view that there is no such thing as science, for they do not accept that rational criteria for assessing such arguments exist.

The problem of whether or not there are thought to be any universal standards of rationality arises in acute form whenever people from the modern West try to understand and explain cultures in which modern forms of 'rationality', as found in sciences and technologies, are absent. An earlier generation of anthropologists, working in the first few decades of the twentieth century, produced mainly descriptive studies of the way of life, including the beliefs and ritual practices, of people living in pre-literate societies. These belief systems, often termed 'primitive religions', 'witchcraft' and 'magic', were explicitly or implicitly compared with modern science. For example, studies were made of the attempts by pre-literate peoples to cure illnesses using magic, or to explain why someone fell ill as the result of the work of witchcraft. A classic of this kind of anthropological research, based upon fieldwork, was that of Evans-Pritchard, as in the selection from his study of Azande witchcraft in this volume.

The work of empirical, field research orientated anthropologists led to many social scientists adopting a relativistic position about other cultures; that is to say, some of them adopted an approach which refused to make judgements, on the basis of modern scientific assumption, about other cultures' values, beliefs and ritual practices, such as those involved in magic and witchcraft. All beliefs, values, rituals and symbols were seen as having some plausibility in their own social settings, and should not be judged by western standards of rationality. Such relativism seemed to be consistent with a broadly liberal, tolerant approach, which many western social scientists accepted. It was challenged by events in Europe, especially with the rise of fascism and Nazism during the economic crises of the early part of the twentieth century. It was all very well to be tolerant of other cultures which were made known to Europeans and Americans by anthropologists; it was quite another matter to be tolerant of the new ideologies which emerged in Europe. The belief systems of tribal groups could be invested with a degree of plausibility by westerners, but not those of fascists, Nazis and racists, by such groups of liberal-minded social scientists. Relativism was found to have its limitations in this period of European and American history.

The effects of these developments are still operating in recent debates about nationality and cultural relativism. For instance, some writers, such as Steven Lukes (1970, in this volume) argue that there are some universal rational criteria which must be used in understanding what members of any society are trying to assert, criteria which include the concept of negation, the laws of identity and non-contradiction, within logic. Lukes holds a position which is influenced by those who thought that social scientists cannot be complete relativists, and he can be seen as an example of someone inclined towards a non-relativist position, but who avoids the simple error of cultural ethnocentrism. Others have taken a less universalistic position about the existence of some basic logical laws and concepts which operate in all cultures, and are more inclined to raise questions about the supposed rational, scientific, ethical and technological superiority of the west at the end of the twentieth century compared with some other cultures. In part, this is held on the grounds that western culture is not a unity, and is full of contradictions which can produce a sense of futility and aimlessness among some groups. (Hirst and Woolley are close to a position of this kind; see the selection from their work in this volume.)

Religion, conflict and legitimation

Some of these cultural contradictions within western capitalist societies have been the subject matter of debates about the role that religion has played in ideological contestation, particularly with regard to the Industrial Revolution in England. This was a subject that attracted the attentions of Weber, Marx and Engels, and also of some French historians who contrasted the revolutionary enthusiasm of their own country with the religious enthusiasm of the English. It was suggested that the channelling of ideological enthusiasm in a religious direction, particularly by Methodism, Evangelicalism and the Sunday school movement, was a crucial distraction in the formation of the English working class. This topic is examined at length in Section II, where we consider some of the various theses that have been put forward on this subject, especially the Halévy thesis (deriving from the French historian of that name) and that of E. P. Thompson in his *The Making of the English Working Class*. The arguments as they relate to the part played by the Sunday schools in this period are considered in the extract from Thomas Walter Laqueur's *Religion and Respectability: Sunday Schools and Working Class Culture 1788–1850*.

Another major area where the contradictions and lack of unity to be found in contemporary western culture appears in sharp focus is in the variations which exist in relationship to religion. Christianity has been the major religion historically in the west, but it is no longer so dominant as perhaps it once was. Sociologists have contributed to the analysis and understanding of the role of religion in modern societies, especially in the emphasis they have given to the social and psychological functions of religion, as distinct from its cognitive beliefs. (Here the work of Durkheim, Marx, Weber and Freud, has been especially significant.) As a cognitive explanatory system, Christianity has appeared weak when compared with the sciences of physics, astronomy, biology and even the social sciences. However, as a symbolic system offering values backed by sacred authority, legitimation to a variety of political views and positions and emotional, therapeutic compensations throughout the life-cycle to those who can find comfort in religious symbolism and rituals, it remains largely unrivalled. Even modern political ideologies such as communism, fascism and national socialism have not achieved the hold over both the collective and the personal lives of people in the ways in which traditional religions, and the more recent forms of religious sectarianism, have achieved in the past and the present. (The ideological potency of such sectarian religious movements is illustrated in the case of Jamaica which is analysed in Section IV.)

In Britain, there is a particular ideological use of some of the symbols of Christianity which is found in the 'civil religion', as it might be called, of the rituals surrounding the monarch and the other members of the Royal Family. It is here that some sociologists and social theorists per-ceive an ideological role for Britain's civil religion in the creation and legitimation of major cultural and political values, especially in the area of gender roles and sexual morality. (See J. Weeks, 1980, in this book.) These cultural values come to appear to be backed up by the sacred authority of the Church, in part because the monarch is Head of the Church of England and of the Church of Scotland, as well as being Head of State. (See R. Bocock, 1985, in this book.) Other sociologists and social theorists do not attach much, if any, weight to the civil religion of Britain in the maintenance of its economic and political structures, seeing the cultus of royalty as not much more than a popular diversion, created and sustained by the mass media, and of no major political or socio-cultural significance. The economic and political structures are seen by these sociologists as being maintained and reproduced by more direct material interests and pressures operating upon different classes. (See B. Turner, 1983, in this book.) It is possible to argue that both of these positions have some plausibility if a distinction is made between the role of civil religion in reproducing patriarchal cultural definitions of gender and sexuality, and the legitimation of capitalism as a mode of production on the one hand, and the actual social and economic processes involved in the re-production of capitalist social relations in the spheres of production and consumption on the other. If such a distinction is made then there is no necessary contradiction between the two broad types of analysis which are represented in Section III – 'Religion as social cement' (in this book).

Conclusion

We are suggesting that, on the one hand, a purely materialistic social theory, which perceives only material interests lying behind ideologies and religions, cannot do justice to the relative autonomy of religious symbolism and values in many societies both in the past and in the world since the end of the Second World War. On the other hand, social theories, in sociology or elsewhere, which treat religious symbolism in isolation from the social formation in which such symbolism is located, fail to acknowledge that religion is part of a wider cultural, economic and political set of relations. In so doing such approaches ignore the 'elective affinity' between a status group or class and a particular road to salvation, and the influence this had on the development of religious symbolism – an influence which whilst it is not fully determining is often important in giving a particular stamp to a religious belief system. In this way, it is possible to see ideological elements in a particular religion, that is, aspects of its belief and value systems which bear the imprint of the classes and status groups which have been its main bearers, or carriers, and in whose interests it may have been modified. But this is a two-way process – the carriers, themselves, are constituted in part by ideology and bear its imprint.

I   THE SOCIOLOGY OF BELIEF
(a) Classical statements

This section provides an introduction to some of the classic statements about the relations between religion and society that have served as an inspiration for subsequent discussions of religion as ideology.

Marx and Engels provided the major inspiration for debates about ideology within both Marxism and sociology. However, their references to religion in this context are relatively unsystematic and brief. In Marx's early philosophical writings, religion is treated as an aspect of alienation and false consciousness. It is described as reflecting the alienating condition of social relations, especially economic relations, and as mystifying or obscuring the real nature of those relations; in other words, it is an imaginary representation which inverts and obscures reality. The ideological effects of religion, according to Marx and Engels, are that it functions as a source of solace and compensation for the deprived and exploited, and for those who do the exploiting or benefit from such relations it serves the function of helping to maintain their social control. This latter view is emphasised in Engels' commentaries on current political events in Britain and in his references to the functions served by Christianity in earlier periods. It is an 'interest theory' of ideology: the form and attraction of an ideology, including religion, is explained in terms of its function in serving class interests, particularly the interests of the dominant class (although it also serves certain psychological functions for the subordinate classes).

However, an interest theory of ideology is not the only one that can be derived from Marx's writings. It is possible to find there elements of a more subtle theory of ideology concerned with disclosing common structuring principles underlying the ideas and practices of different institutions (e.g. religion, economics, politics, the arts etc.), which cause the latter to articulate together as a complex ideological whole. Furthermore, there are grounds for thinking that Marx did not view ideology as a passive reflection of some more real and dynamic entity, but appreciated that it was itself the site of struggle and that it entered into the constitution of social 'subjects' such as classes and institutions.

Weber's work dealt much more directly and extensively with religion than that of Marx and in consequence he was able to present a more elaborate and detailed account of the links between religion and social structures. He rejected the cruder aspects of the interest theory of ideology as applied to religion, stating that the specific nature of a religion was not simply a 'function' or reflection of a social group's material or interest situation. He wished to give due weight to the relative autonomy of religion as a cultural sphere in which symbolic formulations and motivations were intrinsic to that sphere and not simply determined by some other factor, such as economic interests. However, Weber took care not to imply that ideas directly determine the actions of people; he believed with Marx that interests rather than ideas, in conjunction with structural conditions, determine conduct. But Weber emphasised that not only economic interests operate in this way; the relevant interests might, for example, concern the religious standing of the individual. The significance of ideas was that they affected people's perceptions and interpretations of their interests, and so channelled those interests into relevant actions. He examined the different religious ways in which various classes or strata typically seek to interpret their situation, and to adjust to it or adapt it in religious terms; there were 'elective affinities' between the life situation and interests of classes and certain belief systems that they inclined to favour.

Durkheim concentrated his attention on demonstrating that the forms taken by religious beliefs and practices corresponded to certain fundamental principles of social structuration in each society. His analyses are particularly valuable for the light they shed on the ways in which religious and moral beliefs gain their authority, their sacred character, which sets them apart from the mundane world. He explained this in terms of the process by which the sacred symbolises the quintessential forms of the society itself – the transcendent entity which stands above the individual and yet is instilled into the individual consciousness.

For Freud, the last of the major thinkers featured in this section, this process of instilling the individual conscience with social demands and repressions was the root cause of the discontents produced by modern civilisation.

1 K. MARX and F. ENGELS

On religion

From *On Religion* by K. Marx and F. Engels, 1955. Reproduced by permission of the publishers, Foreign Languages Publishing House, Moscow.

1.1 Contribution to the critique of Hegel's philosophy of right
(first published in 1844) – Marx

For Germany the *criticism of religion* is in the main complete, and criticism of religion is the premise of all criticism.

The *profane* existence of error is discredited after its *heavenly oratio pro aris et focis* [speech for the altars and hearths] has been rejected. Man, who looked for a superman in the fantastic reality of heaven and found nothing there but the *reflexion* of himself, will no longer be disposed to find but the *semblance* of himself, the non-human [*Unmensch*] where he seeks and must seek his true reality.

The basis of irreligious criticism is: *Man makes religion,* religion does not make man. In other words, religion is the self-consciousness and self-feeling of man who has either not yet found himself or has already lost himself again. But *man* is no abstract being squatting outside the world. Man is *the world of man,* the state, society. This state, this society, produce religion, *a reversed world-consciousness,* because they are *a reversed world.* Religion is the general theory of that world, its encyclopaedic compendium, its logic in a popular form, its spiritualistic *point d'honneur,* its enthusiasm, its moral sanction, its solemn completion, its universal ground for consolation and justification. It is the *fantastic realization* of the human essence because the *human essence* has no true reality. The struggle against religion is therefore mediately the fight against *the other world,* of which religion is the spiritual *aroma.*

Religious distress is at the same time the *expression* of real distress and the *protest* against real distress. Religion is the sigh of the oppressed creature, the heart of a heartless world, just as it is the spirit of a spiritless situation. It is the *opium* of the people.

The abolition of religion as the *illusory* happiness of the people is required for their *real* happiness. The demand to give up the illusions about its condition is the *demand to give up a condition which needs illusions*. The criticism of religion is therefore *in embryo the criticism of the vale of woe*, the *halo* of which is religion.

Criticism has plucked the imaginary flowers from the chain not so that man will wear the chain without any fantasy or consolation but so that he will shake off the chain and cull the living flower. The criticism of religion disillusions man to make him think and act and shape his reality like a man who has been disillusioned and has come to reason, so that he will revolve round himself and therefore round his true sun. Religion is only the illusory sun which revolves round man as long as he does not revolve round himself.

The task of history, therefore, once the *world beyond the truth* has disappeared, is to establish the *truth of this world*. The immediate *task of philosophy*, which is at the service of history, once the *saintly form* of human self-alienation has been unmasked, is to unmask self-alienation in its *unholy forms*. Thus the criticism of heaven turns into the criticism of the earth, the *criticism of religion* into the *criticism of right* and the *criticism of theology* into the *criticism of politics* [...]

The philosophers have only *interpreted* the world, in various ways; the point, however, is to *change* it.

1.2   **German ideology** (from Chapter 1, written in 1845–6 – Marx and Engels)

... The fact is, therefore: definite persons who are productively active in definite ways enter into definite social and political relations. Empiric observation must in every single case reveal the connection of the social and political organization with production, empirically and without any mystification or speculation. The social organization and the state constantly arise from the life-process of definite individuals, of those individuals not as they or other people imagine them to be, but as they are *really*, i.e., as they act, as they materially produce, consequently as they are active under definite material limitations, provisions and conditions which do not depend on their free will.[1]

The production of notions, ideas and consciousness is from the beginning directly interwoven with the material activity and the material intercourse of human beings, the language of real life. The production of men's ideas, thinking, their spiritual intercourse, here appear as the direct efflux of their material condition. The same applies to spiritual production as represented in the language of politics, laws, morals, religion, metaphysics, etc. of a people. The producers of men's ideas, notions, etc., are men, but real active men as determined by a definite development of

their productive forces and the intercourse corresponding to those productive forces up to its remotest form. Consciousness [*das Bewußtsein*]
can never be anything else but conscious being [*das bewußte Sein*], and
the being of men is their real life-process. If in the whole of ideology men
and their relations appear upside down as in a *camera obscura* this is due
as much to their historical life-process as the inversion of objects on the
retina is due to their immediate physical life-process.

In direct opposition to German philosophy, which comes down from
heaven to earth, here there is ascension from earth to heaven. That means
that we proceed not from what men say, fancy or imagine, nor from men
as they are spoken of, thought, fancied, imagined in order to arrive from
them at men of flesh and blood; we proceed from the really active men
and see the development of the ideological reflexes and echoes of their
real life-process as proceeding from that life-process. Even the nebulous
images in the brain of men are necessary sublimates of their material,
empirically observable, materially preconditioned, life-process. Thus,
morals, religion, metaphysics and other forms of ideology and the forms
of consciousness corresponding to them no longer retain their apparent
independence. They have no history, they have no development, but
men, developing their material production and their material intercourse,
with this, their reality, their thinking and the products of their thinking
also change. It is not consciousness that determines life, but life that
determines consciousness. In the first view one proceeds from consciousness as from the living individuals; in the second, in conformity with real
life, from the real living individuals themselves, considering consciousness only as *their* consciousness.

Consciousness is therefore from the start a product of society, and it
remains such as long as men exist at all. At the beginning consciousness
is of course only consciousness of the *immediate* sensuous surroundings
and consciousness of the limited connection with other persons and
things outside the individual becoming conscious of itself; at the same
time it is consciousness of nature, which at the beginning confronts man
as a completely alien, almighty and unassailable power to which man's
attitude is a purely animal one and to which he submits like a beast; it
is therefore a purely animal consciousness of nature (nature worship).

It is immediately obvious that this nature worship or this definite
attitude to nature is determined by the form of society and conversely.
Here as everywhere the identity of man and nature is so apparent that
the limited attitude of men towards nature conditions their limited
attitude to one another and their limited attitude to one another determines their limited attitude towards nature for the very reason that nature
has yet hardly been modified by history; on the other hand, consciousness

of the necessity of intercourse with surrounding individuals is the beginning of consciousness of living in society at all. This beginning is as animal-like as social life itself at this stage; it is mere herd consciousness, and man is distinguished from the sheep only by his consciousness taking the place of instinct or by his instinct being a conscious one.

1   In the manuscript the following is crossed out: 'The ideas that these individuals have are ideas either of their relation to nature or of their relation to one another or of their own constitution. It is clear that in all these cases these ideas are the conscious expression – true or illusionary – of their real relations and activity, of their production, their intercourse, their social and political organization. The opposite assumption is possible only when besides the spirit of the real materially determined individuals another spirit apart is presupposed. If the conscious expression of the real relations of these individuals is illusory, if in their ideas they turn reality upside down, this again is a result of their limited material activity and their consequent limited social relations.'

1.3 Manifesto of the Communist Party
(Extracts from Chapters II and III, written in 1847–8) –
Marx and Engels

... The charges against communism made from a religious, a philosophical, and, generally, from an ideological standpoint, are not deserving of serious examination.

Does it require deep intuition to comprehend that man's ideas, views and conceptions, in one word, man's consciousness, changes with every change in the conditions of his material existence, in his social relations and in his social life?

What else does the history of ideas prove, than that intellectual production changes its character in proportion as material production is changed? The ruling ideas of each age have ever been the ideas of its ruling class.

When people speak of ideas that revolutionize society, they do but express the fact that within the old society the elements of a new one have been created, and that the dissolution of the old ideas keeps even pace with the dissolution of the old conditions of existence.

When the ancient world was in its last throes, the ancient religions were overcome by Christianity. When Christian ideas succumbed in the eighteenth century to rationalist ideas, feudal society fought its death battle with the then revolutionary bourgeoisie. The ideas of religious liberty and freedom of conscience merely gave expression to the sway of free competition within the domain of knowledge.

'Undoubtedly,' it will be said, 'religious, moral, philosophical and juridical ideas have been modified in the course of historical development.

But religion, morality, philosophy, political science, and law, constantly survived this change.'

'There are, besides, eternal truths, such as Freedom, Justice, etc., that are common to all states of society. But communism abolishes eternal truths, it abolishes all religion, and all morality, instead of constituting them on a new basis; it therefore acts in contradiction to all past historical experience.'

What does this accusation reduce itself to? The history of all past society has consisted in the development of class antagonisms, antagonisms that assumed different forms at different epochs.

But whatever form they may have taken, one fact is common to all past ages, viz., the exploitation of one part of society by the other. No wonder, then, that the social consciousness of past ages, despite all the multiplicity and variety it displays, moves within certain common forms, or general ideas, which cannot completely vanish except with the total disappearance of class antagonisms.

The communist revolution is the most radical rupture with traditional property relations; no wonder that its development involves the most radical rupture with traditional ideas.

... As the parson has ever gone hand in hand with the landlord, so has Clerical Socialism with Feudal Socialism.

Nothing is easier than to give Christian asceticism a Socialist tinge. Has not Christianity declaimed against private property, against marriage, against the State? Has it not preached in the place of these, charity and poverty, celibacy and mortification of the flesh, monastic life and Mother Church? Christian Socialism is but the holy water with which the priest consecrates the heart-burnings of the aristocrat....

1.4 Capital, Book I
(Extracts; first published in 1867) – Marx

... The religious world is but the reflex of the real world. And for a society based upon the production of commodities, in which the producers in general enter into social relations with one another by treating their products as commodities and values, whereby they reduce their individual labour to the standard of homogeneous human labour – for such a society, Christianity with its *cultus* of abstract man, more especially in its bourgeois developments, Protestantism, Deism, &c., is the most fitting form of religion. In the ancient Asiatic and other ancient modes of production, we find that the conversion of products into commodities, and therefore the conversion of men into producers of commodities, holds a subordinate place, which, however, increases in importance as the primitive communities approach nearer and nearer to their dissolution. Trading nations, properly so called, exist in the ancient world only in its interstices, like the gods of Epicurus in the Intermundia, or like Jews in the pores of Polish society. Those ancient social organisms of production are, as compared with bourgeois society, extremely simple and transparent. But they are founded either on the immature development of man individually, who has not yet severed the umbilical cord that unites him with his fellowmen in a primitive tribal community, or upon direct relations of subjection. They can arise and exist only when the development of the productive power of labour has not risen beyond a low stage, and when, therefore, the social relations within the sphere of material life, between man and man, and between man and nature, are correspondingly narrow. This narrowness is reflected in the ancient worship of nature, and in the other elements of the popular religions. The religious reflex of the real world can, in any case, only then finally vanish, when the practical relations of every-day life offer to man none but perfectly intelligible and reasonable relations with regard to his fellowmen and to nature....

1.5 **Anti-Dühring** (written in 1878) – Engels

... All religion ... is nothing but the fantastic reflection in men's minds of those external forces which control their daily life, a reflection in which the terrestrial forces assume the form of supernatural forces. In the beginnings of history it was the forces of nature which were first so reflected and which in the course of further evolution underwent the most manifold and varied personifications among the various people. This early process has been traced back by comparative mythology, at least in the case of the Indo-European peoples, to its origin in the Indian Vedas, and in its further evolution it has been demonstrated in detail among the Indians, Persians, Greeks, Romans, Germans and, so far as material is available, also among the Celts, Lithuanians and Slavs. But it is not long before, side by side with the forces of nature, social forces begin to be active – forces which confront man as equally alien and at first equally inexplicable, dominating him with the same apparent natural necessity as the forces of nature themselves. The fantastic figures, which at first only reflected the mysterious forces of nature, at this point acquire social attributes, become representatives of the forces of history. At a still further stage of evolution, all the natural and social attributes of the numerous gods are transferred to *one* almighty god, who is but a reflection of the abstract man. Such was the origin of monotheism, which was historically the last product of the vulgarized philosophy of the later Greeks and found its incarnation in the exclusively national god of the Jews, Jehovah. In this convenient, handy and universally adaptable form, religion can continue to exist as the immediate, that is, the sentimental form of men's relation to the alien natural and social forces which dominate them, so long as men remain under the control of these forces. However, we have seen repeatedly that in existing bourgeois society men are dominated by the economic conditions created by themselves, by the means of production which they themselves have produced, as if by an alien force. The actual basis of the reflective activity that gives rise to religion therefore continues to exist, and with it the religious reflection itself. And although bourgeois political economy has given a certain insight into the causal connection of this alien domination, this makes no essential difference. Bourgeois economics can neither prevent crises in general, nor protect the individual capitalists from losses, bad debts and bankruptcy, nor secure the individual workers against unemployment and destitution. It is still true that man proposes and God (that is, the alien domination of the capitalist mode of production) disposes. Mere knowledge, even if it went much further and deeper than that of bourgeois economic science, is not enough to bring social forces under the domination of society. What is above all necessary for this, is a social *act*. And when this act has been accomplished, when society, by taking possession of all means of production and using them on a planned basis, has freed itself and all its members from the bondage in which they are now held by these means of production which they themselves have produced but which confront them as an irresistible alien force; when therefore man no longer merely proposes, but also disposes – only then will the last alien force which is still reflected in religion vanish; and with it will also vanish the religious reflection itself, for the simple reason that there will be nothing left to reflect.

1.6 Introduction to the English edition of 'Socialism: Utopian and Scientific' (written in 1892) – Engels

... I have mentioned the fact that, about forty or fifty years ago, any cultivated foreigner settling in England was struck by what he was then bound to consider the religious bigotry and stupidity of the English respectable middle class. I am now going to prove that the respectable English middle class of that time was not quite as stupid as it looked to the intelligent foreigner. Its religious leanings can be explained [...].

Thus, if materialism became the creed of the French Revolution, the God-fearing English bourgeois held all the faster to his religion. Had not the reign of terror in Paris proved what was the upshot, if the religious instincts of the masses were lost? The more materialism spread from France to neighbouring countries, and was reinforced by similar doctrinal currents, notably by German philosophy, the more, in fact, materialism and free thought generally became on the Continent, the necessary qualifications of a cultivated man, the more stubbornly the English middle class stuck to its manifold religious creeds. These creeds might differ from one another, but they were, all of them, distinctly religious, Christian creeds.

While the Revolution ensured the political triumph of the bourgeoisie in France, in England Watt, Arkwright, Cartwright, and others initiated an industrial revolution, which completely shifted the centre of gravity of economic power. The wealth of the bourgeoisie increased considerably faster than that of the landed aristocracy. Within the bourgeoisie itself, the financial aristocracy, the bankers, etc., were more and more pushed into the background by the manufacturers. The compromise of 1689, even after the gradual changes it had undergone in favour of the bourgeoisie, no longer corresponded to the relative position of the parties to it. The character of these parties, too, had changed; the bourgeoisie of 1830 was very different from that of the preceding century. The political power still left to the aristocracy, and used by them to resist the pretensions of the new industrial bourgeoisie, became incompatible with the new economic interests. A fresh struggle with the aristocracy was necessary; it could end only in a victory of the new economic power. First, the Reform Act was pushed through, in spite of all resistance, under the impulse of the French Revolution of 1830. It gave to the bourgeoisie a recognized and powerful place in Parliament. Then the Repeal of the Corn Laws, which settled, once for all, the supremacy of the bourgeoisie, and especially of its most active portion, the manufacturers, over the landed aristocracy. This was the greatest victory of the bourgeoisie; it was, however, also the last it gained in its own exclusive interest. Whatever triumphs it obtained later on, it had to share with a new social power, first its ally, but soon its rival.

The industrial revolution had created a class of large manufacturing capitalists, but also a class – and a far more numerous one – of manufacturing work-people. This class gradually increased in numbers, in proportion as the industrial revolution seized upon one branch of manufacture after another, and in the same proportion it increased in power. This power it proved as early as 1824, by forcing a reluctant Parliament to repeal the acts forbidding combinations of workmen. During the Reform agitation, the working-men constituted the Radical wing of the Reform party; the Act of 1832 having excluded them from the suffrage, they formulated their demands in the People's Charter, and constituted themselves, in opposition to the great bourgeois Anti-Corn Law party, into an independent party, the Chartists, the first working-men's party of modern times.

Then came the Continental revolutions of February and March 1848, in which the working people played such a prominent part, and, at least in Paris, put forward demands which were certainly inadmissible from the point of view of capitalist society. And then came the general reaction. First the defeat of the Chartists on the 10th April, 1848, then the crushing of the Paris working-men's insurrection in June of the same year, then the disasters of 1849 in Italy, Hungary, South Germany, and at last the victory of Louis Bonaparte over Paris, 2nd December, 1851. For a time, at least, the bugbear of working-class pretensions was put down, but at what cost! If the British bourgeois had been convinced before of the necessity of maintaining the common people in a religious mood, how much more must he feel that necessity after all these experiences? Regardless of the sneers of his Continental compeers, he continued to spend thousands and tens of thousands, year after year, upon the evangelization of the lower orders; not content with his own native religious machinery, he appealed to Brother Jonathan, the greatest organizer in existence of religion as a trade, and imported from America revivalism, Moody and Sankey, and the like; and, finally, he accepted the dangerous aid of the Salvation Army, which revives the propaganda of early Christianity, appeals to the poor as the elect, fights capitalism in a religious way, and thus fosters an element of early Christian class antagonism, which one day may become troublesome to the well-to-do people who now find the ready money for it [...]

And now came the triumph of British respectability over the free thought and religious laxity of the Continental bourgeois. The workmen of France and Germany had become rebellious. They were thoroughly infected with socialism, and, for very good reasons, were not at all particular as to the legality of the means by which to secure their own ascendency. The *puer robustus*, here, turned from day to day more *malitiosus*. Nothing remained to the French and German bourgeoisie as a last resource but to silently drop their free thought, as a youngster, when seasickness creeps upon him, quietly drops the burning cigar he brought swaggeringly on board; one by one, the scoffers turned pious in outward behaviour, spoke with respect of the Church, its dogmas and rites, and even conformed with the latter as far as could not be helped. French bourgeois dined *maigre* on Fridays, and German ones sat out long Protestant sermons in their pews on Sundays. They had come to grief with materialism. '*Die Religion muss dem Volk erhalten werden,*' – religion must be kept alive for the people – that was the only and the last means to save society from utter ruin. Unfortunately for themselves, they did not find this out until they had done their level best to break up religion for ever. And now it was the turn of the British bourgeois to sneer and to say: 'Why, you fools, I could have told you that two hundred years ago!'

However, I am afraid neither the religious stolidity of the British, nor the *post festum* conversion of the Continental bourgeois will stem the rising Proletarian tide. Tradition is a great retarding force, is the *vis inertiae* of history, but, being merely passive, is sure to be broken down; and thus religion will be no lasting safeguard to capitalist society. If our juridical, philosophical, and religious ideas are the more or less remote offshoots of the economical relations prevailing in a given society, such ideas cannot, in the long run, withstand the effects of a complete change in these relations. And, unless we believe in supernatural revelation, we must admit that no religious tenets will ever suffice to prop up a tottering society.

2 M. WEBER

The sociology of religion

From *The Sociology of Religion* by M. Weber, trans. by Ephraim Fischoff. Originally published in German by J.C.B. Mohr. English translation © 1963 by Beacon Press. Reproduced by permission.

The rise of religions

To define 'religion,' to say what it *is*, is not possible at the start of a presentation such as this. Definition can be attempted, if at all, only at the conclusion of the study. The essence of religion is not even our concern, as we make it our task to study the conditions and effects of a particular type of social behavior.

The external courses of religious behavior are so diverse that an understanding of this behavior can only be achieved from the viewpoint of the subjective experiences, ideas, and purposes of the individuals concerned – in short, from the viewpoint of the religious behavior's 'meaning' (*Sinn*).

The most elementary forms of behavior motivated by religious or magical factors are oriented to *this* world. 'That it may go well with thee ... and that thou mayest prolong thy days upon the earth' (Deut. 4:40) expresses the reason for the performance of actions enjoined by religion or magic [...] Furthermore, religiously or magically motivated behavior is relatively rational behavior, especially in its earliest manifestations. It follows rules of experience, though it is not necessarily action in accordance with a means-end schema. Rubbing will elicit sparks from pieces of wood, and in like fashion the simulative actions of a magician will evoke rain from the heavens. The sparks resulting from twirling the wooden sticks are as much a 'magical' effect as the rain evoked by the manipulations of the rainmaker. Thus, religious or magical behavior or thinking must not be set apart from the range of everyday purposive conduct, particularly since even the ends of the religious and magical actions are predominantly economic...

Religion of non-privileged classes

... From the time of its inception, ancient Christianity was character-istically a religion of artisans. Its savior was a semi-rural artisan, and his missionaries were wandering apprentices, the greatest of them a wander-ing tent maker, so alien to the land that in his epistles he actually em-ploys in a reverse sense a metaphor relating to the process of grafting. The earliest communities of original Christianity were, as we have already seen, strongly urban throughout ancient times, and their adherents were recruited primarily from artisans, both slave and free. Moreover, in the Middle Ages the lower middle class remained the most pious, if not always the most orthodox stratum of society. But in Christianity as in other religions, widely different currents found a warm reception simul-taneously within the lower middle class. Thus, there were the ancient pneumatic prophecies which cast out demons, the unconditionally orthodox (institutionally ecclesiastical) religiosity of the Middle Ages, and the monasticism of the mendicant type. In addition, there were cer-tain types of medieval sectarian religiosity such as that of the *Humiliati*, who were long suspected of heterodoxy, there were Baptist movements of all kinds, and there was the piety of the various Reformed churches, including the Lutheran.

This is indeed a highly checkered diversification, which at least proves that a uniform determinism of religion by economic forces never existed among the artisan class. Yet there is apparent in these lower middle classes, in contrast to the peasantry, a definite tendency towards con-gregational religion, towards religion of salvation, and finally towards rational ethical religion. But this contrast between the middle class and the peasantry is far from implying any uniform determinism [...]

Yet it is still true in theory that the middle class, by virtue of its distinc-tive pattern of economic life, inclines in the direction of a rational ethical religion, wherever conditions are present for the emergence of a rational ethical religion. When one compares the life of a lower-middle-class person, particularly the urban artisan or the small trader, with the life of the peasant, it is clear that middle-class life has far less connection with nature. Consequently, dependence on magic for influencing the irrational forces of nature cannot play the same role for the urban dweller as for the farmer. At the same time, it is clear that the economic foundation of the urban man's life has a far more rational essential character, viz., calcul-ability and capacity for purposive manipulation. Furthermore, the artisan and in certain circumstances even the merchant lead economic existences which influence them to entertain the view that honesty is the best policy, that faithful work and the performance of obligations will find their reward and are 'deserving' of their just compensation. For these reasons, small traders and artisans are disposed to accept a rational world view incorporating an ethic of compensation. We shall see presently that this is the normal trend of thinking among all non-privileged classes. The peasants, on the other hand, are much more remote from this notion of compensation and do not acquire it until the magic in which they are immersed has been eliminated by other forces. By contrast, the artisan is very frequently active in effecting the elimination of this very process of magic. It follows that the belief in ethical compensation is even more alien to warriors and to financial magnates who have economic interests in war and in the political manifestations of power. These groups are the least accessible to the ethical and rational elements in any religion.

The artisan is deeply immersed in magical encumbrances in the early stages of occupational differentiation. Every specialized art that is uncommon and not widely disseminated is regarded as a magical charisma, either personal or, more generally, hereditary, the acquisition and maintenance of which is guaranteed by magical means. Other elements of this early belief are that the bearers of this charisma are set off by taboos, occasionally of a totemic nature, from the community of ordinary people (peasants), and frequently that they are to be excluded from the ownership of land. One final element of this early belief in the magical charisma of every specialized art must be mentioned here. Wherever crafts had remained in the hands of ancient groups possessing raw materials, who had first offered their arts as intruders in the community and later offered their craftsmanship as individual strangers settled within the community, the belief in the magical nature of special arts condemned such groups to pariah status and stereotyped with magic their manipulations and their technology. But wherever this magical frame of reference has once been broken through (this happens most readily in newly settled cities), the effect of the transformation may be that the artisan will learn to think about his labor and the small trader will learn to think about his enterprise much more rationally than any peasant thinks. The craftsman in particular will have time and opportunity for reflection during his work, in many instances. Consequently, the workers in occupations which are primarily of the indoor variety, e.g., in textile mills in our climate, are strongly infused with sectarian or religious trends. This is true to some extent even for the workers in modern factories with mechanized weaving, but very much more true for the workers at the looms in the textile mills of the past.

Wherever the attachment to purely magical or ritualistic views has been broken by prophets or reformers, there has frequently been a tendency for artisans, craftsmen and middle-class people to incline toward a rather primitively rationalistic ethical and religious view of life. Furthermore, their very occupational specialization makes them the bearers of an integrated pattern of life of a distinctive kind. Yet there is certainly no uniform determination of religion by these general conditions in the life of artisans and middle-class groups [...]

Only a congregational religion, especially one of the rational and ethical type, could conceivably win followers easily, particularly among the urban lower middle classes, and then, given certain circumstances, exert a lasting influence on the pattern of life of these classes. This is what actually happened.

Finally, the classes of the greatest economic disability, such as slaves and free day laborers, have hitherto never been the bearers of a distinctive type of religion. In the ancient Christian communities the slaves belonged to the lower middle classes in the cities [...]

Handicraft apprentices have at all times tended to share the characteristic religion of the lower middle classes, since they are normally distinguished from the independent lower middle classes only by the factor of *Karenzzeit* (the time during which a person employed at some manufactory is pledged to refrain from entering any rival establishment in that locality). The apprentice group also tended to evince a conspicuous inclination toward various forms of unofficial religion of the sect type, which found particularly fertile soil among the lower occupational strata of the city, in view of their workaday struggles with everyday needs, the fluctuations in the price of their daily bread, their quest for jobs, and their dependence on fraternal assistance. Furthermore, the class of small artisans and craft apprentices was generally represented in the numerous secret or half-tolerated communities of 'poor folk' that espoused congregational religions which were by turn revolutionary, pacifistic-communistic and ethical-rational, chiefly for the technical reason that wandering handicraft apprentices are the available missionaries of every mass congregational religion. This process is illustrated in the extraordinarily rapid expansion of Christianity across the tremendous area from the Orient to Rome in just a few decades.

Insofar as the modern proletariat has a distinctive religious position, it is characterized by indifference to or rejection of religions common to large groups of the modern bourgeoisie. For the modern proletariat, the sense of dependence on one's own achievements is supplanted by a consciousness of dependence on purely societal factors, economic conjunctures, and power relationships guaranteed by law. Any thought of dependence upon the course of natural or meteorological processes, or upon anything that might be regarded as subject to the influence of magic or providence, has been completely eliminated, as Sombart has already demonstrated in fine fashion. Therefore, the rationalism of the proletariat, like that of the bourgeoisie of developed capitalism when it has come into the full possession of economic power, of which indeed the proletariat's rationalism is a complementary phenomenon, cannot in the nature of the case easily possess a religious character and certainly cannot easily generate a religion. Hence, in the sphere of proletarian rationalism, religion is generally supplanted by other ideological surrogates.

The lowest and the most economically unstable strata of the proletariat, for whom rational conceptions are the least congenial, and also the proletaroid or permanently impoverished lower middle-class groups who are in constant danger of sinking into the proletarian class, are nevertheless readily susceptible to being influenced by religious missionary enterprise. But this religious propaganda has in such cases a distinctively magical form or, where real magic has been eliminated, it has certain characteristics which are substitutes for the magical-orgiastic supervention of grace. Examples of these are the soteriological orgies of the Methodist type, such as are engaged in by the Salvation Army. Undoubtedly, it is far easier for emotional rather than rational elements of a religious ethic to flourish in such circumstances. In any case, ethical religion scarcely ever arises primarily in this group.

Only in a limited sense is there a distinctive class religion of disprivileged social groups. Inasmuch as the *substantive* demands for social and political reform in any religion are based on god's will, we shall have to devote a brief discussion to this problem when we discuss ethics and natural law. But insofar as our concern is with the character of the religion as such, it is immediately evident that a need for salvation in the widest sense of the term has as one of its foci, but not the exclusive or primary one, as we shall see later, disprivileged classes. Turning to the 'sated' and privileged strata, the need for salvation is remote and alien to warriors, bureaucrats, and the plutocracy.

A religion of salvation may very well have its origin within socially privileged groups. For the charisma of the prophet is not confined to membership in any particular class; and furthermore, it is normally associated with a certain minimum of intellectual cultivation. Proof for both of these assertions is readily available in the various characteristic prophecies of intellectuals. But as a rule, the aforementioned relationship between salvation religion and privileged classes changes its character as soon as the religion has reached lay groups who are not particularly or professionally concerned with the cultivation of intellectualism, and certainly changes its character after it has reached into the disprivileged social strata to whom intellectualism is both economically and socially inaccessible. One characteristic element of this transformation, a product of the inevitable accommodation to the needs of the masses, may be formulated generally as the emergence of a personal, divine or human-divine savior as the bearer of salvation, with the additional consequence that the religious relationship to this personage becomes the precondition of salvation.

We have already seen that one form of the adaptation of religion to the needs of the masses is the transformation of cultic religion into mere wizardry. A second typical form of adaptation is the shift into savior religion, which is naturally related to the aforementioned change into magic by the most numerous transitional stages. The lower the social class, the more radical are the forms assumed by the need for a savior, once this need has emerged [...]

The religious need of the middle and lower bourgeoisie expresses itself less in the form of heroic myths than in rather more sentimental legend, which has a tendency toward inwardness and edification. This corresponds to the peaceableness and the greater emphasis upon domestic and family life of the middle classes, in contrast to the ruling strata. This middle-class transformation of religion in the direction of domesticity is illustrated by the emergence of the god-suffused *bhakti* piety in all Hindu cults, both in the creation of the Bodhisattva figure as well as in the cults of Krishna; and by the popularity of the edifying myths of the child Dionysos, Osiris, the Christ child, and their numerous parallels [...]

The soteriological myth with its god who has assumed human form or its savior who has been deified is, like magic, a characteristic concept of popular religion, and hence one that has arisen quite spontaneously in very different places. On the other hand, the notion of an impersonal and ethical cosmic order that transcends the deity and the ideal of an exemplary type of salvation are intellectualistic conceptions which are definitely alien to the masses and possible only for a laity that has been educated along rational and ethical lines. The same holds true for the development of a concept of an absolutely transcendent god. With the exception of Judaism and Protestantism, all religions and religious ethics have had to reintroduce cults of saints, heroes or functional gods in order to accommodate themselves to the needs of the masses. Thus, Confucianism permitted such cults, in the form of the Taoist pantheon, to continue their existence by its side. Similarly, as popularized Buddhism spread to many lands, it allowed the various gods of these lands to live on as recipients of the Buddhist cult subordinated to the Buddha. Finally, Islam and Catholicism were compelled to accept local, functional, and occupational gods as saints, the veneration of which constituted the real religion of the masses in everyday life.

The religion of the disprivileged classes, in contrast to the aristocratic cults of the martial nobles, is characterized by a tendency to allot equality to women. There is a great diversity in the scope of the religious participation permitted to women, but the greater or lesser, active or passive participation (or exclusion) of women from the religious cults is everywhere a function of the degree of the group's relative pacification or militarization (present or past) [...]

What gave Christianity its extraordinary superiority, as it conducted its missionary enterprises among the lower middle classes, over its most important competitor, the religion of Mithra, was that this extremely masculine cult excluded women [...]

The specific importance of salvation religion for politically and economically disprivileged social groups, in contrast to privileged groups, may be viewed from an even more comprehensive perspective. In our subsequent discussion of castes and classes we shall have a good deal to say about the sense of honor or superiority characteristic of the non-priestly classes that claimed the highest social privileges, particularly the nobility. Their sense of self-esteem rests on their awareness that the perfection of their life pattern is an expression of their underived, ultimate, and qualitatively distinctive *being*; indeed, it is in the very nature of the case that this should be the basis of the elite's feeling of worth. On the other hand, the sense of honor of disprivileged classes rests on some concealed promise for the future which implies the assignment of some function, mission, or vocation to them. What they cannot claim to *be*, they replace by the worth of that which they will one day *become*, to which they will be called in some future life here or hereafter; or replace, very often concomitantly with the motivation just discussed, by their sense of what they signify and achieve in the world as seen from the point of view of providence. Their hunger for a worthiness that has not fallen to their lot, they and the world being what it is, produces this conception from which is derived the rationalistic idea of a providence, a significance in the eyes of some divine authority possessing a scale of values different from the one operating in the world of man.

This psychological condition, when turned outward toward the other social classes, produces certain characteristic contrasts in what religion must provide for the various social strata. Since every need for salvation is an expression of some distress, social or economic oppression is an effective source of salvation beliefs, though by no means the exclusive source. Other things being equal, classes with high social and economic privilege will scarcely be prone to evolve the idea of salvation. Rather, they assign to religion the primary function of legitimizing their own life pattern and situation in the world. This universal phenomenon is rooted in certain basic psychological patterns. When a man who is happy compares his position with that of one who is unhappy, he is not content with the fact of his happiness, but desires something more, namely the right to this happiness, the consciousness that he has earned his good fortune, in contrast to the unfortunate one who must equally have earned his misfortune. Our everyday experience proves that there exists just such a psychological need for reassurance as to the legitimacy or deservedness of one's happiness, whether this involves political success, superior economic status, bodily health, success in the game of love, or anything else. What the privileged classes require of religion, if anything at all, is this psychological reassurance of legitimacy [...]

In practically every ethical religion found among privileged classes and the priests who serve them, the privileged or disprivileged social position of the individual is regarded as somehow merited from the religious point of view. What varies is only the form by which good fortune is legitimized.

Correspondingly different is the situation of the disprivileged. Their particular need is for release from suffering. They do not always experience this need for salvation in a religious form, as shown by the example of the modern proletariat. Furthermore, their need for religious salvation, where it exists, may assume diverse forms. Most important, it may be conjoined with a need for just compensation, envisaged in various ways but always involving reward for one's own good deeds and punishment for the unrighteousness of others. This hope for and expectation of just compensation, a fairly calculating attitude, is, next to magic (indeed, not unconnected with it), the most widely diffused form of mass religion all over the world. Even religious prophecies, which rejected the more mechanical forms of this belief, tended as they underwent popularization and routinization to slip back into these expectations of compensation. The type and scope of these hopes for compensation and salvation varied greatly depending on the expectations aroused by the religious promises, especially when these hopes were projected from the earthly existence of the individual into a future life [...]

A theodicy of disprivilege, in some form, is a component of every salvation religion which draws its adherents primarily from the disprivileged classes. Wherever a developing priestly ethic met a theodicy of disprivilege halfway, the theodicy became a component of congregational religion, as happened with the pious Hindu and with the Asiatic Buddhist. That these religions lack virtually any kind of social-revolutionary ethics can be explained by reference to their theodicy of rebirth, according to which the caste system itself is eternal and absolutely just. The virtues or sins of a former life determine birth into a particular caste, and one's behavior in the present life determines one's chances of improvement in the next rebirth. Those living under this theodicy experienced no trace of the conflict experienced by the Jews between the social claims based on God's promises and the actual conditions of dishonor under which they lived. This conflict precluded any possibility of finding ease in this life for the Jews, who lived in continuous tension with their actual social position and in perpetually fruitless expectation and hope. The Jews' theodicy of disprivilege was greeted by the pitiless mockery of the godless heathen, but for the Jews the theodicy had the consequence of transforming religious criticism of the godless heathen into ever-watchful concern over their own fidelity to the law. This preoccupation was frequently tinged with bitterness and threatened by secret self-criticism [...]

It would be erroneous to portray the need for salvation, theodicy, or congregational religion as something that developed only among disprivileged social classes or as a product of resentment, and hence merely as the outcome of a 'slave revolt in morality'. This would not even be true of ancient Christianity, although it directed its promises most emphatically to the poor in spirit and in worldly goods. [...]

Not even Jesus' own warnings, according to the tradition, of the dangers presented by wealth to the attainment of salvation were motivated by asceticism. Certainly the motivation of his preaching against wealth was not resentment, for the tradition has preserved many evidences of Jesus' intercourse, not only with publicans (who in the Palestine of that period were mostly small moneylenders), but also with many wealthy people of the upper class. Furthermore, resentment cannot be regarded as the primary motivation of Jesus' doctrines regarding wealth, in view of the Gospels' impressive indifference to mundane affairs, an indifference based upon the importance attributed to eschatological expectations. To be sure, the rich young man was bidden to unconditionally take his leave of the world if he desired to be a perfect disciple. But it is stated that for God all things are possible, even the salvation of the wealthy. The rich man who is unable to decide to part with his wealth may nonetheless achieve salvation, despite the difficulties in the way. There were no 'proletarian instincts' in the doctrine and teaching of Jesus, the prophet of acosmistic love. He brought to the poor in spirit and to the good people of this world the happy tidings of the immediate coming of the Kingdom of God and of freedom from the domination of evil spirits. Similarly, any proletarian denunciation of wealth would have been equally alien to the Buddha, for whom the absolute precondition of salvation was unconditional withdrawal from the world.

The limited occurrence of the factor of *ressentiment* and the dubiousness of applying the conceptual schema of 'repression' almost universally appear most clearly when the Nietzschean schema is applied erroneously to the altogether inappropriate example of Buddhism. Buddhism constitutes the most radical anti-thesis to every type of *ressentiment* morality. Buddhism clearly arose as the salvation doctrine of an intellectual class, originally recruited almost entirely from the privileged castes, especially the warrior caste, which proudly and aristocratically rejected the illusions of life, both here and hereafter. Buddhism may be compared in social provenience to the salvation doctrines of the Greeks, particularly the Neo-Platonic, Manichean, and Gnostic manifestations, even though they are radically different in content. The Buddhist *bhikshu* does not begrudge the entire world, even a rebirth into paradise, to the person who does not desire *Nirvana*.

Precisely this example of Buddhism demonstrates that the need for salvation and ethical religion has yet another source besides the social condition of the disprivileged and the rationalism of the middle classes, which are products of their practical way of life. This additional factor is intellectualism as such, more particularly the metaphysical needs of the human mind as it is driven to reflect on ethical and religious questions, driven not by material need but by an inner compulsion to understand the world as a meaningful cosmos and to take up a position toward it.

3 M. WEBER

The social psychology of the world religions

Adapted from *Max Weber: Essays in Sociology*, edited and translated by H. H. Gerth and C. W. Mills. Copyright 1946 by Oxford University Press, Inc. Renewed 1973 by Hans H. Gerth. Reprinted by permission of the publisher.

... An economic ethic is not a simple 'function' of a form of economic organization; and just as little does the reverse hold, namely, that economic ethics unambiguously stamp the form of the economic organization.

No economic ethic has ever been determined solely by religion. In the face of man's attitudes towards the world – as determined by religious or other (in our sense) 'inner' factors – an economic ethic has, of course, a high measure of autonomy. Given factors of economic geography and history determine this measure of autonomy in the highest degree. The religious determination of life-conduct, however, is also one – note this – only one, of the determinants of the economic ethic. Of course, the religiously determined way of life is itself profoundly influenced by economic and political factors operating within given geographical, political, social, and national boundaries. We should lose ourselves in these discussions if we tried to demonstrate these dependencies in all their singularities. Here we can only attempt to peel off the directive elements in the life-conduct of those social *strata* which have most strongly influenced the practical ethic of their respective religions. These elements have stamped the most characteristic features upon practical ethics, the features that distinguish one ethic from others; *and*, at the same time, they have been important for the respective economic ethics.

By no means must we focus upon only one stratum. Those strata which are decisive in stamping the characteristic features of an economic ethic may change in the course of history. And the influence of a single stratum is never an exclusive one. Nevertheless, as a rule one may determine the strata whose styles of life have been at least predominantly decisive for certain religions. Here are some examples, if one may anticipate:

Confucianism was the status ethic of prebendaries, of men with literary educations who were characterized by a secular rationalism. If one did not belong to this *cultured* stratum he did not count. The religious (or if one wishes, irreligious) status ethic of this stratum has determined the Chinese way of life far beyond the stratum itself.

Earlier Hinduism was borne by a hereditary caste of cultured literati, who, being remote from any office, functioned as a kind of ritualist and spiritual advisers for individuals and communities. They formed a stable center for the orientation of the status stratification, and they placed their stamp upon the social order. Only Brahmans, *educated* in the Veda, formed, as bearers of tradition, the fully recognized religious status group. And only later a non-Brahman status group of ascetics emerged by the side of the Brahmans and competed with them. Still later, during the Indian Middle Ages, Hinduism entered the plain. It represented the ardent sacramental religiosity of the savior, and was borne by the lower strata with their plebeian mystagogues.

Buddhism was propagated by strictly contemplative, mendicant monks, who rejected the world and, having no homes, migrated. Only these were full members of the religious community; all others remained religious laymen of inferior value: objects, not subjects, of religiosity.

During its first period, Islamism was a religion of world-conquering warriors, a knight order of disciplined crusaders. They lacked only the sexual asceticism of their Christian copies of the age of the Crusades. But during the Islamic Middle Ages, contemplative and mystical Sufism attained at least an equal standing under the leadership of plebeian technicians of orgiastics. The brotherhoods of the petty bourgeoisie grew out of Sufism in a manner similar to the Christian Tertiarians, except they were far more universally developed.

Since the Exile, Judaism has been the religion of a civic 'pariah people.' We shall in time become acquainted with the precise meaning of the term. During the Middle Ages Judaism fell under the leadership of a stratum of intellectuals who were trained in literature and ritual, a peculiarity of Judaism. This stratum has represented an increasingly quasi-proletarian and rationalist petty-bourgeois intelligentsia.

Christianity, finally, began its course as a doctrine of itinerant artisan journeymen. During all periods of its mighty external and internal development it has been a quite specifically urban, and above all a civic, religion. This was true during Antiquity, during the Middle Ages, and in Puritanism. The city of the Occident, unique among all other cities of the world – and citizenship, in the sense in which it has emerged only in the Occident – has been the major theatre for Christianity. This holds for the pneumatic piety of the ancient religious community, for the mendicant monk orders of the high Middle Ages, and for the [Protestant] sects of the reformation up to pietism and methodism.

It is not our thesis that the specific nature of a religion is a simple 'function' of the social situation of the stratum which appears as its characteristic bearer, or that it represents the stratum's 'ideology,' or that it is a 'reflection' of a stratum's material or ideal interest-situation. On the contrary, a more basic misunderstanding of the standpoint of these discussions would hardly be possible.

However incisive the social influences, economically and politically determined, may have been upon a religious ethic in a particular case, it receives its stamp primarily from religious sources, and, first of all, from the content of its annunciation and its promise. Frequently the very next generation reinterprets these annunciations and promises in a fundamental fashion. Such reinterpretations adjust the revelations to the needs of the religious community. If this occurs, then it is at least usual that religious doctrines are adjusted to *religious needs*. Other spheres of interest could have only a secondary influence; often, however, such influence is very obvious and sometimes it is decisive.

For every religion we shall find that a change in the socially decisive strata has usually been of profound importance. On the other hand, the type of a religion, once stamped, has usually exerted a rather far-reaching influence upon the life-conduct of very heterogeneous strata. In various ways people have sought to interpret the connection between religious ethics and interest-situations in such a way that the former appear as mere 'functions' of the latter. Such interpretation occurs in so-called historical materialism – which we shall not here discuss – as well as in a purely psychological sense.

A quite general and abstract class-determination of religious ethics might be deduced from the theory of 'resentment', known since Friedrich Nietzsche's brilliant essay and since then spiritedly treated by psychologists. As is known, this theory regards the moral glorification of mercy and brotherliness as a 'slave revolt in morals' among those who are disadvantaged, either in their natural endowments or in their opportunities as determined by life-fate. The ethic of 'duty' is thus considered a product of 'repressed' sentiments for vengeance on the part of banausic men who 'displace' their sentiments because they are powerless, and condemned to work and to money-making. They resent the way of life of the lordly stratum who live free of duties. A very simple solution of the most important problems in the typology of religious ethics would obviously result if this were the case. However fortunate and fruitful the disclosure of the psychological significance of resentment as such has been, great caution is necessary in estimating its bearing for social ethics.

Later we shall have to discuss the motives that have determined the different forms of ethical 'rationalization' of life conduct, *per se*. In the main, these have had nothing whatsoever to do with resentment. But that the evaluation of *suffering* in religious ethics has been subject to a typical change is beyond doubt. If properly understood, this change carries a certain justification for the theory first worked out by Nietzsche. The primeval attitude towards suffering has been thrown into relief most drastically during the religious festivities of the community, especially in the treatment of those haunted by disease or other cases of obstinate misfortune. Men, permanently suffering, mourning, diseased, or otherwise unfortunate, were, according to the nature of their suffering, believed either to be possessed by a demon or burdened with the wrath of a god whom they had insulted. To tolerate such men in the midst of the cultic community could result in disadvantages for it. In any case, they were not allowed to participate in cultic feasts and sacrifices, for the gods did not enjoy the sight of them and could be incited to wrath by it. The sacrificial feasts were occasions for rejoicing – even in Jerusalem during times of siege.

In treating suffering as a symptom of odiousness in the eyes of the gods and as a sign of secret guilt, religion has psychologically met a very general need. The fortunate is seldom satisfied with the fact of being fortunate. Beyond this, he needs to know that he has a *right* to his good fortune. He wants to be convinced that he 'deserves' it, and above all, that he deserves it in comparison with others. He wishes to be allowed the belief that the less fortunate also merely experiences his due. Good fortune thus wants to be 'legitimate' fortune.

If the general term 'fortune' covers all the 'good' of honor, power, possession, and pleasure, it is the most general formula for the service of legitimation, which religion has had to accomplish for the external and the inner interests of all ruling men, the propertied, the victorious, and the healthy. In short, religion provides the theodicy of good fortune for those who are fortunate. This theodicy is anchored in highly robust ('pharisaical') needs of man and is therefore easily understood, even if sufficient attention is often not paid to its effects [...]

The annunciation and the promise of religion have naturally been addressed to the masses of those who were in need of salvation. They and their interests have moved into the center of the professional organization for the 'cure of the soul,' which, indeed, only therewith originated. The typical service of magicians and priests becomes the determination of the factors to be blamed for suffering, that is, the confession of 'sins.' At first, these sins were offenses against ritual commandments. The magician and priest also give counsel for behavior fit to remove the suffering. The material and ideal interests of magicians and priests could thereby actually and increasingly enter the service of specifically *plebeian* motives. A further step along this course was signified when, under the pressure of typical and ever-recurrent distress, the religiosity of a 'redeemer' evolved. This religiosity presupposed the myth of a savior, hence (at least relatively) of a *rational* view of the world. Again, suffering became the most important topic [...]

The figure of the savior has been of varying stamp. In the late form of Zoroastrianism with its numerous abstractions, a purely constructed figure assumed the role of the mediator and savior in the economy of salvation. The reverse has also occurred: a historical person, legitimized through miracles and visionary reappearances, ascends to the rank of savior. Purely historical factors have been decisive for the realization of these very different possibilities. Almost always, however, some kind of theodicy of suffering has originated from the hope for salvation.

The promises of the religions of salvation at first remained tied to ritualist rather than to ethical preconditions. Thus, for instance, both the worldly and the other worldly advantages of the Eleusinian mysteries were tied to ritual purity and to attendance at the Eleusinian mass. When law gained in significance, these special deities played an increasing role, and the task of protecting the traditional order, of punishing the unjust and rewarding the righteous, was transferred to them as guardians of juridical procedure.

Where religious development was decisively influenced by a prophecy, naturally 'sin' was no longer a mere magical offense. Above all, it was a sign of disbelief in the prophet and in his commandments. Sin figured as the basic cause of all sorts of misfortunes.

The prophet has not regularly been a descendant or a representative of depressed classes. The reverse, as we shall see, has almost always been the rule. Neither has the content of the prophet's doctrine been derived preponderantly from the intellectual horizon of the depressed classes. As a rule, however, the oppressed, or at least those threatened by distress, were in need of a redeemer and prophet; the fortunate, the propertied, the ruling strata were not in such need. Therefore, in the great majority of cases, a prophetically announced religion of redemption has had its permanent locus among the less-favored social strata. Among these, such religiosity has either been a substitute for, or a rational supplement to, magic.

Wherever the promises of the prophet or the redeemer have not sufficiently met the needs of the socially less-favored strata, a secondary salvation religion of the masses has regularly developed beneath the official doctrine. The rational conception of the world is contained in germ within the myth of the redeemer. A rational theodicy of misfortune has, therefore, as a rule, been a development of this conception of the world. At the same time, this rational view of the world has often furnished suffering as such with a 'plus' sign, which was originally quite foreign to it [...]

The need for an ethical interpretation of the 'meaning' of the distribution of fortunes among men increased with the growing rationality of conceptions of the world. As the religious and ethical reflections upon the world were increasingly rationalized and primitive, and magical notions were eliminated, the theodicy of suffering encountered increasing difficulties. Individually 'undeserved' woe was all too frequent; not 'good' but 'bad' men succeeded – even when 'good' and 'bad' were measured by the yardstick of the master stratum and not by that of a 'slave morality.'

One can explain suffering and injustice by referring to individual sin committed in a former life (the migration of souls), to the guilt of ancestors, which is avenged down to the third and fourth generation, or – the most principled – to the wickedness of all creatures *per se*. As compensatory promises, one can refer to hopes of the individual for a better life in the future in this world (transmigration of souls) or to hopes for the successors (Messianic realm), or to a better life in the hereafter (paradise).

The metaphysical conception of God and of the world, which the ineradicable demand for a theodicy called forth, could produce only a few systems of ideas on the whole – as we shall see, only three. These three gave rationally satisfactory answers to the questioning for the basis of the incongruity between destiny and merit: the Indian doctrine of Kharma, Zoroastrian dualism, and the predestination decree of the *deus abscondidus*. These solutions are rationally closed; in pure form, they are found only as exceptions.

The rational need for a theodicy of suffering and of dying has had extremely strong effects. As a matter of fact, this need has molded important traits of such religions as Hinduism, Zoroastrism, and Judaism, and, to a certain extent, Paulinian and later Christianity. Even as late as 1906, a mere minority among a rather considerable number of proletarians gave as reasons for their disbelief in Christianity conclusions derived from modern theories of natural sciences. The majority, however, referred to the 'injustice' of the order of this world – to be sure, essentially because they believed in a revolutionary compensation in this world.

The theodicy of suffering can be colored by resentment. But the need of compensation for the insufficiency of one's fate in this world has not, as a rule, had resentment as a basic and decisive color. Certainly, the need for vengeance has had a special affinity with the belief that the unjust are well off in this world only because hell is reserved for them later. Eternal bliss is reserved for the pious; occasional sins, which, after all, the pious also commit, ought therefore to be expiated in this world. Yet one can readily be convinced that even this way of thinking, which occasionally appears, is not always determined by resentment, and that it is by no means always the product of socially oppressed strata. We shall see that there have been only a few examples of religion to which resentment contributed essential features. Among these examples only one is a fully developed case. All that can be said is that resentment *could* be, and often and everywhere has been, significant as one factor, among others, in influencing the religiously determined rationalism of socially disadvantaged strata. It has gained such significance, in highly diverse and often minute degrees, in accordance with the nature of the promises held out by different religions.

In any case, it would be quite wrong to attempt to deduce 'asceticism' in general from these sources. The distrust of wealth and power, which as a rule exists in genuine religions of salvation, has had its natural basis primarily in the experience of redeemers, prophets, and priests. They understood that those strata which were 'satiated' and favored in this world had only a small urge to be saved, regardless of the kind of salvation offered. Hence, these master strata have been less 'devout' in the sense of salvation religions. The development of a rational religious ethic has had positive and primary roots in the inner conditions of those social strata which were less socially valued.

Strata in solid possession of social honor and power usually tend to fashion their status-legend in such a way as to claim a special and intrinsic quality of their own, usually a quality of blood; their sense of dignity feeds on their actual or alleged being. The sense of dignity of socially repressed strata or of strata whose status is negatively (or at least not positively) valued is nourished most easily on the belief that a special 'mission' is entrusted to them; their worth is guaranteed or constituted by an *ethical imperative*, or by their own functional *achievement*. Their value is thus moved into something beyond themselves, into a 'task' placed before them by God. One source of the ideal power of ethical prophecies among socially disadvantaged strata lies in this fact. Resentment has not been required as a leverage; the rational interest in material and ideal compensations as such has been perfectly sufficient.

There can be no doubt that prophets and priests through intentional or unintentional propaganda have taken the resentment of the masses into their service. But this is by no means always the case. This essentially negative force of resentment, so far as is known, has never been the source of those essentially metaphysical conceptions which have lent uniqueness to every salvation religion. Moreover, in general, the nature of a religious promise has by no means necessarily or even predominantly been the mere mouthpiece of a class interest, either of an external or internal nature.

By themselves, the masses, as we shall see, have everywhere remained engulfed in the massive and archaic growth of magic – unless a prophecy that holds out specific promises has swept them into a religious movement of an ethical character. For the rest, the specific nature of the great religious and ethical systems has been determined by social conditions of a far more particular nature than by the mere contrast of ruling and ruled strata [...]

The kind of empirical state of bliss or experience of rebirth that is sought after as the supreme value by a religion has obviously and necessarily varied according to the character of the stratum which was foremost in adopting it. The chivalrous warrior class, peasants, business classes, and intellectuals with literary education have naturally pursued different religious tendencies. As will become evident, these tendencies have not by themselves determined the psychological character of religion; they have, however, exerted a very lasting influence upon it. The contrast between warrior and peasant classes, and intellectual and business classes, is of special importance. Of these groups, the intellectuals have always been the exponents of a rationalism which in their case has been relatively theoretical. The business classes (merchants and artisans) have been at least possible exponents of rationalism of a more practical sort. Rationalism of either kind has borne very different stamps, but has always exerted a great influence upon the religious attitude.

Above all, the peculiarity of the intellectual strata in this matter has been in the past of the greatest importance for religion. At the present time, it matters little in the development of a religion whether or not modern intellectuals feel the need of enjoying a 'religious' state as an 'experience,' in addition to all sorts of other sensations, in order to decorate their internal and stylish furnishings with paraphernalia guaranteed to be genuine and old. A religious revival has never sprung from such a source. In the past, it was the work of the intellectuals to sublimate the possession of sacred values into a belief in 'redemption.' The conception of the idea of redemption, as such, is very óld, if one understands by it a liberation from distress, hunger, drought, sickness, and ultimately from suffering and death. Yet redemption attained a specific significance only where it expressed a systematic and rationalized 'image of the world' and represented a stand in the face of the world. For the meaning as well as the intended and actual psychological quality of redemption has depended upon such a world image and such a stand. Not ideas, but material and ideal interests, directly govern men's conduct. Yet very frequently the 'world images' that have been created by 'ideas' have, like switchmen, determined the tracks along which action has been pushed by the dynamic of interest. 'From what' and 'for what' one wished to be redeemed and, let us not forget, 'could be' redeemed, depended upon one's image of the world.

There have been very different possibilities in this connection: One could wish to be saved from political and social servitude and lifted into a Messianic realm in the future of this world; or one could wish to be saved from being defiled by ritual impurity and hope for the pure beauty of psychic and bodily existence. One could wish to escape being incarcerated in an impure body and hope for a purely spiritual existence. One could wish to be saved from the eternal and senseless play of human passions and desires and hope for the quietude of the pure beholding of the divine. One could wish to be saved from radical evil and the servitude of sin and hope for the eternal and free benevolence in the lap of a fatherly god. One could wish to be saved from peonage under the astrologically conceived determination of stellar constellations and long for the dignity of freedom and partaking of the substance of the hidden deity. One could wish to be redeemed from the barriers of the finite, which express themselves in suffering, misery and death, and the threatening punishment of hell, and hope for an eternal bliss in an earthly or paradisical future existence. One could wish to be saved from the cycle of rebirths with their inexorable compensations for the deeds of the times past and hope for eternal rest. One could wish to be saved from senseless brooding and events and long for the dreamless sleep. Many more varieties of belief have, of course, existed. Behind them always lies a stand towards something in the actual world which is experienced as specifically 'senseless.' Thus, the demand has been implied: that the world order in its totality is, could, and should somehow be a meaningful 'cosmos.' This quest, the core of genuine religious rationalism, has been borne precisely by strata of intellectuals. The avenues, the results, and the efficacy of this metaphysical need for a meaningful cosmos have varied widely. Nevertheless, some general comments may be made [...]

Of course, the religions of all strata are certainly far from being unambiguously dependent upon the character of the strata we have presented as having special affinities with them. Yet, at first sight, civic strata appear, in this respect and on the whole, to lend themselves to a more varied determination. Yet it is precisely among these strata that elective affinities for special types of religion stand out. The tendency towards a *practical* rationalism in conduct is common to all civic strata; it is conditioned by the nature of their way of life, which is greatly detached from economic bonds to nature. Their whole existence has been based upon technological or economic calculations and upon the mastery of nature and of man, however primitive the means at their disposal. The technique of living handed down among them may, of course, be frozen in traditionalism, as has occurred repeatedly and everywhere. But precisely for these, there has always existed the possibility – even though in greatly varying measure – of letting an *ethical* and rational regulation of life arise. This may occur by the linkage of such an ethic to the tendency of technological and economic rationalism. Such regulation has not always been able to make headway against traditions which, in the main, were magically stereotyped. But where prophecy has provided a religious basis, this basis could be one of two fundamental types of prophecy which we shall repeatedly discuss: 'exemplary' prophecy, and 'emissary' prophecy.

Exemplary prophecy points out the path to salvation by exemplary living, usually by a contemplative and apathetic-ecstatic life. The emissary type of prophecy addresses its *demands* to the world in the name of a god. Naturally these demands are ethical; and they are often of an active ascetic character.

4 E. DURKHEIM

The elementary forms of the religious life

From *The Elementary Forms of the Religious Life* by E. Durkheim, 1915. Translated by J. W. Swain. Reproduced by permission of the publishers, George Allen & Unwin.

... The study which we are undertaking is therefore a way of taking up again, *but under new conditions*, the old problem of the origin of religion. To be sure, if by origin we are to understand the very first beginning, the question has nothing scientific about it, and should be resolutely discarded [...]

What we want to do is to find a means of discerning the ever-present causes upon which the most essential forms of religious thought and practice depend [...]

For a long time it has been known that the first systems of representations with which men have pictured to themselves the world and themselves were of religious origin. There is no religion that is not a cosmology at the same time that it is a speculation upon divine things. If philosophy and the sciences were born of religion, it is because religion began by taking the place of the sciences and philosophy. But it has been less frequently noticed that religion has not confined itself to enriching the human intellect, formed beforehand, with a certain number of ideas; it has contributed to forming the intellect itself. Men owe to it not only a good part of the substance of their knowledge, but also the form in which this knowledge has been elaborated.

At the roots of all our judgments there are a certain number of essential ideas which dominate all our intellectual life; they are what philosophers since Aristotle have called the categories of the understanding: ideas of time, space, class, number, cause, substance, personality, etc. They correspond to the most universal properties of things. They are like the solid frame which encloses all thought; this does not seem to be able to liberate itself from them without destroying itself, for it seems that we cannot think of objects that are not in time and space, which have no number, etc. Other ideas are contingent and unsteady; we can conceive of their being unknown to a man, a society or an epoch; but these others appear to be nearly inseparable from the normal working of the intellect. They are like the framework of the intelligence. Now when primitive religious beliefs are systematically analysed, the principal categories are naturally found. They are born in religion and of religion; they are a product of religious thought. This is a statement that we are going to have occasion to make many times in the course of this work.

This remark has some interest of itself already; but here is what gives it its real importance.

The general conclusion of the book which the reader has before him is that religion is something eminently social. Religious representations are collective representations which express collective realities; the rites are a manner of acting which take rise in the midst of the assembled groups and which are destined to excite, maintain or recreate certain mental states in these groups. So if the categories are of religious origin, they ought to participate in this nature common to all religious facts; they too should be social affairs and the product of collective thought. At least – for in the actual condition of our knowledge of these matters, one should be careful to avoid all radical and exclusive statements – it is allowable to suppose that they are rich in social elements.

Even at present, these can be imperfectly seen in some of them. For example, try to represent what the notion of time would be without the processes by which we divide it, measure it or express it with objective signs, a time which is not a succession of years, months, weeks, days and hours! This is something nearly unthinkable. We cannot conceive of time, except on condition of distinguishing its different moments. Now what is the origin of this differentiation? Undoubtedly, the states of consciousness which we have already experienced can be reproduced in us in the same order in which they passed in the first place; thus portions of our past become present again, though being clearly distinguished from the present. But howsoever important this distinction may be for our private experience, it is far from being enough to constitute the notion or category of time. This does not consist merely in a commemoration, either partial or integral, of our past life. It is an abstract and impersonal frame which surrounds, not only our individual existence, but that of all humanity. It is like an endless chart, where all duration is spread out before the mind, and upon which all possible events can be located in relation to fixed and determined guide lines. It is not *my time* that is thus arranged; it is time in general, such as it is objectively thought of by everybody in a single civilization. That alone is enough to give us a hint that such an arrangement ought to be collective. And in reality, observation proves that these indispensable guide lines, in relation to which all things are temporally located, are taken from social life. The divisions into days, weeks, months, years, etc., correspond to the periodical recurrence of rites, feasts, and public ceremonies. A calendar expresses the rhythm of the collective activities, while at the same time its function is to assure their regularity.

It is the same thing with space [...]

All known religious beliefs, whether simple or complex, present one common characteristic: they presuppose a classification of all the things, real and ideal, of which men think, into two classes or opposed groups, generally designated by two distinct terms which are translated well enough by the words *profane* and *sacred* (*profane, sacré*). This division of the world into two domains, the one containing all that is sacred, the other all that is profane, is the distinctive trait of religious thought; the beliefs, myths, dogmas and legends are either representations or systems of representations which express the nature of sacred things, the virtues and powers which are attributed to them, or their relations with each other and with profane things [...]

But if a purely hierarchic distinction is a criterium at once too general and too imprecise, there is nothing left with which to characterize the sacred in its relation to the profane except their heterogeneity. However, this heterogeneity is sufficient to characterize this classification of things and to distinguish it from all others, because it is very particular: *it is absolute*. In all the history of human thought there exists no other example of two categories of things so profoundly differentiated or so radically opposed to one another. The traditional opposition of good and bad is nothing beside this; for the good and the bad are only two opposed species of the same class, namely morals, just as sickness and health are two different aspects of the same order of facts, life, while the sacred and the profane have always and everywhere been conceived by the human mind as two distinct classes, as two worlds between which there is nothing in common. The forces which play in one are not simply those which are met with in the other, but a little stronger; they are of a different sort [...]

Thus we arrive at the first criterium of religious beliefs. Undoubtedly there are secondary species within these two fundamental classes which, in their turn, are more or less incompatible with each other. But the real characteristic of religious phenomena is that they always suppose a bipartite division of the whole universe, known and knowable, into two classes which embrace all that exists, but which radically exclude each other. Sacred things are those which the interdictions protect and isolate; profane things, those to which these interdictions are applied and which must remain at a distance from the first. Religious beliefs are the representations which express the nature of sacred things and the relations which they sustain, either with each other or with profane things. Finally, rites are the rules of conduct which prescribe how a man should comport himself in the presence of these sacred objects [...]

However, this definition is not yet complete, for it is equally applicable to two sorts of facts which, while being related to each other, must be distinguished nevertheless: these are magic and religion.

Magic, too, is made up of beliefs and rites. Like religion, it has its myths and its dogmas; only they are more elementary, undoubtedly because, seeking technical and utilitarian ends, it does not waste its time in pure speculation [...]

Here is how a line of demarcation can be traced between these two domains.

The really religious beliefs are always common to a determined group, which makes profession of adhering to them and of practising the rites connected with them. They are not merely received individually by all the members of this group; they are something belonging to the group, and they make its unity. The individuals which compose it feel themselves united to each other by the simple fact that they have a common faith. A society whose members are united by the fact that they think in the same way in regard to the sacred world and its relations with the profane world, and by the fact that they translate these common ideas into common practices, is what is called a Church [...]

It is quite another matter with magic. To be sure, the belief in magic is always more or less general; it is very frequently diffused in large masses of the population, and there are even peoples where it has as many adherents as the real religion. But it does not result in binding together those who adhere to it, nor in uniting them into a group leading a common life. *There is no Church of magic.* Between the magician and the individuals who consult him, as between these individuals themselves, there are no lasting bonds which make them members of the same moral community, comparable to that formed by the believers in the same god or the observers of the same cult. The magician has a clientele and not a Church, and it is very possible that his clients have no other relations between each other, or even do not know each other; even the relations which they have with him are generally accidental and transient; they are just like those of a sick man with his physician [...]

Thus we arrive at the following definition: *A religion is a unified system of beliefs and practices relative to sacred things, that is to say, things set apart and forbidden – beliefs and practices which unite into one single moral community called a Church, all those who adhere to them.* The second element which thus finds a place on our definition is no less essential than the first; for by showing that the idea of religion is inseparable from that of the Church, it makes it clear that religion should be an eminently collective thing.

Origin of the idea of the totemic principle or mana

The proposition established in the preceding chapter determines the terms in which the problem of the origins of totemism should be posed. Since totemism is everywhere dominated by the idea of a quasi-divine principle, imminent in certain categories of men and things and thought of under the form of an animal or vegetable, the explanation of this religion is essentially the explanation of this belief; to arrive at this, we must seek to learn how men have been led to construct this idea and out of what materials they have constructed it.

It is obviously not out of the sensations which the things serving as totems are able to arouse in the mind; we have shown that these things are frequently insignificant [...]

Thus the totem is before all a symbol, a material expression of something else. But of what?

From the analysis to which we have been giving our attention, it is evident that it expresses and symbolizes two different sorts of things. In the first place, it is the outward and visible form of what we have called the totemic principle or god. But it is also the symbol of the determined society called the clan. It is its flag; it is the sign by which each clan distinguishes itself from the others, the visible mark of its personality, a mark borne by everything which is a part of the clan under any title whatsoever, men, beasts or things. So if it is at once the symbol of the god and of the society, is that not because the god and the society are only one? How could the emblem of the group have been able to become the figure of this quasi-divinity, if the group and the divinity were two distinct realities? The god of the clan, the totemic principle, can therefore be nothing else than the clan itself, personified and represented to the imagination under the visible form of the animal or vegetable which serves as totem.

But how has this apotheosis been possible, and how did it happen to take place in this fashion?

In a general way, it is unquestionable that a society has all that is necessary to arouse the sensation of the divine in minds, merely by the power that it has over them; for to its members it is what a god is to his worshippers. In fact, a god is, first of all, a being whom men think of as superior to themselves, and upon whom they feel that they depend. Whether it be a conscious personality, such as Zeus or Jahveh, or merely abstract forces such as those in play in totemism, the worshipper, in the one case as in the other, believes himself held to certain manners of acting which are imposed upon him by the nature of the sacred principle with which he feels that he is in communion. Now society also gives us the sensation of a perpetual dependence. Since it has a nature which is peculiar to itself and different from our individual nature, it pursues ends which are likewise special to it; but, as it cannot attain them except through our intermediacy, it imperiously demands our aid. It requires that, forgetful of our own interest, we make ourselves its servitors, and it submits us to every sort of inconvenience, privation and sacrifice, without which social life would be impossible. It is because of this that at every instant we are obliged to submit ourselves to rules of conduct and of thought which we have neither made nor desired, and which are sometimes even contrary to our most fundamental inclinations and instincts.

Even if society were unable to obtain these concessions and sacrifices from us except by a material constraint, it might awaken in us only the idea of a physical force to which we must give way of necessity, instead of that of a moral power such as religions adore. But as a matter of fact, the empire which it holds over consciences is due much less to the physical supremacy of which it has the privilege than to the moral authority with which it is invested. If we yield to its orders, it is not merely because it is strong enough to triumph over our resistance; it is primarily because it is the object of a venerable respect.

We say that an object, whether individual or collective, inspires respect when the representation expressing it in the mind is gifted with such a force that it automatically causes or inhibits actions, *without regard for any consideration relative to their useful or injurious effects*. When we obey somebody because of the moral authority which we recognize in him, we follow out his opinions, not because they seem wise, but because a certain sort of physical energy is imminent in the idea that we form of this person, which conquers our will and inclines it in the indicated direction. Respect is the emotion which we experience when we feel this interior and wholly spiritual pressure operating upon us [...]

Since it is in spiritual ways that social pressure exercises itself, it could not fail to give men the idea that outside themselves there exist one or several powers, both moral and, at the same time, efficacious, upon which they depend. They must think of these powers, at least in part, as outside themselves, for these address them in a tone of command and sometimes even order them to do violence to their most natural inclinations. It is undoubtedly true that if they were able to see that these influences which they feel emanate from society, then the mythological system of interpretations would never be born. But social action follows ways that are too circuitous and obscure, and employs psychical mechanisms that are too complex to allow the ordinary observer to see when it comes. As long as scientific analysis does not come to teach it to them, men know well that they are acted upon, but they do not know by whom. So they must invent by themselves the idea of these powers with which they feel themselves in connection, and from that, we are able to catch a glimpse of the way by which they were led to represent them under forms that are really foreign to their nature and to transfigure them by thought.

But a god is not merely an authority upon whom we depend; it is a force upon which our strength relies. The man who has obeyed his god and who for this reason, believes the god is with him, approaches the world with confidence and with the feeling of an increased energy. Likewise, social action does not confine itself to demanding sacrifices, privations and efforts from us. For the collective force is not entirely outside of us; it does not act upon us wholly from without; but rather, since society cannot exist except in and through individual consciousness, this force must also penetrate us and organize itself within us; it thus becomes an integral part of our being and by that very fact this is elevated and magnified.

There are occasions when this strengthening and vivifying action of society is especially apparent. In the midst of an assembly animated by a common passion, we become susceptible of acts and sentiments of which we are incapable when reduced to our own forces; and when the assembly is dissolved and when, finding ourselves alone again, we fall back to our ordinary level, we are then able to measure the height to which we have been raised above ourselves. History abounds in examples of this sort [...]

Besides these passing and intermittent states, there are other more durable ones, where this strengthening influence of society makes itself felt with greater consequences and frequently even with greater brilliancy. There are periods in history when, under the influence of some great collective shock, social interactions have become much more frequent and active. Men look for each other and assemble together more than ever. That general effervescence results which is characteristic of revolutionary or creative epochs [...]

Also, in the present day just as much as in the past, we see society constantly creating sacred things out of ordinary ones. If it happens to fall in love with a man and if it thinks it has found in him the principal aspirations that move it, as well as the means of satisfying them, this man will be raised above the others and, as it were, deified. Opinion will invest him with a majesty exactly analogous to that protecting the gods. This is what has happened to so many sovereigns in whom their age had faith: if they were not made gods, they were at least regarded as direct representatives of the deity. And the fact that it is society alone which is the author of these varieties of apotheosis, is evident since it frequently chances to consecrate men thus who have no right to it from their own merit. The simple deference inspired by men invested with high social functions is not different in nature from religious respect. It is expressed by the same movements: a man keeps at a distance from a high personage; he approaches him only with precautions; in conversing with him, he uses other gestures and language than those used with ordinary mortals. The sentiment felt on these occasions is so closely related to the religious sentiment that many peoples have confounded the two.

In addition to men, society also consecrates things, especially ideas. If a belief is unanimously shared by a people, then, for the reason which we pointed out above, it is forbidden to touch it, that is to say, to deny it or to contest it. Now the prohibition of criticism is an interdiction like the others and proves the presence of something sacred. Even to-day, howsoever great may be the liberty which we accord to others, a man who should totally deny progress or ridicule the human ideal to which modern societies are attached, would produce the effect of a sacrilege. There is at least one principle which those the most devoted to the free examination of everything tend to place above discussion and to regard as untouchable, that is to say, as sacred: this is the very principle of free examination.

All these facts allow us to catch glimpses of how the clan was able to awaken within its members the idea that outside of them there exist forces which dominate them and at the same time sustain them, that is to say in fine, religious forces: it is because there is no society with which the primitive is more directly and closely connected. The bonds uniting him to the tribe are much more lax and more feebly felt. Although this is not at all strange or foreign to him, it is with the people of his own clan that he has the greatest number of things in common; it is the action of this group that he feels the most directly; so it is this also which, in preference to all others, should express itself in religious symbols.

The life of the Australian [Aboriginal] societies passes alternately through two distinct phases. Sometimes the population is broken up into little groups who wander about independently of one another, in their various occupations; each family lives by itself, hunting and fishing, and in a word, trying to procure its indispensable food by all the means in its power. Sometimes, on the contrary, the population concentrates and gathers at determined points for a length of time varying from several days to several months. This concentration takes place when a clan or a part of the tribe is summoned to the gathering, and on this occasion they celebrate a religious ceremony, or else hold what is called a corrobbori in the usual ethnological language.

These two phases are contrasted with each other in the sharpest way. In the first, economic activity is the preponderating one, and it is generally of a very mediocre intensity. Gathering the grains or herbs that are necessary for food, or hunting and fishing are not occupations to awaken very lively passions. The dispersed condition in which the society finds itself results in making its life uniform, languishing and dull. But when a corrobbori takes place, everything changes. Since the emotional and passional faculties of the primitive are only imperfectly placed under the control of his reason and will, he easily loses control of himself. Any event of some importance puts him quite outside himself [...]

We are now able to understand how the totemic principle, and in general, every religious force, comes to be outside of the object in which it resides. It is because the idea of it is in no way made up of the impressions directly produced by this thing upon our senses or minds. Religious force is only the sentiment inspired by the group in its members, but projected outside of the consciousnesses that experience them, and objectified. To be objectified, they are fixed upon some object which thus becomes sacred; but any object might fulfil this function. In principle, there are none whose nature predestines them to it to the exclusion of all others; but also there are none that are necessarily impossible. Everything depends upon the circumstances which lead the sentiment creating religious ideas to establish itself here or there, upon this point or upon that one. Therefore, the sacred character assumed by an object is not implied in the intrinsic properties of this latter: *it is added to them*. The world of religious things is not one particular aspect of empirical nature; *it is superimposed upon it* [...]

Thus social life, in all its aspects and in every period of its history, is made possible only by a vast symbolism. The material emblems and figurative representations with which we are more especially concerned in our present study, are one form of this; but there are many others. Collective sentiments can just as well become incarnate in persons or formulæ: some formulæ are flags, while there are persons, either real or mythical, who are symbols [...]

Our entire study rests upon this postulate that the unanimous sentiment of the believers of all times cannot be purely illusory. Together with a recent apologist of the faith we admit that these religious beliefs rest upon a specific experience whose demonstrative value is, in one sense, not one bit inferior to that of scientific experiments, though different from them. We, too, think that 'a tree is known by its fruits,' and that fertility is the best proof of what the roots are worth. But from the fact that a 'religious experience,' if we choose to call it this, does exist and that it has a certain foundation — and, by the way, is there any experience which has none? — it does not follow that the reality which is its foundation conforms objectively to the idea which believers have of it. The very fact that the fashion in which it has been conceived has varied infinitely in different times is enough to prove that none of these conceptions express it adequately. If a scientist states it as an axiom that the sensations of heat and light which we feel correspond to some objective cause, he does not conclude that this is what it appears to the senses to be. Likewise, even if the impressions which the faithful feel are not imaginary, still they are in no way privileged intuitions; there is no reason for believing that they inform us better upon the nature of their object than do ordinary sensations upon the nature of bodies and their properties. In order to discover what this object consists of, we must submit them to an examination and elaboration analogous to that which has substituted for the sensuous idea of the world another which is scientific and conceptual.

This is precisely what we have tried to do, and we have seen that this reality, which mythologies have represented under so many different forms, but which is the universal and eternal objective cause of these sensations *sui generis* out of which religious experience is made, is society. We have shown what moral forces it develops and how it awakens this sentiment of a refuge, of a shield and of a guardian support which attaches the believer to his cult. It is that which raises him outside himself; it is even that which made him. For that which makes a man is the totality of the intellectual property which constitutes civilization, and civilization is the work of society. This is explained [by] the preponderating rôle of the cult in all religions, whichever they may be. This is because society cannot make its influence felt unless it is in action, and it is not in action unless the individuals who compose it are assembled together and act in common. It is by common action that it takes consciousness of itself and realizes its position; it is before all else an active co-operation. The collective ideas and sentiments are even possible only owing to these exterior movements which symbolize them, as we have established. Then it is action which dominates the religious life, because of the mere fact that it is society which is its source.

In addition to all the reasons which have been given to justify this conception, a final one may be added here, which is the result of our whole work. As we have progressed, we have established the fact that the fundamental categories of thought, and consequently of science, are of religious origin. We have seen that the same is true for magic and consequently for the different processes which have issued from it. On the other hand, it has long been known that up until a relatively advanced movement of evolution, moral and legal rules have been indistinguishable from ritual prescriptions. In summing up, then, it may be said that nearly all the great social institutions have been born in religion. Now in order that these principal aspects of the collective life may have commenced by being only varied aspects of the religious life, it is obviously necessary that the religious life be the eminent form and, as it were, the concentrated expression of the whole collective life. If religion has given birth to all that is essential in society, it is because the idea of society is the soul of religion [...]

But, it is said, what society is it that has thus made the basis of religion? Is it the real society, such as it is and acts before our very eyes, with the legal and moral organization which it has laboriously fashioned during the course of history? This is full of defects and imperfections. In it, evil goes beside the good, injustice often reigns supreme, and the truth is often obscured by error. How could anything so crudely organized inspire the sentiments of love, the ardent enthusiasm and the spirit of abnegation which all religions claim of their followers? These perfect beings which are gods could not have taken their traits from so mediocre, and sometimes even so base a reality.

But, on the other hand, does someone think of a perfect society, where justice and truth would be sovereign, and from which evil in all its forms would be banished for ever? No one would deny that this is in close relations with the religious sentiment; for, they would say, it is towards the realization of this that all religions strive. But that society is not an empirical fact, definite and observable; it is a fancy, a dream with which men have lightened their sufferings, but in which they have never really lived. It is merely an idea which comes to express our more or less obscure aspirations towards the good, the beautiful and the ideal. Now these aspirations have their roots in us; they come from the very depths of our being; then there is nothing outside of us which can account for them. Moreover, they are already religious in themselves; thus it would seem that the ideal society presupposes religion, far from being able to explain it.

But, in the first place, things are arbitrarily simplified when religion is seen only on its idealistic side: in its way, it is realistic. There is no physical or moral ugliness, there are no vices or evils which do not have a special divinity. There are gods of theft and trickery, of lust and war, of sickness and of death. Christianity itself, howsoever high the idea which it has made of the divinity may be, has been obliged to give the spirit of evil a place in its mythology. Satan is an essential piece of the Christian system; even if he is an impure being, he is not a profane one. The anti-god is a god, inferior and subordinated, it is true, but nevertheless endowed with extended powers; he is even the object of rites, at least of negative ones. Thus religion, far from ignoring the real society and making abstraction of it, is in its image; it reflects all its aspects, even the most vulgar and the most repulsive. All is to be found there, and if in the majority of cases we see the good victorious over evil, life over death, the powers of light over the powers of darkness, it is because reality is not otherwise. If the relation between these two contrary forces were reversed, life would be impossible; but, as a matter of fact, it maintains itself and even tends to develop.

But if, in the midst of these mythologies and theologies we see reality clearly appearing, it is none the less true that it is found there only in an enlarged, transformed and idealized form. In this respect, the most primitive religions do not differ from the most recent and the most refined. For example, we have seen how the Arunta place at the beginning of time a mythical society whose organization exactly reproduces that which still exists to-day; it includes the same clans and phratries, it is under the same matrimonial rules and it practises the same rites. But the personages who compose it are ideal beings, gifted with powers and virtues to which common mortals cannot pretend. Their nature is not only higher, but it is different, since it is at once animal and human. The evil powers there undergo a similar metamorphosis: evil itself is, as it were, made sublime and idealized. The question now raises itself of whence this idealization comes.

Some reply that men have a natural faculty for idealizing, that is to say, of substituting for the real world another different one, to which they transport themselves by thought. But that is merely changing the terms of the problem; it is not resolving it or even advancing it. This systematic idealization is an essential characteristic of religions. Explaining them by an innate power of idealization is simply replacing one word by another which is the equivalent of the first; it is as if they said that men have made religions because they have a religious nature. Animals know only one world, the one which they perceive by experience, internal as well as external. Men alone have the faculty of conceiving the ideal, of adding something to the real. Now where does this singular privilege come from? Before making it an initial fact or a mysterious virtue which escapes science, we must be sure that it does not depend upon empirically determinable conditions.

The explanation of religion which we have proposed has precisely this advantage, that it gives an answer to this question. For our definition of the sacred is that it is something added to and above the real: now the ideal answers to this same definition; we cannot explain one without explaining the other. In fact, we have seen that if collective life awakens religious thought on reaching a certain degree of intensity, it is because it brings about a state of effervescence which changes the conditions of psychic activity. Vital energies are over-excited, passions more active, sensations stronger; there are even some which are produced only at this moment. A man does not recognize himself; he feels himself transformed and consequently he transforms the environment which surrounds him. In order to account for the very particular impressions which he receives, he attributes to the things with which he is in most direct contact properties which they have not, exceptional powers and virtues which the objects of every-day experience do not possess. In a word, above the real world where his profane life passes he has placed another which,in one sense, does not exist except in thought, but to which he attributes a higher sort of dignity than to the first. Thus, from a double point of view it is an ideal world.

The formation of the ideal world is therefore not an irreducible fact which escapes science; it depends upon conditions which observation can touch; it is a natural product of social life. For a society to become conscious of itself and maintain at the necessary degree of intensity the sentiments which it thus attains, it must assemble and concentrate itself. Now this concentration brings about an exaltation of the mental life which takes form in a group of ideal conceptions where is portrayed the new life thus awakened; they correspond to this new set of psychical forces which is added to those which we have at our disposition for the daily tasks of existence. A society can neither create itself nor recreate itself without at the same time creating an ideal. This creation is not a sort of work of supererogation for it, by which it would complete itself, being already formed; it is the act by which it is periodically made and remade. Therefore when some oppose the ideal society, like two antagonists which would lead us in opposite directions, they materialize and oppose abstractions. The ideal society is not outside of the real society; it is a part of it. Far from being divided between them as between two poles which mutually repel each other, we cannot hold to one without holding to the other. For a society is not made up merely of the mass of individuals who compose it, the ground which they occupy, the things which they use and the movements which they perform, but above all is the idea which it forms of itself. It is undoubtedly true that it hesitates over the manner in which it ought to conceive itself; it feels itself drawn in divergent directions. But these conflicts which break forth are not between the ideal and reality, but between two different ideals, that of yesterday and that of to-day, that which has the authority of tradition and that which has the hope of the future. There is surely a place for investigating whence these ideals evolve; but whatever solution may be given to this problem, it still remains that all passes in the world of the ideal.

Thus the collective ideal which religion expresses is far from being due to a vague innate power of the individual, but it is rather at the school of collective life that the individual has learned to idealize. It is in assimilating the ideals elaborated by society that he has become capable of conceiving the ideal. It is society which, by leading him within its sphere of action, has made him acquire the need of raising himself above the world of experience and has at the same time furnished him with the means of conceiving another. For society has constructed this new world in constructing itself, since it is society which this expresses. Thus both with the individual and in the group, the faculty of idealizing has nothing mysterious about it. It is not a sort of luxury which a man could get along without, but a condition of his very existence. He could not be a social being, that is to say, he could not be a man, if he had not acquired it. It is true that in incarnating themselves in individuals, collective ideals tend to individualize themselves. Each understands them after his own fashion and marks them with his own stamp; he suppresses certain elements and adds others. Thus the personal ideal disengages itself from the social ideal in proportion as the individual personality develops itself and becomes an autonomous source of action. But if we wish to understand this aptitude, so singular in appearance, of living outside of reality, it is enough to connect it with the social conditions upon which it depends.

Therefore it is necessary to avoid seeing in this theory of religion a simple restatement of historical materialism: that would be misunderstanding our thought to an extreme degree. In showing that religion is something essentially social, we do not mean to say that it confines itself to translating into another language the material forms of society and its immediate vital necessities. It is true that we take it as evident that social life depends upon its material foundation and bears its mark, just as the mental life of an individual depends upon his nervous system and in fact his whole organism. But collective consciousness is something more than a mere epiphenomenon of its morphological basis, just as individual consciousness is something more than a simple efflorescence of the nervous system. In order that the former may appear, a synthesis *sui generis* of particular consciousness is required. Now this synthesis has the effect of disengaging a whole world of sentiments, ideas and images which, once born, obey laws all their own. They attract each other, repel each other, unite, divide themselves, and multiply, though these combinations are not commanded and necessitated by the condition of the underlying reality. The life thus brought into being even enjoys so great an independence that it sometimes indulges in manifestations with no purpose or utility of any sort, for the mere pleasure of affirming itself. We have shown that this is often precisely the case with ritual activity and mythological thought [...]

Thus there is something eternal in religion which is destined to survive all the particular symbols in which religious thought has successively enveloped itself. There can be no society which does not feel the need of upholding and reaffirming at regular intervals the collective sentiments and the collective ideas which make its unity and its personality. Now this moral remaking cannot be achieved except by the means of reunions, assemblies and meetings where the individuals, being closely united to one another, reaffirm in common their common sentiments; hence come ceremonies which do not differ from regular religious ceremonies, either in their object, the results which they produce, or the processes employed to attain these results. What essential difference is there between an assembly of Christians celebrating the principal dates of the life of Christ, or of Jews remembering the exodus from Egypt or the promulgation of the decalogue, and a reunion of citizens commemorating the promulgation of a new moral or legal system or some great event in the national life?

If we find a little difficulty to-day in imagining what these feasts and ceremonies of the future could consist in, it is because we are going through a stage of transition and moral mediocrity [...]

But feasts and rites, in a word, the cult, are not the whole religion. This is not merely a system of practices, but also a system of ideas whose object is to explain the world; we have seen that even the humblest have their cosmology. Whatever connection there may be between these two elements of the religious life, they are still quite different. The one is turned towards action, which it demands and regulates; the other is turned towards thought, which it enriches and organizes. Then they do not depend upon the same conditions, and consequently it may be asked if the second answers to necessities as universal and as permanent as the first.

When specific characteristics are attributed to religious thought, and when it is believed that its function is to express, by means peculiar to itself, an aspect of reality which evades ordinary knowledge as well as science, one naturally refuses to admit that religion can ever abandon its speculative rôle. But our analysis of the facts does not seem to have shown this specific quality of religion. The religion which we have just studied is one of those whose symbols are the most disconcerting for the reason. There all appears mysterious. These beings which belong to the most heterogeneous groups at the same time, who multiply without ceasing to be one, who divide without diminishing, all seem, at first view, to belong to an entirely different world from the one where we live; some have even gone so far as to say that the mind which constructed them ignored the laws of logic completely. Perhaps the contrast between reason and faith has never been more thorough. Then if there has ever been a moment in history when their heterogeneousness should have stood out clearly, it is here. But contrary to all appearances, as we have pointed out, the realities to which religious speculation is then applied are the same as those which later serve as the subject of reflection for philosophers: they are nature, man, society. The mystery which appears to surround them is wholly superficial and disappears before a more painstaking observation: it is enough merely to set aside the veil with which mythological imagination has covered them for them to appear such as they really are. Religion sets itself to translate these realities into an intelligible language which does not differ in nature from that employed by science; the attempt is made by both to connect things with each other, to establish internal relations between them, to classify them and to systematize them. We have even seen that the essential ideas of scientific logic are of religious origin. It is true that in order to utilize them, science gives them a new elaboration; it purges them of all accidental elements; in a general way, it brings a spirit of criticism into all its doings, which religion ignores; it surrounds itself with precautions to 'escape precipitation and bias,' and to hold aside the passions, prejudices and all subjective influences. But these perfectionings of method are not enough to differentiate it from religion. In this regard, both pursue the same end; scientific thought is only a more perfect form of religious thought. Thus it seems natural that the second should progressively retire before the first, as this becomes better fitted to perform the task.

And there is no doubt that this regression has taken place in the course of history. Having left religion, science tends to substitute itself for this latter in all that which concerns the cognitive and intellectual functions. Christianity has already definitely consecrated this substitution in the order of material things. Seeing in matter that which is profane before all else, it readily left the knowledge of this to another discipline, *tradidit mundum hominum disputationi,* 'He gave the world over to the disputes of men'; it is thus that the natural sciences have been able to establish themselves and make their authority recognized without very great difficulty. But it could not give up the world of souls so easily; for it is before all over souls that the god of the Christians aspires to reign. That is why the idea of submitting the psychic life to science produced the effect of a sort of profanation for a long time; even to-day it is repugnant to many minds. However, experimental and comparative psychology is founded and to-day we must reckon with it. But the world of the religious and moral life is still forbidden. The great majority of men continue to believe that here there is an order of things which the mind cannot penetrate except by very special ways. Hence comes the active resistance which is met with every time that someone tries to treat religious and moral phenomena scientifically. But in spite of these oppositions, these attempts are constantly repeated and this persistence even allows us to foresee that this final barrier will finally give way and that science will establish herself as mistress even in this reserved region.

That is what the conflict between science and religion really amounts to. It is said that science denies religion in principle. But religion exists; it is a system of given facts; in a word, it is a reality. How could science deny this reality? Also, in so far as religion is action, and in so far as it is a means of making men live, science could not take its place, for even if this expresses life, it does not create it; it may well seek to explain the faith, but by that very act it presupposes it. Thus there is no conflict except upon one limited point. Of the two functions which religion originally fulfilled, there is one, and only one, which tends to escape it more and more: that is its speculative function. That which science refuses to grant to religion is not its right to exist, but its right to dogmatize upon the nature of things and the special competence which it claims for itself for knowing man and the world. As a matter of fact, it does not know itself. It does not even know what it is made of, nor to what need it answers. It is itself a subject for science, so far is it from being able to make the law for science! And from another point of view, since there is no proper subject for religious speculation outside that reality to which scientific reflection is applied, it is evident that this former cannot play the same rôle in the future that it has played in the past.

However, it seems destined to transform itself rather than to disappear.

We have said that there is something eternal in religion: it is the cult and the faith. Men cannot celebrate ceremonies for which they see no reason, nor can they accept a faith which they in no way understand. To spread itself or merely to maintain itself, it must be justified, that is to say, a theory must be made of it. A theory of this sort must undoubtedly be founded upon the different sciences, from the moment when these exist; first of all, upon the social sciences, for religious faith has its origin in society; then upon psychology, for society is a synthesis of human consciousnesses; and finally upon the sciences of nature, for man and society are a part of the universe and can be abstracted from it only artificially. But howsoever important these facts taken from the constituted sciences may be, they are not enough; for faith is before all else an impetus to action, while science, no matter how far it may be pushed, always remains at a distance from this. Science is fragmentary and incomplete; it advances but slowly and is never finished; but life cannot wait. The theories which are destined to make men live and act are therefore obliged to pass science and complete it prematurely. They are possible only when the practical exigencies and the vital necessities which we feel without distinctly conceiving them push thought in advance, beyond that which science permits us to affirm. Thus religions, even the most rational and laicized, cannot and never will be able to dispense with a particular form of speculation which, though having the same subjects as science itself, cannot be really scientific: the obscure intuitions of sensation and sentiment too often take the place of logical reasons. On one side, this speculation resembles that which we meet with in the religions of the past; but on another, it is different. While claiming and exercising the right of going beyond science, it must commence by knowing this and by inspiring itself with it. Ever since the authority of science was established, it must be reckoned with; one can go farther than it under the pressure of necessity, but he must take his direction from it. He can affirm nothing that it denies, deny nothing that it affirms, and establish nothing that is not directly or indirectly founded upon principles taken from it. From now on, the faith no longer exercises the same hegemony as formerly over the system of ideas that we may continue to call religion. A rival power rises up before it which, being born of it, ever after submits it to its criticism and control. And everything makes us foresee that this control will constantly become more extended and efficient, while no limit can be assigned to its future influence.

5 S. FREUD

Civilization and its discontents

From *The Complete Psychological Works of Sigmund Freud*, translated and edited by James Strachey. Reproduced by permission of Sigmund Freud Copyrights Limited, The Institute of Psycho-Analysis and The Hogarth Press.

... The two processes, that of the cultural development of the group and that of the cultural development of the individual, are, as it were, always interlocked. For that reason some of the manifestations and properties of the super-ego can be more easily detected in its behaviour in the cultural community than in the separate individual.

The cultural super-ego has developed its ideals and set up its demands. Among the latter, those which deal with the relations of human beings to one another are comprised under the heading of ethics. People have at all times set the greatest value on ethics, as though they expected that it in particular would produce especially important results. And it does in fact deal with a subject which can easily be recognized as the sorest spot in every civilization. Ethics is thus to be regarded as a therapeutic attempt – as an endeavour to achieve, by means of a command of the super-ego, something which has so far not been achieved by means of any other cultural activities. As we already know, the problem before us is how to get rid of the greatest hindrance to civilization – namely, the constitutional inclination of human beings to be aggressive towards one another; and for that very reason we are especially interested in what is probably the most recent of the cultural commands of the super-ego, the commandment to love one's neighbour as oneself. In our research into, and therapy of, a neurosis, we are led to make two reproaches against the super-ego of the individual. In the severity of its commands and prohib-itions it troubles itself too little about the happiness of the ego, in that it takes insufficient account of the resistances against obeying them – of the instinctual strength of the id [in the first place], and of the diffi-culties presented by the real external environment [in the second]. Consequently we are very often obliged, for therapeutic purposes, to oppose the super-ego, and we endeavour to lower its demands. Exactly the same objections can be made against the ethical demands of the cultural super-ego. It, too, does not trouble itself enough about the facts of the mental constitution of human beings. It issues a command and does not ask whether it is possible for people to obey it. On the contrary, it assumes that a man's ego is psychologically capable of anything that is required of it, that his ego has unlimited mastery over his id. This is a mistake; and even in what are known as normal people the id cannot be controlled beyond certain limits. If more is demanded of a man, a revolt will be produced in him or a neurosis, or he will be made unhappy. The commandment, 'Love thy neighbour as thyself', is the strongest defence against human aggressiveness and an excellent example of the unpsychological proceedings of the cultural super-ego. The commandment is impossible to fulfil; such an enormous inflation of love can only lower its value, not get rid of the difficulty. Civilization pays no attention to all this; it merely admonishes us that the harder it is to obey the precept the more meritorious it is to do so. But anyone who follows such a precept in present-day civilization only puts himself at a disadvantage *vis-à-vis* the person who disregards it. What a potent obstacle to civilization aggressiveness must be, if the defence against it can cause as much unhappiness as aggressiveness itself! 'Natural' ethics, as it is called, has nothing to offer here except the narcissistic satisfaction of being able to think oneself better than others. At this point the ethics based on religion introduces its promises of a better after-life. But so long as virtue is not rewarded here on earth, ethics will, I fancy, preach in vain. I too think it quite certain that a real change in the relations of human beings to possessions would be of more help in this direction than any ethical commands; but the recognition of this fact among socialists has been obscured and made useless for practical purposes by a fresh idealistic misconception of human nature.

I believe the line of thought which seeks to trace in the phenomena of cultural development the part played by a super-ego promises still further discoveries. I hasten to come to a close. But there is one question which I can hardly evade. If the development of civilization has such a far-reaching similarity to the development of the individual and if it employs the same methods, may we not be justified in reaching the diagnosis that, under the influence of cultural urges, some civilizations, or some epochs of civilization – possibly the whole of mankind – have become 'neurotic'? An analytic dissection of such neuroses might lead to therapeutic recommendations which could lay claim to great practical interest. I would not say that an attempt of this kind to carry psychoanalysis over to the cultural community was absurd or doomed to be fruitless. But we should have to be very cautious and not forget that, after all, we are only dealing with analogies and that it is dangerous, not only with men but also with concepts, to tear them from the sphere in which they have originated and been evolved. Moreover, the diagnosis of communal neuroses is faced with a special difficulty. In an individual neurosis we take as our starting-point the contrast that distinguishes the patient from his environment, which is assumed to be 'normal'. For a group all of whose members are affected by one and the same disorder no such background could exist; it would have to be found elsewhere. And as regards the therapeutic application of our knowledge, what would be the use of the most correct analysis of social neuroses, since no one possesses authority to impose such a therapy upon the group? But in spite of all these difficulties, we may expect that one day someone will venture to embark upon a pathology of cultural communities.

For a wide variety of reasons, it is very far from my intention to express an opinion upon the value of human civilization. I have endeavoured to guard myself against the enthusiastic prejudice which holds that our civilization is the most precious thing that we possess or could acquire and that its path will necessarily lead to heights of unimagined perfection. I can at least listen without indignation to the critic who is of the opinion that when one surveys the aims of cultural endeavour and the means it employs, one is bound to come to the conclusion that the whole effort is not worth the trouble, and that the outcome of it can only be a state of affairs which the individual will be unable to tolerate. My impartiality is made all the easier to me by my knowing very little about all these things. One thing only do I know for certain and that is that man's judgements of value follow directly his wishes for happiness – that, accordingly, they are an attempt to support his illusions with arguments. I should find it very understandable if someone were to point out the obligatory nature of the course of human civilization and were to say, for instance, that the tendencies to a restriction of sexual life or to the institution of a humanitarian ideal at the expense of natural selection were developmental trends which cannot be averted or turned aside and to which it is best for us to yield as though they were necessities of nature. I know, too, the objection that can be made against this, to the effect that in the history of mankind, trends such as these, which were considered unsurmountable, have often been thrown aside and replaced by other trends. Thus I have not the courage to rise up before my fellow-men as a prophet, and I bow to their reproach that I can offer them no consolation: for at bottom that is what they are all demanding – the wildest revolutionaries no less passionately than the most virtuous believers.

The fateful question for the human species seems to me to be whether and to what extent their cultural development will succeed in mastering the disturbance of their communal life by the human instinct of aggression and self-destruction. It may be that in this respect precisely the present time deserves a special interest. Men have gained control over the forces of nature to such an extent that with their help they would have no difficulty in exterminating one another to the last man. They know this, and hence comes a large part of their current unrest, their unhappiness and their mood of anxiety. And now it is to be expected that the other of the two 'Heavenly Powers', eternal Eros, will make an effort to assert himself in the struggle with his equally immortal adversary. But who can foresee with what success and with what result?[1]

Note

1   The final sentence was added in 1931 – when the menace of Hitler was already beginning to be apparent.

I   THE SOCIOLOGY OF BELIEF
(b) Rationality, culture and ideology

In this subsection, there are some selections from a number of authors concerned with debates and issues which have arisen both within anthropology (in the pieces by Geertz, Douglas and Evans-Pritchard), and about issues raised by anthropological research in philosophy and social theory (in the selections from Hirst and Woolley, and from Lukes). The main debate here has been concerned with the issue of whether or not there are any universal norms of rationality such that people from one culture can make judgements about the beliefs, values and practices in another culture which is different from the one into which they were socialised.

In part, this debate concerns the distinction between science and ideology, and between both of these types of belief systems and religion, as the two pieces by Geertz illustrate. This is not just a terminological dispute, but is an important debate rooted in differences in philosophy and epistemology. Geertz makes an attempt to avoid becoming entangled in philosophical issues by concentrating upon the stylistic differences between science and ideology in his article 'Ideology as a cultural system'. Science, he says, is 'restrained, spare, resolutely analytic', while ideology's style is 'ornate, vivid, deliberately suggestive: by objectifying moral sentiment through the same devices that science shuns, it seeks to motivate action'. In his call for an analysis of the symbolic action in a religion, in his article on 'Religion as a cultural system', a similar emphasis upon symbols and stylistic devices emerges.

Geertz's approach stresses the importance of symbolism as a semi-autonomous level which gives a sense of reality and naturalness to the phenomena it portrays. Sociologists need to pay more attention to the symbolic level in its own right, Geertz would claim, especially in an area such as the sociology of religion, before questions about the interrelationships between political-economic structures and cultural components such as religion can be dealt with in a satisfactory way.

A more recent group of writers, represented here by the selections from

Hirst and Woolley, and Lukes, have been concerned with the issue about rationality and its cultural universality or variability. The social scientist cannot avoid this issue as the concrete cases of the analysis of Azande witchcraft (by Evans-Pritchard, 1929), and of pollution (by M. Douglas, 1970) illustrate. Some position has to be taken about which cultural definitions of 'reality' are treated as being most rational, or even true, even if the position is that there is no way of deciding this, as Mary Douglas argues.

Lukes holds that some fundamental criteria of rationality, what he calls 'rational [1] criteria' in the article included in this book, are necessary if meaningful communication is to be possible between members of diverse cultures. Such inter-cultural communication is possible both logically and in practice. Complete relativism, which would claim that no such universal criteria and understandings are possible, is incoherent and cannot be stated in a satisfactory form on this view. However, Lukes also holds that social scientists must give careful attention to the particular context in which a set of beliefs operates in order to grasp the specific criteria of rationality used in a cultural group, as in the example of witchcraft among the Azande. These criteria he calls 'rational [2] criteria'.

Mary Douglas (1970, in this volume) provides an example of an attempt to deny that there are great differences between so-called primitive cultures and those of modern societies which contain science. She analyses the idea of 'dirt' in order to show that there were categories of dirt and pollution before modern medicine, for example, developed the germ theory of the transmission of diseases. The notion of 'dirt' Mary Douglas uses in her article is one which is universal – namely that dirt is defined as matter out of place. Some notion of dirt, or of pollution, is found in all cultures but what is seen as dirty, or polluting, depends on the particular category system a cultural group has developed. All classificatory systems will generate some anomalies which will be candidates for being treated as polluting objects, substances or beings. In this way, Mary Douglas is able to provide a plausible explanation for the observation that modern medical practices can develop along-side more traditional beliefs and practices such as those associated with witchcraft in some cultural groups. The two institutions are not seen to be logically contradictory by people who use both, but as comple-mentary to one another.

In another piece included here, Hirst and Woolley (1980) argue that some standards of rational judgement are possible, but, unlike Lukes, they make it explicit that these criteria are not necessarily those found in any western society at any given point in time. Such rational standards can be used to appraise not only magic and witchcraft but also modern societies' use of science and technology. They conclude by saying that: 'Sociology can offer some clarifications, if not answers, to intractable moral and practical questions ... Conduct and organization cannot be separated from categories of morality and metaphysics, equally those categories are not merely matters of personal choice or intellectual conviction – they are part of social relations.'

6 C. GEERTZ

Religion as a cultural system

From *Anthropological Approaches to Religion* edited by M. Banton, 1966. Reproduced by permission of the publishers, Tavistock Publications.

... At least four of the contributions of the men who ... dominate our thought to the point of parochializing it – Durkheim's discussion of the nature of the sacred, Weber's *Verstehenden* methodology, Freud's parallel between personal rituals and collective ones, and Malinowski's exploration of the distinction between religion and common sense – seem to me inevitable starting-points for any useful anthropological theory of religion. But they are starting-points only. To move beyond them we must place them in a much broader context of contemporary thought than they, in and of themselves, encompass. The dangers of such a procedure are obvious: arbitrary eclecticism, superficial theory-mongering, and sheer intellectual confusion. But I, at least, can see no other road of escape from what, referring to anthropology more generally, Janowitz (1963, p. 151) has called the dead hand of competence.

In working toward such an expansion of the conceptual envelope in which our studies take place, one can, of course, move in a great number of directions; and perhaps the most important initial problem is to avoid setting out, like Stephen Leacock's mounted policeman, in all of them at once. For my part, I shall confine my effort to developing what, following Parsons and Shils (1951), I refer to as the cultural dimension of religious analysis. The term 'culture' has by now acquired a certain aura of ill-repute in social anthropological circles because of the multiplicity of its referents and the studied vagueness with which it has all too often been invoked. (Though why it should suffer more for these reasons than 'social structure' or 'personality' is something I do not entirely understand.) In any case, the culture concept to which I adhere has neither multiple referents nor, so far as I can see, any unusual ambiguity: it denotes an historically transmitted pattern of meanings embodied in symbols, a system of inherited conceptions expressed in symbolic forms by means of which men communicate, perpetuate, and develop their knowledge about and attitudes toward life. Of course, terms such as 'meaning', 'symbol', and 'conception' cry out for explication. But that is precisely where the widening, the broadening, and the expanding come in. If Langer (1962, p. 55) is right that 'the concept of meaning, in all its varieties, is the dominant philosophical concept of our time', that 'sign, symbol, denotation, signification, communication ... are our [intellectual] stock in trade', it is perhaps time that social anthropology, and particularly that part of it concerned with the study of religion, became aware of the fact.

As we are to deal with meaning, let us begin with a paradigm: viz. that sacred symbols function to synthesize a people's ethos – the tone, character, and quality of their life, its moral and aesthetic style and mood – and their world-view – the picture they have of the way things in sheer actuality are, their most comprehensive ideas of order (Geertz, 1958). In religious belief and practice a group's ethos is rendered intellectually reasonable by being shown to represent a way of life ideally adapted to the actual state of affairs the world-view describes, while the world-view is rendered emotionally convincing by being presented as an image of an actual state of affairs peculiarly well arranged to accommodate such a way of life. This confrontation and mutual confirmation has two fundamental effects. On the one hand, it objectivizes moral and aesthetic preferences by depicting them as the imposed conditions of life implicit in a world with a particular structure, as mere common sense given the unalterable shape of reality. On the other, it supports these received beliefs about the world's body by invoking deeply felt moral and aesthetic sentiments as experiential evidence for their truth. Religious symbols formulate a basic congruence between a particular style of life and a specific (if, most often, implicit) metaphysic, and in so doing sustain each with the borrowed authority of the other [...]

Without further ado, then, a *religion* is:

(1) a system of symbols which acts to (2) establish powerful, pervasive and long-lasting moods and motivations in men by (3) formulating conceptions of a general order of existence and (4) clothing these conceptions with such an aura of factuality that (5) the moods and motivations seem uniquely realistic.

1. *a system of symbols which acts to ...*

Such a tremendous weight is being put on the term 'symbol' here that our first move must be to decide with some precision what we are going to mean by it. This is no easy task, for, rather like 'culture', 'symbol' has been used to refer to a great variety of things, often a number of them at the same time. In some hands it is used for anything which signifies something else to someone: dark clouds are the symbolic precursors of an oncoming rain. In others it is used only for explicitly conventional signs of one sort or another: a red flag is a symbol of danger, a white of surrender. In others it is confined to something which expresses in an oblique and figurative manner that which cannot be stated in a direct and literal one, so that there are symbols in poetry but not in science, and symbolic logic is misnamed. In yet others, however (Langer, 1953, 1960, 1962), it is used for any object, act, event, quality, or relation which serves as a vehicle for a conception – the conception is the symbol's 'meaning' – and that is the approach I shall follow here. The number 6, written, imagined, laid out as a row of stones, or even punched into the program tapes of a computer is a symbol. But so also is the Cross, talked about, visualized, shaped worriedly in air or fondly fingered at the neck, the expanse of painted canvas called 'Guernica' or the bit of painted stone called a churinga, the word 'reality', or even the morpheme '-ing.' They are all symbols, or at least symbolic elements, because they are tangible formulations of notions, abstractions from experience fixed in perceptible forms, concrete embodiments of ideas, attitudes, judgements, longings, or beliefs. To undertake the study of cultural activity – activity in which symbolism forms the positive content – is thus not to abandon social analysis for a Platonic cave of shadows, to enter into a mentalistic world of introspective psychology or, worse, speculative philosophy, and wander there forever in a haze of 'Cognitions', 'Affections', 'Conations', and other elusive entities. Cultural acts, the construction, apprehension, and utilization of symbolic forms, are social events like any other; they are as public as marriage and as observable as agriculture.

They are not, however, exactly the same thing; or, more precisely, the symbolic dimension of social events is, like the psychological, itself theoretically abstractable from those events as empirical totalities. There is still, to paraphrase a remark of Kenneth Burke's (1941, p. 9), a difference between building a house and drawing up a plan for building a house, and reading a poem about having children by marriage is not quite the same thing as having children by marriage. Even though the building of the house may proceed under the guidance of the plan or – a less likely occurrence – the having of children may be motivated by a reading of the poem, there is something to be said for not confusing our traffic with symbols with our traffic with objects or human beings, for these latter are not in themselves symbols, however often they may function as such. No matter how deeply interfused the cultural, the social, and the psychological may be in the everyday life of houses, farms, poems, and marriages, it is useful to distinguish them in analysis, and, so doing, to isolate the generic traits of each against the normalized background of the other two (Parsons & Shils, 1951).

So far as culture patterns, i.e. systems or complexes of symbols, are concerned, the generic trait which is of first importance for us here is that they are extrinsic sources of information (Geertz, 1964a). By 'extrinsic', I mean only that – unlike genes, for example, – they lie outside the boundaries of the individual organism as such in that intersubjective world of common understandings into which all human individuals are born, in which they pursue their separate careers, and which they leave persisting behind them after they die (Schutz, 1962). By 'sources of information', I mean only that – like genes – they provide a blueprint or template in terms of which processes external to themselves can be given a definite form (Horowitz, 1956). As the order of bases in a strand of DNA forms a coded program, a set of instructions, or a recipe, for the synthesization of the structurally complex proteins which shape organic functioning, so culture patterns provide such programs for the institution of the social and psychological processes which shape public behavior. Though the sort of information and the mode of its transmission are vastly different in the two cases, this comparison of gene and symbol is more than a strained analogy of the familiar 'social heredity' sort. It is actually a substantial relationship, for it is precisely the fact that genetically programmed processes are so highly generalized in men, as compared with lower animals, that culturally programmed ones are so important, only because human behavior is so loosely determined by intrinsic sources of information that extrinsic sources are so vital (Geertz, 1962). To build a dam a beaver needs only an appropriate site and the proper materials – his mode of procedure is shaped by his physiology. But man, whose genes are silent on the building trades, needs also a conception of what it is to build a dam, a conception he can get only from some symbolic source – a blueprint, a textbook, or a string of speech by someone who already knows how dams are built, or, of course, from manipulating graphic or linguistic elements in such a way as to attain for himself a conception of what dams are and how they are built.

This point is sometimes put in the form of an argument that cultural patterns are 'models', that they are sets of symbols whose relations to one another 'model' relations among entities, processes or what-have-you in physical, organic, social, or psychological systems by 'paralleling', 'imitating', or 'simulating' them (Craik, 1952). The term 'model' has, however, two senses – an 'of' sense and a 'for' sense – and though these are but aspects of the same basic concept they are very much worth distinguishing for analytic purposes. In the first, what is stressed is the manipulation of symbol structures so as to bring them, more or less closely, into parallel with the pre-established non-symbolic system, as when we grasp how dams work by developing a theory of hydraulics or constructing a flow chart. The theory or chart models physical relationships in such a way – i.e. by expressing their structure in synoptic form – as to render them apprehensible: it is a model *of* 'reality'. In the second, what is stressed is the manipulation of the non-symbolic systems in terms of the relationships expressed in the symbolic, as when we construct a dam according to the specifications implied in an hydraulic theory or the conclusions drawn from a flow chart. Here, the theory is a model under whose guidance physical relationships are organized; it is a model *for* 'reality'. For psychological and social systems, and for cultural models that we would not ordinarily refer to as 'theories', but rather as 'doctrines', 'melodies', or 'rites', the case is in no way different. Unlike genes, and other non-symbolic information sources, which are only models *for*, not models *of*, culture patterns have an intrinsic double aspect: they give meaning, i.e. objective conceptual form, to social and psychological reality both by shaping themselves to it and by shaping it to themselves [...]

The perception of the structural congruence between one set of processes, activities, relations, entities, etc. and another set for which it acts as a program, so that the program can be taken as a representation, or conception – a symbol – of the programmed, is the essence of human thought. The inter-transposability of models *for* and models *of* which symbolic formulation makes possible is the distinctive characteristic of our mentality.

2.   ... *to establish powerful, pervasive, and long-lasting moods and motivations in men by* ...
So far as religious symbols and symbol systems are concerned this inter-transposability is clear [...]

Whether one sees the conception of a personal guardian spirit, a family tutelary or an immanent God as synoptic formulations of the character of reality or as templates for producing reality with such a character seems largely arbitrary, a matter of which aspect, the model *of* or model *for*, one wants for the moment to bring into focus.

3.   ... *by formulating conceptions of a general order of existence and* ...
That the symbols or symbol systems which induce and define dispositions we set off as religious and those which place those dispositions in a cosmic framework are the same symbols ought to occasion no surprise. For what else do we mean by saying that a particular mood of awe is religious and not secular except that it springs from entertaining a conception of all-pervading vitality like mana and not from a visit to the Grand Canyon? Or that a particular case of asceticism is an example of a religious motivation except that it is directed toward the achievement of an unconditioned end like nirvana and not a conditioned one like weight-reduction? If sacred symbols did not at one and the same time

induce dispositions in human beings and formulate, however obliquely, inarticulately, or unsystematically, general ideas of order, then the empirical differentia of religious activity or religious experience would not exist. A man can indeed be said to be 'religious' about golf, but not merely if he pursues it with passion and plays it on Sundays: he must also see it as symbolic of some transcendent truths.

The extreme generality, diffuseness, and variability of man's innate (i.e. genetically programmed) response capacities means that without the assistance of cultural patterns he would be functionally incomplete, not merely a talented ape who had, like some under-privileged child, un-fortunately been prevented from realizing his full potentialities, but a kind of formless monster with neither sense of direction nor power of self-control, a chaos of spasmodic impulses and vague emotions (Geertz, 1962). Man depends upon symbols and symbol systems with a dependence so great as to be decisive for his creatural viability and, as a result, his sensitivity to even the remotest indication that they may prove unable to cope with one or another aspect of experience raises within him the gravest sort of anxiety [...]

There are at least three points where chaos – a tumult of events which lack not just interpretations but *interpretability* – threatens to break in upon man: at the limits of his analytic capacities, at the limits of his powers of endurance, and at the limits of his moral insight. Bafflement, suffering, and a sense of intractable ethical paradox are all, if they become intense enough or are sustained long enough, radical challenges to the proposition that life is comprehensible and that we can, by taking thought, orient ourselves effectively within it – challenges with which any religion, however 'primitive', which hopes to persist must attempt somehow to cope.

Of the three issues, it is the first which has been least investigated by modern social anthropologists (though Evans-Pritchard's (1937) classic discussion of why granaries fall on some Azande and not on others, is a notable exception).

... Where the more intellective aspects of what Weber called the Problem of Meaning are a matter of affirming the ultimate explicability of experience, the more affective aspects are a matter of affirming its ultimate sufferableness. As religion on one side anchors the power of our symbolic resources for formulating analytic ideas in an authoritative conception of the overall shape of reality, so on another side it anchors the power of our, also symbolic, resources for expressing emotions – moods, sentiments, passions, affections, feelings – in a similar concep-tion of its pervasive tenor, its inherent tone and temper. For those able to embrace them, and for so long as they are able to embrace them, religious symbols provide a cosmic guarantee not only for their ability to comprehend the world, but also, comprehending it, to give a precision to their feeling, a definition to their emotions which enables them, morosely or joyfully, grimly or cavalierly, to endure it [...]

The problem of meaning ... is a matter of affirming, or at least recognizing, the inescapability of ignorance, pain, and injustice on the human plane while simultaneously denying that these irrationalities are characteristic of the world as a whole. And it is in terms of religious symbolism, a symbolism relating man's sphere of existence to a wider sphere within which it is conceived to rest, that both the affirmation and the denial are made.

4. ... *and clothing those conceptions with such an aura of factuality that ...*

There arises here, however, a profounder question: how is it that this denial comes to be believed? how is it that the religious man moves from a troubled perception of experienced disorder to a more or less settled conviction of fundamental order? just what does 'belief' mean in a religious context? [...]

It seems to me that it is best to begin any approach to this issue with frank recognition that religious belief involves not a Baconian induction from everyday experience – for then we should all be agnostics – but rather a prior acceptance of authority which transforms that experience [...]

In tribal religions authority lies in the persuasive power of traditional imagery; in mystical ones in the apodictic force of supersensible experience; in charismatic ones in the hypnotic attraction of an extraordinary personality. But the priority of the acceptance of an authoritative criterion in religious matters over the revelation which is conceived to flow from that acceptance is not less complete than in scriptural or hieratic ones. The basic axiom underlying what we may perhaps call 'the religious perspective' is everywhere the same: he who would know must first believe.

But to speak of 'the religious perspective' is, by implication, to speak of one perspective among others. A perspective is a mode of seeing, in that extended sense of 'see' in which it means 'discern', 'apprehend', 'understand', or 'grasp'. It is a particular way of looking at life, a particular manner of construing the world, as when we speak of an historical perspective, a scientific perspective, an aesthetic perspective, a common-sense perspective, or even the bizarre perspective embodied in dreams and in hallucinations. The question then comes down to, first, what is 'the religious perspective' generically considered, as differentiated from other perspectives; and second, how do men come to adopt it.

If we place the religious perspective against the background of three of the other major perspectives in terms of which men construe the world – the common-sensical, the scientific, and the aesthetic – its special character emerges more sharply. What distinguishes common sense as a mode of 'seeing' is, as Schutz (1962) has pointed out, a simple accept-ance of the world, its objects, and its processes as being just what they seem to be – what is sometimes called naïve realism – and the pragmatic motive, the wish to act upon that world so as to bend it to one's practical purposes, to master it, or so far as that proves impossible, to adjust to it. The world of everyday life, itself, of course, a cultural product, for it is framed in terms of the symbolic conceptions of 'stubborn fact' handed down from generation to generation, is the established scene and given object of our actions. Like Mt. Everest it is just there and the thing to do with it, if one feels the need to do anything with it at all, is to climb it. In the scientific perspective it is precisely this givenness which dis-appears (Schutz, 1962). Deliberate doubt and systematic inquiry, the suspension of the pragmatic motive in favor of disinterested observation, the attempt to analyze the world in terms of formal concepts whose relationship to the informal conceptions of common sense become increasingly problematic – there are the hallmarks of the attempt to grasp the world scientifically. And as for the aesthetic perspective, which under the rubric of 'the aesthetic attitude' has been perhaps most exquis-itely examined, it involves a different sort of suspension of naïve realism and practical interest, in that instead of questioning the credentials of everyday experience that experience is merely ignored in favor of an eager dwelling upon appearances, an engrossment in surfaces, an absorption in things, as we say, 'in themselves': 'The function of artistic illusion is not "make-believe" ... but the very opposite, disengagement from belief – the contemplation of sensory qualities without their usual meanings of "here's that chair", "That's my telephone" ... etc. The knowledge that what is before us has no practical significance in the world is what enables us to give attention to its appearance as such' (Langer, 1957, p. 49). And like the common-sensical and the scientific (or the historical, the philosophical, and the autistic), this perspective, this 'way of seeing' is not the product of some mysterious Cartesian chemistry, but is induced, mediated, and in fact created by means of symbols. It is the artist's skill which can produce those curious quasi-objects – poems, dramas, sculptures, symphonies – which, dissociating themselves from the solid world of common sense, take on the special sort of eloquence only sheer appearances can achieve.

The religious perspective differs from the common-sensical in that, as already pointed out, it moves beyond the realities of everyday life to wider ones which correct and complete them, and its defining concern is not action upon those wider realities but acceptance of them, faith in them. It differs from the scientific perspective in that it questions the realities of every-day life not out of an institutionalized scepticism which dissolves the world's givenness into a swirl of probabilistic hypotheses, but in terms of what it takes to be wider, non-hypothetical truths. Rather than detachment, its watchword is commitment; rather than analysis, encounter. And it differs from art in that instead of effecting a disengagement from the whole question of factuality, deliberately manufacturing an air of semblance and illusion, it deepens the concern with fact and seeks to create an aura of utter actuality. It is this sense of the 'really real' upon which the religious perspective rests and which the symbolic activities of religion as a cultural system are devoted to producing, intensifying, and, so far as possible, rendering inviolable by the discordant revelations of secular experience. It is, again, the imbuing of a certain specific complex of symbols – of the metaphysic they formulate and the style of life they recommend – with a persuasive authority which, from an analytic point of view is the essence of religious action.

Which brings us, at length, to ritual. For it is in ritual – i.e. consecrated behavior – that this conviction that religious conceptions are veridical and that religious directives are sound is somehow generated. It is in some sort of ceremonial form – even if that form be hardly more than the recitation of a myth, the consultation of an oracle, or the decoration of a grave – that the moods and motivations which sacred symbols induce in men and the general conceptions of the order of existence which they formulate for men meet and reinforce one another. In a ritual, the world as lived and the world as imagined, fused under the agency of a single set of symbolic forms, turn out to be the same world, producing thus that idiosyncratic transformation in one's sense of reality to which Santayana refers [...]

The acceptance of authority that underlies the religious perspective that the ritual embodies thus flows from the enactment of the ritual itself. By inducing a set of moods and motivations – an ethos – and defining an image of cosmic order – a world-view – by means of a single set of symbols, the performance makes the model *for* and model *of* aspects of religious belief mere transpositions of one another [...]

5. ... *that the moods and motivations seem uniquely realistic*
But no one, not even a saint, lives in the world religious symbols formulate all of the time, and the majority of men live in it only at moments. The everyday world of common-sense objects and practical acts is, as Schutz (1962, pp. 226ff.) says, the paramount reality in human experience – paramount in the sense that it is the world in which we are most solidly rooted, whose inherent actuality we can hardly question (however much

we may question certain portions of it), and from whose pressures and requirements we can least escape. A man, even large groups of men, may be aesthetically insensitive, religiously unconcerned, and unequipped to pursue formal scientific analysis, but he cannot be completely lacking in common sense and survive. The dispositions which religious rituals induce thus have their most important impact – from a human point of view – outside the boundaries of the ritual itself as they reflect back to color the individual's conception of the established world of bare fact [...]

The tracing of the social and psychological role of religion is thus not so much a matter of finding correlations between specific ritual acts and specific secular social ties – though these correlations do, of course, exist and are very worth continued investigation, especially if we can contrive something novel to say about them. More, it is a matter of understanding how it is that men's notions, however implicit, of the 'really real' and the dispositions these notions induce in them, color their sense of the reasonable, the practical, the humane, and the moral.

References

Burke, K. 1941. *The Philosophy of Literary Form*, n.p.: Louisiana State University Press.
Craik, K. 1952. *The Nature of Explanation*. Cambridge: Cambridge University Press.
Evans-Pritchard, E. E. 1937. *Witchcraft, Oracles and Magic Among the Azande*. Oxford: Clarendon Press.
Geertz, C. 1958. Ethos, World-View and the Analysis of Sacred Symbols. *Antioch Review*, Winter (1957–8): 421–37.
Geertz, C. 1962. The Growth of Culture and the Evolution of Mind. In J. Scher (ed.), *Theories of the Mind*. New York: The Free Press, pp. 713–40.
Geertz, C. 1964a. Ideology as a Cultural System. In D. Apter (ed.), *Ideology of Discontent*. New York: The Free Press.
Horowitz, N. H. 1956. The Gene. *Scientific American*, February.
Janowitz, M. 1963. Anthropology and the Social Sciences. *Current Anthropology* 4: 139, 146–54.
Langer, S. 1953. *Feeling and Form*. New York: Scribner's.
Langer, S. 1960. *Philosophy in a New Key*. Fourth Edition. Cambridge, Mass.: Harvard University Press.
Langer, S. 1962. *Philosophical Sketches*. Baltimore: Johns Hopkins.
Parsons, T. & Shils, E. 1951. *Toward a General Theory of Action*. Cambridge, Mass.: Harvard University Press.
Santayana, G. 1905–6. *Reason in Religion*. Vol. 2 of *The Life of Reason, or The Phases of Human Progress*. London: Constable; New York: Scribner's.
Schutz, A. 1962. *The Problem of Social Reality* (vol. 1 of *Collected Papers*). The Hague: Martinus Nijhoff.

7 C. GEERTZ

Ideology as a cultural system

From *Ideology and Discontent*. Edited by D. Apter, 1964. Reproduced by permission of the publishers, Collier–Macmillan, Free Press.

... There are curently two main approaches to the study of the social determinants of ideology: the interest theory and the strain theory.[1] For the first, ideology is a mask and a weapon; for the second, a symptom and a remedy. In the interest theory, ideological pronouncements are seen against the background of a universal struggle for advantage; in the strain theory, against the background of a chronic effort to correct sociopsychological disequilibrium. In the one, men pursue power; in the other, they flee anxiety. As they may, of course, do both at the same time – and even one by means of the other – the two theories are not necessarily contradictory; but the strain theory (which arose in response to the empirical difficulties encountered by the interest theory), being less simplistic, is more penetrating, less concrete, more comprehensive.

The fundamentals of the interest theory are too well known to need review; developed to perfection of a sort by the Marxist tradition, they are now standard intellectual equipment of the man-in-the-street, who is only too aware that in political argumentation it all comes down to whose ox is gored. The great advantage of the interest theory was and is its rooting of cultural idea-systems in the solid ground of social structure, through emphasis on the motivations of those who profess such systems and on the dependence of those motivations in turn upon social position, most especially social class. Further, the interest theory welded political speculation to political combat by pointing out that ideas are weapons and that an excellent way to institutionalize a particular view of reality – that of one's group, class, or party – is to capture political power and enforce it. These contributions are permanent; and if interest theory has not now the hegemony it once had, it is not so much because it has been proved wrong as because its theoretical apparatus turned out to be too rudimentary to cope with the complexity of the interaction among social, psychological, and cultural factors it itself uncovered. Rather like Newtonian mechanics, it has not been so much displaced by subsequent developments as absorbed into them.

The main defects of the interest theory are that its psychology is too anemic and its sociology too muscular. Lacking a developed analysis of motivation, it has been constantly forced to oscillate between a narrow and superficial utilitarianism that sees men as impelled by rational calculation of their consciously recognized personal advantage and a broader, but no less superficial, historicism that speaks with a studied vagueness of men's ideas as somehow 'reflecting', 'expressing', 'corresponding to', 'emerging from', or 'conditioned by' their social commitments [...]

On the other hand, the view that social action is fundamentally an unending struggle for power leads to an unduly Machiavellian view of ideology as a form of higher cunning and, consequently, to a neglect of its broader, less dramatic social functions. The battlefield image of society as a clash of interests thinly disguised as a clash of principles turns attention away from the role that ideologies play in defining (or obscuring) social categories, stabilizing (or upsetting) social expectations, maintaining (or undermining) social norms, strengthening (or weakening) social consensus, relieving (or exacerbating) social tensions. Reducing ideology to a weapon in a *guerre de plume* gives to its analysis a warming air of militancy, but it also means reducing the intellectual compass within which such analysis may be conducted to the constricted realism of tactics and strategy. The intensity of interest theory is – to adapt a figure from Whitehead – but the reward of its narrowness.

As 'interest', whatever its ambiguities, is at one and the same time a psychological and sociological concept – referring both to a felt advantage of an individual or group of individuals and to the objective structure of opportunity within which an individual or group moves – so also is 'strain', for it refers both to a state of personal tension and to a condition of societal dislocation. The difference is that with 'strain' both the motivational background and the social structural context are more systematically portrayed, as are their relations with one another. It is, in fact, the addition of a developed conception of personality systems (basically Freudian), on the one hand, and of social systems (basically Durkheimian) on the other, and of their modes of interpenetration – the Parsonian addition – that transforms interest theory into strain theory.[2]

The clear and distinct idea from which strain theory departs is the chronic malintegration of society. No social arrangement is or can be completely successful in coping with the functional problems it inevitably faces. All are riddled with insoluble antinomies: between liberty and political order, stability and change, efficiency and humanity, precision and flexibility, and so forth. There are discontinuities between norms in different sectors of the society – the economy, the polity, the family, and so forth. There are discrepancies between goals within the different sectors – between the emphases on profit and productivity in business firms or between extending knowledge and disseminating it in universities, for example. And there are the contradictory role expectations of which so much has been made in recent American sociological literature on the foreman, the working wife, the artist, and the politician. Social friction is as pervasive as is mechanical friction – and as irremovable.

Further, this friction or social strain appears on the level of the individual personality – itself an inevitably malintegrated system of conflicting desires, archaic sentiments, and improvised defenses – as psychological strain. What is viewed collectively as structural inconsistency is felt individually as personal insecurity, for it is in the experience of the social actor that the imperfections of society and contradictions of character meet and exacerbate one another. But at the same time, the fact that both society and personality are, whatever their shortcomings, organized systems, rather than mere congeries of institutions or clusters of motives, means that the sociopsychological tensions they induce are also systematic, that the anxieties derived from social interaction have a form and order of their own. In the modern world at least, most men live lives of patterned desperation.

Ideological thought is, then, regarded as (one sort of) response to this desperation: 'Ideology is a patterned reaction to the patterned strains of a social role.'[3] It provides a 'symbolic outlet' for emotional disturbances generated by social disequilibrium. And as one can assume that such disturbances are, at least in a general way, common to all or most occupants of a given role or social position, so ideological reactions to the disturbances will tend to be similar, a similarity only reinforced by the presumed commonalities in 'basic personality structure' among members of a particular culture, class, or occupational category. The model here is not military but medical: An ideology is a malady (Sutton, *et al.*, mention nail-chewing, alcoholism, psychosomatic disorders, and 'crotchets' among the alternatives to it) and demands a diagnosis. 'The concept of strain is not in itself an explanation of ideological patterns but a generalized label for the kinds of factors to look for in working out an explanation.'[4]

But there is more to diagnosis, either medical or sociological, than the identification of pertinent strains; one understands symptoms not merely etiologically but teleologically – in terms of the ways in which they act as mechanisms, however unavailing, for dealing with the disturbances that have generated them. Four main classes of explanation have been most frequently employed: the cathartic, the morale, the solidarity, and the advocatory. By the 'cathartic explanation' is meant the venerable safety-valve or scapegoat theory. Emotional tension is drained off by being displaced onto symbolic enemies ('The Jews', 'Big Business', 'The Reds', and so forth). The explanation is as simple-minded as the device, but that, by providing legitimate objects of hostility (or, for that matter, of love), ideology may ease somewhat the pain of being a petty bureaucrat, a day laborer, or a small-town storekeeper is undeniable. By the 'morale explanation' is meant the ability of an ideology to sustain individuals (or groups) in the face of chronic strain, either by denying it outright or by legitimizing it in terms of higher values. Both the struggling small businessman rehearsing his boundless confidence in the inevitable justness of the American system and the neglected artist attributing his failure to his maintenance of decent standards in a Philistine world are able, by such means, to get on with their work. Ideology bridges the emotional gap between things as they are and as one would have them be, thus insuring the performance of roles that might otherwise be abandoned in despair or apathy. By the 'solidarity explanation' is meant the power of ideology to knit a social group or class together. To the extent that it exists, the unity of the labor movement, the business community, or the medical profession obviously rests to a significant degree on common ideological orientation; and the South would not be The South without the existence of popular symbols charged with the emotions of a pervasive social predicament. Finally, by the 'advocatory explanation' is meant the action of ideologies (and ideologists) in articulating, however partially and indistinctly, the strains that impel them, thus forcing them into the public notice [...]

It is here, however, in the investigation of the social and psychological roles of ideology, as distinct from its determinants, that strain theory itself begins to creak and its superior incisiveness, in comparison with interest theory, to evaporate. The increased precision in the location of the springs of ideological concern does not, somehow, carry over into the discrimination of its consequences, where the analysis becomes, on the contrary, slack and ambiguous [...]

The reason for this weakness is the virtual absence in strain theory (or in interest theory either) of anything more than the most rudimentary conception of the processes of symbolic formulation. There is a good deal of talk about emotions 'finding a symbolic outlet' or 'becoming attached to appropriate symbols' – but very little idea of how the trick is really done. The link between the causes of ideology and its effects seems adventitious because the connecting element – the autonomous process of symbolic formulation – is passed over in virtual silence. Both interest theory and strain theory go directly from source analysis to consequence analysis without ever seriously examining ideologies as systems of interacting symbols, as patterns of interworking meanings [...]

Asking the question that most students of ideology fail to ask – what, precisely, do we mean when we assert that sociopsychological strains are 'expressed' in symbolic forms? – gets one, therefore, very quickly into quite deep water indeed; into, in fact, a somewhat untraditional and apparently paradoxical theory of the nature of human thought as a public and not, or at least not fundamentally, a private activity.[5] The details of such a theory cannot be pursued any distance here, nor can any significant amount of evidence be marshalled to support it. But at least its general outlines must be sketched if we are to find our way back from the elusive world of symbols and semantic process to the (apparently) solider one of sentiments and institutions, if we are to trace with some circumstantiality the modes of interpenetration of culture, personality, and social system.

The defining proposition of this sort of approach to thought *en plein air* – what, following Galanter and Gerstenhaber, we may call 'the extrinsic theory' – is that thought consists of the construction and manipulation of symbol systems, which are employed as models of other systems, physical, organic, social, psychological, and so forth, in such a way that the structure of these other systems – and, in the favorable case, how they may therefore be expected to behave – is, as we say, 'understood'.[6] Thinking, conceptualization, formulation, comprehension, understanding, or what-have-you consists not of ghostly happenings in the head but of a matching of the states and processes of symbolic models against the states and processes of the wider world [...]

As a road map transforms mere physical locations into 'places', connected by numbered routes and separated by measured distances, and so enables us to find our way from where we are to where we want to go, so a poem like, for example, Hopkins's 'Felix Randal' provides, through the evocative power of its charged language, a symbolic model of the emotional impact of premature death, which, if we are as impressed with its penetration as with the road map's, transforms physical sensations into sentiments and attitudes and enables us to react to such a tragedy not 'blindly' but 'intelligently'. The central rituals of religion – a mass, a pilgrimage, a corroboree – are symbolic models (here more in the form of activities than of words) of a particular sense of the divine, a certain sort of devotional mood, which their continual re-enactment tends to produce in their participants. Of course, as most acts of what is usually called 'cognition' are more on the level of identifying a rabbit than operating a wind tunnel, so most of what is usually called 'expression' (the dichotomy is often overdrawn and almost universally misconstrued) is mediated more by models drawn from popular culture than from high art and formal religious ritual. But the point is that the development, maintenance, and dissolution of 'moods', 'attitudes', 'sentiments', and so forth are no more 'a ghostly process occurring in streams of consciousness we are debarred from visiting' than is the discrimination of objects, events, structures, processes, and so forth in our environment. Here, too, 'we are describing the ways in which ... people conduct parts of their predominantly public behavior'.

Whatever their other differences, both so-called 'cognitive' and so-called 'expressive' symbols or symbol-systems have, then, at least one thing in common: They are extrinsic sources of information in terms of which human life can be patterned – extrapersonal mechanisms for the perception, understanding, judgment, and manipulation of the world. Culture patterns – religious, philosophical, aesthetic, scientific, ideological – are 'programs'; they provide a template or blueprint for the organization of social and psychological processes, much as genetic systems provide such a template for the organization of organic processes [...]

The reason such symbolic templates are necessary is that, as has been often remarked, human behavior is inherently extremely plastic. Not strictly but only very broadly controlled by genetic programs or models – intrinsic sources of information – such behavior must, if it is to have any effective form at all, be controlled to a significant extent by extrinsic ones. Birds learn how to fly without wind tunnels, and whatever reactions lower animals have to death are in great part innate, physiologically preformed. The extreme generality, diffuseness, and variability of man's innate response capacities mean that the particular pattern his behavior takes is guided predominantly by cultural rather than genetic templates, the latter setting the over-all psychophysical context within which precise activity sequences are organized by the former. The tool-making, laughing, or lying animal, man, is also the incomplete – or, more accurately, self-completing – animal. The agent of his own realization, he creates out of his general capacity for the construction of symbolic models the specific capabilities that define him. Or – to return at last to our subject – it is through the construction of ideologies, schematic images of social order, that man makes himself for better or worse a political animal.

Further, as the various sorts of cultural symbol-system are extrinsic sources of information, templates for the organization of social and psychological processes, they come most crucially into play in situations where the particular kind of information they contain is lacking, where institutionalized guides for behavior, thought, or feeling are weak or absent. It is in country unfamiliar emotionally or topographically that one needs poems and road maps. So too with ideology [...]

It is a confluence of sociopsychological strain and an absence of cultural resources by means of which to make (political, moral, or economic) sense of that strain, each exacerbating the other, that sets the stage for the rise of systematic (political, moral, economic) ideologies.

And it is, in turn, the attempt of ideologies to render otherwise incomprehensible social situations meaningful, to so construe them as to make it possible to act purposefully within them, that accounts both for the ideologies' highly figurative nature and for the intensity with which, once accepted, they are held. As metaphor extends language by broadening its semantic range, enabling it to express meanings it cannot or at least cannot yet express literally, so the head-on clash of literal meanings in ideology – the irony, the hyperbole, the overdrawn antithesis – provides novel symbolic frames against which to match the myriad 'unfamiliar somethings' that, like a journey to a strange country, are produced by a transformation in political life. Whatever else ideologies may be – projections of unacknowledged fears, disguises for ulterior motives, phatic expressions of group solidarity – they are, most distinctively, maps of problematic social reality and matrices for the creation of collective conscience [...]

As both science and ideology are critical and imaginative 'works' (that is symbolic structures), an objective formulation both of the marked differences between them and of the nature of their relationship to one another seems more likely to be achieved by proceeding from such a concept of stylistic strategies than from a nervous concern with comparative epistemological or axiological status of the two forms of thought. No more than scientific studies of religion ought to begin with unnecessary questions about the legitimacy of the substantive claims of their subject matter ought scientific studies of ideology to begin with such questions. The best way to deal with Mannheim's as with any true paradox is to circumvent it by reformulating one's theoretical approach so as to avoid setting off yet once more down the well-worn path of argument that led to it in the first place.

The differentiae of science and ideology as cultural systems are to be sought in the sorts of symbolic strategy for encompassing situations that they respectively represent. Science names the structure of situations in such a way that the attitude contained toward them is one of disinterestedness. Its style is restrained, spare, resolutely analytic: By shunning the semantic devices that most effectively formulate moral sentiment, it seeks to maximize intellectual clarity. But ideology names the structure of situations in such a way that the attitude contained toward them is one of commitment. Its style is ornate, vivid, deliberately suggestive: By objectifying moral sentiment through the same devices that science shuns, it seeks to motivate action. Both are concerned with the definition of a problematic situation and are responses to a felt lack of needed information. But the information needed is quite different, even in cases where the situation is the same. An ideologist is no more a poor social scientist than a social scientist is a poor ideologist. The two are – or at least they ought to be – in quite different lines of work, lines so different that little is gained and much obscured by measuring the activities of the one against the aims of the other.[8]

Where science is the diagnostic, the critical, dimension of culture, ideology is the justificatory, the apologetic, one – it refers 'to that part of culture which is actively concerned with the establishment and defense of patterns of belief and value'.[9] That there is natural tendency for the two to clash, particularly when they are directed to the interpretation of the same range of situations, is thus clear; but that the clash is inevitable and that the findings of (social) science necessarily will undermine the validity of the beliefs and values that ideology has chosen to defend and propagate seem most dubious assumptions.

Notes

1 F.S. Sutton *et al.*, The American Business Creed, Cambridge, Mass., pp. 11–12, 303–10.

2 For the general schema, see Parsons, *The Social System* (New York, 1951), especially Chaps. I, VII. The fullest development of the strain theory is in Sutton, *et al.*, *op. cit.*, especially Chap. XV.

3 Sutton, *et al.*, *op. cit.*, pp. 307–8.

4 Parsons, 'An Approach to the Sociology of Knowledge', *Transactions of the Fourth World Congress of Sociology*, Milan and Stressa, 1959.

5 G. Ryle, *The Concept of Mind* (New York, 1949).

6 E. Galanter and M. Gerstenhaber, 'On Thought: the Extrinsic Theory', *Psychological Review*, 63 (1956), 218–27.

7 The quotations are from Ryle, *op. cit.*, p. 51.

8 This point is, however, not quite the same as saying that the two sorts of activity may not in practice be carried on together, any more than a man cannot, for example, paint a portrait of a bird that is both ornithologically accurate and aesthetically effective. Marx is, of course, the outstanding case, but for a more recent successful synchronization of scientific analysis and ideological argument, see E. Shils, *The Torment of Secrecy* (New York, 1956). Most such attempts to mix genres are, however, distinctly less happy.

9 Fallers, *op. cit.* The patterns of belief and value defended may be, of course, those of a socially subordinate group, as well as those of a socially dominant one, and the 'apology' therefore for reform or revolution.

8 P. HIRST and P. WOOLLEY

Witchcraft, rationality and other cultures

From *Social Relations and Human Attributes* by P. Hirst and P. Woolley, 1980. Reproduced by permission of the publishers, Tavistock Publications.

One of the more interesting and intense debates in contemporary philosophy and social science has concerned the concept of 'rationality'. This debate has primarily dealt with two questions: first, whether there is a general set of criteria for assessing the rationality of human conduct, and secondly, whether human beings are in general constrained to attempt to act 'rationally'. This debate has not surprisingly centred on the assessment of witchcraft beliefs and practices in 'primitive' societies. Are men attempting to act rationally in warding off witchcraft or practising magic, but simply using inappropriate technologies? Do witchcraft beliefs evidence a failure of that critical, empirical, assessment of beliefs and circumstances which is essential to rational conduct? Are there objective limits to illusion and irrational conduct, constraints imposed by the very nature of our world and our adaptation to it? [...]

E. E. Evans-Pritchard's *Witchcraft, Oracles and Magic among the Azande* (original date 1937, abridged edition 1976) is the point of departure for this debate.[1] It is *the* classic modern anthropological study of witchcraft beliefs, rituals, and practices. Its pre-eminence is explained by the fact that it offered a paradigm of a method of analysis: beliefs were to be examined in the context of the social practices they articulated or accompanied, by means of detailed fieldwork observation and the collection of 'texts' from native informants. In analysing witchcraft beliefs the central issue was the determination of the social relationships in which they were implicated and which motivated them. Witchcraft accusations thus indicate particular sources of tension in relations between neighbours, and provide the society in question with a mechanism for the exposure and resolution of these tensions. As Evans-Pritchard presents it, witchcraft is a central feature of Azande society, an ever-present force and source of concern. It cannot be dismissed as a marginal or residual belief of little relevance to daily activity.

A characteristic feature of the book, the problem around which it is structured, is a fundamental ambiguity of attitude towards witchcraft on Evans-Pritchard's part. This ambiguity is no external inference as to his thoughts and motives. It is a central thematic component of his text and part of the way in which the book is written. The two poles of the ambiguity are a consequence of two quite distinct belief systems being brought together; the assumptions of the ideologies surrounding Western 'scientific' practices, and the participation by a sympathetic observer in native beliefs. First, Azande beliefs are founded on error: 'Witches, as the Azande conceive them, clearly exist' (1976, p. 18). Witchcraft beliefs therefore need *accounting for*. The entities posited by witchcraft beliefs cannot exist because of what is claimed about them. The issue is then to explain why people *capable of rationality* persist in practices deriving from mystical beliefs about non-existent entities. They do so, on the one hand, because the structure of their thought does not permit them to discover their error and, on the other, because their beliefs are implicated in social relationships which they cannot dispense with. Thus, even though a man may doubt the claim that he is a witch, he is forced to act, and therefore to believe, in certain ways to preserve his relationships with others:

We must remember that since witchcraft has no real existence a man does not know that he has bewitched another, even if he is aware that he bears him no ill-will. But, at the same time, he believes firmly in the existence of witchcraft and in the accuracy of the poison oracle so that when the oracle says he is killing a man by his witchcraft, he is probably thankful for having been warned in time. (Evans-Pritchard 1976, p. 44)

Secondly, Evans-Pritchard was a sympathetic observer who participated as fully as he could in native life and belief. He draws his own, uncomfortable conclusion from this immersion:

In no department of their life was I more successful in 'thinking black' ... than in the sphere of witchcraft. I, too, used to react to misfortunes in the idiom of witchcraft, and it was often an effort to check this lapse into unreason. (1976, p. 45)

Apart from its threat to his 'reason' this lapse presented him with no real difficulties. The life of a Zande was viable and had its own adequate means of organization. Thus Evans-Pritchard found the poison-oracle, despite its foundation in 'unreason', an adequate means of conducting affairs:

I always kept a supply of poison for the use of my household and neighbours and we regulated our affairs in accordance with the oracle's decisions. I may remark that I found this as satisfactory a way of running my home and affairs as any other I know of. (1976, p. 126)

Native practices, furthermore, stand up in the face of the tests of illness and pain: 'When you have lived for some time in Zandeland you will have ample evidence of the therapeutic value of the kind of treatment which witch-doctors employ' (1976, p. 108).

Evans-Pritchard tries to resolve this contradiction by explaining, on the one hand, why the Zande do not uncover the falsity at the heart of their beliefs and, on the other, why in spite of this falsity those beliefs can serve as a viable medium of conduct. He lists twenty-two reasons 'why Azande do not perceive the futility of their magic' (1976, p. 201). Here we will group them into five main explanatory themes, and then comment on his explanations.

1 Social structural obstacles to the generalization of beliefs and the collation of information

Social situations and mores determine the concept to be applied in a given case. The doctrine of witchcraft does not explain *any* misfortune, only a class of sudden and inexplicable deaths, illnesses, and failures. No one will take an inexperienced potter seriously if he blames witchcraft for the breaking of a pot in finishing. A man who kills another with a spear will be dealt with as a murderer. Beliefs are 'functions of situations' (1976, p. 221). They articulate specific contexts of action and conduct. Beliefs are thus fragmented across a series of situations and are never present at the same time. This means that contradictions *between* context-specific beliefs do not emerge. The structure of accusations is also serial, so that the implications of the pattern of accusations for the claims made in beliefs remains hidden. If this pattern were examined, given Zande beliefs about the hereditability of 'witchcraft substance', then virtually everybody would be a witch. This occlusion of the contradictions implicit in the pattern of accusations was reinforced by the weakening of central political authority by the British. Witchcraft ceased to be a crime punishable, and therefore examinable, by the royal courts.

2 'Categorical' reasons

The Azande make no distinction between 'natural' and 'supernatural' phenomena in the way that the ideologies of contemporary Western 'common sense' or the 'scientific attitude' do. They therefore lack the categorical conditions for the exclusion of phenomena as beyond the realm of demonstrable causality. This does not mean that the Azande ignore what we would count as 'natural' causality, nor do they deny it a place in the events surrounding witchcraft. They employ what would be in our terms a plural or multiple scheme of causation. They are aware, for example, that a man died by being crushed by a falling house. That is *how* he died. But they go on to ask *why* was it that it collapsed at the precise moment the man happened to be sitting beneath it. Witchcraft explains the conjunction of elements in the event. This latter question permits explanations of an order we would not permit. The conjunction of elements is for us a matter of coincidence or chance.

3 Limits in the mode of experimentation practised by the Azande

The Azande both incorporate the results of 'experience' into their conduct and are often sceptical of the reliability of oracles, the power of witch doctors, etc. But this reference to 'experience' and this scepticism alike operate to *confirm* the basic structure of belief, for they can account for experiences of failure in divination and healing. This is exemplified by the practices surrounding the poison oracle, the most important and reliable of the oracles the Zande use and only brought into operation to confirm a lesser oracle. It consists in administering a poison called *benge* to fowls. The oracle is questioned in a complex form, a sequence of questions using more than one fowl which includes a cross check on erroneous answers due to the failure of bad poison or the intervention of witchcraft. *Benge* is an *intelligent substance* which should 'understand' the questions put to it. It is discriminating, killing some fowls or letting others live in response to questions. If all the fowls die or all live, then it is a sign that the poison is bad, i.e. indiscriminate. The use of the oracle makes no sense if it works as a natural 'poison' in our meaning of the term. It is the *question* put to the oracle, not the chemical composition of the poison, which should decide the result.

The Azande thus use procedures of testing and checks as to the efficacy of practices. But they do not experiment *systematically* to test whether their beliefs as such are true or not. Failures of the poison oracle cannot therefore serve to disconfirm the structure of their beliefs surrounding it. Experiment takes place within a framework of 'mystical notions'. The failure of the oracle, therefore, is 'explained' by reference to the intervention of entities or forces which depend on other or the very same mystical notions: *benge* has lost its virtue or a witch is distracting it.

4   The absence of the technology of reason

The Azande lack means of the rationalization of existence, of memory, of movement, and calculation of forces such that they could make an objective assessment of states of affairs. Having no clock, they are unable to measure and therefore to recognize that the ritual of placing a stone in a tree in no way retards the arrival of sunset.[2]

5   Thought as a 'mental structure'

Evans-Pritchard was troubled by the implications of Lévy-Bruhl's notion of 'mentalities', but he treats the Zande as people capable of and often using 'common sense' who are nonetheless trapped within a self-reinforcing structure of 'mystical notions'. Witchcraft, oracles, and magic form a coherent and self-reinforcing system, each element of which explains away the contradictions and problems raised by others. Zande reasoning is trapped within the 'web' of their own thought, and they cannot think outside a mesh of 'mystical notions':

> And yet the Azande do not see that their oracles tell them nothing! Their blindness is not due to stupidity: they reason excellently in the idiom of their beliefs but they cannot reason outside, or against, their beliefs because they have no other idiom in which to express their thoughts.
> (1976, p.59)

Given this dominance of entities specified by mystical notions, it is difficult to see how many of their activities could 'fail'. Magic is employed against mystical powers, and as these powers transcend experience they can hardly be contradicted by it.

Evans-Pritchard's explanations are wholly dependent on his asking a particular question: why the *Azande* cannot recognize the 'problem' in their own system of thought, that it is founded on error. Yet the error is *attributed to it*. Similar questions could be asked, from other metaphysical premises, of the beliefs surrounding Western natural scientific activities. The question 'are there witches?' cannot be answered except within a definite system of thought to which attach unprovable metaphysical postulates and theoretical criteria of what is to count as an explanation. Evans-Pritchard is always uncomfortably close to recognizing this. Much of his account could be taken simply as a map of the differences in the assumptions and procedures implicated in Zande beliefs and those of what is called Western 'common sense'. Each of his explanatory themes can either be applied to *Western* belief systems or shown not to be a problem *within the context* of Zande thought. Let us consider them in turn.

(i) Evans-Pritchard recognizes that there are analogous plural causalities in Western thought, and that the type of explanation offered depends on a social situation. We insist upon naturalistic explanations of disease and insanity, reducing statements and behaviour produced in a fever or delirium to consequences of pathology. But in matters of 'normal' conduct we insist on a voluntaristic account of statements and behaviour; we refuse to treat crime as a pathological behaviour at par with those produced by certain diseases. Evans-Pritchard says, 'We accept scientific explanations of the causes of disease, and even of the causes of insanity, but we deny them in crime and sin because they militate against laws and morals which are axiomatic' (1976, p. 27). We may use doctors to certify disease and insanity, but they do so in relation to *conventional categories of classes of action*. Crime is not a scientific concept, but a class of acts dependent on convention. Notions surrounding the category of 'crime' treat human beings as autonomous agents capable of self-reflection and volition. The person as a *subject*, as the author of its actions, is, for all its pervasiveness in our culture, a category which orders experience and one with implications as metaphysical as those of 'witch'. When the judge refuses to consider poverty, a dreadful upbringing, or a man's criminal ancestors as adequate explanations of his behaviour, he is asking the question *why* in a way analogous to our Zande informant in the case of the house.

(ii) If the Azande suffer problems from the lack of a distinction between the natural and supernatural, that distinction itself brings problems in its train. The category 'supernatural' is a means of limiting the classes of phenomena capable of explanation. It rests on a metaphysical limitation of the entities which *can* exist, and it limits phenomena to those ascertainable by certain means. Certain forms of 'experience' are denied. Whereas Zande thought lacks means of exclusion of entities as 'impossible', our means of exclusion are probably too powerful. A whole range of entities from regularly attested 'paranormal' phenomena like precognition and telepathy, to the manifestations of the unconscious or various 'psychosomatic' interactions have been strongly condemned as contrary to common sense and scientific reason. Now it is precisely in this region, and in the sphere of herbal medicine, that claims for the effectiveness of divination and magical therapy tend to be advanced. Most anthropologists place the question of the efficacy of magical and shamanistic practices to one side. Discounting the truth of witchcraft beliefs, they tend to explain their persistence in terms of their foundation in, and consequences for, social relations. Hardly anyone wants to get the reputation of a 'crank', by considering efficacy seriously, which may mean doing so in terms of concepts analogous to those of native informants. Further, in many cases the prospect of such an assessment is long past – native relations of authority, confidence in their own beliefs, and knowledge and skills have often been destroyed or reduced to a shadow of their former selves. Arseniev's informant Darsu did not merely believe that one could talk to tigers.[3] He claimed to have survived 'conversations' with them. His beliefs and the skills associated with them perished with or were disarticulated by Westernization.

(iii) The Zande experiment with *benge* in the context of beliefs that it is an intelligent substance. Western natural scientists engage in many different practices of experiment, but in doing so they do not set out to contradict their basic concepts of causality, or the basic forms of entity specified by them. Indeed, they *could* not do so for it is these very concepts which make possible particular practices of experimental questioning of relationships between phenomena. Thus the famous nineteenth-century experimental physiologist, Claude Bernard, wrote in his methodological textbook, *An Introduction to the Study of Experimental Medicine*, that 'there never are any unsuccessful experiments' (1957, p. 117). If an expected phenomenon is not produced in an experiment as it should be according to the schema of causation adopted and in contradiction to previous results, the causes of this divergence must be sought in conditions outside those predicted for and controlled. This explaining of the phenomena which intervened to change the result leads to a progressive specification and control of the conditions of experimentation.[4] Clearly, the Zande attributing the failure of *benge* to a variety of intervening factors and causes is not engaged in the same practice as Bernard's experimental physiologist. But the physiologist, like the Zande, is not questioning the basic structure of his theory or mode of thinking, and he cannot do so if experimental procedures are to be productive. The scientist must use categories of determinism and of consistency of causal action in order to engage in experimentation. The results, although generally consistent with those categories, are predicated on them and do not independently confirm them. The scientist is no less a prisoner of his premises than the Zande engaged in divination.

(iv) The Zande may lack means of the 'rationalization' of existence, such as clocks, but the primary objective of their procedures could not be furthered by clocks and calculation based on them. Thus the Zande ritual with the stone displaces worry about the fall of night, something a glance at one's watch could only reinforce. The dangers of calculating journeys in terms of time and distance are repeatedly confirmed by many travellers in Africa.[5] Again with oracles, the procedure may seem to be an absurd way to decide when to make a journey or where to build a new house. But, like astrology, the objective is to produce *decisions*, means of ordering action. The non-manipulable oracle delivers such a decision. As Evans-Pritchard admitted,[6] it was as good a way of conducting life as any other. This is particularly true where the elements in a decision are not subject to calculation. It should not be assumed that the conduct of activities in terms of clocks and other forms of measurement promotes 'rationality' or makes decisions more calculable. Modern war is a good example. It is governed by clocks, calculations of distance and times of movement, the scale of resources required, etc. But these activities of staff officers coexist with forms of thought and decision on the part of the mass of soldiers that would make a Zande with his poison oracle appear a veritable technician. For ordinary participants, war is a mass of incidents and incalculables, which cannot be reduced to order. Yet decisions *have* to be taken and the conduct appropriate for survival depends on morale. Soldiers' lives are riddled with the equivalent of the Zande's stone in a tree: whether to stay in a shell hole or leave it; whether one will die today or not. These are questions of vital importance, questions whose resolution is in no way aided by the possession of a watch, a ruler, or the latest casualty statistics. Soldiers develop positively 'mystical notions': in the value of talismans, that one will anticipate one's death, that a particular shell is destined to meet a certain soldier, and so on.[7] And for soldiers, one can read miners, farmers, and so on. Self-advancing pit props and the substances of Messrs Fisons have not yet killed the Zande in us. Technology – clocks, computers, and cannons – create conditions just as haphazard and undecideable as the possible rogue elephant on one's journey through the bush, conditions which still require us to decide and to order our conduct. Oracles and rituals order conduct and make decisions where other forms of calculation cannot, and where a full recognition of the haphazard nature of the situation would paralyse any action.

(v) Zande beliefs form a 'mental structure', a self-reinforcing set of mutually confirmatory notions which govern the interpretations placed on experience. Interestingly enough that is almost exactly how the philosopher Thomas Kuhn (1970) conceives the basic theoretical structures in the natural sciences, which he calls 'paradigms'. At any given moment there is one dominant paradigm in a particular scientific field. This includes a set of assumptions and concepts which structure perception, which govern the kinds of questions that can be asked and the types of answers given. In a period of 'normal science', scientific work consists in 'puzzle-solving', answering questions set by the paradigm according to its rules of adequacy. In a period of scientific revolution when a paradigm tends to accumulate problems and anomalies it cannot answer, change takes place only when another paradigm which is capable of 'covering' the problems unanswerable in the first comes into being. Paradigms are never 'refuted'. They are abandoned for other 'incommensurable' schemes with different basic assumptions. Scientific change is change in the ruling 'mental structures' which govern the scientific community's perception of reality. Kuhn's *The Structure of Scientific Revolutions* (1970) is a controversial work. What particularly exercised critics is the radical relativism implied in the notion of paradigms as 'incommensurable' schemes for ordering our perception of the world, schemes which cannot in themselves be subjected to verification. But Kuhn's position is not an aberration. A number of modern philosophers challenge the verificationist account of the sciences and problematize the very idea that scientific theories are or can be 'refuted' by reference to 'reality'.[8]

Evans-Pritchard's attempt to differentiate Zande thought by pointing to its closed and irrefutable nature only works if there is a form of thought to counterpose to it which is open to empirical criticism. This is just what writers like Kuhn are challenging. Evans-Pritchard is committed to the view of the natural sciences as bodies of propositions which are verified by independent reference to the pertinent facts in their domain. Kuhn challenges this notion of a realm of neutral and independently accessible facts by means of which we can assess theories. Scientific analysis can only take place on the basis of a structure of unverifiable beliefs and concepts which determine what phenomena we *can* see and how we can explain them.

This is not to say that we accept Kuhn's view or consider it unproblematic. Kuhn's conception shares the weakness of Lévy-Bruhl's notion of a distinct pre-logical 'primitive mentality' – a tendency to convert theories and forms of thought into wholly incommensurable mental universes. As a result the contradictions *within* conceptual schemes tend to be obliterated, and the possible co-presence of a number of different or alternative belief systems or theoretical schemes is denied. If 'paradigms' were completely incommensurable or the 'primitive mentality' wholly illogical, then it would be impossible to move from one paradigm or thought system to another. The main strength of positions such as Kuhn's is that they challenge the tendency to privilege of one form of thought over another, and the assertion that Western rationality is closer to 'reality'. Thus, when Evans-Pritchard points to the unresolved contradictions and 'mystical notions' which are part of the web of Zande thought and which prevent them from recognizing error, it can be pointed out that unresolved contradictions abound in the modern natural sciences. Modern theoretical physics consists in a number of competing and incompatible accounts of sub-atomic structure and the structure of the universe. Evans-Pritchard defines 'mystical notions' as 'patterns of thought which attribute to phenomena supra-sensible qualities which ... are not derived from observation, or cannot be logically inferred from it, and which they do not possess' (1956, p. 12). Sub-atomic physics is entirely concerned with 'supra-sensible' entities, such as neutrons.

If 'sensible' means the ordinary human capacities of sight, touch, etc., then these entities are outside 'common sense', for they can be neither directly observed nor inferred from observation. What qualities these supra-sensible phenomena 'possess' can only be determined by scientific instruments constructed by means of theories and where the results of the employment of these instruments are matters for interpretation by theory. As to the existence of these entities we are wholly dependent on the scientists' theoretical account of them. Evans-Pritchard's criterion for differentiating mystical and non-mystical thought depends on the notion of a direct and independent sensory access to 'reality'. As we shall see in discussing Peter Winch's contribution to the debate on rationality it is just this notion which is problematic.

One final point ought to be made before turning to that contribution. Kuhn and Evans-Pritchard have one tendency in common and that is to refer to forms of mentality such as 'science' or 'common sense' *grosso modo*.[9] Yet a mass of distinct discourses and practices is to be encountered in that domain we signal by the concept 'the natural sciences', for example. Epistemological doctrines purport to unify this complex. Similarly the notion of 'common sense' attempts to unify all human 'practical' thought, as the basic human outlook consistent with sense experience and a rational adjustment to the facts of the sensible world. In our discussion of witchcraft beliefs we have consistently spoken not of 'common sense', as if it were a real and present human attitude, but of the 'ideology' of contemporary common sense, and likewise, we have spoken of the epistemological 'doctrines' associated with the modern natural sciences. These ideologies or doctrines purport to govern the discourses and practices they refer to, but the relationship is one of claim rather than undisputed dominion. Definite discursive structures (for example, Neo-Platonism and its philosophical alternatives in the Renaissance) and conditions of practice do constrain what can be said and done, what can be argued or constructed. But these structures and conditions are not 'mentalities' – that is, a collective mode of 'thought' which is prior to and which governs its expressions. Such a concept of 'mentality' merely restores the worst defects and excesses of Durkheim's 'collective consciousness' or para-Hegelian notions of *Zeitgeist*. However, discursive structures and conditions of practice are effective and operative only through the mode in which a discourse is written and continued, through the process of a trial or an experiment. The notion of forms of 'mentality' has its value, particularly in challenging universalist notions of human nature, but it also has its limits. To enter fully into these limits would entail writing a different, far more theoretical, and even less accessible book.

Peter Winch in his paper 'Understanding a Primitive Society' (1979)

poses clearly the problem of the 'rationality' of witchcraft beliefs torment-
ing Evans-Pritchard. The practice of falsification of Zande beliefs would
involve reference to *another thought system*. We, guided by 'rationality'
and 'common sense', can see the error at the heart of Zande beliefs. Evans-
Pritchard clearly believes he is doing more than use the alternative criteria
of his own belief system to assess what phenomena can or cannot exist.
To do that would be simply to presume the validity of one's own system
and would in no way demonstrate it. The central question, therefore, is
the putative *independence* of the tests and criticisms of beliefs proposed
in Western 'rationality' from the beliefs from which those tests derive.
That is, the refutation of beliefs is based on their independent reference
to reality itself. In other words, the claim is that Western rationality
or science is able to avoid the trap of its own beliefs and assumptions
because those very beliefs give it access to an independently existing and
intelligible reality.

Evans-Pritchard is in fact thereby put into the same metaphysical camp as Pareto:
for both of them the conception of 'reality' must be regarded as intelligible and
applicable *outside* the context of scientific reasoning itself, since it is that to which
scientific notions do, and unscientific notions do not, have a relation.
(Winch 1979, p. 81)

Winch contends that Western science is not the only system of thought
to conceive the real as independent of the knower and intelligible in itself.
Many religious beliefs do just this on the grounds that the world was made
by God and bears witness to His intelligent action. Winch argues that
Evans-Pritchard is trying to work with a concept of 'reality' which is not
determined by its form of use in the conventions of a language:

What Evans-Pritchard wants to be able to say is that the criteria applied in scientific experimentation constitute a true link between our ideas and an independent
reality, whereas those characteristic of other systems of thought – in particular,
magical methods of thought – do not. It is evident that the expressions 'true link'
and 'independent reality' in the previous sentence cannot themselves be explained
by reference to the scientific universe of discourse, as this would beg the question.
We have then to ask how, by reference to what established universe of discourse,
the use of those expressions is to be explained: and it is clear that Evans-Pritchard
has not answered this question.
(Winch 1979, pp. 82–3)

Winch is contending that all statements about 'reality' are interpretative
and that they stem from definite 'universes of discourse' which are not
'reality' itself. He is denying that reality is intelligible *independent of
discourse*. Such an idea of independence has two basic ways of formulation. One is the positivist philosopher's notion of an independent *observation language* against which theoretical languages are measured, and

the other is of a directly meaningful 'experience' of nature or God, a poetic or religious revelation.[10] In both cases language is inscribed *within the real*, a neutral *language* of observation, the voice of nature or of God which speaks directly to the soul of the poet or mystic. This notion of reality itself serving to signify the 'true link', to confirm or disconfirm our ideas, rests on assumptions which transcend observation: that the world of appearances is coherent and intelligible, that is does not consist in a mass of sense impressions dispersed apart from the forms of order we impose on them. In order to make the *claim* for a neutral observation language it is necessary to present an argument which depends on non-observational terms.

Winch makes his argument in terms of the Austrian philosopher Ludwig Wittgenstein's later theory of meaning.[11] It is not necessary to elaborate or to agree with this theory to agree with the point Winch makes. Briefly, however, Wittgenstein denies his own earlier view that meaningful statements consist in propositions which model states of affairs and argues that the meaning of statements is dependent on their context of use and the rules specifying usage. Language is not a model of reality; and there are no necessary limits to meaning other than those imposed by systems of language rules and the 'forms of life' to which they relate. Different conceptions or uses of words like 'reality', 'existence', or 'entity' are, therefore, possible. The positivist philosopher and the mystic will make use of these words in different ways. Both work in terms of a discursive doctrine of possible entities and both have concepts of what types of tests of adequacy are to count. Both may utilize a concept of experience. The positivist has to choose by convention not to count the mystic's world. Both have doctrines of the entities which are possible and these doctrines transcend and limit observation and experience. The question of which entities are to count can only be settled *within* a form of discourse by the rules it proposes, and not *between* discourses. Evans-Pritchard can deal with the Azande in the terms of Western thought or in terms of their own belief systems. He cannot, despite the claims of certain Western doctrines of scientific method, use the one to *independently* or objectively refute the other by reference to 'reality'.

Winch points to the inescapable relativity of distinct theoretical schemes and belief systems. That one can assess phenomena only within a system or scheme, and that the tests one uses depend on but do not validate that system or scheme. Alasdair MacIntyre (1979) is strongly critical of Winch precisely because of this relativism. MacIntyre argues that it *is* possible to settle whether or not Zande beliefs can be assessed as rational or irrational. That assessment *must* be relative to Western scientific knowledge. Societies are *not* equivalent. Social development provides new means and standards for explaining the world and controlling it. Relativism can only be sustained by setting that process of development to one side:

> It seems to me that one could only hold the belief of the Azande rationally *in the absence of* any practice of science and technology in which criteria of effectiveness, ineffectiveness and kindred notions had been built up. But to say this is to recognize the appropriateness of scientific criteria of judgement from our standpoint ... It is only *post eventum* in the light of later and more sophisticated understanding that their belief and concepts can be evaluated at all.
> (MacIntyre 1979a, p. 67)

We cannot dispense with our own criteria because, relative to other beliefs, they *are* rational. To ask for a meta-proof of these criteria is to seek a philosophical realm outside the actual dialectical process of development of rationality. That dialectic is one of a pluralism and conflict of views: it means that in society undergoing development there will be alternative views in contest. It is these transitions from one system of belief to another that make it possible to choose between alternative views:

> In seventeenth century Scotland, for example, the question could not be raised, 'But are there witches?' If Winch asks, from within what way of life, under what system of belief was this question asked, the only answer is that it was asked by men who confronted alternative systems and were able to draw out of what confronted them independent criteria of judgement. Many Africans today are in the same situation.
> (MacIntyre 1976b, p. 129)

The problem with this account is the notion of 'independent criteria of judgement'. Independent of what? We have seen all too clearly that the critics of the legal persecution of witches did *not* have criteria independent of Christian religious beliefs. To have had such criteria would have led them to the stake or at least to utter marginality. Lacking independent criteria and dependent on the premises of their opponents, their criticisms were effectively discounted as incompatible with both received religion and experience. Further, the field of debate was primarily *forensic*. The question 'But are there witches?' was actually posed as 'Should people who *believe themselves to be* or are accused as witches be tried and punished?' That question could be answered by denying certain of the claims following from witch beliefs and yet insisting that 'witches' be tried for *what they thought*, which was sin enough. The question 'But are there witches?' could not be satisfactorily answered within the terms of debate or the 'alternative' means of discourse available; nor did a negative answer lead to an end to the legal process. Africans' transitions are all too typically between their tribal pagan beliefs and some variant of Christianity, a step to social promotion and, if possible, a comfortable urban existence. How one measures the relative merits in terms of 'rationality' of traditional paganism and, say, Methodism or Pentacostalism, is a question MacIntyre does not try to answer. But this is the typical pattern of such 'transitions' from one set of beliefs and practices with undemonstrable metaphysical premises to another.

And not all transitions are so cosy. The mass of native peoples never encountered Western beliefs and practices as a higher, more ordered, and rational world. To the Aztecs dying *en masse* of Old World diseases and subject to the Spanish fury, to the South Sea Islanders dying of the same diseases and drink, to the American Indians or the Eskimos, Western civilization came as a calamity.[12] It shattered their confidence in their own beliefs and practices. It left them as the slaves or ethnographical museum pieces of their Western conquerors. It brought them next to nothing. It dealt them blows whose only Western standard of measure is the scale of the Lisbon earthquake or Hiroshima.

In thus shattering viable and often prosperous ways of life, developed cultures and civilizations, Western penetration did not bring 'progress'.[13] It brought new, and often more problematic and ecologically less viable, conditions of living for reduced and servile populations. On the other hand, it would be dubious to use population growth as a measure of progress. The populations of areas of Western imperial conquest, India, China, Latin America, have grown rapidly in this century. This owes something to economic intervention and to public health measures – benefits of Western 'rationality'. But it would be unwise to over-emphasize the role technology or medicine has played in population growth or to ignore the problems that growth has brought in train. China's population, for example, grew throughout epidemics, famines, a declining standard of living, conditions of administrative incompetence, and collapse of public order directly connected with and even fostered by imperialist intervention. Most Chinese, until 1949, were born, lived, and died without the benefits of Western medicine and public health, and with all the evils imperialism can visit on a country.

'Post eventum', growing numbers of Westerners are less than happy with the 'criteria of effectiveness' of Western science and technology. To judge our civilization 'superior' by its own standards of technique is to ignore the objectives those techniques are required to serve, and the unintended consequences they bring in train. Those objectives and consequences raise moral and practical problems which cannot be solved by waving the wand of 'rationality'. It would be possible to reply to MacIntyre thus: in a world busily consuming its non-renewable forms of stored energy, probably dependent for the continued maintenance of its current scientific and technical order on the hazards of nuclear power,

and possessing the means to create conditions of life in which the sur-
vivors would envy the Azande, we raise the question of the relative
'rationality' of forms of belief at our peril. Is a nuclear bomber pilot trained
to unhesitatingly obey an order to destroy a city containing millions of
people superior to or more rational than a public prosecutor or Inquisitor
sending perhaps hundreds to the stake as a consequence of witch trials?
Is a man dying of some incurable disease alone in an American hospital
crammed with techniques and at a cost which ruins his family better
served in his last hours than is a 'primitive' with the ministrations of the
shaman and the attention of his relatives?

There are no 'independent criteria of judgement' to answer these
questions. Indeed, if we are honest it is hard to answer them at all. Few
of us would leave for the bush. 'Alternative' views are riddled with contradictions and are part of what they oppose [...] It would be too facile to
attribute the role of an emergent rationality to the critics of the excesses
of Western technology and economic growth. It is difficult to see any
props on which MacIntyre's 'dialectic' can fix itself. Things look a good
deal less comfortable than they did twenty years ago, and we cannot feel
so confident about the place from where *we* speak.

Our discussion has taken the case of the Azande because their thought
– presented to us through anthropological reconstruction – poses the
question of 'rationality' in its starkest form, and not because we believe
primitive societies are in some way 'better' than our own. The celebration
of primitivism is no less problematic than the complacent acceptance of
Western science and technology. It is as deep-seated a Western response as
the belief in 'progress' and the 'rationality' of modern Western standards
and techniques. Primitive societies had and have their savageries and
suffering. They often pale in comparison with the savageries and suffering our civilization inflicts upon itself and others. We might leave those
others with the dignity of being, if not better, then at least different and
no worse.

... Sociology can offer some clarifications, if not answers, to intractable
moral and practical questions. To recognize the otherness and the nagging
possibility of the moral and epistemological equivalence of values and
beliefs we do not share, and perhaps only half understand, is not necessarily to enter some relativistic limbo. On the other hand, we cannot find
in that otherness 'independent criteria of judgement'; that is too much
to hope for. What we can find is some answers to *why* we are stuck with
certain of the values and beliefs we do have; to see how those beliefs and
values serve as media of conduct and conditions of social organization.
At the same time we can see the limits to some of the metaphysical and
ontological *claims* made by the doctrines which accompany and support

those beliefs and values. Claims that 'progress' and 'rationality', 'liberty' or 'justice' are human actualities or realizable states of affairs cannot be swallowed whole. But neither can the categories which sustain such claims be simply rejected outright. We would be infinitely worse off if there were no appeals to liberty and justice. To reject them would be the equivalent of a Zande confronted with 'evidence' of his witchcraft quoting Evans-Pritchard and MacIntyre – supposing we were able to do so. Not only would this be no defence, it could resolve none of the dilemmas of conduct which confront the man nor the problems of organization which confront his social relations. Conduct and organization cannot be separated from categories of morality and metaphysics, equally those categories are not merely matters of personal choice or intellectual conviction – they are part of social relations.

Notes

1   E. Evans-Pritchard – *Witchcraft, Oracles, and Magic among the Azande*, 1976, abridged edition.
2   Evans-Pritchard (1976, p. 203).
3   See S. M. Shirokogoroff 'Talking to Tigers not to Bears' (1954).
4   See P. Q. Hirst *Durkheim, Bernard and Epistemology* (1975: Ch. 1).
5   See, for example, Graham Greene's remarks on this point in *Journey without Maps*.
6   Evans-Pritchard (1976, p. 126).
7   For an account of war as a situation of conduct for the ordinary soldier, see J. Keegan *The Face of the Battle* (1976); for instances of such rituals and superstitious beliefs in World War One see D. Winter *Death's Men* (1979) and Paul Fussell *The Great War and Modern Memory* (1975).
8   A notable Anglo-Saxon example is Paul Feyerabend's *Against Method* (1975) [...]
9   This is particularly true of the paper by Robin Horton, 'African Thought and Western Science', reprinted in B. Wilson (ed.) *Rationality* (1979) – in which not only traditional thought but also Western 'science', in the singular, is treated as a single 'mentality', with an essentially common outlook, method, and procedure. Such a 'science' exists only in the imaginations of certain positivist philosophers.
10   This distinction between theoretical language and a neutral observation language is made by the philosopher, Rudolf Carnap (1956).
11   Presented in his work, *Philosophical Investigations* (1963): his earlier theory of language is to be found in his *Tractatus Logico-Philosophicus* (1961) [...]
12   For an assessment of the demographic disaster produced by the Spaniards see S. F. Cook and W. Borah (1971–73) [...]
13   For a positive revaluation of the living standards possible in hunting and gathering societies, which are all too often considered to be – by their very nature – at the margins of subsistence, see M. Sahlins 'The Original Affluent Society' in *Stone Age Economics* (1974).

References

MacIntyre, A. 1979a. 'Is Understanding Religion Compatible with Believing?'
  in Wilson, B. (ed.) *Rationality*, Oxford, Basil Blackwell
MacIntyre, A. 1979b. 'The Idea of a Social Science' in Wilson op. cit.
Winch, P. 1979. 'Understanding a Primitive Society' in Wilson op. cit.

9 S. LUKES

Some problems about rationality

From 'Some Problems About Rationality' by S. Lukes, 1970 in B. R. Wilson (ed.) *Rationality* (Basil Blackwell). Reproduced by permission of the editors, *European Journal of Sociology*, where the article first appeared.

In what follows I shall discuss a philosophical problem arising out of the practice of anthropologists and sociologists which may be stated, in a general and unanalysed form, as follows: when I come across a set of beliefs which appear *prima facie* irrational, what should be my attitude towards them? Should I adopt a critical attitude, taking it as a fact about the beliefs that they *are* irrational, and seek to explain how they came to be held, how they manage to survive unprofaned by rational criticism, what their consequences are, etc? Or should I treat such beliefs charitably: should I begin from the assumption that what appears to me to be ir-rational may be interpreted as rational when fully understood in its context? More briefly, the problem comes down to whether or not there are alternative standards of rationality.

There are, of course, a number of different issues latent in the problem as I have stated it. In particular, it will be necessary to distinguish between the different ways in which beliefs may be said to be irrational. There are, for example, important differences and asymmetries between falsehood, inconsistency and nonsense. Also there are different sorts of belief; indeed there are difficult problems about what is to count as a belief. Let us, however, leave the analysis of the problem until a later stage in the argument.

... I shall set out a number of different answers to it that have been offered by anthropologists and philosophers with respect to primitive magical and religious beliefs. In doing so I make no claim to comprehen-siveness. These and related issues have been widely debated throughout the history of anthropology; all I aim to do here is to compare a number of characteristic positions. It is, however, worth stressing at this point that I do not pose the problem as a problem *in* anthropology but rather as a philosophical problem[1] raised in a particularly acute form by the practice of anthropology. It is raised, though in a less clearcut form, by all sociological and historical inquiry that is concerned with beliefs [...]

Let us compare for plausibility five different answers to the problem.

(i) First, there is the view that the seeming irrationality of the beliefs involved in primitive religion and magic constitutes no problem, for those beliefs are to be interpreted as *symbolic*. Take, for instance, the following passages from Dr Leach:

> [...] a very large part of the anthropological literature on religion concerns itself almost wholly with a discussion of the content of belief and of the rationality or otherwise of that content. Most such arguments seem to me to be scholastic nonsense. As I see it, myth regarded as a statement in words 'says' the same thing as ritual regarded as a statement in action. To ask questions about the content of belief which are not contained in the content of ritual is nonsense [...] In parts of this book I shall make frequent reference to Kachin mythology but I shall make no attempts to find any logical coherence in the myths to which I refer. Myths for me are simply one way of describing certain types of human behaviour [...][2]

Professor Firth argues, in a similar fashion, that judgment about the rationality of beliefs is irrelevant to the purposes of the anthropologist. It is, he writes, 'not important for an anthropological study whether witches exist or not [...] we are dealing here only with human relations [...]'[3]

The most systematic recent statement of this position is by Dr Beattie.[4] According to Beattie, beliefs associated with ritual are essentially expressive and symbolic. Thus, '[f]or the magician, as for the artist, the basic question is not whether his ritual is true in the sense of corresponding exactly with some empirically ascertainable reality, but rather whether it says, in apt symbolic language, what it is sought, and held important, to say' [...][5]

Thus the first answer to our problem amounts to the refusal to answer it, on the grounds that it is nonsensical (Leach), or irrelevant (Firth), or misdirected (Beattie).[6]

(ii) The second answer to the problem comes down to the claim that there are certain criteria which we can apply both to modern and to primitive beliefs which show the latter to be quite incomprehensible. (I leave until later the question of whether this claim is itself intelligible.)

As an example, take the following passage from Elsdon Best:

> The mentality of the Maori is of an intensely mystical nature [...] We hear of many singular theories about Maori beliefs and Maori thought, but the truth is that we do not understand either, and, what is more, we never shall. We shall never know the inwardness of the native mind. For that would mean tracing our steps, for many centuries, back into the dim past, far back to the time when we also possessed the mind of primitive man. And the gates have long closed on that hidden road.[7]

A similar view was expressed by the Seligmans about the tribes of the Pagan Sudan:

On this subject [of magic] the black man and the white regard each other with amazement: each considers the behaviour of the other incomprehensible, totally unrelated to everyday experience, and entirely disregarding the known laws of cause and effect.[8]

(iii) The third answer amounts to the hypothesis that primitive magical and religious beliefs are attempted explanations of phenomena. This involves the claim that they satisfy certain given criteria of rationality by virtue of certain rational procedures of thought and observation being followed; on the other hand they are (more or less) mistaken and to be judged as (more or less) unsuccessful explanations against the canons of science (and modern common sense).

The classical exponents of this position were Taylor and Frazer, especially in their celebrated 'intellectualist' theory of magic. Professor Evans-Pritchard has succinctly summarized their standpoint as follows:

They considered that primitive man had reached his conclusions about the efficacy of magic from rational observation and deduction in much the same way as men of science reach their conclusions about natural laws. Underlying all magical ritual is a rational process of thought. The ritual of magic follows from its ideology. It is true that the deductions of a magician are false – had they been true they would have been scientific and not magical – but they are nevertheless based on genuine observation. For classification of phenomena by the similarities which exist between them is the procedure of science as well as of magic and is the first essential process of human knowledge. Where the magician goes wrong is in inferring that because things are alike in one or more respects they have a mystical link between them whereas in fact the link is not a real link but an ideal connexion in the mind of the magician. [...] A causal relationship exists in his mind but not in nature. It is subjective and not an objective connexion. Hence the savage mistakes an ideal analogy for a real connexion.[9]

Their theory of religion was likewise both rationalistic and derogatory: Frazer in particular held religion to be less rational (though more complex) than the Occult Science of magic because it postulated a world of capricious personal beings rather than a uniform law-governed nature.

There has recently been elaborated a highly sophisticated version of this position on the part of a number of writers, who have stressed the explanatory purport of primitive magical and religious beliefs. In a brilliant paper,[10] Dr Robin Horton treats traditional African religious systems as theoretical models akin to those of the sciences, arguing that many of the supposed differences between these two modes of thought result, more than anything else, from differences of idiom used in their

respective theoretical models. His aim is to break down the contrast
between traditional religious thought as 'non-empirical' and scientific
thought as 'empirical'.

Horton's case is not that traditional magico-religious thought is
a variety of scientific thought but that both aim at and partially succeed
in grasping causal connexions. He also, of course, maintains that 'scientific method is undoubtedly the surest and most efficient tool for arriving
at beliefs that are successful in this respect'[11] and examines the different
ways in which traditional and scientific thought relate to experience:
his case is that these can ultimately be traced to the differences between
'closed' traditional cultures 'characterized by lack of awareness of
alternatives, sacredness of beliefs, and anxiety about threats to them'
and 'open' scientifically-orientated cultures 'characterized by awareness
of alternatives, diminished sacredness of beliefs, and diminished anxiety
about threats to them'.[12]

Thus the third answer to our problem involves the application of
given rational criteria to *prima facie* irrational beliefs which shows
them to be largely rational in method, purpose and form, though unscientific, and more or less (for Taylor and Frazer, entirely; for Horton,
less than we thought) irrational in content [...]

(iv) The fourth position we are to consider is that of Lucien Lévy-
Bruhl (until the time of writing *Les Carnets*). This is, as we shall see,
crucially ambiguous on the point of concern to us.[13]

Lévy-Bruhl's central theme was to emphasize the differences between
the content of two types of beliefs (seen as Durkheimian *représentations
collectives*):[14] those characteristic of primitive societies and those
characteristic of 'scientific' thinking. He tried to bring out those aspects
in which these two types of belief differed: as he wrote 'I intended
to bring fully to light the mystical *aspect* of primitive mentality in
contrast with the rational *aspect* of the mentality of our societies'.[15]
Thus primitive beliefs were characteristically mystical, in the sense
of being committed to 'forces, influences, powers imperceptible to
the senses, and never the less real'.[16] Indeed,

[...] the reality in which primitives move is itself mystical. There is not a
being, not an object, not a natural phenomenon that appears in their collective
representations in the way that it appears to us. Almost all that we see therein
escapes them, or is a matter of indifference to them. On the other hand, they
see many things of which we are unaware.[17]

Furthermore, their thought is (in his confusing but revealing term)
'pre-logical':[18] that is

[it] is not constrained above all else, as ours is, to avoid contradictions. The
same logical exigencies are not in its case always present. What to our eyes

is impossible or absurd, it sometimes will admit without seeing any difficulty [...][19]

Lévy-Bruhl's position is an uneasy compromise, maintaining that primitive 'mystical' and 'pre-logical' beliefs are on our standards irrational, but that on other (unspecified) standards they are about 'real' phenomena and 'logical'.[20]

(v) The fifth answer to our problem asserts that there is a strong case for assuming that, in principle, seemingly irrational belief-systems in primitive societies are to be interpreted as rational. [This] has been most clearly stated by Professor Peter Winch [...][21] According to Winch's view, when an observer is faced with seemingly irrational beliefs in a primitive society, he should seek contextually given criteria according to which they may appear rational.

Winch objects to Evans-Pritchard's approach in *Witchcraft, Oracles and Magic among the Azande* on the grounds that the criteria of rationality which he applies there are alien to the context. According to Evans-Pritchard,

It is an inevitable conclusion from Zande descriptions of witchcraft that it is not an objective reality. The physiological condition which is said to be the seat of witchcraft, and which I believe to be nothing more than food passing through the small intestine, is an objective condition, but the qualities they attribute to it and the rest of their beliefs about it are mystical. Witches, as Azande conceive them, cannot exist.[22]

Winch objects to this position on the ground that it relies upon a notion of 'objective reality' provided by science: for Evans-Pritchard 'the scientific conception agrees with what reality actually is like, whereas the magical conception does not',[23] but, Winch maintains, it is a mistake to appeal to any such independent or objective reality. What counts as real depends on the context and the language used (thus 'it is *within* the religious use of language that the conception of God's reality has its place');[24] moreover, '[w]hat is real and what is unreal shows itself *in* the sense that language has [...] we could not in fact distinguish the real from the unreal without understanding the way this distinction operates in the language'.[25] Thus European scepticism is misplaced and (we must suppose) Zande witchcraft is real.

Again, Winch objects to Evans-Pritchard's account of contradictions in the Zande belief-system. The Zande believe that a suspect may be proved a witch by post-mortem examination of his intestines for witchcraft-substance; they also believe that this is inherited through the male line. Evans-Pritchard writes:

To our minds it appears evident that if a man is proven a witch the whole of his clan are *ipso facto* witches, since the Zande clan is a group of persons related biologically to one another through the male line. Azande see the sense of this argument but they do not accept its conclusions, and it would involve the whole notion of witchcraft in contradiction were they to do so. [...] Azande do not perceive the contradiction as we perceive it because they have no theoretical interest in the subject, and those situations in which they express their belief in witchcraft do not force the problem upon them.[26]

Winch's comment on this passage is that

the context from which the suggestion about the contradiction is made, the context of our scientific culture, is not on the same level as the context in which the beliefs about witchcraft operate. Zande notions of witchcraft do not constitute a theoretical system in terms of which Azande try to gain a quasi-scientific understanding of the world. This in its turn suggests that it is the European, obsessed with pressing Zande thought where it would not naturally go – to a contradiction – who is guilty of misunderstanding, not the Zande. The European is in fact committing a category-mistake.[27]

Thus Winch's complaint against Evans-Pritchard's treatment of the Azande is 'that he did not take seriously enough the idea that the concepts used by primitive peoples can only be interpreted in the context of the way of life of these peoples':[28] thus we cannot legislate about what is real for them or what counts as a contradiction in their beliefs.[29] Moreover, Winch goes on to argue, rationality itself is context- or culture-dependent. 'We start', he writes, 'from the position that standards of rationality in different societies do not always coincide; from the possibility, therefore, that the standards of rationality current in S are different from our own [...] what we are concerned with are differences in *criteria of rationality*'.[30] He objects to the view, expressed by Professor MacIntyre, that 'the beginning of an explanation of why certain criteria are taken to be rational in some societies is that they *are* rational. And since this last has to enter into our explanation we cannot explain social behaviour independently of our own norms of rationality'.[31] Winch's case against this is that rationality in the end comes down to 'conformity to norms'; how this notion is to be applied to a given society 'will depend on our reading of their conformity to norms – what counts for them as conformity and what does not' [...][32] I shall suggest that some criteria of rationality are universal, i.e. relevantly applicable to all beliefs, in any context, while others are context-dependent, i.e. are to be discovered by investigating the context and are only relevantly applicable to beliefs in that context. I argue (as against Winch) that beliefs are not only to be evaluated by the criteria that are to be discovered in the context in which they are held; they must also be evaluated by criteria of rationality that simply *are* criteria of rationality, as opposed to criteria of rationality in context [c]. In what follows universal criteria will be called 'rational (1) criteria' and context-dependent criteria 'rational (2) criteria'.

One may conclude that all beliefs are to be evaluated by both rational (1) and rational (2) criteria. Sometimes, as in the case of religious beliefs, rational (1) truth criteria will not take the analysis very far. Often rational (1) criteria of logic do not reveal anything positive about relations between beliefs that are to be explicated in terms of 'provides a reason for'. Sometimes rational (1) criteria appear less important than 'what the situation demands'. In all cases, rational (2) criteria are illuminating. But they do not make rational (1) criteria dispensable. They could not, for the latter, specify the ultimate constraints to which thought is subject: that is, they are fundamental and universal in the sense that any society which possesses what we may justifiably call a language must apply them *in general*, though particular beliefs, or sets of beliefs, may violate them.

If both sorts of criteria are required for the understanding of beliefs (for they enable us to grasp their truth-conditions and their interrelations), they are equally necessary to the explanation of why they are held, how they operate and what their social consequences are. Thus only by the application of rational (1) criteria is it possible to see how beliefs which fail to satisfy them can come to be rationally criticized, or fail to be.[34] On the other hand, it is usually only by the application of rational (2) criteria that the point and significance that beliefs have for those that hold them can be grasped. Rational (1) and rational (2) criteria are necessary both to understand and to explain.

Notes

1   Some have argued that its solution bears directly on anthropological practice (see, e.g. P. Winch, Understanding a Primitive Society, *American Philosophical Quarterly*, where Evans-Pritchard's account of witchcraft among the Azande is held to be partly vitiated by his supposedly mistaken answer to it). I agree with this position, but in this paper I do not seek to substantiate it.

2   E. Leach, *Political Systems of Highland Burma*, London, 1954, pp. 13–14.

3   R. Firth, *Essays on Social Organization and Values*, London, 1964, p. 237.

4   See J. Beattie, *Other Cultures*, London, 1964, Chapters V and XII, and idem, 'Ritual and Social Change', *Man: The Journal of the Royal Anthropological Institute*, I, 1966, 60–74.

5   J. Beattie, loc. cit. (1966), p. 68. Thus, magic is 'the acting out of a situation, the expression of a desire in symbolic terms; it is not the application of empirically acquired knowledge about the properties of natural substances' (Beattie, op. cit. (1964), p. 206). Cf. T. Parsons, *The Structure of Social Action*, New York and London, 1937, p. 431 (2nd edition 1949): 'Ritual actions are not [...] either simply irrational, or pseudo rational, based on prescientific erroneous knowledge, but are of a different character altogether and as such not to be measured by the standards of intrinsic rationality at all' (cited in Beattie, loc. cit. 1966). Parsons wrongly attributes this position to Durkheim.

6   Beattie appeals to the authority of Suzanne Langer (Beattie, 'Ritual and

Social Change', loc. cit. p. 66), but I am unsure how far his allegiance to her views goes. I do not know whether he would wish to argue, as she does, that rationality and even logic can be ascribed to expressive symbolism and whether he would subscribe to her general view that '[rationality] is the essence of mind and symbolic transformation its elementary process. It is a fundamental error, therefore, to recognize it only in the phenomenon of systematic, explicit reasoning. That is a mature and precarious product. Rationality, however, is embodied in every mental act [...]' (idem *Philosophy in a new Key*, Harvard, 1942, p. 99; 3rd edition 1963. Miss Langer's is in any case a special sense of 'rationality'. As I hope to show, the fundamental meaning of rationality is essentially linked to the phenomenon of systematic, explicit reasoning.

7   'Maori Medical Lore', *Journal of Polynesian Society*, XIII, 1904, p. 219, cited in L. Lévy-Bruhl, *Les fonctions mentales dans les sociétés inférieures*, Paris, 1910, p. 69 (2nd edition 1912).

8   C. G. and B. Z. Seligman, *Pagan Tribes of the Nilotic Sudan*, London, 1932, p. 25, cited in E. E. Evans-Pritchard, Lévy-Bruhl's Theory of Primitive Mentality, *Bulletin of the Faculty of Arts*, II, 1934, 1–36.

9   E. E. Evans-Pritchard, 'The Intellectualist (English) Interpretation of Magic', *Bulletin of the Faculty of Arts*, I, 1933, 282–311. Cf. also idem, *Theories of Primitive Religion*, Oxford, 1965, Chapter II.

10   R. Horton, 'African Traditional Thought and Western Science', in B. Wilson (ed.), *Rationality*, 1970, Oxford.

11   See Horton, in B. Wilson, 1970, op. cit., p. 140.

12   Ibid. pp. 155–6.

13   See *Les Carnets de Lucien Lévy-Bruhl*, Paris, 1949, passim, where it is made explicit and partially resolved.

14   It is worth noting that Durkheim differed crucially from Lévy-Bruhl, emphasizing the continuities rather than the differences between primitive and modern scientific thought: see E. Durkheim, *Les formes élémentaires de la vie religieuse*, pp. 336–42, and Review of L. Lévy-Bruhl, *Les fonctions mentales dans les sociétés inférieures*, and E. Durkheim, *Les formes élémentaires de la vie religieuse*, in *Année sociologique*, XII, 1913, 33–7.

15   L. Lévy-Bruhl, 'A Letter to E. E. Evans-Pritchard', *British Journal of Sociology*, III, 1952, 117–23.

16   L. Lévy-Bruhl, *Les fonctions mentales dans les sociétés inférieures*, Paris, 1910, p. 30.

17   Ibid. pp. 30–31.

18   He eventually abandoned it: see *Les Carnets de L. Lévy-Bruhl*, op. cit. pp. 47–51, 60–62, 69–70, 129–35, etc.

19   L. Lévy-Bruhl, *La mentalité primitive* (Herbert Spencer Lecture), Oxford, 1931, p. 21.

20   Lévy-Bruhl's final position was as follows: 'there is no primitive mentality which is distinguished from the other by *two* characteristic features (being mystical and pre-logical). There is one mystical mentality that is more marked and more easily observable among 'primitives' than in our societies, but present in every human mind'. (*Les Carnets ...*, p. 131.)

21   P. Winch, Understanding a Primitive Society, pp. 78ff.

22   E. E. Evans-Pritchard, *Witchcraft, Oracles and Magic among the Azande*, Oxford, 1937, p. 63.

23   P. Winch, Understanding a Primitive Society, loc. cit., p. 81.

24   Ibid. p. 82.

25 Ibid., p. 82.

26 *Witchcraft* ..., op. cit. pp. 24–5.

27 'Understanding a Primitive Society', p. 93.

28 Ibid.

29 The philosophical basis for this position is to be found in P. Winch, *The Idea of a Social Science and its Relation to Philosophy*, London, 1958.

30 P. Winch, 'Understanding ...', loc. cit. p. 97.

31 A. MacIntyre, 'A Mistake about Causality in Social Science', in P. Laslett and W. G. Runciman (eds.), *Philosophy, Politics and Society*, Second Series, Oxford, 1962, p. 61. This formulation suffers from its emphasis on the location of these norms rather than on their nature.

32 P. Winch, 'Understanding ...', loc. cit. p. 100.

33 Cf. E. E. Evans-Pritchard, *Witchcraft, Oracles and Magic among the Azande*, Oxford, 1937, pp. 475–78, where twenty-two reasons are given why the Azande 'do not perceive the futility of their magic'.

10 M. DOUGLAS

Purity and danger

From *Purity and Danger* by M. Douglas, London, 1970. Reproduced by permission of the publishers, Routledge and Kegan Paul PLC.

[Mary Douglas is here discussing the pollution rules governing the daily lives of Havik Brahmin in India] ... All bodily emissions, even blood or pus from a wound, are sources of impurity. Water, not paper, must be used for washing after defecating, and this is done only with the left hand, while food may be eaten only with the right hand. To step on animal faeces caused impurity. Contact with leather causes impurity. If leather sandals are worn they should not be touched with the hands, and should be removed and the feet be washed before a temple or house is entered.

Precise regulations give the kinds of indirect contact which may carry pollution. A Havik, working with his untouchable servant in his garden, may become severely defiled by touching a rope or bamboo at the same time as the servant. It is the simultaneous contact with the bamboo or rope which defiles. A Havik cannot receive fruit or money directly from an Untouchable. But some objects stay impure and can be conductors of impurity even after contact. Pollution lingers in cotton cloth, metal cooking vessels, cooked food. Luckily for collaboration between the castes, ground does not act as a conductor. But straw which covers it does [...]

The more deeply we go into this and similar rules, the more obvious it becomes that we are studying symbolic systems. Is this then really the difference between ritual pollution and our ideas of dirt: are our ideas hygienic where theirs are symbolic? Not a bit of it: I am going to argue that our ideas of dirt also express symbolic systems and that the difference between pollution behaviour in one part of the world and another is only a matter of detail.

Before we start to think about ritual pollution we must go down in sack-cloth and ashes and scrupulously re-examine our own ideas of dirt. Dividing them into their parts, we should distinguish any elements which we know to be the result of our recent history.

There are two notable differences between our contemporary European ideas of defilement and those, say, of primitive cultures. One is that dirt avoidance for us is a matter of hygiene or aesthetics and is not related to our religion [...] The second difference is that our idea of dirt is dominated by the knowledge of pathogenic organisms. The bacterial transmission of disease was a great nineteenth-century discovery. It produced the most radical revolution in the history of medicine. So much has it transformed our lives that it is difficult to think of dirt except in the context of pathogenicity. Yet obviously our ideas of dirt are not so recent. We must be able to make the effort to think back beyond the last 100 years and to analyse the bases of dirt-avoidance, before it was transformed by bacteriology; for example, before spitting deftly into a spittoon was counted unhygienic.

If we can abstract pathogenicity and hygiene from our notion of dirt, we are left with the old definition of dirt as matter out of place. This is a very suggestive approach. It implies two conditions: a set of ordered relations and a contravention of that order. Dirt, then, is never a unique, isolated event. Where there is dirt there is system. Dirt is the by-product of a systematic ordering and classification of matter, in so far as ordering involves rejecting inappropriate elements. This idea of dirt takes us straight into the field of symbolism and promises a link-up with more obviously symbolic systems of purity.

We can recognize in our own notions of dirt that we are using a kind of omnibus compendium which includes all the rejected elements of ordered systems. It is a relative idea. Shoes are not dirty in themselves, but it is dirty to place them on the dining-table; food is not dirty in itself, but it is dirty to leave cooking utensils in the bedroom, or food bespattered on clothing; similarly, bathroom equipment in the drawing room; clothing lying on chairs; out-door things in-doors; upstairs things downstairs; under-clothing appearing where over-clothing should be, and so on. In short, our pollution behaviour is the reaction which condemns any object or idea likely to confuse or contradict cherished classifications.

We should not force ourselves to focus on dirt. Defined in this way it appears as a residual category, rejected from our normal scheme of classifications. In trying to focus on it we run against our strongest mental habit. For it seems that whatever we perceive is organized into patterns for which we, the perceivers, are largely responsible. Perceiving is not a matter of passively allowing an organ – say of sight or hearing – to receive a ready-made impression from without, like a palette receiving a spot of paint. Recognizing and remembering are not matters of stirring up old images of past impressions. It is generally agreed that all our impressions are schematically determined from the start. As perceivers we select from all the stimuli falling on our senses only those which interest us, and our interests are governed by a pattern-making tendency, sometimes called *schema*. In a chaos of shifting impressions, each of us constructs a stable world in which objects have recognizable shapes, are located in depth, and have permanence. In perceiving we are building, taking some cues and rejecting others. The most acceptable cues are those which fit most easily into the pattern that is being built up. Ambiguous ones tend to be treated as if they harmonized with the rest of the pattern. Discordant ones tend to be rejected. If they are accepted the structure of assumptions has to be modified. As learning proceeds objects are named. Their names then affect the way they are perceived next time: once labelled they are more speedily slotted into the pigeon-holes in future.

As time goes on and experiences pile up, we make a greater and greater investment in our system of labels. So a conservative bias is built in. It gives us confidence. At any time we may have to modify our structure of assumptions to accommodate new experience, but the more consistent experience is with the past, the more confidence we can have in our assumptions. Uncomfortable facts, which refuse to be fitted in, we find ourselves ignoring or distorting so that they do not disturb these established assumptions. By and large anything we take note of is pre-selected and organized in the very act of perceiving. We share with other animals a kind of filtering mechanism which at first only lets in sensations we know how to use [...]

But it is not always an unpleasant experience to confront ambiguity. Obviously it is more tolerable in some areas than in others. There is a whole gradient on which laughter, revulsion and shock belong at different points and intensities. The experience can be stimulating. The richness of poetry depends on the use of ambiguity, as Empson has shown. The possibility of seeing a sculpture equally well as a landscape or as a reclining nude enriches the work's interest. Ehrenzweig has even argued that we enjoy works of art because they enable us to go behind the explicit structures of our normal experience. Aesthetic pleasure arises from the perceiving of inarticulate forms.

I apologize for using anomaly and ambiguity as if they were synonymous. Strictly they are not: an anomaly is an element which does not fit a given set or series; ambiguity is a character of statements capable of two interpretations. But reflection on examples shows that there is very little advantage in distinguishing between these two terms in their practical application. Treacle is neither liquid nor solid; it could be said to give an ambiguous sense-impression. We can also say that treacle is anomalous in the classification of liquids and solids, being in neither one nor the other set [...]

There are several ways of treating anomalies. Negatively, we can ignore, just not perceive them, or perceiving we can condemn. Positively we can deliberately confront the anomaly and try to create a new pattern of reality in which it has a place. It is not impossible for an individual to revise his own personal scheme of classifications. But no individual lives in isolation and his scheme will have been partly received from others.

Culture, in the sense of the public, standardized values of a community, mediates the experience of individuals. It provides in advance some basic categories, a positive pattern in which ideas and values are tidily ordered. And above all, it has authority, since each is induced to assent because of the assent of others. But its public character makes its categories more rigid. A private person may revise his pattern of assumptions or not. It is a private matter. But cultural categories are public matters. They cannot so easily be subject to revision. Yet they cannot neglect the challenge of aberrant forms. Any given system of classification must give rise to anomalies, and any given culture must confront events which seem to defy its assumptions. It cannot ignore the anomalies which its scheme produces, except at risk of forfeiting confidence. This is why, I suggest, we find in any culture worthy of the name various provisions for dealing with ambiguous or anomalous events.

First, by settling for one or other interpretation, ambiguity is often reduced. For example, when a monstrous birth occurs, the defining lines between humans and animals may be threatened. If a monstrous birth can be labelled an event of a peculiar kind the categories can be restored. So the Nuer treat monstrous births as baby hippopotamuses, accidentally born to humans and, with this labelling, the appropriate action is clear. They gently lay them in the river where they belong.[1]

Second, the existence of anomaly can be physically controlled. Thus in some West African tribes the rule that twins should be killed at birth eliminates a social anomaly, if it is held that two humans could not be born from the same womb at the same time. Or take night-crowing cocks. If their necks are promptly wrung, they do not live to contradict the definition of a cock as a bird that crows at dawn.

Third, a rule of avoiding anomalous things affirms and strengthens the definitions to which they do not conform. So where Leviticus[2] abhors crawling things, we should see the abomination as the negative side of the pattern of things approved.

Fourth, anomalous events may be labelled dangerous. Admittedly individuals sometimes feel anxiety confronted with anomaly. But it would be a mistake to treat institutions as if they evolved in the same way as a person's spontaneous reactions. Such public beliefs are more likely to be produced in the course of reducing dissonance between individual and general interpretations. Following the work of Festinger it is obvious that a person, when he finds his own convictions at variance with those of friends, either wavers or tries to convince the friends of their error. Attributing danger is one way of putting a subject above dispute. It also helps to enforce conformity, as we shall show below in a chapter on morals.

Fifth, ambiguous symbols can be used in ritual for the same ends as they are used in poetry and mythology, to enrich meaning or to call attention to other levels of existence. We shall see in the last chapter how ritual, by using symbols of anomaly, can incorporate evil and death along with life and goodness, into a single, grand, unifying pattern.

To conclude, if uncleanness is matter out of place, we must approach it through order. Uncleanness or dirt is that which must not be included if a pattern is to be maintained. To recognize this is the first step towards insight into pollution. It involves us in no clear-cut distinction between sacred and secular. The same principle applies throughout. Furthermore, it involves no special distinction between primitives and moderns: we are all subject to the same rules. But in the primitive culture the rule of patterning works with greater force and more total comprehensiveness. With the moderns it applies to disjointed, separate areas of existence.

Notes

1   E. E. Evans-Pritchard, 1956, 'Nuer Religion'. Oxford University Press, p. 84.
2   This refers to Leviticus in the Bible; the 'Old Testament' of the Christian Church. – Eds.

11   E. E. EVANS-PRITCHARD

Witchcraft amongst the Azande

From 'Witchcraft amongst the Azande' by E. E. Evans-Pritchard, 1929, in *Sudan Notes and Records*, vol. 12. Reproduced by permission.

Witchcraft (*mangu*) and magic (*ngwa*) have quite different connotations in Zande culture and should be clearly distinguished in an ethnological account. In certain respects witchcraft and sorcery are similar. Probably neither, certainly not *mangu*, has any real existence. Both have common functions, since they are used for pernicious private ends against the lives and property of law-abiding citizens. But their technique is quite different. Zande magic comprises the common characteristics of magic the world over, rite, spell, ideas, traditions, and moral opinion associated with its use, taboo and other conditions of the magician and the rite (Evans-Pritchard, 1929; Hubert and Mauss, 1902–3; Malinowski, 1926). All these are traditional facts transmitted from one generation to another. Witchcraft operates through different channels though in similar situations to sorcery.

Let us commence our analysis of Zande witchcraft from its concrete elements, for as the nuclear equipment of sorcery is a concrete, generally botanical, medicine, so the nuclear equipment of witchcraft is an abdominal condition (*mangu*). We have never actually seen a *mangu*, but it has often been described to us as an oval, blackish swelling or sack which sometimes contains various small objects. In size about the elbow-width of a man's bent fore-arm, it is situated somewhere in the upper abdomen near the bile tract. It cannot be observed from the outside during a man's lifetime, but in the past it used often to be extracted by a post-mortem operation, and was sometimes placed hanging from a tree bordering one of the main paths leading to a chief's court. We are ignorant about the real nature of this abdominal condition, but think that it is probably the gall-bladder or the stomach itself in certain digestive periods [...]

Here we wish to state the main attributes of *mangu* in a preliminary manner before discussing the part the concept of witchcraft plays in native life and the complex and often contradictory notions associated with it in Zande mentality. The first of these attributes is its physical character. It is a physical or physiological fact, a thing, which is situated, so far as we have been able to gather, in the abdomen just below where the breast-bones meet. The second important fact which we wish to bring out about *mangu* is that it is an hereditary anatomical endowment which is transmitted in unilinear descent from parents to children. There is sex dichotomy in the biological transmission of witchcraft. Thus whilst the sons of a male witch are all witches his daughters are not, and whilst all the daughters of a female witch are also witches her sons are not.[1] Witchcraft thus regarded as an inherited biological trait transmitted along the lines of sex does not run counter to Zande ideas of kinship and descent, but is complementary to their notions about procreation and their eschatalogical beliefs. We will summarize these briefly in so far as they concern our subject.

The birth of a child results from a union of spiritual properties in the womb of a woman with spiritual properties in the sperm of a man. The foetus is derived from the union of two principles, male and female. When the spirit (*mbisimo*) of the male is stronger than that of the female a boy child is born. When the woman's spirit (*mbisimo*) is stronger, a girl child will be born. Thus, whilst a child is thought to partake of the spirits of both parents, a girl is believed to partake more of the spirit of her mother, and a boy of his father, but in certain respects a child takes after one or other parent according to its sex, in the inheritance of sexual characteristics [and] of *mangu* [...]

Some nocturnal birds and animals are very definitely associated with witchcraft and are thought to be the servants of human witches, and to be in league with them. Such are bats, which are universally feared for their evil attributes, and owls, which hoot forebodings of misfortune in the night. These nocturnal creatures are associated with witches because witchcraft is especially active at night, where it may sometimes be seen in motion.

For, like many primitive peoples, the Azande believe that witchcraft emits a bright light which can only be seen in the daylight by witch-doctors and by witches themselves, but which is occasionally visible at night to persons who are neither witches (all such being *amukundu*) nor witch-doctors.[2] The light of *mangu* is described as being similar to the little lights of firefly beetles, which move about like sparks kicked from a log-fire, only it is ever so much larger than they. The beetles themselves arouse no suspicion of witchcraft, but the Zande compares their phosphorescence to the emanation of *mangu*, adding that it is a poor comparison, since *mangu* has a so much greater and brighter light [...]

We will naturally wonder what the light [is], whether it [is] the actual witch stalking his prey or whether it [is] some emanation which he [emits] to do the murder. On this point Zande theory is quite decided.

The witch is asleep during the period of his activity on his bed in his hut, but he has despatched the spirit of his *mangu* to accomplish his ends. The spirit of *mangu* removes parts of the spirit of the victim's flesh and devours it. The whole act of vampirism is a spiritual one; the spirit of *mangu* removes and devours the spirit of the body. I have never been able to obtain a more precise explanation of witchcraft activities by enquiring into the meaning of *mbisimo mangu* and *mbisimo pasie*. The Zande knows that people are killed in such a way, but only a witch himself could give a circumstantial account of what exactly happens.

Witches usually combine in their destructive activities and subsequent ghoulish feasts. They assist each other in crime and they arrange their nefarious schemes in concert. They are believed to possess a special kind of ointment (*mbiro mangu*) with which they rub their bodies and little drums which they beat to summon others to congress, where their discussions are presided over by old and experienced members of the brotherhood. For witches have their hierarchy and status and leadership in the same way as all other Zande social groupings have. Experience must first be obtained under tuition of elder witches before a man is able to kill his neighbours. Growth in experience goes hand in hand with physical growth of *mangu* itself.

A child born of a witch parent of its own sex has such a small *mangu* that it can do little injury to others. It is possible that his *mangu* will remain inoperative or largely so throughout life, but generally it grows both in size and in exercise of its powers. Hence, a child is never accused of murder, and even grown boys and girls are not suspected by adults of serious offences of witchcraft, though they may be a more serious menace to their child contemporaries. Generally speaking, the older a man grows the more potent becomes his *mangu* and the more violent and unscrupulous its use. The reason for this genetic concept of witchcraft will become apparent when we explain its situations in Zande social life and its place in their system of morals.

Sooner or later, a witch will probably fall a victim to vengeance or, even if he is clever enough to avoid retribution, he will be killed by another witch or by sorcery. Is the distinction between witches (*aboro mangu*) and non-witches (*amukundu*) operative beyond the grave? We have never been given a spontaneous statement to this effect, but in answer to direct and leading questions we have been told that at death witches become ... evil spirits ... known as *agilisa* [...]

Mangu is ubiquitous. It plays its part in every activity of Zande life, in agricultural, fishing, and hunting pursuits; in domestic life of homesteads as well as in communal life of district and court; it is the essential theme of mental life, in which it forms the background of a vast panorama of magic; its influence is plainly stamped on law and morals, etiquette and religion; it is prominent in such different spheres as technology and language; [there is] no niche or corner of Zande culture into which it does not twist itself. If blight seizes the ground-nut crop it is *mangu*; if the bush is burnt vainly in pursuit of game it is *mangu*; if women laboriously ladle out water from a pool and are rewarded by but a few small fish it is *mangu*; if termites do not rise when they are due and a cold, useless, night is wasted in waiting for their flight it is *mangu*; if a wife shows herself sulky and unresponsive to her husband it is *mangu*; if a chief is cold and distant with his subject it is *mangu*; if a magical rite fails to achieve its purpose it is *mangu*; if, in fact, any failure or misfortune falls upon anyone at any time and in relation to any of the manifold activities of his life he believes that it is due to *mangu*. Those acquainted either at first hand or through reading with a normal day-to-day life of an agricultural African people will understand that there is no end to possible misfortunes arising in routine tasks and relaxations from miscalculation, incompetence, laziness, but mostly from causes over which the native has no control, since he possesses little scientific knowledge. All these are regarded as being due to *mangu* unless there is strong internal evidence and sub-sequent oracular confirmation that sorcery or one of those species of evil-bringing agents which we have described in the preceding section have been at work. But unless a man had previously had the misfortune of seeing *adandala*,[3] touching his wife's menstrual blood, seeing her anus, or similar experience, he would not attribute any casual misfortune to these causes.

It is strange at first to live amongst the Zande and to listen to their naïve explanation of misfortunes with the most obvious origin as products of witchcraft. A European cannot repress a smile at such crude and childish shelving of responsibility. A boy knocked his foot against a small stump of wood in the centre of a bush path, a daily occurrence in Africa, and suffered considerable pain and inconvenience in consequence. The sore, owing to its position on his toe, was continually receiving dirt and refused to heal. It was *mangu*. I pointed out that it was carelessness and advised him to look out where he was going in future, but he replied that it was quite true witchcraft had nothing to do with the stump of wood being in the path but that he had kept his eyes open, and if he had not been be-witched he would of course have seen the stump. As a conclusive argu-ment for his view he remarked that all sores did not take days to heal, but generally close quickly, since that is the nature of sores and their usual behaviour; why, then, had not this wound closed unless there were *mangu* behind it? This I discovered before long was to be regarded as the general theory of ailments, and that there was little knowledge as to the real causes of disease. Thus, for example, when feeling unfit for several days

I consulted native friends whether they thought that my consumption of bananas could have anything to do with my indisposition, but was at once informed that bananas do not cause sickness however many are eaten unless one is bewitched [...]

Though a Zande will always place his misfortunes at the door of witchcraft, it must not be thought that he regards every enterprise as potentially successful so long as it is not interfered with by *mangu*. He is fully aware that people who traverse the bush will get cuts and scratches, and you will see how carefully he searches the ground in front of his bare feet whilst you, poor stranger, stumble along admiring the rich variety of the bush, but are, fortunately, provided with boots. His knowledge and absence of adequate protection make him careful. It is knowledge which each learns for himself from experience in childhood and uses throughout life. However, in spite of all precautions, cuts are sometimes unavoidable, since stumps of wood are often so close to the ground and so covered with dust or ashes that they are invisible to the most accustomed eye, or night conceals stumps and thorns from the late traveller; or a man must pursue game through sharp-edged grasses and tangled thorny undergrowth, where he can no longer keep to his beloved paths, and his attention to minor discomforts is distracted by excitement in the chase. Moreover, there are several different kinds of magic which protect him against minor injuries of this kind. I know of none which are specifically devoted to ward off bush cuts, but Zande magic is often wide-embracing and gives general protection to travellers and huntsmen away from home. If, in spite of practical caution and protective magic, he receives a nasty cut he will attribute it to the malice of his neighbours who have bewitched him. He will not, however, trouble very much about the matter unless the cut festers or refuses to close. He will then be certain that *mangu* is the cause and will begin to be resentful and possibly he will consult the oracles to find out who is causing such prolonged discomfort and inconvenience [...]

If an illness continues in spite of the precautions taken, the relatives of the sick man will try and find out who is responsible. They will probably commence their enquiries through the *iwa*[4] oracle and then check its verdict with the *benge*[5] oracle. One by one they place the names of people whom they suspect before *iwa*, and, when *iwa* has chosen one of them as the culprit, they ask it whether this is the only man responsible, or whether there are others acting in concert with him. If *iwa* says that this man is acting alone they put his name before *benge*. As we do not wish to enter here into the complicated technicalities of oracle-magic we will suppose that *iwa* chooses the name of one man and that *benge* supports the lesser oracle. The sick man and his relatives now have in their possession the name of the witch. This man was previously suspected, otherwise his name would not have been put before the oracles, and now they are certain that it is he who is bewitching their friend. As the feeling of the sick man and his relations is one of great indignation, and their first impulse is to assault the witch, it is highly important at this juncture that their actions should be well controlled by traditional procedure. There are two lines of action considered socially commendable. They may make a more or less public accusation of the witch face to face in a manner to be described shortly, or they may make a public declaration in his presence without mentioning any names, so that only they and the witch will know whom is being referred to. This latter method has an advantage where the witch is a person of social standing whom they do not wish to offend, or someone enjoying the respect and esteem of his fellow citizens, whom they do not wish to humiliate. This latter method is known as *kuba* [...]

Those who have listened to this dramatic declaration know the voice which has spoken, who is ill, and all the circumstances of his sickness. As the witch listens he knows that his plot is discovered and that, being a marked man, if he continues to torture his victim his name will be revealed, and that, if he kills him, the death will be avenged. Self-preservation and self-respect will make him stop before it is too late. Moreover, he will be honoured by the deference which has been paid to him by concealment of his identity from the general public, so that he may yield to flattery where he will not yield to fear.

If this effort to get the witch to cease his activities is unsuccessful, the relatives of the sick man will resort to the procedure which is generally used alone without being preceded by a *kuba*, for a *kuba* is only used if they think that it is more convenient and if the *iwa* oracle sanctions its use. The normal procedure is to put the names of all suspects before *iwa* and let it select those guilty of causing sickness. Unless the man is dangerously ill, when they will at once make known *iwa*'s selection, they will place the names chosen by *iwa* before the more reliable oracle *benge*. A red strychnic powder is given to chicken, whilst the names of the suspects are mentioned one by one, and by either killing or sparing these chicken the oracle separates the innocent from among the guilty. Maybe several will be found guilty, maybe only one, but the procedure is the same for many as for one. They cut off a wing from the hen which died to the name of the witch and thrust it on to the end of a little pointed stick, spreading its wing out in the shape of a fan, and take it home with them. One of the relatives will then go with it to a neighbouring chief's deputy, since the chief is not always accessible, and does not wish to be troubled with every little affair of this kind, and they will tell him the name of the man denounced by *benge*. Or, instead of going to him, they may again consult *iwa* about several reliable men of good social position in order to choose one of them to notify the witch of *benge*'s verdict. If they go to the chief's deputy, the wiser course, he will promise to notify the witch. He calls one of his dependants and sends him with the fowl's wing to the homestead of the witch and tells him to present him with it, to note what happens and to bring back word accordingly. The messenger goes with the wing and lays it on the ground in front of the witch, saying that his master has sent him with it because of the illness of so-and-so. Generally a witch will protest his innocence of intention and his ignorance of the harm that he is doing to his neighbour. He calls for a gourdful of water, and when his wife brings it he takes a draught, swills it round in his mouth, and blows it out in a spray over the wing. He says aloud, so that the messenger can hear his words, that if he is a witch he is unaware of his possession of *mangu*, and that he is not causing injury to others with intent. He addresses the *mangu* in his stomach beseeching it to become inactive. If he makes this appeal from his heart and not in mere pretence with his lips, then the sick man will recover. The messenger returns to his master with news of what he has seen, and the deputy tells the relatives of the sick man that his duty has been performed satisfactorily. The relatives will wait anxiously for some days to find out what effect this ceremony will have. If the sick man shows signs of recovery they will praise *benge* for having revealed so quickly and surely the name of the witch and opened up a road to recovery. If sickness continues they will again consult the oracles to find out whether the witch was only pretending repentance or whether some new aggressor had arisen to trouble their ill friend, and in this case the same formal ceremony of presentation of hen's wings will again take place.

Though chiefs appear in the past to have sometimes taken more drastic steps to ensure their safety, the procedure described above has always been the normal everyday usage of every section of society. It is an usage which maintains generally an orderly outcome to a situation fraught with considerable emotional stress on both sides for the conferring of a hen's wing upon a man often leads, on the part of the *boro mangu*,[6] to concealed anger and permanent estrangement, whilst the relatives on their part feel themselves face to face with what amounts to murder of their friend and kin. The great authority of the *benge* oracle, the use of an intermediary to carry out the more offensive part of the performance, the social standing of a deputy backed up by the political power of a chief, the stereotyped mode of behaviour expected of a witch under the trying publicity which accompanies his humiliation, are factors which help to tide over this difficult impasse in human relations, whilst at the same time allowing expression of indignation along prescribed channels of conduct. For a man who were to accuse another man wantonly of witchcraft without being able to produce an oracular verdict to back up his statement would be merely laughed at for his pains if he were not beaten into the bargain. A man who went himself to deliver a hen's wing or who sent some unsuitable messenger without first consulting either the oracles or an old man of high social standing would run the risk of initiating a violent scene, and people would say that he got what an ignorant 'provincial' deserves. While, on the other hand, the man who showed temper on being presented with a hen's wing in the proper traditional manner would [...] not only be considered a boor, but his behaviour would reveal blackness of heart and confirm the worst suspicions. The Zande can always tell you what is the correct behaviour in any situation, the ideal of conduct based on tradition; but people are always doing things the wrong way and troublesome consequences arise. Nevertheless, by a traditional sequence of activities from a preliminary consultation of the *iwa* oracle to a consultation of *benge*, from *benge* to *iwa* once more, from *iwa* to a dramatic declaration in the *kuba*, from the *kuba* to *iwa* again, from *iwa* to *benge*, from *benge* to a formal request to a chief's deputy and the sending of a messenger and the carrying out of a simple ceremony in the homestead of a witch, all is regulated by a well-known sequence of traditional moves and a series of behaviour-patterns which give firm social control over the unruly passions of men under severe emotional stress [...]

Notes

1   Lagae (1926, pp. 107–8).
2   Lagae (1926, p. 108).
3   A species of wild cat associated with witchcraft, the sight of which is believed to be fatal (Evans-Pritchard, 1937, p. 51).
4   '... rubbing-board oracle, which operates by means of a wooden instrument' (Evans-Pritchard, 1937, p. 11).
5   '... poison oracle, which operates through the administration of strychnine to fowls, and formerly to human beings also' (Evans-Pritchard, 1937, pp. 10–11).
6   '*Boro* (*ira*) *mangu* witch: a person whose body contains, or is declared by oracles or diviners to contain, witchcraft-substance and who is supposed to practise witchcraft' (Evans-Pritchard, 1937, p. 9).

References

Evans-Pritchard, E. E. (1929), 'The morphology and function of magic', *American Anthropologist*, vol. 31.
Evans-Pritchard, E. E. (1937), *Witchcraft, Oracles and Magic among the Azande*, Clarendon Press.
Hubert, H., and Mauss, M. (1902–3), 'Esquisse d'une théorie générale de la magie', *L'Année Sociologique*, vol. 7; reprinted in M. Mauss (1950), *Sociologie et Anthropologie*, Presses Universitaires de France.

Lagae, C.R. (1926), 'Les Azande ou Niam–Niam', *Bibliothèque Congo*, vol. 18.
Malinowski, B. (1926), 'Magic, science and religion', in J. Needham (ed.), *Science, Religion and Reality*, Macmillan; reprinted in R. Redfield (ed.), *Magic, Science and Religion and Other Essays*, The Free Press, 1948; Doubleday, 1954.

II RELIGION AND SOCIAL CONTROL

This section addresses some of the key questions about the functioning of religion in the field of ideological contestation, specifically with respect to debates about the part that religion played in the ideological struggles that accompanied the Industrial Revolution in England. It was not only Marx and Engels who saw religion as having acted like a drug, offering solace and compensation to the deprived and distressed workers in this period of social and political turmoil. French observers came to the same conclusion when they contrasted the movements of religious enthusiasm in England with the revolutionary political movements in their own country; a detailed explanation for this English situation was provided by the French historian Elie Halévy, and his conclusion about the distraction of the English working class away from revolutionary political consciousness through the absorption of its potential leaders into Methodism and Evangelical religion, became famous as the 'Halévy thesis'. The same phenomenon was addressed by the historian E. P. Thompson in his remarkable, influential study, *The Making of the English Working Class*, giving rise to what he referred to, ironically, as a successor to the Halévy thesis – the 'Thompson thesis'. Both theses, and other explanations are covered in this section, along with a detailed assessment of the evidence for these various explanations as they relate to the specific part played by the Sunday schools, which is presented in an extract from Laqueur's impressive study of those institutions during the period 1780–1850. The first article in this section, 'Religion, class and control', deals with some of the general theoretical issues concerning the various functions that have been attributed to working class religiosity in this period, the location of those religious phenomena within the terrain of ideological contestation, and their relation to other sets of symbols and discourses within the cultural complex of working-class life.

12 K. THOMPSON

Religion, class and control

Grateful acknowledgement is made to the following sources:
Tables 1 and 2: Longman Group Ltd for A.D. Gilbert (1976), *Religion and Society in Industrial England*; Tables 3 and 4: Yale University Press for T.W. Laqueur (1976), *Religion and Respectability*, © Yale University Press.

Theoretical introduction

It is generally agreed that the period of English history from the middle of the eighteenth century to the middle of the nineteenth century was marked by considerable social upheaval and intense ideological struggle. We have it on the authority of observers at the time that many workers who flocked, or were herded, into the growing towns experienced acute hardship and distress. It also saw the 'making of the working class', as E.P. Thompson put it, in which, as a result of their common experience 'in the years between 1780 and 1832 most English working people came to feel an identity of interests as between themselves, and as against their rulers and employers' – a class consciousness (Thompson, 1968, p. 12). However, as Thompson suggests, there were certain peculiarities about that consciousness. Although their experiences were determined by the productive relations common to all wage-earners in a capitalist mode of production, the class consciousness of the English working class had its own peculiar characteristics. The way in which they interpreted their experience was affected by the cultural resources at their disposal and the social context in which they existed, with its various institutional structures. One of the most important features of English culture and social structure was its religious formation. In the feudal period the Church had been the dominant ideological institution and subsequent economic and political changes had been accompanied by ideological struggles couched in terms of religious beliefs, the struggles were frequently overtly concerned with religious practices and organisation. It is not surprising, therefore, that the ideological struggles that accompanied the massive social changes entailed in capitalist industrialisation should manifest some of the same tendencies.

The problem of how to analyse the nature and effects of those ideological struggles, as they relate to religion, can be formulated in different ways. One problematic, which fits in with recent Marxist theories of ideology, but pre-dates them and was shared by non-Marxists, such as the French historians who contrasted England with revolutionary France, poses questions about why working-class consciousness was not more often revolutionary consciousness. Answers tend to be sought in terms of the existence of structures, including structures of discourses and intellectual leadership, which impeded the development of such a consciousness.

It will not be possible to arrive at a definitive answer to the question of why revolutionary consciousness did not become stronger or more widespread. However, it is possible to map out some of the key issues as they relate to the part that religion may have played in this connection, and to indicate some of the answers that have been suggested. The key issues are:

How important was religion in forming a non-revolutionary working class consciousness; and why did it take the form that it did?

These issues can be broken down into a number of sub-questions and hypothetical answers:

1 Was there an affinity between pre-existing religious cultural elements and the new ideological currents that came to prominence during the Industrial Revolution, e.g. a reservoir of Protestant dissent that could be channelled in different directions?

2 Was there an imposition on the working class of extraneous ideology emanating from the dominant class and transmitted through the agency of its intellectual leadership, e.g. the clergy, Sunday schools, and church building movements funded and encouraged by the state or members of the middle and upper classes?

3 Were there certain functions that religion served for the working class in a period of disruption and hardship that might explain why religious solutions were adopted? Some of the suggested functions are: 'the opium of the people' (Marx); a compensation for those who suffer in this life through the promise of higher status in the spiritual realm (Weber); a transitional ideology helping the workers to adjust to the requirements of capitalist industrialisation or 'modernisation' by inculcating work-discipline (Weber); a form of community that eased the passage from traditionally-based community (*Gemeinschaft*) to a more impersonal, rational and contractually-based social order (*Gesellschaft*) (Gilbert, 1976; and Semmel, 1974).

4 Did religion help to separate off from the working class its leading strata, the so-called 'aristocracy of labour' (Engels' term), those workers who, by virtue of their skill and relative independence, might have been the 'organic intellectuals' (Gramsci) capable of developing revolutionary working-class consciousness? Is it possible to go even further and find evidence that such strata were permeated by, and incorporated into, the

ideology of the dominant class? (This 'dominant ideology thesis' and its relation to the notion of an 'aristocracy of labour' cannot be pursued in detail here, nor can we evaluate the evidence for its possible extensiveness, but some of the subsequent discussions of Methodism, Sunday schools, and occupational community culture are relevant to it. For fuller discussion, see Abercrombie *et al.*, 1980.)

5   What factors might have affected the degree of overlap between the culture of working-class communities and the ideological content of those institutions in which the middle and upper classes performed a dominant leadership role, particularly religious institutions? Ideological contestation, as we will see, tended to be most acute where there was a strongly entrenched working-class culture based on a certain way of life, such as the mining and fishing villages and small towns in Cornwall and similar areas, and the occupational communities of craftsmen in small workshops, where there were rituals and practices involving initiation and funeral rites, and patterns of mutual support, which made them resistant to extraneous ideological influences.

It is hoped that the following discussion, and the accompanying articles in this section, will help to clarify these issues, although we cannot hope to resolve them here. No overall theorisation of the issues will be attempted; indeed, it is doubtful whether an adequate general theory of ideology exists. Most current theories of ideology tend to be either extremely abstract (Thompson, 1978) or, where they are more concrete and specific, they are ill-suited to the task of doing justice to the historical specificity of religion as a cultural system in this earlier period. This is not surprising as the focus of recent theories of ideology has tended to be on the non-emergence of revolutionary working-class consciousness in *mature* capitalism, rather than in *emerging* industrial capitalism. However, some of the ideas and concepts deriving from these theories are potentially useful, particularly Gramsci's discussions of hegemony in terms of ideological leadership, 'organic intellectuals', and cultures as multi-layered (including common sense notions, popular traditions, as well as various sorts of philosophies) (Gramsci, 1971). These ideas find their nearest parallel in the sociology of religion in the work of Max Weber (Weber, 1965, and the article by Weber in this volume, pp. 31–40). Weber can be criticised for not having developed a more dynamic view of the 'elective affinities' between ideologies and various social strata. The relationship appears rather passive, unlike Gramsci's picture of the ideological terrain as the site of contestation and struggle. However, Weber did sometimes show an awareness of this, as E.P. Thompson suggests in his account of Methodism and the making of the English working class, when he quotes Weber's statement that:

Wherever modern capitalism has begun its work of increasing the productivity
of human labour by increasing its intensity, it has encountered the immensely
stubborn resistance of ... pre-capitalist labour.
(Thompson, 1968, p. 392)

If recent theories of ideology do not *explain* the specific cultural configuration in the period we are discussing, they do offer a better way of
conceptualising that configuration than the older 'economistic' Marxist
theory according to which religion was viewed as mere superstructure,
or a cultural 'transmission belt' for the interests of the dominant class.
Gramsci rejected this principle of 'reduction' in analysing the relationship between class and ideology, in which an ideology would be reduced
to, or belonged to, a certain class, and which had led to the assumption
that the existence of a dominant class meant that other classes were
automatically subject to, or incorporated into, a dominant ideology.
Gramsci's guiding principle of 'articulation' envisaged a looser set of
relationships in which there was no pure dominant ideology descending
from above, nor a pure working-class ideology emanating from below,
but rather complex forms of interaction of political, cultural and ideological negotiation within and between dominant groups (i.e. aristocracy
and bourgeoisie) and various subordinate groups and classes.

On the whole, the following account of the issues will favour this
Gramscian view of the ideological terrain as the site of contestation and
struggle in which religion can be seen to have provided the language of
dissent and resistance for subordinate classes, as well as being a means
by which the dominant class sought to establish and maintain hegemony.
It follows from this that due weight will be given to the 'positive' features
and functions of working-class religious life – the ways in which people
actively created, adapted and used religion for their own needs. At the
same time, we will consider some of the arguments for religion having
acted as an agency of social control, whether through the splitting-off or
incorporation of working-class leaders, by acting as the 'opium of the
people', or by functioning to instil a work-discipline or a transitional
ideology in the passage from *Gemeinschaft* to *Gesellschaft* forms of social
organisation.

The significance of the period from the latter part of the eighteenth
century through the first few decades of the nineteenth century, as far
as religion and ideology are concerned, is that it was a period of intense
contestation. This means that those involved in religious movements and
disputes will be found to have had an unusually well-developed awareness
of the wider social relevance of their beliefs and practices. In these circumstances, even a narrow definition of ideology, such as that which
designates it as the 'justificatory, apologetic' dimension of culture (cf.
Geertz, in this volume, pp. 82–3), would encompass many of the most

salient ideological features of the religious situation. However, this narrow definition tends to spotlight only those aspects of religion which were most obviously in play as active elements in the ideological struggle along class lines, particularly in relation to the efforts of the governing classes to maintain social order and legitimate their authority. But a narrow view of ideology would miss some of the less obvious ideological elements of religious culture that were at issue in this period, and which helped to form the ideological complex that we associate with the Victorian moral ethos that became established from the middle of the nineteenth century onwards. We need a broad view of ideology that also directs our attention to those underlying structures of 'common sense' and 'presuppositions' by and through which people orientate themselves in their daily lives, and which make them accept such a way of life as natural. (Such a focus is not restricted to, although it gains much from, those who have developed rigorously 'structuralist' methods for analysing culture and ideology, e.g. Lévi-Strauss and Althusser.) This broad view of ideology, which in Gramsci's approach is combined with a sense of the dynamic character of the ideological terrain, is the one that is most likely to make sense of the ideological aspects of religion defined as a cultural system:

A system of symbols which acts to establish powerful, pervasive and long-lasting moods and motivations in men by formulating conceptions of a general order of existence and clothing these conceptions with such an aura of factuality that the moods and motivations seem uniquely realistic.
(Geertz, 1966, pp. 3–4; and in this volume, p. 67)

This broad definition of religion corresponds to the broad view of ideology, and its adoption has similar consequences. For example, in the subsequent discussion of religion in the period of capitalist industrial-isation, it helps to determine whether or where we draw a line between religion and other elements of popular culture in working class com-munities, such as superstitions, traditional recreational activities, and the ritualised aspects of occupational and workplace cultures. On the whole, we will regard them as being closely involved with the more overt-ly religious elements and so part of the same ideological contestation. At times, the authorities will be seen to have had a similar recognition of their interconnectedness, viewing popular religious movements and other aspects of popular culture as posing the same threat. In other cases the ideological connotations of religion and popular culture were more subtle and less obviously representative of a stance towards the political-economic order. This was so with respect to some of the more arcane theological disputes and the message of popular hymns, not all of which conveyed the clear ideological message of those oft-quoted hymn lines:

> The rich man in his castle,
> The poor man at his gate,
> God made them high or lowly,
> And ordered their estate.

But quite often they did play some part in constituting the *discourses* that gave meaning to the social order, and which positioned people as *'subjects'* within that order (cf. Althusser, 1969). There were real ideological implications in the disputes about whether 'Arminian' or 'Calvinist' doctrines shold prevail in Methodism, and about how people were categorised or positioned as 'subjects' within this theological discourse – subjects like 'the saved', 'the elect', 'God's people', 'the damned' and 'the innocent'.

Historical background

The primary aim of this article is to explore and elucidate some of the intricate relations between ideology and social structure (particularly social stratification) as exemplified by English religion between 1740 and 1850. This period marks the emergence and growth to maturity of industrial capitalism, and also the struggle of the Established Church (the Church of England) to maintain and fulfil its role as the pre-eminent ideological institution cementing the social order – a role which it gradually and reluctantly relinquished to secular institutions such as the state system of education. The 1740s saw the rise of Methodism, which seemed to present a challenge to the hegemonic position of the Established Church in the religious sphere as well as appearing to pose a threat to the established social order. We will examine the thesis put forward by the French historian, Elie Halévy, in 1906 (and subsequently readdressed by E. P. Thompson in *The Making of the English Working Class*, 1968), which maintains that, although Methodism may have appeared to pose a threat to the authorities, it served to deflect or channel off any potential revolutionary impulses in the working class. The Church of England answered the challenges posed to it by its religious and secular rivals, and by social upheavals, in ways that came naturally to an established church – it endeavoured to prove its usefulness to the state, and expected the state to fulfil its side of the partnership in return. (For an account of the Church's espousal of this 'utilitarian' rationale, see K. A. Thompson, 1970.) We can mention three ways in which the Church attempted to make a contribution to cementing the social order in the face of external and internal threats: the fostering of nationalism during the French Revolutionary and Napoleonic wars (1793–1815) (cf. Stafford, 1982); the church reforms and building drives that aimed to win the new urban working class (discussed in K.A. Thompson, 1970); and the Sunday school movement, as a means of socialising working-class children into behaviour patterns appropriate to their future roles in a capitalist society (Laqueur, 1976; and in this volume, pp. 183–203). However, although the Church had some success in these respects, it was a very limited success. Nationalism was prominent during the period of the French threat, and church reform building movements increased the number of churches from 11,379 in 1801 to 14,077 in 1851 but the percentage of the population aged fifteen and over attending Easter communion dropped in this period, from 9.9 per cent to 8.1 per cent (Gilbert, 1976, p. 28). The Census of 1851 showed that half of the 5–15 age group attended Sunday school, but the Church of England had only about 40 per cent of the enrolments (Laqueur, 1976). Laqueur makes a plausible case that the Nonconformist Sunday schools may not have played such an important part in the process of indoctrination into bourgeois values, but rather expressed working-class values and aspirations.

Overall, in the period of industrial and demographic expansion, 1740 to 1830, when the English population rose from about 5,500,000 to 13,200,000, the Church of England declined from a position in which it had nearly a monopoly of religious practice to one in which it almost became a minority religious establishment. By 1831 there were only 605,000 Easter Day communicants (7.2 per cent of the population aged 15 and over, compared with 535,000 in 1801), and clergy and church buildings had increased only marginally since 1740 (Gilbert, 1976, 27–9). A massive church building drive was launched in the 1830s with support from the government, but the enormous increase in population to over 34 million by 1914 meant that the Church never really made up the ground lost between 1740 and 1830 (see Table 1).

In the case of Methodism, there was a period of sustained rapid expansion from 1740 to 1840, followed by a period of slower and decelerating expansion until 1906, and then continuing decline. There were also many schisms into small sects (see Table 2).

As for the success of Sunday schools, they made a slow start in the last two decades of the eighteenth century, and then their enrolments climbed steadily from 1800 to 1850, with some acceleration in the late 1820s and 1830s. After 1830, few working-class children could have escaped at least some exposure to Sunday school (see Tables 3 and 4).

Many accounts of the social effects of religion in nineteenth-century Britain emphasise the stabilising effects, by which they mean it counteracted the disruptive effects of capitalist industrialisation. Some accounts suggest that religion acted as a kind of social cement, binding otherwise divided social classes into a common set of beliefs and a religiously defined common identity. Another view is that religion served both to

Table 1   The Church of England
Churches, clergy, and Easter Day communicants, 1801–1914

Year	Churches and chapels	Clergy	Easter Day communicants ('000s)	Easter Day communicant density
1801	11,379	–	535	9.9
1811	11,444	14,531	550	8.9
1821	11,558	–	570	7.9
1831	11,883	14,933	605	7.2
1841	12,668	15,730	755	7.9
1851	14,077	16,194	875	8.1
1861	14,731	17,966	995	8.3
1871	15,522	19,411	1,110	8.2
1881	16,300	20,341	1,225	7.9
1891	16,956	22,753	1,490	8.4
1901	17,368	23,670	1,945	9.4
1911	–	23,193	2,293	9.8
1914	–	–	2,226	9.2

Notes
1   In 1966 Anglican 'churches', 'clergy', and 'Easter Day communicants' numbered 17,761, 20,008, and 1,899,000 respectively. The 1966 Easter Day Communicant density index was 5.4.
2   The density index expresses Easter Day communicant figures as a percentage of the population aged fifteen and over.
3   The figures on 'clergy' for 1811–41 include a few hundred Welsh clergy. Welsh clergy have been excluded from the subsequent figures. The increase of clergy in the 1840s consequently was greater than the series indicates.
(*Source:* Gilbert, 1976, p. 28)

Table 2   Methodist membership in England, 1767–1914

A.   Wesleyan membership, 1767–96

1767	22,410	1776	30,875	1791	56,605
1771	26,119	1781	37,131	1796	77,402
		1786	46,559		

B.   Wesleyan, New Connexion, and total Methodist membership, 1801–1819

	W	NC	Total		W	NC	Total
1801	87,010	4,815	91,825	1816	181,631	8,146	189,777
1806	103,549	5,586	109,135	1819	184,998	9,672	194,670
1811	135,863	7,448	143,311				

(**Table 2** – *continued on p. 134*)

Table 2 – *continued*

C.   *Wesleyan, New Connexion, Primitive Methodist, Bible Christian, United Methodist Free Churches, and total Methodist membership, 1821–1906*

	W	NC	PM	BC	UMFC	Total
1821	188,668	10,404	16,394			215,466
1826	217,486	10,233	–	6,433		267,652
1831	232,883	11,433	37,216	6,650		288,182
1836	273,588	18,248	62,306	10,499		364,641
1841	305,682	20,506	75,967	11,353		435,591
1846	319,770	15,610	85,500	12,181		452,238
1851	285,000	16,962	106,074	13,324		490,000
1856	242,296	18,380	104,178	13,894		443,493
1861	291,288	22,732	127,772	16,866	52,970	513,628
1866	303,500	24,064	140,905	18,758	60,386	547,613
1871	319,495	22,870	148,597	18,050	61,924	570,936
1876	342,612	23,055	160,737	19,665	64,777	610,846
1881	349,695	25,797	168,807	21,209	65,067	630,575
1886	378,518	27,720	179,726	23,614	66,964	676,542
1891	387,779	28,756	180,518	25,769	67,200	690,022
1896	395,588	29,932	181,079	26,306	69,509	702,411
1901	412,194	32,324	187,260	28,315	72,568	732,668
1906	447,474	37,017	203,103	32,317	80,323	800,234

D.   *Wesleyan Methodist Association and Wesleyan Reformers membership, 1837–1856*

	WMA		WMA		WMA	WR
1837	21,262	1846	19,177	1856	18,136	46,609
1841	22,074	1851	20,557			

E.   *Wesleyan, Primitive Methodist, United Methodist, and total Methodist membership, 1911–1914*

	W	PM	UM	Total
1911	436,356	202,479	144,888	783,723
1914	432,370	202,420	143,096	777,886

F.   Total Methodist membership as a percentage of the adult English population, 1801–1914

1801	1.6	1841	4.5	1881	4.0
1806	1.9	1846	4.3	1886	4.0
1811	2.3	1851	4.4	1891	3.8
1816	2.8	1856	3.8	1896	3.6
1821	2.9	1861	4.1	1901	3.5
1826	3.3	1866	4.2	1906	3.6
1831	3.4	1871	4.1	1911	3.3
1836	4.0	1876	4.1	1914	3.2

Notes

1   The *Total Methodist Membership* Series is based on an aggregation of the following connexional memberships: 1801–19, Wesleyan and New Connexion; 1821, Wesleyan, New Connexion, and Primitive Methodist; 1826–36, Wesleyan, New Connexion, Primitive Methodist, and Bible Christian; 1836–56, Wesleyan, Methodist Association, and (1851 and 1856) the Wesleyan Reformers; 1861–1906,

Table 3   Numbers of Sunday schools built or founded 1780–1850 distinguishing Anglican and Non-Anglican*

Years to:	Total no.	No. belonging to C. of E.	Percentage of total no. belonging to C. of E.
1801	2,290	1,282	56.4
1811	4,687	2,288	48.8
1821	8,236	3,766	45.7
1831	11,910	5,371	45.0
1841	17,168	7,815	45.0
1851	23,135	10,427	45.0

Table 4   Enrolment in English Sunday schools 1788–1850**

Year	Number	Percentage of population	Percentage of those age 5–15	Percentage of working class age 5–15
1788	59,980	–	–	–
1795	94,100	–	–	–
1801	206,100	2.5	10.3	13.8
1811	415,000	4.4	18.2	24.2
1818	452,325	4.2	17.6	23.4
1821	730,000	6.5	27.0	36.0
1831	1,096,000	8.4	37.2	49.6
1833	1,363,170	10.2	45.0	60.0
1841	1,679,000	11.4	49.8	66.4
1851	2,099,611	12.5	56.5	75.4

* Prepared from *Census: Education* 1852–53 [1692] xc, Table 25. Those schools for which no date of founding or constructing of building is given, 1,071 Anglican, 420 Dissenting, were distributed equally over seven decades. There is no basis for a more sophisticated distribution of the undated schools.
** Numbers of 1788 and 1795 are, at best, educated guesses arrived at through the use of the following formula:

$$\text{no. in schools aided by the Sunday School Society in 1788 and 1795} \quad \times \quad \frac{\text{no. of schools founded by 1801}}{\text{no. of schools aided by the Sunday School Society in 1801}}$$

(*Source:* Laqueur, 1976, p. 44)

Notes (*to Table 2 continued*)
Wesleyan, New Connexion, Primitive Methodist, Bible Christian, and United Methodist Free Churches; 1911–14, Wesleyan, Primitive Methodist, and United Methodist Church.
2   For the purpose of computing the density series of Section F (above), 'Adult population' has been defined as the population aged fifteen years and over.
3   Wesleyan density in 1767 was around 0.5.
4   In 1968 membership of the Methodist Church in England was 603,100 and Methodist density was 1.7. Following the Union of 1932 these figues represent a continuation of the *Total Methodist Membership* series.
(*Source:* Gilbert, 1976, pp. 31–2)

legitimate the superior position of the upper classes and to console the lower classes (acting like a drug – 'the opium of the people', as Marx called it). The home missionary effort to build hundreds of new churches in working class areas, the Evangelical movement in the Church of England and the Sunday school movement, have all been interpreted as conscious or unconscious attempts to provide a social cement, or to promote acquiescence to the status quo and consolation for the miseries of the lower classes. Even the growth of Methodism, which at first caused alarm and opposition among the upper classes, has been viewed as an ideological distraction taking away working-class revolutionary potential (Thompson, 1968, and in this volume, pp. 154–82). On the basis of historical evidence, as we shall see, it is possible to make a case for each of these explanations having a certain amount of plausibility (exactly how plausible is less easily established). However, a full picture of the social effects of religion in the nineteenth century must take account of evidence of religion operating in ways contrary to those encompassed by the 'social cement' and 'opium of the people' theories. In some respects religion exacerbated social divisions and deepened class conflict; indeed, the very phrase about religion being an opium of the people was first used by a clergyman, the Reverend Charles Kingsley. It will be necessary, there-fore, to examine ways in which religion furnished the language and beliefs for dissent and opposition to the status quo. Also, it is possible to find evidence of a 'split consciousness' among subordinate classes, in that they seem to 'simultaneously produce their own view of the world and inhale the religious atmosphere produced by the dominant culture of the dominant class' (Turner, 1983, p. 85). It may be that a better description would be that of an 'amalgam' rather than a 'split', as the culture of the lower classes in nineteenth-century Britain seems to have been a complicated mixture of traditional popular beliefs, practices and super-stitions, elements of workplace culture and trades societies' rituals, and more orthodox Christian beliefs that they shared with other classes. This would correspond to Gramsci's view of ideological complexes.

We will endeavour to provide a sociological analysis of religion in these various ideological complexes and their functioning, whilst at the same time examining some of the evidence that historians have used to test what has been described as 'one of the most persistent, appealing, and useful hypotheses used to interpret English history in the eighteenth and nineteenth centuries', which runs as follows:

On 24 May 1738 Wesley was converted. From that moment, so it is argued, a corrupt and lifeless Established Church was faced with the shock of the Methodist Revival. The Methodists, persecuted by mobs and forbidden to preach in many Anglican churches, were at length driven from the Church of England. Their impact, however, continued through their spiritual descendents, the Evangelicals.

These Evangelicals (to continue the hypothesis) did not effect a takeover of the Church of England, but rather a takeover of the whole nation, imbuing it with their values and creating Victorianism. The Methodists' main appeal was to the working classes. Besides accomplishing the civilization of a section of those classes, the Methodists imposed a degree of conservatism upon them which was providential, since the French Revolution and the Industrial Revolution together created uniquely powerful tensions which otherwise might have brought about the disintegration of society.
(Armstrong, 1973, p. 7).

This is certainly a simplification of a complicated set of religious developments and we will be looking at some of the wider social ramifications of religious beliefs and practices, but Armstrong's formulation does provide a useful story-line. It received its classic statement in the form of the question posed by Halévy: 'Why was it that of all the countries of Europe England has been the most free from revolutions, violent crises and sudden change?' The answer, he believed, did not lie in England's political or economic institutions, but in English religion, especially the effect of the Evangelical movement on the thinking of the potential leaders of a revolution:

We have sought in vain to find the explanation by an analysis of her political institutions and economic organization. Her political institutions were such that society might easily have lapsed into anarchy had there existed in England a bourgeoisie animated by the spirit of revolution. And a system of economic production that was in fact totally without organization of any kind would have plunged the kingdom into violent revolution had the working classes found in the middle class leaders to provide it with a definite ideal, a creed, a practical programme. But the elite of the working class, the hard-working and capable bourgeois, had been imbued by the Evangelical movement with a spirit from which the established order had nothing to fear.
(Halévy, 1938, Book 3, p. 47)

Methodism and the working class

The Methodist Revival flourished at the same time as the Industrial Revolution and the French Revolution; consequently it is not surprising that there have been constant efforts to discern the connections. One of the first was by Robert Southey in the year of Peterloo, 1819, who, while attacking the Methodists for their irrationality and spiritual tyranny, admitted that their conversions might have a great effect in improving the morality of individuals, and he commended Wesley's insistence on strict control over personal expenditure and the avoidance of personal indulgence. W. E. H. Lecky, in his *History of England in the Eighteenth Century* (vol. 3, Longmans, 1878), also criticised the Methodists' irrationality and spiritual tyranny, but argued that the new religious enthusiasm was one of the things that saved England from anything like the French Revolution. The thesis was elaborated by the French historian, E. Halévy, in articles published in the *Revue de Paris* in 1906, and in his *History of the English People in the Nineteenth Century* (1913, English translation, 1924 Penguin edn 1938). The idea of Methodism as an antidote to revolution in Britain had already been promulgated by nineteenth-century French writers such as Taine and Guizot, and Halévy's thesis was in line with this French view (Semmel, 1971).

He also maintained that it was characteristic of social change in England that it took religious forms, and Nonconformism was a transitional phase for those who were upwardly socially mobile:

Nonconformity ... tended to become a transitional creed, a stage in the history of an English family. The unskilled workman becomes in turn a skilled workman, an artisan, the head of a small business, a businessman possessed of a modest capital, and as he rises out of the barbarism in which the working class was plunged, he becomes a Nonconformist. If he himself rises still higher on the social ladder, or if his children rise after his death, he or they go over to the Church of England.
(Halévy, 1938, III, p.46)

Harold Perkin, in his *Origins of Modern English Society 1780–1880* (1969), developed Halévy's observation on the connections between a person's rise in social status and his change in religion. In the birth of the modern class structure Perkin pictures religion as the 'midwife', in the sense that it enabled men to escape from dependence upon the gentry, and it gave them 'a model of class organization'.

E.P. Thompson's *The Making of the English Working Class* (1968) argues that Methodism had a disastrous effect on the English working class, for three reasons:

(i) working class radicalism was inhibited by the Methodist insistence on submissiveness;
(ii) Wesley's stress on the virtues of work, discipline and thrift played into the hands of the industrialists;
(iii) the Methodist concentration on the emotions had harmful psychological effects.

Methodism has been accused at various times of being both radical and conservative in its effects. Coinciding as it did with the French Revolution and the Industrial Revolution, it seemed to many of its contemporaries that Methodism was a further threat to the established social and ideological order. Its teachings were radical in that they emphasised human sinfulness and the need for redemption, and the condemnation applied to all classes. In a more important sense, Methodism attacked the structures of society; it undermined the ideology inscribed in institutional practices:

Visibly, the Methodist meeting – either outside or in one of the new chapels with the sexes segregated and seated on benches on the principle of first come, first seated – was in as sharp a contrast as could be imagined to the hierarchically ordered congregation at the parish church, surrounded as it was with hatchments, memorials, and decorated pews. Less obviously, the attack on the parish was also an attack on the elaborate complex of property rights in which clergy and land-owners shared.
(Armstrong, op. cit., p. 113)

In its early years, Methodism was accused of all sorts of dangerous tendencies and the meetings were subject to attacks by gangs, which gave rise to riots. One bishop even accused the Methodists of administering drugs to people to induce hysteria (George Lavington, Bishop of Exeter, in his *Enthusiasm of Methodists and Papists compared*, 1749–51).

The simple version of the historical hypothesis about the ideological functions of Methodism – that it imposed a degree of conservatism on the working class – is inadequate. It is important to take account of the quite different and varied functions that a religious ideology can serve. The strength of a highly developed and successful ideology lies in its capacity to serve a multiplicity of functions and to have an affinity or con-gruity with a variety of aspects in the culture and experiences of the groups to whom it appeals. It is often the case that a sociologist or his-torian has emphasised one set of functions or aspects and ignored or downplayed others as a result of adopting a particular perspective, or as the result of a judgement about what was most important in terms of the scholar's own set of values. This has to be kept in mind when comparing different accounts of the functions of Methodism, as – for example – Gilbert (1976) and E.P. Thompson (1968). According to Gilbert, Thompson's account emphasises the repressive 'utility' of Methodism in inculcating a 'work discipline' rather than a more attractive obverse aspect of its legitimation of self-improvement and economic endeavour. Thompson is accused of writing with some distaste for Methodist beliefs and values, evidently out of a conviction that the best they could offer was 'consolation' to those who felt 'defeated and hopeless'. Gilbert main-tains that this was a minor function in the total ideological impact of Methodism; its most widespread appeal was to groups whose economic and social positions were improving, and it echoed the aspirations rather than the despair of the working classes.

In fact, Thompson's approach is potentially more complicated than this summary might suggest. He sees Methodism as serving functions for both the 'exploiters' and the 'exploited' (Thompson, 1968, p. 412). He gives three reasons for this: (1) it served the exploiters' interest in exercising social control through indoctrination of the workers, especial-ly through the Sunday schools; (2) it could 'offer to the uprooted and abandoned people of the Industrial Revolution some kind of community to replace the older community-patterns which were being displaced' (ibid., pp.416–17); (3) it offered compensation for disappointed this-worldly hopes, including political hopes, by emphasising the after-life – it was the 'chiliasm of despair' (ibid., p.419). On balance, however, Thompson's account emphasises the counter-revolutionary effects of Methodism, which is seen as serving the function of social control.

The issue of which of the ideological functions served by Methodism and Evangelicalism was the most important cannot be resolved by a simple appeal to neutral empirical evidence because such evidence is never completely independent of any conceptual structure. However, such evidence can clear away over-simplification and generalisations that are too broad. A comparison of the different accounts provided by Gilbert and Thompson reveals that certain functions relate to some groups of Methodist adherents but not others, and that this also varied from one period to another. For example, until the demoralising introduction of the powerloom had its impact on handloom weavers after the Napoleonic Wars, weavers joined Methodism in large numbers and found there an 'overall congruity' between the religious culture and the spirit of inde-pendence and self-reliance which characterised their socio-economic situation. As we will see, different ideological functions of Methodism might be emphasised depending on whether we concentrate on a 'social control' perspective or look at it in terms of the ways in which it served as an expression of working-class cultures and aspirations. Gilbert stresses the positive functions of the chapel communities, which were largely created and sustained by working-class lay members; whereas Thompson sees them more as instruments of the middle class for exer-cising social control and instilling discipline in the working class. The same contrast, between an imposed social control perspective and an approach which emphasises the ways in which working-class religion was an expression or translation in a religious idiom of people's aspirations and communal values, occurs in accounts of the functions served by the Sunday school movement (in the excerpt from Laqueur, 1976, in this volume), and with regard to the relations between Methodism, popular beliefs and village culture (discussed in Rule, 1982).

In comparing the different accounts of the social functions of Method-ism by Gilbert and Thompson, it is worth noting the different styles of the two accounts: Thompson builds up a powerful case emphasising the social control functions of Methodism and Evangelicalism – functions that mainly served the interests of the emerging system of industrial capitalism. Gilbert emphasises more strongly the functions that Method-ism, Nonconformity and Evangelicalism served for certain sections of the working class in a period of transition. The point of these remarks about the two accounts is not to suggest that one is right and the other is wrong – they both offer 'true' observations in terms of the theoretical perspective adopted for the task of guiding and interpreting observation. (Also, in many respects, the two approaches offer complementary insights.) The main point to be borne in mind when evaluating historical accounts such as those concerning the social functions or effects of Methodism is the need to discern the explicit and implicit theoretical perspectives used in producing these accounts, which can help to explain why, on balance, they give different emphases to some facts and less to others.

'Social control' and 'social expression' might be seen as just two of the functional relationships between ideology and social classes or groups within the complex and dynamic field of ideology as mapped out by Gramsci.

Another functional relationship that has been posited between Methodism/Evangelicalism and both the working class and the bourgeoisie, is that of providing a transitional ideology for integrating those classes into the capitalist industrial state, and for supplying an 'effective nourishing ground for English nationalism' (Semmel, 1974, p. 80). According to Semmel, this was achieved through Evangelical Arminianism, a theological synthesis elaborated by Wesley and extended by his successors, 'uniting the emotional force of the quasi-mystical primitive Christianity of the Reformation – with its powerful capacity to create ''new men'' – with the ''modernity'' of Arminian doctrine ... Evangelical Arminianism was the ''ideology'' of the Methodist Revolution' (Semmel, ibid.).[1]

The modernity of Arminianism stemmed from the fact that it saw the relationship between Christ and his worshippers as akin to a commercial contract:

Arminians saw Christ as having, by his sacrifice, both *purchased* favourable *terms* or *conditions* for men, and also as having restored to men a great part of their ability to fulfill these conditions of which they had been deprived by Adam's sin. God seemed as much bound by the contract, which offers a *quid pro quo* as was the individual worshipper ... In thus stipulating that salvation was dependent upon man's rational, responsible behaviour, the Arminians were asking for the kind of conduct which 'modern' political and economic life would find essential, and which, especially so far as the lower classes were concerned, was almost non-existent in the traditional order.
(Semmel, op. cit., p. 12)

The genius of Wesley as an ideologist was that he managed to synthesise, or mediate between, different ideological streams and tendencies, and appeal to classes with seemingly different interests and cultures. In theological terms, 'Wesley appealed to both the Puritan sense of man's degenerate state, with its passionate plea for God's grace so essential to salvation, as well as to the Arminian insistence on personal responsibility, on free will and good works' (Semmel, op. cit., p. 13). In class terms, he not only united Puritanism and Arminianism into an instrument for the evangelisation of the growing industrial proletariat, but also inspired a similar fusion by Anglican Evangelicals and Dissenters which permeated the bourgeoisie and even some of the aristocracy.

Sunday schools and social control

One of the main agencies of transmission of bourgeois values to the working class is reputed to have been the Sunday school movement, according to E. P. Thompson and other historians who adopt the Halévy thesis about the counter-revolutionary effects of religion in Britain. However, Laqueur (1976) provides a markedly different conclusion as a result of his study of the Sunday school movement:

The period 1780–1850 witnessed the birth of a working-class culture that was deeply rooted in that ethic of education, religion and respectability which was embodied in the Sunday school. English working-class politics lacked a revolutionary ideology, a rhetoric of 1789, less because of religious education than because England did not experience a '1789'. And this latter fact is due to the stability of English society and the cohesion of its ruling class and not to the failure of ideology taken as an independent variable. The religious, educational and social institutions of the working class must be seen as significant cultural achievements in their own right and not merely as spurs or restraints in the development of revolutionary politics. Sunday schools were largely a creation of the community they served and 'helped to keep the soul alive in a population living under conditions that degrade the mind'.
(Laqueur, 1976, p. 245)

The issue as to whether the working class was successfully incorporated into a dominant, bourgeois ideology is not easily resolved, but it is certainly the case that the one area of high working-class involvement in religion, that of the Sunday school movement, does not provide unequivocal evidence of incorporation. Although E. P. Thompson is successful in showing that the middle-class founders and management committees of Sunday schools often had that purpose in mind, Laqueur concludes that the working-class Sunday school teachers and parents did not share that intention. Many Nonconformist Sunday schools seemed to have grown out of the demand from within the working class for basic education and the transmission to children of the values of the 'respectable' working class, or 'labour aristocracy' – industry, thrift, self-discipline, improvement, communalism and egalitarianism. Laqueur sees such Sunday schools as genuinely popular institutions that promoted working-class culture, and therefore akin to trade unions, friendly societies, co-operatives, building societies, savings banks, and various institutions for intellectual improvement. Certainly the authorities in the Church of England and in Wesleyan Methodism feared that the Sunday schools could have such effects, and in the 1820s they prohibited the teaching of writing to Sunday school pupils. The original Methodist emphasis, on the values of equality of all people before God and the community of believers within the church, resonated with the democratic-egalitarian and communal-activist values of the working class, and were a source of acute tension within Wesleyanism as the representatives of bourgeois values – the clergy and leading laymen – promoted centralisation, inegalitarianism, and support for the existing social order. This led to splits and some branches of Methodism, especially the Primitive Methodists, were closely connected with radical working-class movements and supported political action (Hobsbawm, 1957, 1959). Even E. P. Thompson, who paints a negative political picture of Methodism, admits that some Methodists did display confrontationist, class-conscious, proletarian values in the early nineteenth century (Thompson, 1968, p. 430).

The truth of the matter is that the evidence about working-class beliefs is somewhat sketchy and incomplete. There are few first-hand accounts of such beliefs and practices until after the mid-nineteenth century and the spread of literacy. The amalgam of beliefs probably varied considerably between areas, between sections of the working class, and depending on the degree of penetration of middle-class agencies of transmission of bourgeois values. Literacy and the printed word provided the most potent agency for indoctrination into bourgeois values and for exercising social control. However, this should not be regarded as a straightforward, one-way process; the working-class communities were not 'clay', open to the imprint of whatever values were pressed upon them, nor were values exclusively class related or derived. Firstly, as we have suggested with regard to Sunday schools, the learning and organisational abilities developed in the Sunday schools could be used in working-class radicalism. Secondly, the actual content of the 'texts' used in the Sunday schools – scriptures and hymns – were open to a variety of interpretations; they were not, after all, statements of bourgeois utilitarianism, but highly symbolic and potent images of various sorts. The political radicals wrote and thought in the metaphors of the Bible. As an opponent of Sunday schools and advocate of secular education put it in a report on the Kentish peasant risings, 'The narratives and lessons contained in the sacred writings may be turned, as they often have been, not merely into sources of error, but into authorities for wrong' (Liardet, 1839, quoted in Laqueur, 1976, p. 244). The hymns of Wesley, which were widely loved and sung, even at Chartist and Luddite meetings, had more in common with Romanticism than with rational utilitarianism, as we will see in

144   *K. Thompson*

the next section. The third set of factors that need to be considered, which hindered or complicated the penetration and indoctrination of working-class culture by more specifically bourgeois beliefs and values, relate to the pre-existing culture of working-class communities, whether at the workplace or in certain localities and occupations.

According to E. P. Thompson and others who judge religion to have been a counter-revolutionary force, one of the most important means by which nineteenth-century religion functioned to exercise social control was through the Sunday school movement and the influence of certain dominant ideas purveyed through that movement, which not only influenced children but also – through them – the parents' generation. But Sunday school teaching was not a direct transmission of dominant bourgeois values. An important motif in the thought of the Sunday school movement was a kind of Romanticism, a set of ideas concerned with childlike innocence, counterposed against adult sinfulness. One explanation for the popularity and success of the Sunday school movement may lie in the content of its teaching and the character of the relations between teachers and pupils. Laqueur argues that the content of the teaching, especially in Wesleyan and Evangelical Sunday schools, tended to resolve the tension inherent in Protestant doctrines concerning the moral state of the child in favour of its innocence. Whereas strict Calvinist theology had proclaimed that each soul's fate was predestined from eternity, and some were reprobate from the womb, Wesleyan Methodism had elements of an Arminian theology which sometimes softened that doctrine. It maintained that infants who died before they could choose redemption were destined for heaven because of their birthright of innocence. Although the hymns of John and Charles Wesley contained some of the usual Christian ambivalence about the moral state of the child, their metaphorical structure included the image of the innocent child. The hymn on the text, 'Suffer the little children to come unto me', proclaimed of children that they were formally born in sin:

> Born they are, like us, in sin
> Touch the unconscious lepers clean;
> Purchase of thy blood they are,
> Save them by Thy dying prayer.
> (quoted in Laqueur, 1976, p. 13)

But a few lines later, under the text, 'For such is the kingdom of God' the hymn develops the metaphor of the soul regaining childlike innocence in order to enter paradise:

> Thy church is here with saints supplied
> Who childlike innocence regain;
> And every babe that ever dies
> Shall in thy heavenly kingdom reign.
> (ibid., p. 13)

Another famous example is to be found in the hymn for children, 'Gentle Jesus, meek and mild / Look upon a little child', which continues,

> I shall live the simple life
> Free from sin's uneasy strife:
> Sweetly ignorant of ill,
> Innocent and happy still.
>
> Keep me from the great offence,
> Guard my helpless innocence,
> Hide me, from all evil hide,
> Self and stubbornness, and pride.

There was a new softness and sentimentality in the late eighteenth-century and early nineteenth-century attitude towards children that suffused the Sunday school movement. That is not to say there was none of the old Calvinist thunder against immorality, disobedience and sin. There were also many arguments in favour of Sunday schools which emphasised their utility for the purpose of maintaining social order and overcoming class divisions, as in the statement that they offered the hope that the links of the 'great chain of society which has too long been broken and separated', the chain which once 'united rich and poor', could somehow be reforged (quoted in Laqueur, op. cit., p. 7). But the Sunday school movement cannot be understood solely in terms of its social utility; it shared with the high culture of romanticism a streak of anti-rationalism; 'children because of their relative ignorance, their innocence and their simplicity were more likely to perceive religious reality and to accept the Holy Spirit than were adults' (Laqueur, p. 15). Like Wordsworth, the Sunday schools took as their dictum, 'the child is the father of the man'. The child not only epitomised the characteristics that would find favour in God's eyes, but he or she might also be the means of converting adults. This theme was put forward in one of the most widely read pieces of popular literature, Leigh Richmond's *The Dairyman's Daughter*, the sales of which exceeded half a million before 1850.

The character of the relations between Sunday school teachers and pupils also differed from those that prevailed in other institutions, such as the factory or the day schools. One reason may have been that the teachers were much younger in the Sunday schools – more like older brothers and sisters. Certainly the ideal of that relationship, as set forth in guides to Sunday school teaching or organisation, stressed that the good teacher was 'affectionate in manner and mild in expression' and put forward the model of the teacher as an older, wiser and steadier friend (see examples given in Laqueur, op. cit., p. 18). To a large extent the Sunday school movement was staffed by the working class, even though it may have been encouraged and funded initially by middle- and upper-class patrons, who had in mind the need for social control and a disciplined workforce. If we simply take the statements of intention of these latter groups as a guide to the character of the Sunday schools, then we could be misled. The Sunday schools may have served some of the social functions the upper classes had in mind for them, but they also served other functions for the working class. Many children learned to read in the Sunday schools, and they were communities in which poor children experienced pleasures, affection and kindness that were badly needed. To a certain degree the Sunday schools can be described as predominantly working-class institutions, staffed by members of the skilled or 'respectable' sections of that class, who passed on some of the benefits they had gained from their relatively favoured positions, such as the ability to read, instruction in cleanliness, and access to various social services and benefits organised by the Sunday school or the wider community. They had a collective-communalist orientation that was typically working class and therefore differed in practice from the values of bourgeois individualism.

Workplace and occupational culture

One of the problems that we face in evaluating the beliefs and culture of the working class in the first half of the nineteenth century concerns the paucity of information about workplace culture. We know relatively more about those aspects of the affairs of the working class that were conducted in public, such as Chartism and the organised religious activities of the churches. The same cannot be said of workplace culture in that period. There is a good reason for this: studies of the workplace culture in that period (e.g. Behagg, 1982) suggest that the opacity and secrecy of workplace culture were part of a defensive reaction in which the workers sought to control their immediate working environment in the face of employers' attempts to exercise authority over them, backed by middle-class inspired efforts to 'improve' and 'reform' their morals and behaviour. Those urban missionaries who did manage to penetrate the workplace in places such as Birmingham found it contained many of the values and beliefs most calculated to undermine their efforts. One such missionary, Edward Derrington, drew attention in 1839 to the independence that the experience of work afforded to those who he had hoped would be pliable ex-Sunday school scholars: 'the youths have at a very early age', he complained, 'been their own or nearly their own masters' (quoted in Behagg, op. cit., p. 155). Such work experience threatened to undermine the missionaries' efforts to reform the workers' morals through involvement in 'rational recreation' because the youths who started work at an early age tended, according to Derrington, to be 'the fighters – the pigeon flyers – dog fighters and gamblers' (quoted in Behagg, ibid.). Another missionary, Peter Sebtree, expressed the same concern about a widow who had been left to run her husband's factory and who said 'that her children had been brought under the teaching of the Gospel among the Wesleyans, but now they were unhappily infidel having imbibed the notions from some of the workmen' (ibid., p. 156). Missionaries, such as William Jackson, who evangelised in Birmingham from 1842 until 1847, feared to enter the factories, and when he did enter a nailer's workshop he was stopped and challenged to open debate by an 'infidel' workman (ibid.). His colleague Derrington's most abiding memory of such a visit was of 'an hour's close argument' with an 'infidel' navigator who 'eulogised Robert Owen as a most benevolent man' (ibid., p. 157). The missionaries bemoaned the fact that the infidel culture of the workplace and of the public house permeated into the homes, where the missionaries directed their efforts to converting the wives.

According to Behagg,

The symbiosis of the workplace and the public house represented, to the outsider, a culture that embraced not only drunkenness, violence and sensuality, but also radical politics, Owenite infidelity and, at times, an almost puritanical concept of moral justice. Once within either institution the intruders were confronted by an alternative set of values and beliefs that would intimidate them both physically and intellectually. It is argued here that in the first half of the nine-teenth century the working class deliberately emphasized the distinct nature of their own culture, particularly the separateness of the workplace and their auto-nomous role within it, in an attempt to retain some control over a work process that was undergoing structural change.
(Behagg, 1982, pp. 157–8)

Ritual and secrecy were two of the hallmarks of the trade societies, which is not surprising in view of the fact that trade unions were illegal from 1800 to 1824 and of only dubious legal status thereafter. The ex-clusivity and secrecy of the trade societies was emphasised by their rituals of initiation: oath-swearing, the wearing of surplices and the chanted liturgy of psalms and Old Testament extracts. Similar rituals were to be found in groups as diverse as the Leeds woolcombers, the London tailors, the West Country weavers and the Operative Stone Masons. Sometimes the trade societies would make a show of their exclusive and mysterious culture, as in their funeral processions. An account of a typical trade society funeral in 1834 records that a Derby carpenter was accompanied to his last resting place by a hundred women in white robes and hoods, and the officers of more than eleven trade societies, similarly attired; at other funerals the robbed mourners carried a branch of ivy or a bunch of thyme, which would be dropped on the coffin after the singing of the doxology (Behagg, p. 161). In such ways the workers gave witness to their 'mysterious brotherhood' and emphasised the life-long commitment undertaken at their initiation. The ceremonies expressed visually and in practice the ideological distinctiveness of the working community; the funerals, in particular, showed that the individual who respected collective values was, in turn, deserving of collective respect (Behagg, op. cit.).

Commentators who write from the angle of the study of working-class resistance to capitalist control and exploitation in the workplace tend to interpret these beliefs and practices as a cloak or shield to hide the worker's more 'important' activities from the employers and other authorities. As Behagg puts it:

It was clearly the operation of the trade society, or where this did not exist the work group, within the workplace that were to be cloaked and hidden rather than the ceremonial itself. The actual rules of behaviour by which the workforce governed their own activities and attitudes at the place of work were largely unwritten and it is these rather than the elaborate initiation ritual that constitute the anonymous tradition of early English industrial relations. In order to control the work process, or rather to re-organize it, in a period of structural economic change, so that it answered the needs of capital rather than those of labour, the manufacturer had first to penetrate the collective culture of the workplace. This was a culture based upon assumptions which he did not share, transmitted through face-to-face relationships in which he had no part. Penetration was made doubly difficult where collectivity was underpinned by mystification and ... folk violence.
(Behagg, 1982, pp. 162–3)

This is to interpret these workplace rituals, ceremonies and beliefs in a rather narrowly 'exclusivist' way. Although it is probably true that their secrecy and mysteriousness did serve the important function of preventing the manufacturer from penetrating and controlling the workplace, that was not their only function, nor can their character be understood and appreciated purely in terms of this function. In order to understand the character of these sub-cultures it is necessary to see how they articulated with other cultural layers, especially popular religion, superstition and folklore.

Popular culture and popular religion

Workplace culture did not come into existence to serve the function of withstanding capitalist control; it was part of a wider popular and traditional working-class culture that included Old Testament and Christian elements, folk beliefs and rituals, superstitions and revelries. The historian Gareth Steadman Jones has pointed out that there is a danger in making the concept of 'social control' central to accounts of developments in popular culture in the nineteenth century; it can lead us to view cultures too much in oppositional terms, in which one culture is on the defensive (traditional popular culture) and the other is on the offensive (the reforming cultures of evangelicals, Methodists, civil elites and capitalist employers, intent on imposing rational recreation on the working class as part of the process of incorporating it into the capitalist scheme of things). The 'social control' concept is suggestive of the attempted *imposition* of new forms of behaviour upon the working class by *external* forces. In some respects there were cultural oppositions: Methodism and teetotalism were opposed to the 'revelry' aspect of traditional popular culture. As Harrison has pointed out, it was over attempts to dominate popular leisure that the churches and the working class came most frequently into contact in the nineteenth century:

Nineteenth century Christians deplored that recreational complex of behaviour which included gambling, adultery, drinking, cruel sports and sabbath breaking and blasphemy – all of which took place together at the race course, the drinking place, the theatre, the 'feast' and the 'fair'.
(Harrison, 1966, p. 2)

In other respects, however, there was less opposition and Methodism in particular merged with popular religion and superstition and other aspects of traditional popular culture. Indeed, the success of Methodism in some areas was due to the ease with which it could assimilate traditional forms of belief and action. In one of its most successful areas, among the miners and fishermen of Cornwall, for example, Methodism did not so much replace folk beliefs as translate them into a religious idiom. The appeal of Methodism was not dissimilar to the appeal of witchcraft beliefs (discussed earlier in this book although mainly with respect to African examples):

Neither witchcraft nor spirit-agency as an explanation of events precludes commonsense empirical observation. Men die because they happen to be at a moment in time under a fall of rock. What needs explaining is why that man was in that place at that time. Witchcraft, as Max Gluckman has observed, explains that singularity of misfortune which the agnostic or scientific mind prefers to see as 'chance'. In modern British history no church of comparable weight has allowed a greater degree of comprehensiveness or frequency to divine or satanic intervention than did early Methodism. The idea of an omnipotent deity and a malicious devil can explain singularity of misfortune as well as can witches or evil spirits. The retributive anger of God can explain the most widespread of disasters.
(Rule, 1982, pp. 63–4)

One of the reasons for John Wesley's success in appealing to the common people was probably that despite his learning he was fascinated by, and in touch with, some of the ingredients of popular superstition and belief. As Armstrong puts it:

Yet attempts to make Wesley a man representative of his time must fail. Conversion and assurance – his most obvious doctrines – were obvious throwbacks to the previous age. The practice of determining a course of action by opening the Bible at random (which he took from the Moravians) was likewise out of tune with the eighteenth century. Witchcraft he would never reject, and he collected the most circumstantial accounts of witches. Before retailing a lengthy narrative of one Elizabeth Hobson in his Journal for 25 May, 1768, he observed:

> It is true likewise, that the English in general and indeed most of the men of learning in Europe, have given up all accounts of witches and apparitions, as mere old wives' fables. I am sorry for it ... The wisest and best men in all ages and nations ... well know that giving up witchcraft is, in effect, giving up the Bible.

(Armstrong, 1973, p. 82)

Conclusion

The case for the strong thesis that religion served a predominantly and crucially counter-revolutionary function in England during the period from the late eighteenth century to the end of the nineteenth century has been examined with respect to two of its most important elements – the influence of Methodism, and Sunday schools. The discussion has centred on the cultural content of these two movements in relation to working-class culture and its penetration or incorporation by bourgeois values. Although it is difficult to judge the degree of penetration or incorporation achieved, partly because the evidence from first-hand accounts is limited, it has not been established that it was sufficient, of itself, to prevent a revolutionary class consciousness developing. At the most, the thesis could only be applied to the potential leaders of such a revolution (which is what Halévy's formulation of the thesis did imply), because it has been noted that the working-class involvement in organised religion, apart from Sunday schools, was very low. Membership of Methodist sects ranged from 3.6 to 4.4 per cent of the English population throughout the nineteenth century; Church of England communicants on Easter Day were in the range of 7.2 to 8.9 per cent; and Roman Catholics attending mass were in the region of 4 per cent as a result of Irish immigration after 1850 (Gilbert, 1976). In the rural areas, those members of the working class who were religious seem to have held an amalgam of beliefs that was completely antithetical to the bourgois values of industrialism, being made up of Christian elements intermixed with superstitions, magic and folklore (Obelkevich, 1976). This was also the case among Cornish miners and similar occupational groups who were numerically prominent in Methodism (Rule, 1982), and even in the popular Methodism among factory operatives described by E.P. Thompson, not to mention some descriptions of Wesley's own writings.

In so far as religious ideology did serve an anti-revolutionary function, it was probably in an indirect and diffuse way among the bourgeoisie itself. Although Halévy mentioned the working class in his thesis, it was the working-class elite and the bourgeoisie, as the potential leaders of revolution who were described as having been 'imbued by the Evangelical movement with a spirit from which the established order had nothing to fear'. He was contrasting the situation in England with the revolutionary situation in France, where the blocked aspirations of the bourgeoisie led them to provide revolutionary leadership. In England, Evangelical ideology and organisational techniques enabled the bourgeoisie to succeed in their aspirations without having to lead the working class in a revolutionary direction. The stimulus of Wesleyan Methodism brought about a parallel Evangelical movement in the Church of England, and it was principally through the influence of this movement that the ruling class became permeated with the distinctive ideological ethos that we call 'Victorianism'; its political outcome was a programme of individual moral reform, not revolution or even collective social reform.

Rather than viewing religion in terms of whether it overwhelmingly served one function or another, or served the interests of one class or another, this account has suggested that religion should be viewed as part of a cultural system which is also an ideological terrain of contestation. We have spotlighted a number of functional relationships (or 'elective affinities' as Weber preferred to call them) between ideological elements and social classes or groups, all occurring in the same period. It is a tribute to the richness of the symbolic sphere, of which religion provides a pre-eminent example, that it defies analyses which are 'reductionist' or based on crudely mechanical models linking 'base' and 'superstructure'. A further corrective that emerges from consideration of specific examples of ideology such as Methodism and Evangelicalism, is to the theory that ideologies 'belong' to classes, and are primarily used as instruments or 'transmission belts' to secure the interests of a class. This is not to say that groups do not seek to use ideologies for their purposes (the British government legislated to build churches, and benefactors founded Sunday schools, with such purposes in mind). But ideologies are fluid, dynamic and multi-functional: they overlap class cultures, are used for a variety of purposes, and have even more unintended than intended consequences. The English working class was not incorporated into the ideology of the dominant class; but that is not to say that it did not incorporate some of the elements of that ideology into its way of life. After all, the factory or coalmine formed part of that way of life alongside the chapel and Sunday school, and there was a cultural overlap in many instances, such as the inculcation of time-discipline and the notions of individual responsibility and contract. E. P. Thompson chose to interpret the ideological aspects of Methodism in terms of their part in providing the moral repression necessary for capitalist development. Semmel and Gilbert emphasise Methodism's function in creating a new type of man capable of bridging the gap between *Gemeinschaft* and *Gesellschaft*. Others have found this difficult to reconcile with the evidence of the active part played by Primitive Methodists, especially, in working-class politics and trade unionism. They would claim that a 'more balanced view' (Turner and Hill, 1975, p. 160) would be that Methodism, through its class meetings and lay officials, found itself simultaneously 'producing men who revolted against the established order and also disowning them, if their activities seemed to imperil the religious society's existence' (Kent, 1966, p. 137). Clearly a religion can produce all of these ideological effects, and much else.

Note

1   Arminius, a professor of theology at the University of Leiden, led a group of Protestants working in the commercial cities of Holland at the beginning of the seventeenth century, and put forward a new view of the relationship of God and man. In the Remonstrance of 1610, published the year after Arminius' death, his followers proclaimed that because of Christ's sacrifice and atonement, *all* men *might* be saved, not merely a pre-ordained elect as Calvin had stipulated.

References

Abercrombie, N., Hill, S., and Turner, B. S. (1980) *The Dominant Ideology Thesis.* London, Allen and Unwin.

Althusser, L. (1969) *For Marx.* Harmondsworth, Penguin.

Armstrong, A. (1973) *The Church of England, the Methodists and Society 1700–1850.* University of London Press.

Behagg, C. (1982) 'Secrecy, ritual and folk violence: the opacity of the workplace in the first half of the nineteenth century', in Storch (ed.) *Popular Culture and Custom in Nineteenth Century England.* London, Croom Helm.

Gilbert, A. D. (1976) *Religion and Society in Industrial England*, ch. 4, 'The functions of "church" and "chapel"'. London, Longman.

Gramsci, A. (1971) *Selections from the Prison Notebooks.* London, Lawrence and Wishart.

Halévy, E. (1938) *A History of the English People in the Nineteenth Century*, Penguin, 3 vols, edn. First English edn. pub. in London, by T. Fisher, Unwin.

Harrison, B. (1966) 'Religion and recreation in nineteenth century England', *Papers presented to the Past and Present Conference on Popular Religion*, 9 July 1966.

Hobsbawm, E. J. (1967) 'Methodism and the threat of revolution in Britain', in *Labouring Men: Studies in the History of Labour.* London, Weidenfeld and Nicolson, 1964.

Kent, J. (1966) *The Age of Disunity.* London, Epworth.

Laqueur, T.W. (1976) *Religion and Respectability: Sunday Schools and Working Class Culture 1780–1850*, ch.7, 'Sunday schools and social control'. New Haven, Conn., Yale University Press.

Obelkevich, J. (1976) *Religion and Rural Society: South Lindsay, 1825–1875.* Oxford, University Press.

Perkin, H. (1969) *Origins of Modern English Society 1780–1880.* London.

Rule, J. (1982) 'Methodism, popular beliefs and village culture in Cornwall 1800–50', in Storch, R.D. (ed.) *Popular Culture and Custom in Nineteenth Century England.* London, Croom Helm, pp.48–70.

Semmel, B. (ed.) (1971) *The Birth of Methodism.* University of Chicago Press.

Semmel, B. (1974) *The Methodist Revolution.* London, Heinemann.

Stafford, W. (1982) 'Religion and the doctrine of nationalism in England at the time of the French Revolution and Napoleonic wars', in S. Mews (ed.), *Religion and National Identity.* Oxford, Blackwell, pp.381–98.

Thompson, E.P. (1968) *The Making of the English Working Class*, ch.11, 'The transforming power of the cross'. Harmondsworth, Penguin (first published 1963).

Thompson, E.P. (1978) *The Poverty of Theory.* London, Merlin Press.

Thompson, K.A. (1970) *Bureaucracy and Church Reform: the Organizational Response of the Church of England to Social Change 1800–1965.* Oxford, The Clarendon Press.

Turner, B.J. and Hill, M. (1975) 'Methodism and the pietist definition of politics: historical development and contemporary evidence', in M. Hill (ed.), *A Sociological Yearbook of Religions in Britain*, 8, London, SCM Press.

Turner, Bryan S. (1983) *Religion and Social Theory.* London, Heinemann Educational Books.

Weber, M. (1965) *The Sociology of Religion.* London, Methuen (first published in German, 1922).

13 E. P. THOMPSON

The transforming power of the cross

From *The Making of the English Working Class* by E. P. Thompson, 1963.
Reproduced by permission of the publishers, Gollancz Ltd. © E. P.
Thompson, 1963, 1968.

1. Moral machinery

Puritanism – Dissent – Nonconformity: the decline collapses into a
surrender. *Dissent* still carries the sound of resistance to Apollyon and
the Whore of Babylon, *Nonconformity* is self-effacing and apologetic:
it asks to be left alone. Mark Rutherford, one of the few men who
understand the full desolation of the inner history of nineteenth-century
Nonconformity – and who is yet, in himself, evidence of values that
somehow survived – noted in his *Autobiography* the form of service
customary in his youth:

> It generally began with a confession that we were all sinners, but no individual
> sins were ever confessed, and then ensued a kind of dialogue with God, very much
> resembling the speeches which in later years I have heard in the House of Com-
> mons from the movers and seconders of addresses to the Crown at the opening
> of Parliament.

The example is taken from the Calvinistic Independents: but it will
also serve excellently to describe the stance of Methodism before temporal authority. This surrender was implicit in Methodism's origin –
in the Toryism of its founder and in his ambivalent attitude to the Established Church. From the outset the Wesleyans fell ambiguously between
Dissent and the Establishment, and did their utmost to make the worst
of both worlds, serving as apologists for an authority in whose eyes they
were an object of ridicule or condescension, but never of trust. After the
French Revolution, successive Annual Conferences were forever profess-
ing their submission and their zeal in combating the enemies of established order; drawing attention to their activity 'in raising the standard
of public morals, and in promoting loyalty in the middle ranks as well
as subordination and industry in the lower orders of society'.[1] But
Methodists were seldom admitted by the Establishment to audience –
and then only by the back door: never decorated with any of the honours

of status: and if they had been mentioned in despatches it would probably have hindered the kind of moral espionage which they were most fitted to undertake.

The Wars saw a remarkable increase in the Methodist following.[2] They witnessed also (Halévy tells us) 'an uninterrupted decline of the revolutionary spirit' among all the Nonconformist sects. Methodism is most remarkable during the War years for two things: first, its gains were greatest among the new industrial working class: second, the years after Wesley's death see the consolidation of a new bureaucracy of ministers who regarded it as their duty to manipulate the submissiveness of their followers and to discipline all deviant growths within the Church which could give offence to authority.

In this they were very effective. For centuries the Established Church had preached to the poor the duties of obedience. But it was so distanced from them – and its distance was rarely greater than in this time of absenteeism and plural livings – that its homilies had ceased to have much effect. The deference of the countryside was rooted in bitter experience of the power of the squire rather than in any inward conviction. And there is little evidence that the evangelical movement within the Church met with much greater success: many of Hannah More's halfpenny tracts were left to litter the servants' quarters of the great houses. But the Methodists – or many of them – *were* the poor. Many of their tracts were confessions of redeemed sinners from among the poor; many of their local preachers were humble men who found their figures of speech (as one said) 'behind my spinning-jenny'. And the great expansion after 1790 was in mining and manufacturing districts. Alongside older Salems and Bethels, new-brick Brunswick and Hanover chapels proclaimed the Methodist loyalty. 'I hear great things of your amphitheatre in Liverpool,' one minister wrote to the Reverend Jabez Bunting in 1811:

A man will need strong lungs to blow his words from one end of it to the other. In Bradford and in Keighley they are building chapels nearly as large as Carver Street Chapel in Sheffield. To what will Methodism come in a few years?[3]

Jabez Bunting, whose active ministry covers the full half-century, was the dominant figure of orthodox Wesleyanism from the time of Luddism to the last years of the Chartist movement. His father, a Manchester tailor, had been a 'thorough Radical' who 'warmly espoused the cause of the first French revolutionists', but who was not the less a Methodist for that.[4] But in the late 1790s, and after the secession of the Kilhamite New Connexion, a group of younger ministers emerged, of whom Bunting was one, who were above all concerned to remove from Methodism the Jacobin taint. In 1812 Bunting earned distinction by disowning Methodist Luddites; the next year, in Leeds, he counted 'several Tory magistrates of the old school, Church and King people, who, probably, never crossed the threshold of a conventicle before, among his constant hearers'.[5] He and his fellow-ministers – one of the more obnoxious of whom was called the Reverend Edmund Grindrod – were above all organizers and administrators, busied with endless Connexional intrigues and a surfeit of disciplinary zeal. Wesley's dislike of the self-governing anarchy of Old Dissent was continued by his successors, with authority vested in the Annual Conference (weighted down with ministers designated by Wesley himself) and its Committee of Privileges (1803). The Primitive Methodists were driven out because it was feared that their camp meetings might result in 'tumults' and serve as political precedents (as they did); the 'Tent Methodists' and Bible Christians, or Bryanites, were similarly disciplined; female preaching was prohibited; the powers of Conference and of circuit superintendents were strengthened. Espionage into each other's moral failings was encouraged; discipline tightened up within the classes; and, after 1815, as many local preachers were expelled or struck off the 'plan' for political as for religious 'back-slidings'. Here we find an entry in the Halifax Local Preacher's Minute Book: 'Bro. M. charged with attending a political meeting when he should have been at his class' (16 December 1816): there we find a correspondent writing in alarm from Newcastle to Bunting:

... a subject of painful and distressing concern that two of our local preachers (from North Shields) have attended the tremendous Radical Reform Meeting ... I hope no considerable portion of our brethren is found among the Radicals; but a small number of our leaders are among the most determined friends to their spirit and design ... and some of the really pious, misguided sisterhood have helped to make their colours. On expostulation, I am glad to say, several members have quitted their classes (for they have adopted almost the whole Methodist economy, the terms 'Class Leaders', 'District Meetings', etc., etc., being perfectly current among them). If men are to be drilled at Missionary and Bible meetings to face a multitude with recollection, and acquire facilities of address, and then begin to employ the mightly moral weapon thus gained to the endangering the very existence of the Government of the country, *we* may certainly begin to tremble ...

This was in 1819, the year of Peterloo. The response of the Methodist Committee of Privileges to the events of this year was to issue a circular which 'bears clear traces' of Bunting's composition; expressing –

strong and decided disapprobation of certain tumultuous assemblies which have lately been witnessed in several parts of the country; in which large masses of people have been irregularly collected (often under banners bearing the most shocking and impious inscriptions) ... calculated, both from the infidel principles, the wild and delusive political theories, and the violent and inflammatory declamations ... to bring all government into contempt, and to introduce universal discontent, insubordination, and anarchy.[6]

Wesley at least had been a great-hearted warhorse; he had never spared himself; he was an enthusiast who had stood up at the market-cross to be pelted. Bunting, with his 'solid, mathematical way of speaking', is a less admirable character. It was his own advice to 'adapt your principles to your exigencies'. 'In our family intercourse', a friend of his youthful ministry informed his son:

his conversation was uniformly serious and instructive. Like his ministry in the pulpit, every word had its proper place, and every sentence might have been digested previously. ... Sometimes your dear mother's uncontrollable wit suddenly disturbed our gravity; but he was never seen otherwise than in his own proper character as a minister of the gospel of Christ.

Bunting's uncompromising Sabbatarianism stopped just short at the point of his own convenience: 'he did not hesitate, in the necessary prosecution of his ministerial work, to employ beasts; though always with a self-imposed reserve ...' With children it was another matter. We are often tempted to forgive Methodism some of its sins when we recollect that at least it gave to children and adults rudimentary education in its Sunday schools; and Bamford's happy picture is sometimes recalled, of the Middleton school in the late 1790s, attended by 'big collier lads and their sisters', and the children of weavers and labourers from Whittle, Bowlee, Jumbo and the White Moss. But it is exactly *this* picture, of the laxness of the early Methodists, which Bunting was unable to forgive. When, in his ministry at Sheffield in 1808, his eye fell upon children in Sunday school being taught to *write*, his indignation knew no bounds. Here was 'an awful abuse of the Sabbath'. There could be no question as to its theological impropriety – for children to learn to read the Scriptures was a 'spiritual good', whereas writing was a 'secular art' from which 'temporal advantage' might accrue. Battle commenced in Sheffield (with the former 'Jacobin', James Montgomery, defending the children's cause in the *Sheffield Iris*), from which Bunting emerged victorious; it was renewed at Liverpool in the next year (1809) with the same result; and Bunting was in the forefront of a movement which succeeded, very largely, in extirpating this insidious 'violation' of the Lord's Day until the 1840s. This was, indeed, one of the ways in which Bunting won his national spurs.[7]

The spurs were needed, perhaps, to stick into the children's sides during the six days of the week. In Bunting and his fellows we seem to touch upon a deformity of the sensibility complementary to the deformities of the factory children whose labour they condoned. In all the copious correspondence of his early ministries in the industrial heartlands (Manchester, Liverpool, Sheffield, Halifax and Leeds, 1804–15), among endless petty Connexional disputes, moralistic humbug, and prurient inquiries into the private conduct of young women, neither he nor his colleagues appear to have suffered a single qualm as to the consequences of industrialism.[8] But the younger leaders of Methodism were not only guilty of complicity in the fact of child labour by default. They weakened the poor from within, by adding to them the active ingredient of submission; and they fostered within the Methodist Church those elements most suited to make up the psychic component of the work-discipline of which the manufacturers stood most in need.

As early as 1787, the first Robert Peel wrote: 'I have left most of my works in Lancashire under the management of Methodists, and they serve me excellently well.'[9] Weber and Tawney have so thoroughly anatomized the interpenetration of the capitalist mode of production and the Puritan ethic that it would seem that there can be little to add. Methodism may be seen as a simple extension of this ethic in a changing social milieu; and an 'economist' argument lies to hand, in the fact that Methodism, in Bunting's day, proved to be exceptionally well adapted, by virtue of its elevation of the values of discipline and of order as well as its moral opacity, both to self-made mill-owners and manufacturers and to foremen, overlookers, and sub-managerial groups. And this argument – that Methodism served as ideological self-justification for the master-manufacturers and for their satellites – contains an important part of the truth. So much John Wesley – in an often-quoted passage – both foresaw and deplored:

... religion must necessarily produce both industry and frugality, and these cannot but produce riches. But as riches increase, so will pride, anger, and love of the world. ... How then is it possible that Methodism, that is, a religion of the heart, though it flourishes now as a green bay tree, should continue in this state? For the Methodists in every place grow diligent and frugal; consequently they increase in goods. Hence they proportionately increase in pride, in anger, in the desire of the flesh, the desire of the eyes, and the pride of life. So, although the form of religion remains, the spirit is swiftly vanishing away.

Many a Methodist mill-owner – and, indeed, Bunting himself – might serve as confirmation of this in the early nineteenth century.[10] And yet the argument falters at a critical point. For it is exactly at this time that Methodism obtained its greatest success in serving *simultaneously* as the religion of the industrial bourgeoisie (although here it shared the field with other Nonconformist sects) and of wide sections of the proletariat. Nor can there be any doubt as to the deep-rooted allegiance of many working-class communities (equally among miners, weavers, factory workers, seamen, potters and rural labourers) to the Methodist Church. How was it possible for Methodism to perform, with such remarkable vigour, this double service?

This is a problem to which neither Weber nor Tawney addressed themselves. Both were mainly preoccupied with Puritanism in the six-teenth and seventeenth centuries, and with the genesis of commercial capitalism; both addressed themselves, in the main, to the psychic and social development of the middle class, the former stressing the Puritan concept of a 'calling', the latter the values of freedom, self-discipline, individualism and acquisitiveness. But it is intrinsic to both arguments that puritanism contributed to the psychic energy and social coherence of middle-class groups which felt themselves to be 'called' or 'elected' and which were engaged (with some success) in acquisitive pursuits. How then should such a religion appeal to the forming proletariat in a period of exceptional hardship, whose multitudes did not dispose them to any sense of group calling, whose experiences at work and in their communi-ties favoured collectivist rather than individualist values, and whose frugality, discipline or acquisitive virtues brought profit to their masters rather than success to themselves?

Both Weber and Tawney, it is true, adduce powerful reasons as to the *utility*, from the point of view of the employers, of the extension of Puritan or pseudo-Puritan values to the working class. Tawney anatomiz-ed the 'New Medicine for Poverty', with its denunciation of sloth and improvidence in the labourer, and its convenient belief that − if suc-cess was a sign of election − poverty was itself evidence of spiritual turpitude.[11] Weber placed more emphasis on the question which, for the working class, is crucial: work-discipline. 'Wherever modern capitalism has begun its work of increasing the productivity of human labour by increasing its intensity,' wrote Weber, 'it has encountered the immensely stubborn resistance of ... precapitalistic labour.'

The capitalistic economy of the present day is an immense cosmos into which the individual is born, and which presents itself to him ... as an unalterable order of things in which he must live. It forces the individual, in so far as he is involved in the system of market relationships, to conform to capitalistic rules of action.

But, as industrial capitalism emerged, these rules of action appeared as unnatural and hateful restraints: the peasant, the rural labourer in the unenclosed village, even the urban artisan or apprentice, did not measure the return of labour exclusively in money-earnings, and they rebelled against the notion of week after week of disciplined labour. In the way of life which Weber describes (unsatisfactorily) as 'traditionalism', 'a man does not "by nature" wish to earn more and more money, but simply to live as he is accustomed to live and to earn as much as is necessary for that purpose'. Even piece-rates and other incentives lose effectiveness at a certain point if there is no inner compulsion; when enough is earned the peasant leaves industry and returns to his village, the artisan goes on a drunken spree. But at the same time, the opposite discipline of low wages is ineffective in work where skill, attentiveness or responsibility is required. What is required – here Fromm amplifies Weber's argument – is an 'inner compulsion' which would prove 'more effective in harnessing all energies to work than any outer compulsion can ever be':

> Against external compulsion there is always a certain amount of rebelliousness which hampers the effectiveness of work or makes people unfit for any differentiated task requiring intelligence, initiative and responsibility. ... Undoubtedly capitalism could not have been developed had not the greatest part of man's energy been channelled in the direction of work.

The labourer must be turned 'into his own slave driver'.[12]

The ingredients of this compulsion were not new.[13] Weber has noted the difficulties experienced by employers in the 'putting-out' industries – notably weaving – in the seventeenth century, as a result of the irregular working habits (drunkenness, embezzlement of yarn and so on) of the workers. It was in the West of England woollen industry – at Kidderminster – that the Presbyterian divine, Richard Baxter, effected by his ministry a notable change in labour relations; and many elements of the Methodist work-discipline may be found fully-formed in his *Christian Directory* of 1673.[14] Similar difficulties were encountered by mineowners and northern woollen and cotton manufacturers throughout the eighteenth century. Colliers generally received a monthly pay; it was complained that 'they are naturally turbulent, passionate, and rude in manners and character':

> Their gains are large and *uncertain*, and their employment is a species of task work, the profit of which can very rarely be previously ascertained. This circumstance gives them the wasteful habits of a gamester ...
>
> Another trait in the character of a collier, is his predilection to change of situation ... Annual changes are almost as common with the pitman as the return of the seasons ... Whatever favours he may have received, he is disposed to consider them all cancelled by the refusal of a single request.[15]

The weaver-smallholder was notorious for dropping his work in the event of any farming emergency; most eighteenth-century workers gladly exchanged their employments for a month of harvesting; many of the adult operatives in the early cotton mills were 'of loose and wandering habits, and seldom remained long in the establishment'.[16] A few of the managerial problems in early enterprises are suggested by the list of fines at Wedgwood's Etruria works:

> ... Any workman striking or likewise abusing an overlooker to lose his place.
> Any workman conveying ale or liquor into the manufactory in working hours, forfeit 2/ – .
> Any person playing at fives against any of the walls where there are windows, forfeit 2/ – ...[17]

Whether his workers were employed in a factory or in their own homes, the master-manufacturer of the Industrial Revolution was obsessed with these problems of discipline. The out-workers required (from the employers' point of view) education in 'methodical' habits, punctilious attention to instructions, fulfilment of contracts to time, and in the sinfulness of embezzling materials. By the 1820s (we are told by a contemporary) 'the great mass of Weavers' were 'deeply imbued with the doctrines of Methodism'. Some of the self-made men, who were now their employers, were Methodists or Dissenters whose frugality – as Wesley had foreseen – had produced riches. They would tend to favour fellow-religionists, finding in them a 'guarantee for good conduct' and 'a consciousness of the value of character'.[18] The 'artisan' traditions of the weavers, with their emphasis on the values of independence, had already prepared them for some variant of Puritan faith.[19] What of the factory operatives?

It is in Dr Andrew Ure's *Philosophy of Manufactures* (1835) – a book which, with its Satanic advocacy, much influenced Engels and Marx – that we find a complete anticipation of the 'economist' case for the function of religion as a work-discipline. The term *Factory*, for Ure:

involves the idea of a vast automaton, composed of various mechanical and intellectual organs, acting in uninterrupted concert for the production of a common object, all of them being subordinated to a self-regulated moving force.

'The main difficulty' of the factory system was not so much technological but in the 'distribution of the different members of the apparatus into one cooperative body', and, above all, 'in training human beings to renounce their desultory habits of work, and to identify themselves with the unvarying regularity of the complex automaton':

To devise and administer a successful code of factory discipline, suited to the necessities of factory diligence, was the Herculean enterprise, the noble achievement of Arkwright. Even at the present day, when the system is perfectly organized, and its labour lightened to the utmost, it is found nearly impossible to convert persons past the age of puberty, whether drawn from rural or from handicraft occupations, into useful factory hands. After struggling for a while to conquer their listless or restive habits, they either renounce the employment spontaneously, or are dismissed by the overlookers on account of inattention.

'It required, in fact, a man of a Napoleonic nerve and ambition, to subdue the refractory tempers of work-people accustomed to irregular paroxysms of diligence ... Such was Arkwright.' Moreover, the more skilled a workman, the more intractable to discipline he became, 'the more self-willed and ... the less fit a component of a mechanical system, in which, by occasional irregularities, he may do great damage to the whole'. Thus the manufacturers aimed at withdrawing any process which required 'peculiar dexterity and steadiness of hand ... from the *cunning* workman' and placing it in charge of a 'mechanism, so self-regulating, that a child may superintend it'. 'The grand object therefore of the modern manufacturer is, through the union of capital and science, to reduce the task of his work-people to the exercise of vigilance and dexterity, – faculties ... speedily brought to perfection in the young.'[20]

For the children, the discipline of the overlooker and of the machinery might suffice; but for those 'past the age of puberty' inner compulsions were required. Hence it followed that Ure devoted a section of his book to the 'Moral Economy of the Factory System', and a special chapter to religion. The unredeemed operative was a terrible creature in Ure's sight; a prey to 'artful demagogues'; chronically given to secret cabals and combinations; capable of any atrocity against his masters. The high wages of cotton-spinners enabled them 'to pamper themselves into nervous ailments by a diet too rich and exciting for their indoor occupations':

Manufactures naturally condense a vast population within a narrow circuit; they afford every facility for secret cabal ...; they communicate intelligence and energy to the vulgar mind; they supply in their liberal wages the pecuniary sinews of contention ...

In such circumstances, Sunday schools presented a 'sublime spectacle'. The committee of a Stockport Sunday school, erected in 1805, congratulated itself upon the 'decorum' preserved in the town, in 1832, at a time of 'political excitement' elsewhere: 'it is hardly possible to approach the town ... without encountering one or more of these quiet fortresses, which a wise benevolence has erected against the encroachments of vice and ignorance'. And Ure drew from this a moral, not only as to general political subordination, but as to behaviour in the factory itself:

The neglect of moral discipline may be readily detected in any establishment by a practised eye, in the disorder of the general system, the irregularities of the individual machines, the waste of time and material ...

Mere wage-payment could never secure 'zealous services'. The employer who neglected moral considerations and was himself 'a stranger to the self-denying graces of the Gospel' –

knows himself to be entitled to nothing but eye-service, and will therefore exercise the most irksome vigilance, but in vain, to prevent his being overreached by his operatives – the whole of whom, by natural instinct as it were, conspire against such a master. Whatever pains he may take, he can never command superior workmanship ...

It is, therefore, excessively the interest of every mill-owner *to organize his moral machinery on equally sound principles with his mechanical*, for otherwise he will never command the steady hands, watchful eyes, and prompt cooperation, essential to excellence of product ... There is, in fact, no case to which the Gospel truth, 'Godliness is great gain,' is more applicable than to the administration of an extensive factory.[21]

The argument is thus complete. The factory system demands a transformation of human nature, the 'working paroxysms' of the artisan or
outworker must be methodized until the man is adapted to the discipline
of the machine.[22] But how are these disciplinary virtues to be inculcated
in those whose Godliness (unless they become overlookers) is unlikely
to bring any temporal gain? It can only be by inculcating 'the first and
great lesson ... that man must expect his chief happiness, not in the
present, but in a future state'. Work must be undertaken as a '*pure act
of virtue* ... inspired by the love of a transcendent Being, operating ... on
our will and affections':

Where then shall mankind find this transforming power? – in the cross of Christ.
It is the sacrifice which removes the guilt of sin: it is the motive which removes
love of sin: it mortifies sin by showing its turpitude to be indelible except by such
an awful expiation; it atones for disobedience; it excites to obedience; it purchases
strength for obedience; it makes obedience practicable; it makes it acceptable;
it makes it in a manner unavoidable, for it constrains to it; it is, finally, not only
the motive to obedience, but the pattern of it.[23]

Ure, then, is the Richard Baxter of Cottonopolis. But we may descend,
at this point, from his transcendental heights to consider, more briefly,
mundane matters of theology. It is evident that there was, in 1800,
casuistry enough in the theology of all the available English churches to
reinforce the manufacturer's own sense of moral self-esteem. Whether
he held an hierarchic faith, or felt himself to be elected, or saw in his
success the evidence of grace or godliness, he felt few promptings to
exchange his residence beside the mill at Bradford for a monastic cell on
Bardsey Island. But Methodist theology, by virtue of its promiscuous op-
portunism, was better suited than any other to serve as the religion of a
proletariat whose members had not the least reason, in social experience,
to feel themselves to be 'elected'. In his theology, Wesley appears to have
dispensed with the best and selected unhesitatingly the worse elements
of Puritanism: if in class terms Methodism was hermaphroditic, in doctrinal terms it was a mule. We have already noted Methodism's rupture
with the intellectual and democratic traditions of Old Dissent. But
Luther's doctrines of submission to authority might have served as the
text for any Wesleyan Conference in the years after 1789:

Even if those in authority are evil or without faith, nevertheless the authority
and its power is good and from God ...
    God would prefer to suffer the government to exist, no matter how evil, rather
than allow the rabble to riot, no matter how justified they are in doing so ...

(Jabez Bunting, however, unlike Luther, could never have admitted the
notion that the rabble could ever be 'justified'.) The general Lutheran bias
of Wesleyanism has often been noted.[24] Wesley's espousal of the doctrine of the universality of grace was incompatible with the Calvinist

notion of 'election'. If grace was universal, sin was universal too. Any man who came to a conviction of sin might be visited by grace and know himself to be ransomed by Christ's blood. Thus far it is a doctrine of spiritual egalitarianism: there is at least equality of opportunity in sin and grace for rich and poor. And as a religion of 'the heart' rather than of the intellect, the simplest and least educated might hope to attain towards grace. In this sense, Methodism dropped all doctrinal and social barriers and opened its doors wide to the working class. And this reminds us that Lutheranism was also a religion of the poor; and that, as Munzer proclaimed and as Luther learned to his cost, spiritual egalitarianism had a tendency to break its banks and flow into temporal channels, bringing thereby a perpetual tension into Lutheran creeds which Methodism also reproduced.

But Christ's ransom was only provisional. Wesley's doctrine here was not settled. He toyed with the notion of grace being perpetual, once it had visited the penitent; and thus a dejected form of Calvinism (the 'elected' being now the 'saved') re-entered by the back door. But as the eighteenth century wore on the doctrine of justification by faith hardened – perhaps because it was so evident that multitudes of those 'saved' in the revivalist campaigns slid back to their old ways after years or only months. Thus it became doctrine that forgiveness of sin lasted only so long as the penitent went and sinned no more. The brotherhood and sisterhood who were 'saved' were in a state of conditional, provisory election. It was always possible to 'backslide'; and in view of human frailty this was, in the eyes of God and of Jabez Bunting, more than likely. Moreover, Bunting was at pains to point out God's view that –

Sin ... is not changed in its nature, so as to be made less 'exceedingly sinful' ... by the pardon of the sinner. The penalty is remitted; and the obligation to suffer that penalty is dissolved; but it is still naturally due, though graciously remitted. Hence appears the propriety and the duty of continuing to confess and lament even pardoned sin. Though released from its penal consequences by an act of divine clemency, we should still remember, that the dust of self-abasement is our proper place before God ...[25]

But there are further complexities to the doctrine. It would be presumptuous to suppose that a man might save *himself* by an act of his own will. The saving was the prerogative of God, and all that a man could do was to prepare himself, by utter abasement, for redemption. Once convinced of grace, however, and once thoroughly introduced to the Methodist brotherhood, 'backsliding' was no light matter to a working man or woman. It might mean expulsion from the only community-group which they knew in the industrial wilderness; and it meant the ever-present fear as to an eternity of lurid punishment to come:

> There is a dreadful hell
>   And everlasting pains,
> Where sinners must with devils dwell
>   In darkness, fire and chains.

How, then, to keep grace? Not by good works, since Wesley had elevated faith above works: 'You have nothing to do but save souls.' Works were the snares of pride and the best works were mingled with the dross of sin; although – by another opportunist feint – works might be a *sign* of grace. (A vestigial Calvinism here for the mill-owners and shopkeepers.) Since this world is the ante-room to eternity, such temporal things as wealth and poverty matter very little: the rich might show the evidence of grace by serving the Church (notably, by building chapels for their own work-people). The poor were fortunate in being less tempted by 'the desire of the flesh, the desire of the eyes, and the pride of life'. They were more likely to remain graced, not because of their 'calling', but because they faced fewer temptations to backslide.

Three obvious means of maintaining grace presented themselves. First, through service to the Church itself, as a class leader, local preacher, or in more humble capacities. Second, through the cultivation of one's own soul, in religious exercises, tract-reading, but – above all – in attempts to reproduce the emotional convulsions of conversion, conviction of sin, penitence, and visitation by grace. Third, through a methodical discipline in every aspect of life. Above all, in labour itself (which, being humble and unpleasant, should not be confused with good works), undertaken for no ulterior motives but (as Dr Ure has it) as 'a pure act of virtue' there is an evident sign of grace. Moreover, God's curse over Adam, when expelled from the Garden of Eden, provided irrefutable doctrinal support as to the blessedness of hard labour, poverty, and sorrow 'all the days of thy life'.

We can now see the extraordinary correspondence between the virtues which Methodism inculcated in the working class and the desiderata of middle-class Utilitarianism.[26] Dr Ure indicates the point of junction, in his advice to the mill-owner 'to organize his moral machinery on equally sound principles with his mechanical'. From this aspect, Methodism was the desolate inner landscape of Utilitarianism in an era of transition to the work-discipline of industrial capitalism. As the 'working paroxysms' of the hand-worker are methodized and his unworkful impulses are brought under control, so his emotional and spiritual paroxysms increase. The abject confessional tracts are the other side of the dehumanized prose style of Edwin Chadwick and Dr Kay. The 'march of intellect' and the repression of the heart go together.

But it was Wesley's claim that Methodism was, above all things, a 'religion of the heart'. It was in its 'enthusiasm' and emotional transports that it differed most evidently from the older Puritan sects.[27] We might note some of the approved stages in religious experience, taken from a characteristic tract which describes the conversion of a sailor, Joshua Marsden, in the 1790s. These tracts normally follow a conventional pattern. First, there are descriptions of a sinful youth: swearing, gaming, drunkenness, idleness, sexual looseness or merely 'desire of the flesh'.[28] There follows either some dramatic experience which makes the sinner mindful of death (miraculous cure in mortal illness, shipwreck or death of wife or children); or some chance-hap encounter with God's word, where the sinner comes to jeer but remains to learn the way to salvation. Our sailor had all these experiences. A shipwreck left him 'trembling with horror upon the verge both of the watery and the fiery gulph ... the ghosts of his past sins stalked before him in ghastly forms'. A severe illness 'sent him often weeping and broken-hearted to a throne of grace', 'consumed and burned up sensual desires', and 'showed the awfulness of dying without an interest in Christ'. Invited by a friend to a Methodist class meeting, 'his heart was melted into a child-like weeping frame ... Tears trickled down his cheeks like rivulets.' There follows the long ordeal of intercession for forgiveness and of wrestling with temptations to relapse into the former life of sin. Only grace can unloose 'the seven seals with which ignorance, pride, unbelief, enmity, self-will, lust and covetousness bind the sinner's heart'. Again and again the penitent in his 'novitiate' succumbs to obscurely-indicated 'temptations'.[29]

In spite of all, he was sometimes borne away by the violence and impetuosity of temptation, which brought upon him all the anguish of a broken spirit. After being overtaken with sin he would redouble his prayers ... Sometimes the fear of dying in an unpardoned state greatly agitated his mind, and prevented his falling asleep for fear of awakening in the eternal world.

When the 'desire of the flesh' is to some degree humbled, the 'Enemy' places more subtle spiritual temptations in the penitent's path. Chief among these are *any* disposition which leads to 'hardness of the heart' – levity, pride, but above all the temptation to 'buy salvation' by good works rather than waiting with patience to 'receive it as the free gift of God, through the infinite merits of the bleeding Reconciler'. The doctrine of good works is 'this Hebrew, this Popish doctrine of human merit'. Thus 'hardness of the heart' consists in any character-trait which resists utter submission:

God ... before he can justify us freely ... must wither our gourd, blast the flower of proud hope, take away the prop of self-dependence, strip us of the gaudy covering of christless righteousness, stop the boasting of pharasaical self-sufficiency, and bring the guilty, abased, ashamed, blushing, self-despairing sinner, to the foot of the Cross.

At this point of abasement, 'all his prospects appeared like a waste howling wilderness'. But 'the time of deliverance was now at hand'. At a love-feast in the Methodist chapel, the penitent knelt in the pew 'and, in an agony of soul, began to wrestle with God'. Although 'the enemy raged and rolled upon him like a flood',

Some of the leaders, with some pious females, came into the gallery, and united in interceding for him at a throne of grace: the more they prayed, the more his distress and burthen increased, till finally he was nearly spent; and sweat ran off him ... and he lay on the floor of the pew with little power to move. This, however, was the moment of deliverance ... He felt what no tongue can ever describe; a something seemed to rest upon him like the presence of God that went through his whole frame; he sprang on his feet, and felt he could lay upon Christ by faith.

From this time forward the 'burthen of sin fell off'. 'The new creation was manifested by new moral beauties – love, joy, hope, peace, filial fear, delight in Jesus, tender confidence, desire after closer communion, and fuller conformity ... A new kingdom of righteousness was planted in the heart.' God's glory became 'the end of each action'. But salvation was conditional; the conviction of grace coexisted with the knowledge that man 'is a poor, blind, fallen, wretched, miserable and (without divine grace) helpless sinner'.[30]

Our sinner has now been 'translated from the power of Satan to the kingdom and image of God's dear Son'. And we may see here in its lurid figurative expression the psychic ordeal in which the character-structure of the rebellious pre-industrial labourer or artisan was violently recast into that of the submissive industrial worker. Here, indeed, is Ure's 'transforming power'. It is a phenomenon, almost diabolic in its penetration into the very sources of human personality, directed towards the repression of emotional and spiritual energies. But 'repression' is a misleading word; these energies were not so much inhibited as displaced from expression in personal and in social life, and confiscated for the service of the Church. The box-like, blackening chapels stood in the industrial districts like great traps for the human psyche. Within the Church itself there was a constant emotional drama of backsliders, confessions, forays against Satan, lost sheep; one suspects that the pious sisterhood, in particular, found in this one of the great 'consolations' of religion. For the more intellectual there was the spiritual drama of:

trials, temptations, heart sinkings, doubts, struggles, heaviness, manifestations, victories, coldness, wanderings, besetments, deliverances, helps, hopes, answers to prayer, interpositions, reliefs, complaints ... workings of the heart, actings of faith, leadings through the mazes of dark dispensations ... fiery trials, and succour in the sinking moment.[31]

But what must be stressed is the *intermittent character* of Wesleyan emotionalism. Nothing was more often remarked by contemporaries of the workaday Methodist character, or of Methodist home-life, than its methodical, disciplined and repressed disposition. It is the paradox of a 'religion of the heart' that it should be notorious for the inhibition of all spontaneity. Methodism sanctioned 'workings of the heart' only upon the occasions of the Church; Methodists wrote hymns but no secular poetry of note; the idea of a passionate Methodist lover in these years is ludicrous. ('Avoid all manner of passions', advised Wesley.) The word is unpleasant; but it is difficult not to see in Methodism in these years a ritualized form of psychic masturbation. Energies and emotions which were dangerous to social order, or which were merely unproductive (in Dr Ure's sense) were released in the harmless form of sporadic love-feasts, watch-nights, band-meetings or revivalist campaigns. At these love-feasts, after hymns and the ceremonial breaking of cake or water-biscuit, the preacher then spoke, in a raw emotional manner, of his spiritual experiences, temptations and contests with sin:

While the preacher is thus engaged, sighs, groans, devout aspirations, and ... ejaculations of prayer or praise, are issuing from the audience in every direction.

In the tension which succeeded, individual members of the congregation then rose to their feet and made their intimate confessions of sin or temptation, often of a sexual implication. An observer noted the 'bashful-ness, and evident signs of inward agitation, which some of the younger part of the females have betrayed, just before they have risen to speak'.[32]

The Methodists made of religion (wrote Southey) 'a thing of sensation and passion, craving perpetually for sympathy and stimulants'.[33] These Sabbath orgasms of feeling made more possible the single-minded week-day direction of these energies to the consummation of productive labour. Moreover, since salvation was never assured, and temptations lurked on every side, there was a constant inner goading to 'sober and industrious' behaviour – the visible sign of grace – every hour of the day and every day of the year. Not only 'the sack' but also the flames of hell might be the consequence of indiscipline at work. God was the most vigilant overlooker of all. Even above the chimney breast 'Thou God Seest Me' was hung. The Methodist was taught not only to 'bear his Cross' of poverty and humiliation; the crucifixion was (as Ure saw) the very pat-tern of his obedience: 'True followers of our bleeding Lamb, Now on Thy daily cross we die ...'[34] Work was the Cross from which the 'trans-formed' industrial worker hung.

But so drastic a redirection of impulses could not be effected without a central disorganization of the human personality. We can see why Hazlitt described the Methodists as 'a collection of religious invalids'.[35] If Wesley took from Luther his authoritarianism, from Calvinism and from the English Puritan divines of the seventeenth century Methodism took over the joylessness: a methodical discipline of life 'combined with the strict avoidance of all spontaneous enjoyments'.[36] From both it took over the almost-Manichaean sense of guilt at man's depravity. And, as gratuitous additions, the Wesleys absorbed and passed on through their hymns and writings the strange phenomenon of early eighteenth-century necrophily and the perverse imagery which is the least pleasant side of the Moravian tradition. Weber has noted the connexion between sexual repression and work-discipline in the teachings of such divines as Baxter:

The sexual asceticism of Puritanism differs only in degree, not in fundamental principle, from that of monasticism; and on account of the Puritan conception of marriage, its practical influence is more far-reaching than that of the latter. For sexual intercourse is permitted, even within marriage, only as the means willed by God for the increase of His glory according to the commandment, 'Be fruitful and multiply.' Along with a moderate vegetable diet and cold baths, the same prescription is given for all sexual temptations as is used against religious doubts and a sense of moral unworthiness: 'Work hard in your calling.'[37]

Methodism is permeated with teaching as to the sinfulness of sexuality, and as to the extreme sinfulness of the sexual organs. These – and especially the male sexual organs (since it became increasingly the convention that women could not feel the 'lust of the flesh') – were the visible fleshly citadels of Satan, the source of perpetual temptation and of countless highly unmethodical and (unless for deliberate and Godly procreation) unproductive impulses.[38] But the obsessional Methodist concern with sexuality reveals itself in the perverted eroticism of Methodist imagery. We have already noted, in John Nelson's conversion, the identification of Satan with the phallus. God is usually a simple father image, vengeful, authoritarian and prohibitive, to whom Christ must intercede, the sacrificial Lamb 'still bleeding and imploring Grace / For every Soul of Man'. But the association of feminine – or, more frequently, ambivalent – sexual imagery with Christ is more perplexing and unpleasant.

Here we are faced with layer upon layer of conflicting symbolism. Christ, the personification of 'Love' to whom the great bulk of Wesleyan hymns are addressed, is by turns maternal, Oedipal, sexual and sado-masochistic. The extraordinary assimilation of wounds and sexual imagery in the Moravian tradition has often been noted. Man as a sinful 'worm' must find 'Lodging, Bed and Board in the Lamb's Wounds'. But the sexual imagery is easily transferred to imagery of the womb. The 'dearest little opening of the sacred, precious and thousand times beautiful little side' is also the refuge from sin in which 'the Regenerate rests and breathes':

> There in one Side-hole's joy divine,
> I want to spend my life in thee ...
> There in one Side-hole's joy divine,
> I'll spend all future Days of mine.
> Yes, yes, I will for ever sit
> There, where thy Side was split.[39]

Sexual and 'womb-regressive' imagery appears here to be assimilated. But, after the Wesleys broke with the Moravian brethren, the language of their hymns and the persistent accusation of Antinomian heresy among Moravian communities had become a public scandal. In the hymns of John and Charles Wesley overt sexual imagery was consciously repressed, and gave way to imagery of the womb and the bowels:

> Come, O my guilty brethren, come,
> Groaning beneath your load of sin!
> His bleeding heart shall make you room,
> His open side shall take you in ...

This imagery, however, is subordinated to the overpowering sacrificial imagery of blood, as if the underground traditions of Mithraic blood-sacrifice which troubled the early Christian Church suddenly gushed up in the language of eighteenth-century Methodist hymnody. Here is Christ's 'bleeding love', the blood of the sacrificial Lamb in which sinners must bathe, the association of sacrifice with the penitent's guilt. Here is the 'fountain' that 'gushes from His side, / Open'd that all may enter in':

> Still the fountain of Thy blood
> Stands for sinners open'd wide;
> Now, even now, my Lord and God,
> I wash me in Thy side.

And sacrificial, masochistic, and erotic language all find a common nexus in the same blood-symbolism:

> We thirst to drink Thy precious blood,
> We languish in Thy wounds to rest,
> And hunger for immortal food,
> And long on all Thy love to feast.

The union with Christ's love, especially in the eucharistic 'marriage-feast' (which the Church collectively 'offers herself to God' by 'offering to God the Body of Christ'),[40] unites the feelings of self-mortification, the yearning for the oblivion of the womb, and tormented sexual desire, 'harbour'd in the Saviour's breast':

> 'Tis there I would always abide,
> And never a moment depart,
> Conceal'd in the cleft of Thy side,
> Eternally held in Thy heart.[41]

It is difficult to conceive of a more essential disorganization of human life, a pollution of the sources of spontaneity bound to reflect itself in every aspect of personality. Since joy was associated with sin and guilt, and pain (Christ's wounds) with goodness and love, so every impulse became twisted into the reverse, and it became natural to suppose that man or child only found grace in God's eyes when performing painful, laborious or self-denying tasks. To labour and to sorrow was to find pleasure, and masochism was 'Love'.

This strange imagery was perpetuated during the years of the Industrial Revolution, not only in Methodist hymnody but also in the rhetoric of sermons and confessions. Nor did it pass unnoticed. 'The Deity is personified and embodied in the grossest of images,' Leigh Hunt commented in an essay 'On the Indecencies and Profane Rapture of Methodism'. 'If God must be addressed in the language of earthly affection, why not address him as a parent rather than a lover?'[42] But by the end of the eighteenth century, the Methodist tradition was undergoing a desolate change. The negation or sublimation of love was tending towards the cult of its opposite: death. Charles Wesley himself had written more than one hymn which presages this change:

> Ah, lovely Appearance of Death!
> No Sight upon Earth is so fair.
> Not all the gay Pageants that *breathe*
> Can with a dead Body compare.

The Methodist tradition here is ambivalent. On the one hand, Methodist preachers perfected techniques to arouse paroxysms of fear of death and of the unlimited pains of Hell. Children from the age that they could speak, were terrified with images of everlasting punishment for the slightest misbehaviour. Their nights were made lurid by Foxe's *Book of Martyrs* and similar reading.[43] But at the same time, those who could read were deluged throughout the early nineteenth century, with the tracts which celebrated 'Holy Dying'. No Methodist or evangelical magazine, for the mature or for children, was complete without its death-bed scene in which (as Leigh Hunt also noted) death was often anticipated in the langauge of bride or bridegroom impatient for the wedding-night. Death was the only goal which might be desired without guilt, the reward of peace after a lifetime of suffering and labour.

So much of the history of Methodism has, in recent years, been written by apologists or by fair-minded secularists trying to make allowances for a movement which they cannot understand, that one notes with a sense of shock Lecky's judgement at the end of the nineteenth century:

A more appalling system of religious terrorism, one more fitted to unhinge a tottering intellect and to darken and embitter a sensitive nature, has seldom existed.[44]

Over the Industrial Revolution there brooded the figure of the Reverend Jabez Branderham (almost certainly modelled upon Jabez Bunting) who appears in Lockwood's grim nightmare at the opening of *Wuthering Heights*: 'good God! what a sermon; divided into *four hundred and ninety parts* ... and each discussing a separate sin!' It is against this all-enveloping 'Thou Shalt Not!', which permeated *all* religious persuasions in varying degree in these years, that we can appreciate at its full height the stature of William Blake. It was in 1818 that he emerged from his densely alle-gorical prophetic books into a last phase of gnomic clarity in *The Ever-lasting Gospel*. Here he reasserted the values, the almost-Antinomian affirmation of the joy of sexuality, and the affirmation of innocence, which were present in his earlier songs. Almost every line may be seen as a declaration of 'mental war' against Methodism and Evangelicalism.[45] Their 'Vision of Christ' was his vision's 'greatest Enemy'. Above all, Blake drew his bow at the teaching of humility and submission. It was this nay-saying humility which 'does the Sun & Moon blot out', 'Distorts the Heavens from Pole to Pole',

> Rooting over with thorns & stems
> The buried Soul & all its Gems.

2. The chiliasm of despair

The utility of Methodism as a work-discipline is evident. What is less easy to understand is why so many working people were willing to submit to this form of psychic exploitation. How was it that Methodism could perform with such success this dual rôle as the religion of both the exploiters and the exploited?

During the years 1790–1830[46] three reasons may be adduced: direct indoctrination, the Methodist community-sense, and the psychic con-sequences of the counter-revolution.

The first reason – indoctrination – cannot be overstated. The evan-gelical Sunday schools were ever-active, although it is difficult to know how far their activities may be rightly designated as 'educational'. The Wesleyans had inherited from their founder a peculiarly strong convic-tion as to the aboriginal sinfulness of the child; and this expressed – in Wesley's case – with a force which might have made some Jesuits blench:

Break their wills betimes. Begin this work before they can run alone, before they can speak plain, perhaps before they can speak at all. Whatever pains it costs, break the will if you would not damn the child. Let a child from a year old be taught to fear the rod and to cry softly; from that age make him do as he is bid, if you whip him ten times running to effect it ... Break his will now, and his soul shall live, and he will probably bless you to all eternity.[47]

At Wesley's Kingswood School only severely workful 'recreations' were allowed – chopping wood, digging and the like – since games and play were 'unworthy of a Christian child'. ('I will kill or cure,' said Wesley, who rarely said things he did not mean: 'I *will* have one or the other – a Christian school, or none at all.') A brief glance at the 'educational' materials in common use in Sunday schools in the first decades of the nineteenth century exposes their true purpose. The Wesleys' lurid hymns, employed in the adult services, were replaced by Isaac Watts' *Divine Songs of Children*, or moralistic variants by later writers. Toddlers were taught to sing that they were 'By nature and by practice too, A wretched slave to sin.' The All-seeing God's 'piercing eye' looked upon their most 'secret actions':

> There's not a sin that we commit,
> Nor wicked word we say,
> But in thy dreadful book 'tis writ,
> Against the judgement-day.

A characteristic moral story of the time exemplifies the general tendency of this 'teaching'.[48] John Wise is the son of 'a very poor man, who had many children, and could scarce get bread for them all by hard labour. He had to work with all his might each day in the week, and lived on oatcake, and oatmeal boiled up with water.' His father, notwithstanding, was a good 'prayerful' man, repeatedly giving thanks for his blessings: for example, 'Some of us might have died, but we are all in the land of the living.' John's mother taught him Watts' hymn of the work-disciplined sun:

> When from the chambers of the east
> His morning race begins,
> He never tires, nor stops to rest,
> But round the world he shines,
>
> So, like the sun, would I fulfil
> The duties of this day,
> Begin my work betimes, and still
> March on my heavenly way.

John's parents teach him the sanctity of the Sabbath, and deliver various homilies on duty, obedience and industry. Then comes the awful story of Betty, John's wicked sister, who goes for a walk on Sunday, and comes back wet and muddy, having lost a shoe. Her father rebukes her, and reads to the family Moses' decree that the man who gathered sticks on the Sabbath should be stoned to death. Betty's sin is much worse than this man's, but this time she is pardoned. But worse sins follow: some children play truant from Sunday school and play *football* instead! The next Sunday the children are admonished, and told the story of the forty-two children who mocked the aged Elisha and who were torn in pieces, at the behest of a merciful God. The infants then carol another of Watts' hymns:

> When children in their wanton play,
>   Serv'd old Elisha so;
> And bid the prophet go his way,
>   'Go up, thou bald-head, go:'
> GOD quickly stopt their wicked breath,
>   And sent two raging bears,
> That tore them limb from limb to death,
>   With blood, and groans, and tears.

In the end, the piety of John and of his father are rewarded by an inheritance from a stranger, deeply moved by their patience and submission to poverty.

One might laugh; but the psychological atrocities committed upon children were terribly real to them. One may doubt the emphasis placed by a recent writer upon the repressive effect of Puritan infant-binding (in tight swaddling clothes) and anal training, although the point cannot be dismissed.[49] But despite all the platitudes repeated in most textbooks as to the 'educational initiatives' of the Churches at this time, the Sunday schools were a dreadful exchange even for village dame's schools. Eighteenth-century provision for the education of the poor – inadequate and patchy as it was – was nevertheless provison *for education*, in some sort, even if (as with Shenstone's schoolmistress) it was little more than naming the flowers and herbs. In the counter-revolutionary years this was poisoned by the dominant attitude of the Evangelicals, that the function of education began and ended with the 'moral rescue' of the children of the poor.[50] Not only was the teaching of writing discouraged, but very many Sunday school scholars left the schools unable to read, and in view of the parts of the Old Testament thought most edifying this at least was a blessing. Others gained little more than the little girl who told one of the Commissioners on Child Labour in the Mines: 'if I died a good girl I should go to heaven – if I were bad I should have to be burned in brimstone and fire: they told me that at school yesterday, I did not know it before'.[51] Long before the age of puberty the child was subject at Sunday school and at home (if his parents were pious) to the worst kind of emotional bullying to confess his sins and come to a sense of salvation; and many, like young Thomas Cooper, went 'into secret places twenty times a day, to pray for pardon ...'[52]

Lecky's epithet, 'religious terrorism', is in fact by no means an excessive term to apply to a society which provided no alternative educational arrangements for the children of the poor – at least until the Lancastrian charity school movement, in which the notion of 'moral rescue' was modified by genuine educational intentions and by the utilitarian concern for equipping children for industrial occupations.[53] But – and here we come to our second reason – we should beware of giving too bleak and too unqualified a picture of the evangelical churches from the evidence of Sunday school primers, or from the dogmas of such men as Bunting. What the orthodox Methodist minister intended is one thing; what actually happened in many communities may be another. The old 'Arminian' Methodists had a more humane attitude to Sunday school teaching; the Methodists of the New Connexion were always more intellectual in their approach than those of the Wesleyan orthodoxy; we have noted that James Montgomery (of the *Sheffield Iris*) led the fight among the Sheffield Non-conformists to retain the teaching of writing in the Sunday school syllabus. The lay teachers, who volunteered their services, were less likely to be doctrinaire; and there was a continuous tension which could at times produce unlikely results. 'Even our Sunday Schools', a Bolton minister wrote to the Duke of Portland in 1798:

may become in some Instances the Seminaries of Faction. We have discovered one if not two who have taken the Oaths of United Englishmen, who are acting in the capacity of S. Schoolmasters *gratis* ...[54]

The 'quiet fortress' of the Stockport Sunday schools, which Dr Ure so commended in the 1830s, nevertheless had been besieged with a vengeance (and to some degree actually displaced) between 1817 and 1820, when the Reverend Joseph Harrison and the Stockport Political Union sponsored a Radical Sunday School movement which must have been staffed, in part, by former teachers and scholars of the orthodox schools.[55]

And this should be seen, not only in the schools, but also in relation to the general influence of the Methodist churches. As a dogma Methodism appears as a pitiless ideology of work. In practice, this dogma was in varying degrees softened, humanized, or modified by the needs, values, and patterns of social relationship of the community within which it was placed. The Church, after all, was more than a building, and more than the sermons and instructions of its minister. It was embodied also in the class meetings: the sewing groups: the money-raising activities: the local preachers who tramped several miles after work to attend small functions at outlying hamlets which the minister might rarely visit. The picture of the fellowship of the Methodists which is commonly presented is too euphoric; it has been emphasized to the point where all other characteristics of the Church have been forgotten.[56] But it remains both true and important that Methodism, with its open chapel doors, did offer to the uprooted and abandoned people of the Industrial Revolution some kind of community to replace the older community-patterns which were being displaced. As an unestablished (although undemocratic) Church, there was a sense in which working people could make it their own; and the more closely knit the community in which Methodism took root (the mining, fishing or weaving village) the more this was so.

Indeed, for many people in these years the Methodist 'ticket' of church-membership acquired a fetishistic importance; for the migrant worker it could be the ticket of entry into a new community when he moved from town to town. Within this religious community there was (as we have seen) its own drama, its own degrees of status and importance, its own gossip, and a good deal of mutual aid. There was even a slight degree of social mobility, although few of the clergy came from proletarian homes. Men and women felt themselves to have some place in an otherwise hostile world when within the Church. They obtained recognition, perhaps for their sobriety, or chastity, or piety. And there were other positives, such as the contribution to the stability of the family and the home, to which we shall return. The Puritan character-structure, more-over, was not something which could be confiscated solely for the service of the Church and the employer. Once the transference was made, the same dedication which enabled men to serve in these rôles, will be seen in the men who officered trade unions and Hampden Clubs, educated themselves far into the night, and had the responsibility to conduct working-class organizations. In analysing the ideology of Methodism, we have presented an intellectualized picture. In the fluency of social life, plain common sense, compassion, the obstinate vitality of older com-munity traditions, all mingle to soften its forbidding outlines.

There is a third reason, however, why working people were exception-ally exposed to the penetration of Methodism during the years of the Napoleonic Wars. It is, perhaps, the most interesting reason of all, but it has been scarcely noticed. It may best be approached by recalling the hysterical aspect of Methodist and Baptist revivalism, and of the smaller sects. During the worst years of the Industrial Revolution, real opiates were used quite widely in the manufacturing districts. And Charles Kingsley's epithet, 'the opium of the masses', reminds us that many working people turned to religion as a 'consolation', even though the dreams inspired by Methodist doctrine were scarcely happy. The methods of the revivalist preachers were noted for their emotional violence; the tense opening, the vivid descriptions of sudden death and catastrophe, the unspecific rhetoric on the enormity of sin, the dramatic offer of redemption. And the open-air crowds and early congregations of Method-ism were also noted for the violence of their 'enthusiasm' – swooning, groaning, crying out, weeping and falling into paroxysms. Southey, indeed, suggested that revivalism was akin to Mesmerism: Wesley 'had produced a new disease, and he accounted for it by a theological theory instead of a physical one'.[57] Sometimes these symptoms took the form of violent mass hysteria, as in the incident at Bristol recorded in Wesley's *Journal* in March 1788 when a 'vehement noise ... shot like lightning through the whole congregation':

> The terror and confusion was inexpressible. You might have imagined it was a city taken by storm. The people rushed upon each other with the utmost violence, the benches were broken in pieces, and nine tenths of the congregation appeared to be struck with the same panic.

At Chapel-en-le-Frith, he recorded in 1786, this hysteria had already become habit-forming:

> Some of them, perhaps many, scream all together as loud as they possibly can. Some of them use improper, yea, indecent expressions in prayer. Several drop down as dead, and are as still as a corpse, but in a while they start up and cry, Glory, glory ...

Such excesses of hysteria Wesley condemned, as 'bringing the real work into contempt'.[58] But throughout the Industrial Revolution more muted forms of hysteria were intrinsic to Methodist revivalism. Tight communities, miners, hill-farmers or weavers, might at first resist the campaign of field-preaching and prayer-meetings among them; then there might be 'a little moving among the dry bones'; and then 'the fire broke out; and it was just as when the whins on a common are set on fire, – it blazed gloriously'.[59]

The example is taken from propaganda in West Riding weaving villages in 1799–1801, when whole communities declared themselves – at least temporarily – 'saved'. And it is rarely noted that not only did the war years see the greatest expansion of Methodism, notably in the northern working class, but that this was also accompanied by renewed evidence of hysteria. For example, in the years 1805–6, when numbers flocked to the Methodists in Bradford, 'no sooner, in many cases, was the text announced, than the cries of persons in distress so interrupted the preacher, that the service ... was at once exchanged for one of general and earnest intercession'.[60] 'Three fell while I was speaking,' a preacher of the Bible Christian in Devon noted complacently in his diary in 1816: 'we prayed, and soon some more fell; I think six found peace.' The ministrations of this sect among the moorland farmers and labourers were often accompanied by agonies, prostrations, 'shouts of praise', and 'loud and piteous cries of penitents'.[61]

Methodism may have inhibited revolution; but we can affirm with certainty that its rapid growth during the Wars was a component of the psychic processes of counter-revolution. There is a sense in which any religion which places great emphasis on the after-life is the chiliasm of the defeated and the hopeless. 'The utopian vision aroused a contrary vision. The chiliastic optimism of the revolutionaries ultimately gave birth to the formation of the conservative attitude of resignation ...' – the words of Karl Mannheim's describing another movement. And he also gives us a clue to the nature of the psychic process:

Chiliasm has always accompanied revolutionary outbursts and given them their spirit. When this spirit ebbs and deserts these movements, there remains behind in the world a naked mass-frenzy and a despiritualized fury.[62]

Since, in England of the 1790s, the revolutionary impulse was stifled before it reached the point of 'outburst', so also when the spirit ebbed, the reaction does not fall to the point of frenzy. And yet there are many phenomena in these decades which can scarcely be explained in any other way. Authentic millennarialism ends in the late-1790s, with the defeat of English Jacobinism, the onset of the Wars, and the confining of Richard Brothers in a mad-house. But a number of sects of 'New Jerusalemites' prospered in the next fifteen years.[63] Prophet after prophet arose, like Ebenezer Aldred, a Unitarian minister in an isolated village in the Derbyshire Peak (Hucklow):

There he lived in a kind of solitude, became dreamy and wild; laid hold on the prophecies; saw Napoleon in the Book of Revelation: at last fancied himself the Prophet who, standing neither on land nor water, was to proclaim the destruction of a great city ...

and, clothed in a white garment, his grey hair flowing down his shoulders, sailed in a boat on the Thames, distributing booklets and prophesying doom.[64] Radical, mystic and militarist contested for the robes of Revelation: the lost tribes of Israel were discovered in Birmingham and Wapping: and 'evidence' was found that 'the British Empire is the peculiar possession of Messiah, and his promised naval dominion'.[65]

But the most startling evidence of a 'despiritualized fury' is to be found in the movements surrounding – and outliving – the greatest Prophetess of all, Joanna Southcott. It was in 1801 that her first cranky prophetic booklet was published, *The Strange Effects of Faith*. And the general climate of expectant frenzy is shown by the rapidity with which the reputation of the Devon farmer's daughter and domestic servant swept the country [...]

The Methodists, of course, had many advantages over the South-cottians: organizational stability, money, the benign attitude of the authorities. What members they lost to the cult were probably soon regained. But this does not mean that we can dismiss the cult as a mere 'freak', irrelevant to the stolid lines of social growth. On the contrary, we should see the 'Johannas' and the Methodist revival of these years as intimate relations. The Wars were the heyday of the itinerant lay preachers, with their 'pious ejaculations, celestial groans, angelic swoonings'[66] – the 'downright balderdash' which so much enraged Cobbett:

Their heavenly gifts, their calls, their inspirations, their feelings of grace at work within them, and the rest of their canting gibberish, are a gross and outrageous insult to common sense, and a great scandal to the country. It is in vain that we boast of our *enlightened state*, while a sect like this is increasing daily.[67]

As orthodox Wesleyanism throve, so also did breakaway groups of 'Ranters' – the Welsh 'Jumpers' (cousins to the American 'Shakers'), the Primitive Methodists, the 'Tent Methodists', the 'Magic Methodists' of Delemere Forest, who fell into trances or 'visions', the Bryanites or Bible Christians, the 'Quaker Methodists' of Warrington and the 'Independent Methodists' of Macclesfield. Through the streets of war-time and post-war England went the revivalist missionaries, crying out: 'Turn to the Lord and seek salvation!'

One is struck not only by the sense of disequilibrium, but also by the *impermanence* of the phenomenon of Methodist conversion. Rising graphs of Church membership are misleading; what we have, rather, is a revivalist pulsation, or an oscillation between periods of hope and periods of despair and spiritual anguish. After 1795 the poor had once again entered into the Valley of Humiliation. But they entered it unwillingly, with many backward looks; and whenever hope revived, religious revivalism was set aside, only to reappear with renewed fervour upon the ruins of the political messianism which had been overthrown. In this sense, the great Methodist recruitment between 1790 and 1830 may be seen as the chiliasm of despair.

This is not the customary reading of the period; and it is offered as an hypothesis, demanding closer investigation. On the eve of the French Revolution the Methodists claimed about 60,000 adherents in Great Britain. This indicated little more than footholds in all but a few of the industrial districts. Thereafter the figures claimed advance like this: 1800, 90,619; 1810, 137,997; 1820, 191,217; 1830, 248,592.[68] Years especially notable for revivalist recruitment were 1797–1800, 1805–7, 1813–18, 1823–4, 1831–4. These years are so close to those of maximum political awareness and activity that Dr Hobsbawm is justified in directing attention to the 'marked parallelism between the movements of religious, social and political consciousness'.[69] But while the relationship between political and religious excitement is obviously intimate, the nature of the relationship remains obscure: the conclusion that 'Methodism advanced when Radicalism advanced and not when it grew weaker' does not necessarily follow.[70] On the contrary, it is possible that religious revivalism took over just at the point where 'political' or temporal aspirations met with defeat [...]

Notes

1   Cited in E. Halévy, *A History of the English People in 1815*, Penguin edn, Bk 3, III, p. 53. For accounts of Methodism's political stance during these years, see E. R. Taylor, *Methodism and Politics, 1791–1850*; and R. F. Wearmouth, *Methodism and the Working Class Movements of England, 1800–1850* (1937), especially the chapters on 'The Methodist Loyalty' and 'The Methodist Neutrality'. See also J. L. and B. Hammond, *The Town Labourer*, London, Longman & Green, 1917, ch. 13, 'The Defences of the Poor'.

2   See below, p. 179.

3   T. P. Bunting, *Life of Jabez Bunting*, D.D. (1887), p. 338.

4   Ibid., p. 11. It is interesting to note that Oastler's father, a Leeds clothier, was also a Methodist and a 'Tom Painite'. In his maturity, Oastler's opinion of Methodism was scarcely more complimentary than that of Cobbett.

5   J. Wray, 'Methodism in Leeds', Leeds Reference Library.

6   T. B. Bunting, op. cit., pp. 527–8.

7   Ibid., pp. 295–7, 312–14, 322–3; Bamford, *Early Days*, pp. 100–101. It is fair to note that the Established Church and other Nonconformist sects also forbade the teaching of writing on Sundays.

8   The only humanitarian cause to which Methodists like Bunting gave consistent support was Anti-Slavery agitation; but as the years go by, and the issue is trotted out again and again, one comes to suspect that it was less a vestigial social conscience than a desire to disarm criticism which propped this banner up.

9   L. Tyerman, *John Wesley* (1870), III, p. 499. See also J. Sutcliffe, *A Review of Methodism* (York, 1805), p. 37.

10   See W. J. Warner, *The Wesleyan Movement in the Industrial Revolution*, 1930, pp. 168–80.

11   R. H. Tawney, *Religion and the Rise of Capitalism*, 1926, Penguin edn., 1938, pp. 227ff.

12   Max Weber, *The Protestant Ethic and the Spirit of Capitalism*, Allen and Unwin, 1930, esp. pp. 54, 60–67, 160–61, 178; E. Fromm *The Fear of Freedom* (1960 edn), p. 80.

13   Nor is this work-discipline in any sense limited to Methodism. We are discussing Methodism here as the leading example of developments which belong also to the history of Evangelicism and of most Nonconformist sects during the Industrial Revolution.

14   Weber, op. cit., pp. 66–7, 282; Tawney, op. cit., pp. 198ff. Baxter's writings were favoured reading among the early Methodists, and were much reprinted in the early decades of the nineteenth century.

15   *Report of the Society for Bettering the Condition of the Poor*, I (1798), pp. 238ff.; account of the Duke of Bridgewater's colliers (near Manchester). The Duke's colliers were regarded as 'more moral than most, and 'some of the duke's agents are men of a religious cast, and have established Sunday schools ...'

16   A. Redford, *The Economic History of England*, 2nd edn. 1960, pp. 19–20. As late as the 1830s Samuel Greg was complaining of 'that restless and migratory spirit which is one of the peculiar characteristics of the manufacturing population'.

17   V. W. Bladen, 'The Potteries in the Industrial Revolution', *Econ. Journal* (Supplement), 1926–9, p. 130. See also M. McKendrick, 'Josiah Wedgwood and Factory Disciple', *Hist. Journal*, IV, I, 1961, p. 30. It was Wedgwood's aim to 'make such *Machines* of the *Men* as cannot err'.

18   R. Guest, *A Compendious History of the Cotton Manufacture* (1823), pp. 38, 43.

19   In the seventeenth century the Puritan sects had a large weaver following, but – except in the West of England – this tradition had little life in the early eighteenth century.

20   A. Ure, *The Philosophy of Manufactures*, 1835, pp. 13–21. Cf. also p. 23: 'It is in fact the constant aim and tendency of every improvement in machinery to supersede human labour altogether, or to diminish its cost, by substituting the industry of women and children for that of men; or that of ordinary labourers, for trained artisans.' As an expression of the mill-owners' intentions this is interesting, and relevant to the textile industries; but as an expression of the 'law' of capitalist development, Marx and Engels perhaps gave Ure's claims too much credence.

21   Ibid., III, chs. 1 and 3. Thompson's italics.

22   Cf. D. H. Lawrence in *The Rainbow*: 'They believe that they must alter themselves to fit the pits and the place, rather than alter the pits and the place to fit themselves. It is easier.'

23   Ure, op. cit., pp. 423–5.

24   Weber, in his brief discussion of Methodism in *The Protestant Ethic and the Spirit of Capitalism*, exaggerates the Calvinist elements in its theology, and thereby fails to see its special adaptability as a religion of the proletariat. He thus presses too far the sense of a 'calling' among the Wesleyans, especially when he seeks to apply it to the 'calling' of the working man, a doctrine which has less significance in England than those of submission and obedience.

25   Jabez Bunting, *Sermon on Justification by Faith* (Leeds, 1813), p. 11. Bunting's imagery reminds one that in January of this same year (1813) some Luddites had suffered the full 'penal consequences' on the gallows, while others had had their penalty 'graciously remitted' to fourteen years transportation.

26   Weber and Tawney, of course, direct attention to the parallel development of Puritan and Utilitarian dogmas: cf. Tawney, op. cit., p. 219: 'Some of the links in the Utilitarian coat of mail were forged ... by the Puritan divines of the seventeenth century.' It was Methodism, however, which forged the last links of the Utilitarian chains riveted upon the proletariat.

27   Excepting, of course, the Baptists – notably in Wales.

28   For an example, taken from this tract, see Thompson (1968), p. 62.

29   The language often suggests that the objective component of the 'sin' was masturbation. And this might well be deduced from three facts: (1) The introversial nature of penitent self-absorption. (2) The obsessional Methodist teaching as to the sinfulness of the sexual organs. (3) The fact that the children of Methodists were expected to come to a sense of sin at about the age of puberty. See G. R. Taylor, *The Angel-Makers* (1958), p. 326 for the increase in literature on the subject in these years.

30   Joshua Marsden, *Sketches of the Early Life of a Sailor* (an autobiography in the third person) (Hull, n.d.), *passim*.

31   *Sketches of the Early Life of a Sailor*, pp. 104, 111.

32   Joseph Nightingale, *Portraiture of Methodism* (1807), pp. 203ff.

33   R. Southey, *Life of Wesley and Rise and Progress of Methodism* (1890 edn), 381ff.

34   J. E. Rattenbury, *The Eucharistic Hymns of John and Charles Wesley* (1948), p. 240:

> We cast our sins into that fire
>   Which did thy sacrifice consume,
> And every base and vain desire
>   To daily crucifixion doom.

35   W. Hazlitt, 'On the Causes of Methodism', *The Round Table* (1817), *Works*, IV, pp. 57ff.

36   Weber, *op. cit.*, p. 53.

37   Ibid., pp. 158–9.

38   Only an appreciation of the degree to which this obsession came to permeate English culture – and in particular working-class culture – can lead to an understanding of why Lawrence was impelled to write *Lady Chatterley's Lover*.

39   See R. A. Knox, *Enthusiasm* (Oxford, 1950), pp. 408–17, G. R. Taylor, op. cit., pp. 166–7.

40   J. E. Rattenbury, op. cit., p. 132.

41   Ibid., pp. 109–11, 202–4, 224–34; and J. E. Rattenbury, *The Evangelical Doctrines of Charles Wesley's Hymns* (1941), p. 184. This subject is due for renewed and more expert attention. Mr G. R. Taylor's study of *The Angel-Makers* is suggestive, but his attempt to find a 'sexual' explanation of historical change in patrist and matrist child-orientations is pressed to the point of absurdity.

42   The Editor of the Examiner [Leigh Hunt], *An Attempt to Show the Folly and Danger of Methodism* (1809), esp. pp. 54–64, 89–97. The language also laid the Methodists open to charges that love-feasts, watch-nights, and revivalist fervour became occasions for promiscuous sexual intercourse. Among sober critics, Nightingale discounted these accusations, Leigh Hunt supported them, Southey reserved judgement. See such *canaille* as A Professor, *Confessions of a Methodist* (1810).

43   Cf. W. E. H. Lecky, *History of England in the Eighteenth Century* (1891 edn), II, p. 585: 'The ghastly images [the Methodist preachers] continually evoked poisoned their imaginations, haunted them in every hour of weakness or depression, discoloured all their judgements of the world, and added a tenfold horror to the darkness of the grave.'

44   W. E. H. Lecky, *History of the English People in the 18th Century*, 1891, III, pp. 77–8.

45   Cf. Wilberforce, *A Practical View of Christianity*, p. 437: 'Remember that we are all fallen creatures, born in sin, and naturally depraved, Christianity recognizes no *innocence* or *goodness of heart*.'

46   These years cover the period of the rise and dominance of Jabez Bunting and his circle. After 1830 liberalizing tendencies can be seen at work within the Methodist Connexion; and although Bunting fought a determined rearguard action, by the 1840s Methodism entered a new and somewhat softened stage. On the one hand, some second or third generation mill-owners and employers left the Methodists for the respectability of the Established Church. On the other hand, Methodism appears as the authentic outlook of some in the small shop-keeper and clerical and sub-managerial groups, in which a muted radicalism is joined to the ideology of 'self-help'. See E. R. Taylor, op. cit., chs. 5, 6, and W. J. Warner, op. cit. pp. 122–35.

47   R. Southey, *Life of Wesley and the Rise of Methodism*, 1890 edn, p. 561. We can see, for example from Bamford's memoirs of the 1790s, and from Thomas Cooper's *Life* (when as a Methodist schoolmaster in the 1820s he regarded it as a sign of grace that he should *not* strike his pupils) that Wesley's teachings were humanized by many of his late eighteenth-century and early nineteenth-century followers. But see the orthodox utilitarian advocacy of Jabez Bunting in *Sermon on a great work described* (1805).

48   *The History of John Wise, a Poor Boy: Intended for the Instruction of Children* (Halifax, 1810).

49   G.R. Taylor, op. cit.

50   Cf. Raymond Williams, *The Long Revolution* (1961), pp. 135–6.

51   Cited in J.L. and B. Hammond, *Lord Shaftesbury* (Penguin edn), p. 74.

52   T. Cooper, *Life*, p. 37.

53   Those writers today who rightly expose the human depreciation resulting from the commercial abuse of the media of communication, seem to me to have matters out of proportion when they overlook the extent and character of mass indoctrination in earlier periods.

54   Rev. Thomas Bancroft, 12 February 1798, P.C.A. 152.

55   See D. Read, *Peterloo* (Manchester, 1957), pp. 51ff., and below, p. 788.

56   The sense of fellowship in the early years of the Church is expressed sympathetically in L.F. Church, *The Early Methodist People* (19..?). See also, of course, Dr Wearmouth's book, among many others.

57   Southey, op. cit., pp. 382ff.

58   See the discussion of the 'enthusiasm' in R.A. Knox, op. cit., pp. 520–35.

59   F.A. West, *Memoirs of Jonathan Saville* (Halifax, 1844).

60   W.M. Stamp, *Historical Notes of Wesleyan Methodism in Bradford* (1841), p. 85.

61   F.W. Bourne, *The Bible Christians* (1905), pp. 36–42.

62   K. Mannheim, *Ideology and Utopia* (1960 edn), pp. 192–6.

63   In March 1801, Earl Fitzwilliam was enquiring into the activities of the followers of Brothers in Bradford, led by Zacchaus Robinson, a weaver, who 'was for many years a strong Methodist, & what is here called a Class Leader'. Fitzwilliam Papers, F. 45(a).

64   T.A. Ward, op. cit., pp. 188–9; Eben-Eser, *The Little Book* (1811).

65   R. Wedgwood, *The Book of Remembrance* (1814).

66   Halifax Theatre Royal playbill, 1793.

67   *Political Register*, 12 June 1813.

68   Census of Religious Worship, England and Wales, 1851 (1853), p. lxxviii. Orthodox Wesleyan circuits with over 1,000 members in 1815 were claimed to be: London, Bristol, Redruth, St Ives, Birmingham, Burslem, Macclesfield, Manchester, Bolton, Liverpool, Colne, Nottingham, Sheffield, Leeds, Birstal, Bradford, Halifax, Isle of Man, Sunderland, Wakefield, Dewsbury, Epworth, York, Hull, Darlington, Barnard Castle, Newcastle, Shields. See M.E. Edwards, 'The Social and Political Influence of Methodism in the Napoleonic Period' (London Ph.D. Thesis, 1934), p. 244.

69   *Primitive Rebels*, 1959, pp. 129–30.

70   See E.J. Hobsbawm, 'Methodism and the Threat of Revolution', *History today* (1957), VII, p. 124.

14 T.W. LAQUEUR

Sunday schools and social control

From *Religion and Respectability: Sunday Schools and Working Class Culture 1780–1850*, by T. W. Laqueur, 1976. Reproduced by permission of the publishers, © Yale University Press.

Introduction

Modern historians who investigate the social role of Sunday schools agree on two propositions. First, that the schools were agencies of the upper and middle classes which were imposed on the 'lower orders' or the working class. Second, that they were an important agency in suppressing, with a minimum of coercion, traditional lower-class patterns of behavior which were replaced with conduct more suited to an industrial society. Both points appear in numerous guises and with varying degrees of specificity.

The working classes, argues J. F. C. Harrison, 'had no alternative but to accept the instruction offered in middle-class day and Sunday schools'. The breakdown of the old popular culture and its supersession by formal literary instruction based on the three Rs was the conscious aim of middle-class educationalists who provided these schools.[1] Based on the theories of Weber and his successors, historians have sought and found in evangelical religion the source of all those personal traits and values suited to an industrial society.[2] One scholar discusses Sunday schools in the company of 'various other schemes which were used to discipline the lower orders'.[3] Another cites both charity and Sunday schools as 'the principal channels through which the upper and middle classes sought to impose their social ideas upon the working class' while the latter schools, he argues, were 'even more explicitly geared to manning the growing industries than the former'.[4] E. P. Thompson singles out the Sunday school as one of the institutions created by the middle class in order to wean the working classes from their pre-industrial rhythms of work and play and to inculcate in them the 'time thrift' necessary in an industrial society. The military rules of behavior, the insistence on regularity and punctuality of attendance, and undisguised indoctrination are adduced to support the views of some contemporaries that Sunday schools constituted 'a spectacle of order and regularity' which, as a Gloucester manufacturer put it, 'made children more tractable and obedient, less quarrelsome and revengeful'. 'Once within the school gates', Thompson argues, 'the child entered the new universe of disciplined time' leaving behind pre-industrial sloth for modern industry.[5]

His *Making of the English Working Class* develops and extends these themes. Here too it is argued that: 'The pressures towards discipline and order extended from the factory, on one hand, the Sunday school, on the other, into every aspect of life: leisure, personal relationships, speech, manner.'[6] Methodism between 1790 and 1830 acted at the same time as the ideology of the oppressed and the oppressor. Of the three reasons given for this curious state of affairs – direct indoctrination, the Methodist community sense, and the psychic consequences of counter-revolution – he argues that 'the first reason – indoctrination – cannot be overstated'. Furthermore, the Evangelical Sunday school is identified as the main agency of this indoctrination.[7] According to Thompson, these schools acted upon Wesley's doctrines of the aboriginal sinfulness of the child; they practised a kind of religious terrorism on the young, convincing them of their spiritual unworthiness and offering hard work, adherence to duty and submission to the wishes of their betters as a kind of exculpatory act. Far worse than being merely agencies of moral rescue, Sunday schools weakened the wills and corrupted the souls of their inmates, making them the victims of an objectively hostile ideology.[8]

Thompson's view of the Sunday school must be considered in the context of his general thesis. 'And class', he argues, 'happens when some men, as a result of common experiences (inherited or shared), feel and articulate the identity of their interests as between themselves, and as against other men whose interests are different from (and usually opposed to) theirs.'[9] Between 1780 and 1832 a working class in this sense came into being; in these decades 'most English working people came to feel an identity of interests as between themselves, and as against their rulers and employers'.[10] If this model is true, the bourgeois values and precepts of the Sunday school, indeed the institution itself, ought to have become increasingly repugnant to the working classes during the industrial revolution. Furthermore, the richly varied radical working-class culture which Thompson describes presumably ought to have been significantly different from the culture of the Sunday school.

But neither of these things happened. Indeed, the interpretation of Sunday schools developed most fully in the *Making of the English Working Class* is insufficiently subtle to encompass the facts. It is difficult to maintain in any literal sense that Sunday schools constituted an imposition by the middle upon the working class. Many of those active in founding Sunday schools in both the eighteenth and nineteenth century were from the working class. The teachers were almost all from the same social strata as those they taught; after 1810 some sixty per cent of all teachers had once been students themselves. Even in those schools where the managers were manufacturers or shopkeepers, teachers played an important part in deciding the internal policies of the school. While early Sunday schools in both towns and villages were often financed by the dominant social class, the change in the early nineteenth century away from subscriptions to annual sermons as a primary source of funds meant that the community at large played a more significant part in underwriting the schools.

Fund-raising sermons were a popular and important element of working-class community life, reported alike in the *Manchester Guardian* and the *Northern Star*. Indeed, Sunday schools were accepted, patronized, and occasionally idealized precisely because they grew out of the working class as a means of fulfilling the real and perceived needs of the community. Any analysis of Sunday schools as an agency of social control or as an institution through which certain norms and values were transmitted must take these facts into account. Therefore, a model which regards Sunday schools primarily as a weapon in an alleged bourgeois assault on working-class culture simply will not do. The schools were effective in large measure because they worked from within and because they were not merely organs of middle-class propaganda.

Sunday schools and the aims of the middle class

In order to put the question of indoctrination in context, it is important to note that Sunday schools represented the first step in the increased specialization of educational activities during the late eighteenth and nineteenth centuries. Children were taken from, or sent by, their parents each Sunday to a school whose function was to do what the parent, or perhaps the isolated clergyman, could not do. But the emergence of children, even temporarily, from the educational nexus of family relationships had enormous political and social ramifications which were not lost on contemporaries.

Sunday schools were advocated by the eighteenth-century Evangelicals and some of their successors as a means of removing children from the corrupt influence of the parent to a morally and politically more salutary atmosphere. 'The children of the poor, by being drawn out of their obscurity into notice and protection are humanized and civilized,' argued a friend of Hannah More.[11] Teachers must begin their work by 'unlearning the children much of what they have been taught' because 'being from the lowest order of people they have not been taught to associate happiness with virtue'.[12] Mrs Trimmer told potential subscribers to her school that the immoralities of the poor, which 'keep their employers in a constant state of suspicion and uneasiness', would be a thing of the past now that the 'education of poor children is no longer entirely left to their ignorant and corrupt parents'. Only good could result from the fact that 'it has in many places become a public business'.[13] Most bluntly put, Sunday school managers could 'at all times exercise authority under a conciliating title, and, while they patronize the children, can insensibly control the conduct of the parents'.[14]

There is little doubt, moreover, that some Sunday schools intended to play their part in restraining political radicalism among the working class. Those founded by the London based, Evangelical dominated, Sunday School Society or by committees of notables in the provinces were a fundamentally conservative response to what was perceived to be a moral and political crisis. Education generally, and the Sunday school in particular, was welcomed as a means of bringing religion to the lower orders which would, it was thought, elevate them above the mire of sin and deprivation into which they had fallen, and thereby assure the harmony and continuity of an hierarchic society of orders. Only as much learning as was necessary to achieve this end was to be offered in Sunday school, and indeed the public was invited to contribute to the project under the assurance that their funds would be used to ensure social stability.[15]

Sermon after sermon, appeal after appeal, emphasized the value of the new institution in restraining the lower orders and maintaining the relationship between the classes which appeared so threatened by the revolutions in France. Mrs Trimmer vouched for the political safety of her schools by including in her guide for genteel patrons a list of 'virtues' which the children were to learn. Among them were civility and gratitude.

If you are civil you will behave with respect to ladies and gentlemen. You will say, Sir, or Madam, when you speak to them; you will rise from your seat when they come into a room where you are sitting; you will make a curtsey to them when you meet them ... If you have gratitude in your mind you will think yourself much obliged to those who subscribe to the school; and you will take care to improve in every respect, that their money and advice may not be thrown away upon you.[16]

A Baptist preacher noted that: 'Christian knowledge has a tendency to establish the peace of society by teaching each individual to fill up that place which Providence has assigned him', and furthermore that 'a well-instructed Christian peasantry will constitute the support and happiness of the nation.'[17] The horrors of the French Revolution could only be prevented in England, argued an anonymous member of the SPCK, if the poorer classes were preserved from the doctrine, preached among them by evil and designing men, that all men were created equal. Sunday schools, he said, were of particular importance because they impress on the poor 'while still young and tender the duty of behaving lowly and reverently to all their betters ... and to fear God and honour the King'.[18]

Most public declarations of educational policy in the late eighteenth century espoused the conservative doctrines of a Sarah Trimmer, a Hannah More, or a Jonas Hanway. Whether or not Sunday schools in fact inculcated meekness and submission, it remains true that many of their early supporters wanted them to teach 'a superstitious veneration for the church of England, and to bow to every man in a handsome coat'.[19]

There is also evidence that Sunday schools were occasionally used as centers for middle-class propaganda during the nineteenth century. One witness before Sadler's Committee, for example, claimed that during the spinners' turn-out some two or three years earlier manufacturers had come to the Sunday schools of Manchester to tell children that it was a sin to withstand their employers, that they ought to be subject to them, and that they would be well advised to go back to work. Other instances might be cited, according to this informant.[20] A dresser in Robinson's mill, Stockport, told another committee that the schools of Stockport were controlled by manufacturers, were subservient to their interests, and served as an outlet for tracts and lectures pleading the factory owners' case. His denunciations were taken seriously enough to prompt rebuttals from the incumbent of St Thomas and the overlooker in the mill where the witness, Joseph Sadler, had been employed.[21] Radicals and Chartists on occasion made similar assertions and not without some justification. Indeed some factory owners did require their hands to attend a Sunday school, though not necessarily one provided by the employer.

Finally, the politically charged, overtly conservative children's literature of the 1780s and 1790s continued to be distributed by Sunday schools well into the nineteenth century. All of the evidence so far presented seems to constitute an overwhelming indictment of the Sunday school as an agency of class repression. But there is also considerable, and in the end convincing, evidence on the other side.

The decline of the educative family and the removal of the child from the home into the school is in itself a politically neutral occurrence.[22] The Sunday school was, as has been shown, tightly integrated into the working-class community. When children left the home and entered the very different atmosphere of the school they came into contact with the most literate of their class and imbibed the values of artisan respectability taught there. Though the potential for intergenerational change was great, it was not of a kind generally repugnant to working-class parents.

It must also be remembered that the most restrictive definitions of Sunday school education were made as pre-emptive counter-arguments in debate with still more reactionary views. The character modelled on the Author in Hannah More's story of the founding of a Sunday school only advanced the view that her proposed school would be limited to teaching the poor to read the Bible, a book which could only lead to the increased obedience and industry of servants, when the farmer being solicited for funds objected that teaching the poor to read was the surest road to national disaster.[23] The Rev. Johnson Grant's caution to Sunday school scholars to regard all printed work with caution and his conviction that education could only lead to religion and this to loyalty seem less offensive when read beside an ultra-reactionary critique of his words. Sunday schools, noted one such article, had turned out fanatical teachers who led disputations, encouraged scepticism, infidelity and the anti-Christ. 'Those taught to read, to write, to reason', this review concludes, 'we see now grasping with eager curiosity every pernicious treatise within reach.'[24] Evidence of their activities and other publications suggest in fact that when the Sheffield Sunday School Union advertised itself as creating a society with 'each in his station under the final influence of religion' or the Stockport Sunday School devoted most of its 1819 report to recounting its battles against those who would attack Britain's 'matchless Constitution', both institutions were defending themselves against real or imagined threats from the Right rather than expressing the views which activated them during calmer times.[25]

Moreover, by the 1820s a new and more progressive conception of Sunday school education had come into being. The doctrine of self-help and advancement through merit replaced those older views of working-class education as an exercise in the creation of deference. Already in 1794 the Baptist Daniel Turner was pointing out that some of 'the richest jewels of society' had been found among the poor whose advancement should be encouraged through education; the Rev. T. Wood recommended Sunday schools to his fellow Wesleyans by recalling the poverty-to-greatness tradition in English history, and suggesting that the schools would 'excite in some of the children strong desires after further attainments'.[26] The advancement of science and learning that would result from mass education became a common theme. Cardinal Wolsey and Shakespeare were favorite subjects for Sunday school stories because of their rise from poverty to greatness, and stories of lesser men – Sunday scholars who learned the three Rs well enough to become prosperous merchants – abound.[27] There were, of course, still sermons and tracts which wished for the restoration of the old order with its patriarchal benevolence of rich to poor and which valued Sunday schools because of their role in maintaining the social order.[28] But by the late 1840s even the Church of England's Sunday school magazine could praise teaching in its schools as a step in the process of self-culture and self-improvement;

and a widely read children's magazine of evangelical Dissent could include in each of its issues a story of 'Pursuit of Knowledge under Difficulties'.[29] Indeed, by the mid-Victorian era the early nineteenth-century Sunday school was almost a symbol of working-class advancement through self-help. Tens of thousands of men had achieved prominence based on their Sunday school education, declared A. J. Mundella. 'From the kinds of qualifications which will be required in the leading men of another generation or two', according to a sabbatarian tract, 'it is not too hazardous to say, that many of the children of our Sunday-schools will become the rulers or the parents of the rulers of the destinies of the world'.[30] Local school histories proudly proclaimed the success of their alumni; Bradwell Methodist Chapel, for example, produced Ralph Benjamin Somerset, fellow of Trinity College, Cambridge, Thomas Morton, a quartermaster in India, and the owner of a large works in Stocksbridge who in turn employed three other ex-Sunday school men in important positions.[31]

But quite apart from its ideological bent, the coercive and propagandistic powers of the Sunday school were severely limited. Since they met on only one day a week they could not, like the public schools of the aristocracy or the less great boarding schools of the bourgeoisie, organize all aspects of their students' lives. As one commentator noted sadly, 'For one day, partially spent in the company of the pious, the children are exposed, during six, to all the moral contagion and impurity of their own dwellings and neighborhoods.'[32] Furthermore, competition for students between rival religious bodies made coercion impossible in the long run. It must be admitted, however, that there is some evidence of Anglican use of compulsion in the 1780s and 1790s which in many ways resembled the Church's efforts to control Methodism throughout the eighteenth century. In those decades, the Anglican clergy, for fear of losing what hold it had on the populace, sometimes used more than superior teaching to prise children from Dissenting schools. It was alleged that they threatened on occasion to withhold relief and exclude families from parish charities; on occasion they even carried out their threats. There was a widely publicized case in Oxfordshire of over twenty families being excluded from the Christmas feast because they refused to send their children to the Anglican school.[33] A fierce controversy in Warwickshire developed into a full scale pamphleteering war in the best eighteenth-century tradition when a Presbyterian minister and his allies accused the Anglican rector and his curate of first bribing and later threatening with loss of employment and eviction certain families who would not send their children to the Church Sunday school. On the other hand the Dissenters made cash payments to their scholars, which might be regarded as bribes but which they justified on the grounds that the pittance involved was merely compensation for the social services lost by failure to attend the parish institution.[34] As late as 1811 Anglican authorities sought to harrass a Dissenting Sunday school in Portsmouth by bringing a prosecution under the Conventicle Act.[35] But, with only a handful of exceptions the market in Sunday school education was relatively free after the turn of the century.

As noted earlier, factory owners occasionally enforced Sunday school attendance. One employee of the Strutt's mill even had his quarterly gift money stopped for not doing so.[36] But the extreme rarity of such instances, the absence of complaints about them from the working people, and the efforts schools made to attract children suggest that by and large attendance was a matter of choice and not of compulsion. There may have been a few cases in which parents were not actually compelled to send their children to a school on the mill grounds but would lose respect if they did not do so. But again the great majority of schools were not attached to a mill or workplace and moral pressure would have been far more difficult to exercise in the pluralist religious environment which characterized even small communities. Because of this pluralism, raw coercive power played little part in the world of Sunday schools. It is, of course, possible that those who managed Sunday schools exercised a measure of control over children and their parents by excluding, or threatening to exclude, radicals and malcontents from the services and the society of the school. But this kind of control is rare indeed; by and large the Sunday school did not interfere with the political lives of scholars or teachers.

The Stockport Sunday School provides a good case in point. The town in which it was situated lay at the center of radical activity during both the Peterloo and Chartist period and was decidedly industrial. More than any other school in England this one was the creature of the manu-facturing interests. Modern historians use its annual reports again and again as evidence for the repressive nature of Sunday schools.[37] Although its teachers came almost entirely from the working classes and although in their quarterly meeting they exercised some measure of control over the school's internal affairs, the relations of the school with the community were in the hands of a board of managers composed entirely of industrialists.[38] They were by no means all Tories; in fact, most probably supported the 1832 Reform Act, repeal of the corn laws, and other Whig-radical measures. Nevertheless they were opposed to Chartism, trade-union activity, and any other form of independent working-class radicalism. If the Sunday schools of England exercised a powerful control over working-class behavior through their powers of exclusion, the Stockport School, therefore, ought to exhibit this facet of social manipulation to the fullest. It does not. In the history of the school from 1792 to 1850 there was only one case of expulsion as a result of internal subversion, namely, an attempt by working-class teachers to assume some of the powers of the middle-class committee [...]

The managers certainly distributed tracts whose message, insofar as it was political, advocated quiescence and maintenance of the *status quo*; they quite probably delivered the occasional lecture to the same effect; they used a crown and sceptre resting on a Bible as an illustration at the beginning of many of their annual reports. But by and large politics were not central to the life of the school. Except during the years 1818– 20 the managers were content to leave the worldly convictions of students and teachers outside their sphere of interest. In a town which was at the center of radical politics for most of the first half of the century the working classes seemed oblivious to the politics of those who financed the schools. So far as the middle-class board of managers was concerned, they were content to let sleeping dogs lie and to get on with the recreational, religious and educational work of the Sunday school [...]

The inculcation of values: lectures, sermons and patriotic exercises

If the coercive powers of the Sunday school were limited, so also was the time spent on direct propaganda, and the means available. It is true that Sunday schools might have exercised indirect influence on the political attitudes of children through efforts to form their habits of work and play, both of which are discussed below. The more direct methods, however, were limited to three. Through sermons and lectures, through participation in patriotic festivals and most importantly through the literature they distributed, Sunday schools could work on the minds of students to inculcate values which sustained the *status quo*. Sermons and lectures, however, had severe limitations in this regard. Only about twenty per cent of each day was available for direct propaganda by a school's managers; the remainder of the time was spent in the classroom engaged in religious or educational exercises having no direct political importance [...]

Viewed as instruments of bourgeois control the annual encounters with the aristocracy and occasional participation in patriotic exercises were not very important. They were often not organized by the bourgeoisie and in any case were too ephemeral and infrequent to have a major impact. However, they were an important reflection of the relationship of the working class to society and of the subtle ways that class tied itself to the social order.

The inculcation of values: literature, politics, and virtue

A far more significant vehicle of propaganda was the vast body of literature with which the working-class child was bombarded. It can be divided into three categories: tracts and reward books given to scholars in school; magazines and periodicals published by denominational or church organizations, by private individuals, or by Sunday school associations; and finally the textbooks which formed the main body of reading material for the boys and girls during school hours. The literature in the first category is so enormous in scope and number of titles that a proper analysis would be a research project in its own right.[39] They range from the most blatantly propagandist and counter-revolutionary tracts to fanciful accounts of heaven and hell to 'books ... such as relate to Natural History, to Biography, to Travels and Voyages, to the History of England, and even to metaphysics', all of which, one reactionary noted, 'are scarcely publications *fit* for the lowest order of Society'.[40] [...]

The literature discussed so far constituted the great bulk of the reading material associated with English Sunday schools during the period 1780–1850. It was first of all religious. Secondly, it formed part of the working-class culture of self-improvement with its concern for history, the natural sciences, and 'useful' knowledge. Thirdly, it dwelt on a morality advocating honesty and kindness while condemning sabbath breaking, disrespect to parents, lying and similar offences. Direct political propaganda as evidenced in the tracts of Hannah More or in some of the productions of the SPCK was rare. The religious content of working-class political life and the aspiration toward respectability, of which self-improvement was a part, may indeed have limited the revolutionary potential in English society during the period being considered. But it was through such channels, and not through coercion or propaganda, that Sunday schools played a political role. They did, however, promote certain values often associated with industrial society.

The inculcation of values: literature and work discipline

On paper, the ideal Sunday school child was certain to grow up into the ideal capitalist man or woman. The perfect scholar was imbued with the puritan ethic:

> ... of temper sweet and mild
> No angry passions e're were seen
> In this engaging child.

> She very soon could knit and sew
> And help her mother too
> For Hannah would not waste her time
> As idle children do.
>
> Each sabbath morn she rose betimes
> And dressed her clean and neat
> Nor ever utter'd naughty words,
> Or loitered in the street.
>
> She knew that God would never love
> Girls that are bold and rude
> And therefore little Hannah prayed
> That he would make her good.[41]

He, or she, went around reciting ditties like:

> In books, or work, or healthful play
> Let my first years be passed
> That I may give for every day
> Some good account at last.[42]

In short he or she was hard working, clean, conscious of the value of time, obedient, and (although not stated in these rhymes) thrifty as well. Indeed it has been argued that Sunday schools were middle-class agencies designed to inculcate just these virtues, that they were part of an assault on the pre-industrial personality. In support of this view, it could be pointed out, for example, that Sunday schools, particularly in industrial cities, were often founded and financially supported by the manufacturing class; that when asked their views some factory owners remarked that the discipline and instruction of the Sunday school caused the children so educated to be 'more orderly and subordinate than others', 'more tractable, better behaved', 'improved in their general conduct and habits of cleanliness' and taken as a whole, more moral and manageable.[43] The aesthetic vision of the Sunday school and the factory during the nineteenth century were also remarkably similar. Ure talks of the 'sublime spectacle of witnessing crowds of factory children arranged in Sunday school' or of '1,500 boys, and as many girls, regularly seated upon benches, the one set on the right side, the other on the left'.[44] Seventeen thousand children attending the Halifax Sunday School Jubilee were described in the official report as 'an invading and well disciplined army – well clad and cheerful'.[45] For some, the spectacle of tens of thousands of spindles turning through the motion of the same drive shaft was not dissimilar to thousands of children following the orders of one individual. But from the facts that the virtues favored in Sunday schools were those characteristic of the entrepreneurial bourgeoisie, that this class on occasion praised and supported Sunday schools, and that on some occasions certain observers saw a similarity between the schools and new forms of industrial organization it does not follow that Sunday schools were agents of the middle classes for imposing suitable character traits on children of their employees.

Two questions remain. To what extent can the puritan ethic in this period be seen as a form of bourgeois ideology? Secondly, in what ways, and how successfully, did Sunday schools propagate or instil this ethic? Both these questions must be answered in the context of the facts presented in Chapter Two. Sunday schools were by no means a simple outgrowth of the factory system or even of industrialism. In 1818, Wiltshire, Dorset, Buckinghamshire and Bedfordshire ranked fourth, fifth, sixth and seventh respectively among counties in percentage of their population enrolled in Sunday school. Bedfordshire stood first in 1851, with almost a fifth of the population enrolled, while Huntingdonshire, Rutland, Cornwall and Buckinghamshire were all in the top one-quarter of counties based on *per capita* enrolment. Sunday schools began at a time when the factory system had scarcely gained a foothold and grew to contain millions of children before the factory became the dominant organization of production. They were as much a rural as an urban phenomenon, as much part of an agrarian as of an industrial economy. Furthermore, as has been noted already in this chapter, Sunday school teachers were predominantly working class, funds often came from the working-class community, and indeed the lower orders responded as eagerly to the philanthropic surge of the late eighteenth century as did other strata of society. The great majority of Sunday schools were then neither the direct product of industrialism nor of the middle class.

Nevertheless they undoubtedly taught the work ethic that is so often associated with the bourgeoisie. Although texts were primarily religious, diligence, cleanliness, punctuality, thrift and obedience were all pressed on students [...]

It would be a mistake, however, to conflate these precepts or ideals into a distinct bourgeois ideology. Indeed, the puritan ethic found some of its most vehement supporters among the leaders of a nascent working class [...]

It is scarcely surprising that working-class leaders should have adopted so readily the ethic traditionally associated with the entrepreneurial middle class; the personality traits of the successful business man are, after all, not very different from those of the successful political leader, journalist, or trade-union militant. It was as important for the *Northern Star* as for *The Times* or *Guardian* that its copy be handed in on time, that its distributors pick up their bundles regularly, and that payments be reliable.[46] A congruence between the fundamental values of the middle and 'respectable' working classes is thus natural and not difficult to understand.

The inculcation of values: school organization and work discipline

In real life, however, practice is more important than preaching; and the decisive role of the Sunday school in the development of personality had less to do with what was taught than with how things were taught, with the structural and operational organization of the institution. The structure of authority, the discipline of time and place, to a lesser extent the organization of teaching the rules governing appearance, and the system of rewards and punishments all arose out of the school *qua* school. Though they may have had, and in some cases did have, almost obsessional ideological justification as well, this was largely window-dressing on a reality determined by the nature of the institution.[47] A consideration of these features will allow us to understand how they acted to encourage inner drives and outward behavior appropriate to an industrial society.

In the same way that the authority relationships in the family appear as a small-scale version of these relationships in an organic society, the nature of power in the Sunday school was based on reason rather than on deference; on a rule book rather than longstanding tradition. In contrast with the far smaller charity schools, many of these schools issued rule books or sheets setting out in writing the privileges and obligations of various categories of personnel. Some were quite short, the size of a broadsheet, and were read out to the assembled students and teachers once each month in order to remind everyone of the nature of the social system in which they were participating. Other sets of rules were extraordinarily extensive, going on for over fifty pages and defining in the minutest detail the power relationships that governed the school. Perhaps the Napoleonic Wars inspired the military language in which they were couched: superintendents are colonels, inspectors are majors, teachers are captains, monitors are sergeants, and the best students in each class are the corporals.[48] The set of rules from which this is drawn resembles nothing so much as Ambrose Crowley's regulations for the operation and management of his iron works. In the Sunday school as in the liberal state or the large firm, obedience is given to a person not because of who he or she is but because of the position they fill within a system of law. Furthermore, both the teaching and the structure of the Sunday school emphasized that it was rational to act according to these laws. In secular affairs this rationality might imply that one ought not to engage in trade-union activity because it was against the immutable laws of political economy to do so; alternatively, of course, it might encourage working-class trade-union or political activism on different but equally rational grounds [...]

It would be misleading to argue that Sunday schools had a uniform system of teaching or of rewards and punishments. The author of a teacher's manual running to over 350 pages gave up in despair trying to describe the range of rewards and censures, claiming that another book of equal length would be required to do the job.[49] One basic generalization, however, can be made. This is that there was great reluctance in Sunday schools to exercise severe discipline and that stress was always more on rewards than on punishments. The result was that the apparent rigidity of the rules in theory was greatly softened by the unwillingness to enforce them in practice by a system of penalties. Whether the reasons for this laxity were pedagogical theory, theological scruples or a fear of losing pupils does not affect the result. Almost from the beginning of Sunday schools, corporal punishment was condemned as inappropriate for the sabbath; similarly any form of punishment arising out of anger or impatience on the part of the teacher was condemned. That hated figure, the wicked and quick tempered day schoolmaster of working-class autobiographies occurs with extreme rarity in remembrances of Sunday school. The pioneer days when Raikes could burn the fingers of a student on a stove, the managers of a midland school hoist a student up in a basket, or force a child to hold a Bible at arm's length for hours on end were looked back on, after the turn of the century, as regrettable instances of a benighted era. Punishments which induced a sense of shame in scholars were more common. Students might be forced to wear a sign saying 'LATE' or 'SWORE' or 'UNRULY'; they might be made to sit on a form in the center of the room; or they could be threatened with public expulsion during which they would be subjected to a stern lecture and then escorted to the door by a cadre of their former schoolmates.[50] But this too was frowned upon in more enlightened circles, both Anglican and Dissenting. If virtue had to be rewarded at all – and there was some controversy about this – then these rewards should consist of books and tracts or of tickets which could be exchanged for such reading material; punishment should consist of confiscation of rewards or of withholding them altogether. As this view of punishment became more widely accepted, however, it forced managers to give little gifts to all students so that there would be some thing that could be taken away in case of improper behavior. Although there is no way of knowing precisely how various schools operated their reward systems, the inspection of a large number of anniversary accounts leaves the impression that most children on the annual or quarterly feast day were likely to receive something or other. So, as an analogue of the world at large, this aspect of the Sunday school was probably not very effective.

Several other factors softened the impact of the teaching regime and overall discipline in creating suitable work habits. First, while the Sunday school as a whole was a large complex organization, each class was far smaller than that of the modern school. Ten students per teacher was an average, with many groups as small as five or six.[51] A child's experience of the school was therefore less of the large and ordered world of the school at large and more of the less regulated and more family-like atmosphere of the small class. Furthermore, although teachers were expected to follow a definite regime of instruction, ensuring that each student learned systematically and was accordingly tested on what he or she was meant to learn a number of factors made the teacher more like a parent than an impartial mentor. The most basic of these was the ambiguity of goals in the Sunday school; secular learning which could be tested, and even objective biblical knowledge, were only one part of the task. Conversion, a sense of seriousness, and love of God were far more important, at least in the eyes of those who wrote about schools. Teachers were therefore encouraged to develop a highly personal relationship with the children in their class, to get to know their homes, and most importantly to let love and kindness guide their dealings with their classes.[52] This of course conflicted with the far more impersonal role assigned to the instructor in his or her role as purveyor of knowledge alone. For example students who read poorly were nevertheless encouraged so that they would not come to dislike Bible reading; teachers were praised who, though deficient in learning, were highly religious; and the specific relationship a child had toward his parents, arising from the Evangelical ideal of the home, was taken as a model at least as often as the universalistic model of the pupil-teacher relationship in a modern school.

All these features of the school worked against the inculcation of suitable work discipline. They mitigated the rational, orderly, impersonal aspect of the Sunday school and indeed account for the widespread acceptance of the independent schools by communities which at the same time rejected those of the National and the British and Foreign Societies. On the other hand, the Sunday school was far more a part of the industrial world of large-scale enterprise than of the artisan-workshop era. If there was a certain mechanistic quality about their discipline and an aggressive commitment to the puritan virtues, it was not because of the school's specific relationship with factory owners or other managers of large-scale enterprise. It was because both the school and the factory were part of the same stage of historical development in which it was, and is, more difficult to maintain humanistic values.[53]

The inculcation of values: Sunday schools and the use of leisure

The role of Sunday schools in transforming working-class leisure was far more profound and pervasive than their part in political propaganda and repression. Their very being was dependent on the existence of leisure; they constituted an alternative way of spending Sunday and had to compete with other activities for the time of children who worked during the week. The child who spent his or her day in Sunday school was therefore taken out of the street or field, away from football, dice, hoop-spinning, or simply noisily playing about. The schools also sounded the alarm against leisure activities which, though not directly injurious to the cause of sabbath education, offended the aesthetic sensibilities, the ideas of what constituted civilized behavior, or simply the practical economic or political judgments of those who managed or taught in them. In place of the proscribed amusements, the Sunday school offered the 'rational pastimes', the outings, walks, railroad excursions, the teas and meetings which formed the core of respectable working-class leisure until the growth of large-scale public entertainment in the late nineteenth and early twentieth century. Neither in its negative nor its positive modes can the Sunday school be regarded simply as an agent of the bourgeoisie molding a recalcitrant working class into conformity with alien values. A certain puritanism, a passive if not an active rejection of the 'picaresque hedonism' of the lower orders in the eighteenth century, was too much a part of radical working-class culture in the nineteenth century for so unambiguous a class interpretation to be valid. Nevertheless, the ascendency of bourgeois sensibilities – the decline of bear-, bull-, and badger-baiting, the end of the old style pugilism, the growth of the temperance movement, the decline of public violence, and not least the establishment of the Evangelical sabbath – were all part of the cultural underpinnings of the new industrial society which Sunday Schools helped to establish [...]

Undoubtedly, some of those who founded and worked for Sunday schools sought to control working-class leisure in order to control crime in general, and most particularly that crime committed in violation of the sabbath. But others, the great majority of the working men and women who taught in the schools, did so because they believed that leisure on the sabbath and at other free times should be well spent, either in preparing for the next life or in improving oneself for a happier and more prosperous earthly existence. For them the remaking of patterns of leisure was part of the culture of self-help, self-improvement, and, above all, respectability.

Sunday schools waged their battle for the control of children's leisure in three ways. First, through education as itself a morally regenerative enterprise; second, through the support of temperance and other reform campaigns; and third, through the provision of counter-recreation. Like religion, education was thought to have a transforming effect on all it touched. The recreations of the educated man, the man who could use his mind, would not be those of the ignorant; education changed man the beast to man the angel, or so it was thought. Rational amusement, made possible by literacy, was therefore touted from the pulpit and in the bourgeois and the working-class press [...]

Sunday schools were thus undoubtedly advocates of refinement and respectability. It is more difficult, however, to determine if they were therefore on the side of the middle classes against the working classes, or the side of counter-revolution against revolution. There were compelling tactical as well as ideological reasons that kept organized working-class politics out of the politics of moral reform. But the vices condemned by the Sunday school were almost as often condemned in the working-class press and in the writings of important spokesmen. A certain puritanism pervaded many of these writings, which suggests that the division in society between the decadent, pleasure-seeking and idle classes on the one hand and the upright, serious and hard-working classes on the other was as important in the minds of their authors as the imputed antagonism between a middle and a working class [...][54]

Of course, Sunday schools cannot be adduced to explain the general decline of fairs and wakes. Their demise was part of the slow death, already well under way in the eighteenth century, of the traditional order. Some festivals, like the London fairs, were suppressed by the magistracy; others, like the Cotswold games, were prohibited by acts of Parliament, a victim of overlarge crowds and new sensibilities. Religion generally and Sunday schools in particular were only one of the forces making for the new attitudes which rejected old pastimes.[55] Nevertheless, for three reasons the schools were instrumental in the process of reforming working-class leisure. They were part of a larger, systemic transformation of pre-industrial to industrial society. They offered a relatively refined form of leisure activity which many working-class men and women already embraced, at least for their children if not for themselves. And finally, their efforts by and large grew out of the community they sought to influence rather than being imposed on it from the outside.

But by helping to form cultural linkages between classes Sunday schools contributed to the stability of Victorian society and the success of a capitalist economy [...]

Conclusions:

The repressive, middle-class dominated Sunday school of Hannah More or William Fox was a rarity by the early nineteenth century. Within two decades of their founding Sunday schools had become one strand of a uniquely working-class cultural constellation. In their literature and teaching they stressed moral and ethical as against overt social or political values. Honesty, orderliness, punctuality, hard work and refinement of manners and morals may all have been congruent with the industrial system and thus in the interest of the bourgeoisie but they were not therefore middle-class values. The great divisions in early nineteenth century society were not between the middle and the working classes but between the idle and the non-idle classes, between the rough and the respectable, between the religious and the non-religious. All of these divisions ran across class lines. The puritan ethic was therefore not the monopoly of the owners of capital; it was the ideology of those who worked as against those who did not. Sunday schools were effective in the transmission of certain values precisely because these values were those of the working-class men and women who taught in and supported the schools.

Furthermore, the life of the Sunday school mirrored an aspect of working-class life which has received short shrift from historians. In it the comparative strength of cohesive over disintegrative forces in society were reflected. The five years between 1838 and 1843 saw not only the publication of the People's Charter, the Newport risings and the Plug Riots but also a parade in Bolton of 12,000 working-class children celebrating the Queen's coronation.[56] In 1841 as Chartist agitation was growing, 1500 children in Blackburn marched out of the town on Easter Monday for a day of pleasure. 'Masters and servants, parents and children were united in the most innocent sports' under the sponsorship of the Sunday school.[57] The 'Age of the Chartists' witnessed scenes like that of the banker Joseph Gurney standing on the platform in Norwich waving to 5,000 Sunday school scholars as their train left the station. The children responded by singing 'The Fine Old English Gentleman' to the music of the band.[58]

Notes

1   J. F. C. Harrison *Learning and Living, 1790–1960*, (1960) 40.
2   See for example Reinhard Bendix *Work and Authority in Industry* (New York, 1956), 65–8.
3   Maurice Quinlan *Victorian Prelude* (New York, 1941) 44 and generally 44–50.

4   M. W. Flinn 'Social Theory and the Industrial Revolution', in Tom Burns and S. B. Saul, eds. *Social Change and Economic Change* (1967) 14 and 17.

5   E. P. Thompson 'Time, Work Discipline and Industrial Capitalism' *Past and Present* no. 38 (1967) 84.

6   Thompson *Making of the English Working Class* (1963) p. 401.

7   Ibid. p. 375.

8   Thompson *Making of the English Working Class* (1963) pp. 50, 361, and particularly pp. 375–83; a similar interpretation of the social role of religion in general and of Sunday schools in particular is given in Harold Silver *The Concept of Popular Education* (1965) 36–40 and Sydney Pollard *The Genesis of Modern Management* (1965, Penguin ed. 1968) 228–31, 243.

9   Thompson *Making ... p. 9.

10   Ibid. p. 11.

11   George Horne DD *Sunday Schools Recommended: A Sermon* (Oxford, 1786) 11.

12   Rev. Thomas Stevenson *The Difficulties and Encouragements attending the communication of religious instruction to the children of the poor: a sermon delivered April 11, 1814* (1814) 20.

13   Trimmer *The Oeconomy of Charity* (1781) pp. 26–8.

14   [Rev. Richard Raikes] *Considerations on the Alliance between Christianity and Commerce Applied to the Present State of this Country* (1806) 56.

15   See Chapter 5, pp. 125–7: Silver *Popular Education ...* gives the most comprehensive review of Evangelical attitudes toward education.

16   Sarah Trimmer *The Oeconomy of Charity* vol 1 (2 vol. 1801 edn.) 321–2.

17   J. Liddon *General Religious Instruction of the poor* (1792) 13 and 16.

18   *Introductory Address to the Public on the Importance of Sunday Schools at the Present Time* (Canterbury, 1800) 23.

19   William Godwin *An Enquiry Concerning Political Justice* vol. 2 (1798 ed.) 299.

20   *Report from the Select Committee on the Bill to regulate the Labour of Children in the Mills & Factories of the United Kingdom*: together with Minutes of Evidence 1831–32 (706) xv. pp. 327 ff.

21   *First Report of the Factory Commissioners* 1833 (450) xx, D2 114.

22   See F. Musgrove 'The Decline of the Educative Family' *Universities Quarterly* vol. 14 (1959–60) 377–404.

23   'The Sunday School' in Hannah More *Works* vol. 4 (new ed. 1818) 376–9.

24   Johnson Grant *The Abuses and Advantages of Sunday Schools: a Sermon preached at Ormskirk, Nov. 3, 1799 ...* (1800) and *Anti Jacobin Review* vol. 7 (1800) 214–17.

25   'Report of the Sheffield Sunday School Union' quoted in John Salt, 'Early Sheffield Sunday Schools and their Educational Importance' *Trans. of the Hunter Archaeological Society*, vol. 9, part 3 (1967) 183; *Report of the Stockport Sunday School* (1819) 5–13 and particularly 12.

26   Turner *Hints on religious education* (1794) second sermon; Rev. T. Wood *Thoughts on Sunday Schools: Importance of Knowledge to the Lower Classes of Society* (1815) 8.

27   See for example *SS Teachers' Magazine* (18397 135.

28   See for example 'Sermon for Sunday Schools on Prov. xxii, 6' reprinted in *Christian Remembrancer* vol. 14 (1832) 623–8; the Wesleyans could always be counted on for right wing views; see for example the quotation from 'Report of the Wesleyan Methodist Sunday Schools of Lincoln' in Rex Russell *Sunday*

Schools in Lindsey (Lincoln, 1965) 17; or another report in Scruton *Sketches of Old Bradford* p. 103.

29   *C. of E. SS Quarterly Magazine* (1848–49) 274; *The Teachers' Offering or Sunday School Monthly Visitor* (1850).

30   *Prize Essays* (1849) 26–27.

31   Seth Evans *Methodism in Bradwell* 89; or for example, Anon. *Founded upon a rock: A Chronicle of Wesleyan Methodism in Betty Brow* (1897) 17.

32   A. H. Davis *Religious Instruction* (1826) p. 11.

33   *Evangelical Magazine* vol. 30 (1822) 71.

34   For the Dissenting case of this wide-ranging controversy see Rev. William Field *A Letter addressed to the inhabitants of Warwick in answer to the charges against the dissenters* (Birmingham, 1791) and *A second letter in reply to remarks … of the Rev. the Vicar and the Curate of St. Nicholas upon the first letter* (Birmingham, 1791); Rev. Benjamin Carpenter *A Letter to the Rev. R. Foley, rector of Old Swinford in answer to charges brought against the dissenters in Stourbridge … To which is added an account of the proceedings at Lye-waste by J. Scott* (1795); see particularly the section by Scott, pp. 39 ff.; for the Anglican case see Rev. Robert Miller and Rev. Hugh Laugherne *Remarks upon a letter to the printer of the Birmingham Gazette … and also upon a letter … to the inhabitants of Warwick … by W. Field* (Warwick, 1798).

35   *Evangelical Magazine* vol. 19 (1811) 356–8. For full account see the trial report re-printed from the *Times* (7 August 1811) in *Philanthropist* No. 4 (1811) 388–91.

36   R. S. Fitton and A. P. Wadsworth, *The Strutts and the Arkwrights 1758–1830* (Manchester, 1958), pp. 256–7.

37   See note 8 p. 188.

38   Names were secured from the *Annual Reports* and occupations determined from commercial directories. All board members are traceable for 1800, 1820, and 1840.

39   See Chapter 4, pp. 113–19 for a discussion of the scope and volume of publishing for Sunday school audiences.

40   R. Lloyd MA *A letter to a Member of Parliament (in these days of infidelity and sedition) showing the serious and dangerous defects of British and Foreign Schools* (1819).

41   *The Sunday School Scholar's Gift, or a present for a good child* (Wellington, 1814).

42   *Teachers' Offering* vol. 4 (1844) 270; it is prefaced by 'Be industrious. It is a discredit to be idle; children's time is valuable; always be doing something; let every young child take for his motto …'

43   *Reports from each of the four Factory Inspectors on the effects on the Educational Provisions of the Factories Act; together with joint reports 1839* (42) xlii, pp. 11, 29 and 7.

44   Andrew Ure *The Philosophy of Manufactures* (1835) 408 and 411.

45   *SS Teachers' Magazine* (1841) 665.

46   Most issues of the *Northern Star* for example carried a 'notes from the editor' section which *inter alia* contained pleas to contributors asking that they hand in their copy on time, to distributors complaining about tardy or altogether neglected pick-ups, etc.

47   The model in this section is derived, in part, from Talcott Parsons 'The School as a Social System: Some of its functions in American Society' originally published in the *Harvard Educational Review* vol. 24 (Fall 1959) 297–318 and

reprinted in A. H. Halsey *et al.*, eds. *Education, Economy, and Society; A Reader in the Sociology of Education* (New York, 1961) 435–55. Parsons' insights are elaborated in Robert Dreeben *On What is Learned in School* (Reading, Mass., 1968) which provides most of the theoretical framework employed here.

48 *Rules and Regulations of the Sunday School held in the Wesleyan Methodist Chapel, Spring Gardens, Doncaster* (Doncaster, 1815) 41.

49 R. N. Collins *The Teachers' Companion designed to exhibit the principles of Sunday School Instruction and discipline* (1840) 196. He then proceeds to discuss the question for the next 58 pages.

50 J. H. Harris, ed. *Robert Raikes*, (1887), *Centenary Volume of the Bank Str. Sunday School, Manchester* (1907); Collins *Teacher's Companion ...* p. 271; Pratt *Black Country Methodism* p. 172.

51 See Chapter 4, pp. 108–10.

52 See Chapter 1, pp. 17, 18; 'treat them [students] like your family' advises the *Evangelical Review* (1812) 174.

53 This paragraph is based partly on the formulation of the relationship between schools and society in Ivan Illich *Deschooling Society* (1972).

54 See Brian Harrison *Drink and the Victorians* (1971), p. 33 and his 'Religion and Recreation in Nineteenth Century England' *Past and Present* no. 38 (1967) 105–25, esp. 121–2, for a similar hypothesis with respect to moral-reform movements.

55 See further, Robert W. Malcolmson *Popular Recreations in English Society, 1700–1850* (1973).

56 Rothwell *Memorials ...* p. 163.

57 *Sunday School Magazine* (1841) 146.

58 *SS Teachers' Magazine* (1846) 394–6.

III RELIGION AS SOCIAL CEMENT

This section is concerned with the analysis of religion in modern Britain as a form of what has been called 'social cement' – that is with binding together various elements in a social formation. Religions can be seen as involved in the social processes concerned with both establishing and maintaining a sense of collective, ethnic identity among specific groups, and with transmitting and reproducing major values about sexuality and gender in such groups. Religions can be seen as one of the ways in which a social formation is held together over time, despite conflicts over material interests. Religious differences, however, can weaken this process of national 'binding together' under particular historical circumstances, as in Northern Ireland, where religious differences reinforce separate national, ethnic identities, and do not contribute to the establishment of a single 'Northern Irish' identity for everyone. In post-war Britain, on the other hand, which is the main focus in this section, religion does play a part in holding together a conflict-ridden social formation, in spite of all the differences of religious belief and practice to be found in the society.

In both Britain and the United States there is what has been called a 'civil religion' which is not identical to Christianity, but which borrows legitimacy from that world religion. The coronation of the British monarch in 1953 was a major example of the civil religion of Britain. Other Royal Family rituals also form a central part of this British civil religion, which has both a national political aspect, and a private, familial component concerned with sexual morality and gender roles. Some of these issues are discussed in the articles by R. Bocock (1985) and B. Turner (1983) from different perspectives. The former article gives greater emphasis to the role of 'civil religion' in post-war Britain than the latter, which attaches more weight to the material interests which are involved for all groups and classes in keeping the social formation in working order.

The mass media, especially television, but also radio and newspapers, play a major part in creating and forming, not merely transmitting, already existing collective sentiments and values about the Royal Family particularly, as well as other components of Britain's civil religion. The article by D. Chaney (1983) analyses the role of the BBC in transmitting civic rituals.

Moral values and gender roles are transmitted to young people, and reasserted and reaffirmed for everyone, in indirect ways in modern Britain. The Royal Family plays an important, if often indirect, role in the process of generating not only knowledge about what these roles and values are, but also a degree of commitment to them. There have been changes in these moral values, especially in the area of sexual behaviour, and in gender roles since the end of the Second World War. These changes do not just happen; they are in part brought about by social groups trying to achieve change.

Jeffrey Weeks (1981) has argued that in the post-war years there have been three different periods – first, the immediate post-war reconsolidation of the family and traditional perceptions of men, women and children; second, a permissive moment, in which a number of reforms and changes about sexuality and gender were made; and a third phase, in which traditional values about sexuality and gender were reasserted by newly-created religious-based pressure groups. The piece included here from Weeks examines these last two phases, and especially the third one, from a perspective influenced by Foucault, the French social historian. This entails seeing power as being exercised not only by the state, but also by social movements of both radical and a traditional orientation.

Religion in modern Britain

Basic concepts

A religion is a complex mixture of beliefs, values, symbols and rituals. Most major religions, such as Christianity, Islam, Hinduism and Buddhism, contain beliefs and values about *this world*, whatever they may say about another, super-empirical one. It is the influence of the empirical and super-empirical beliefs and values of a religion upon the social, economic, political and cultural activities of various groups of people, especially classes and ethnic groups, which is of concern to sociologists and social theorists. In this context Marx's famous proposition that 'religion is the opium of the people' is not, therefore, to be understood as being about the truth value of a particular religion, but rather about what religion does in a society. The issue of central concern to sociologists is not whether a particular religious claim is true or false, but what consequences believing it has for particular groups in specific circumstances.

Religion can be seen as a part of the ideological sphere of a society when it operates in a way which helps to maintain the political, cultural and economic arrangements of that society over time. The ways in which a religion does this may be either by directly teaching that the social, political and economic order is right and God-given, and that it is sinful to try to change it, or they may be more indirect. For example, religions often offer hope about a better future in this life, or in another life, for those oppressed groups who suffer in the present. The ritual and symbolic practices of a religious group may provide comfort to people who experience suffering, pain, poverty and bereavement. By doing this a religion may indirectly help to maintain the social structure (see C. Geertz, 1964; 1966, in this volume).

To focus upon religion as ideology, as this article will do, is not to make derogatory statements about religion, but rather, to take a central concept within social theory and to try to use it to throw some light upon major aspects of religion in modern Britain. To reiterate the point made earlier, such a sociological analysis of religion is not dependent upon making any claims about the truth value of particular religious beliefs and values.

In this article the role of religion in modern Britain will be examined using a number of key concepts derived from sociological theory rooted originally in the works of Marx, Weber and Durkheim. Unless some theoretical framework is used one would become lost in a plethora of material, there being so many sects, churches and religious groups in modern Britain that it would be impossible to cover them all here. The main theoretical concepts to be employed will be derived from the sociology of religion as this area has developed over the last hundred years or so.

Many people, including some sociologists, define modern western societies such as Britain as being 'secular'. In the sense that such modern societies are no longer dominated by religious institutions in the way the Catholic Church dominated life in the Middle Ages in Europe, then it is possible to say that they are more secular. However, such a description can overestimate both the role of the Church in the past and the decline of the influence of religious groups on many people in present day societies. So some definition of religion and the secular is needed which allows for these complications in a way which the notion of secularisation fails to do. It is also important to avoid an over-cognitive definition of religion, such as those definitions which concentrate upon beliefs in supernatural entities as the defining characteristic of religion (see, for example, R. Robertson, 1970). Many people, for instance, participate in ritual occasions, which take place in churches, who do not think of themselves as believers in any clear set of propositions about the supernatural. This is true of rituals such as funerals, some weddings, and some church services such as those at Christmas time, or on Remembrance Sunday.

An important concept in Durkheim's sociology derived from his distinction between the sacred and the profane. 'The sacred' denoted the 'set apart' from the everyday, secular, utilitarian, profane area of social life. Beliefs, values, symbols, places, objects, people, time periods and ritual actions can all be sacred in this sense. The sacred is special, not part of the everyday world. All societies contain a sacred part of social and cultural life, according to Durkheim and Durkheimians, including communist systems (see C. Lane, 1981). This notion of the sacred forms the basis for a useful definition of religion. Religion can be defined analytically as consisting of those beliefs, values, symbols, rituals, social roles, organisations and groups which are concerned with the sacred, the set-apart from everyday life, according to Durkheim.

Another major concept to be used here is that of legitimation, and its converse – de-legitimation, or protest. This concept is part of both later forms of Marxism, and can be found in Weber's sociology (see A. Giddens, 1971). Religions can be seen as legitimating the ruling groups in a social formation, such as Christianity came to do in the Roman Empire after it became an officially recognised religion under the Emperor Constantine. Christianity can be seen as having begun as a protest movement among the Jews whilst they were subjugated to the imperialism of Rome. After its official recognition by the Emperor Constantine, Christianity became an ideology which could be used for the legitimation of rulers. This continued under feudalism and in early capitalism, although protest movements continually emerged, especially after the Bible became available in the vernacular languages of Europe and elsewhere. The tension between a church type of religion which is willing to compromise with ruling groups in a society, and to legitimate their rule, or at least not actively to oppose them, and sects which do not compromise on some values, such as pacifism, but often condemn some aspects of secular life and form a protest movement is, therefore, built-in within Christianity according to most sociologists of religion (see E. Troelstch, 1931).

As an unintended consequence of social and economic change, churches in modern societies such as Britain and the USA have in effect lost, on the whole, the critical, protest element within Christianity. The concept of privatisation introduced by P. Berger (1968) highlighted one of the ways in which Christianity became neutralised. The notion of privatisation refers to the process whereby religion is located in the private sphere of the family and sexual morality. Religious values are seen as irrelevant to economic, political, military or wider social issues, and any claims to apply morality to these areas are seen as ill-founded by most key groups in these activities – unless the religious leaders are willing to legitimate that which the ruling groups do. In this way, privatisation may be said to operate in ways which help to legitimate the power structures in a society and to remove the critical edge of Christianity from general circulation.

There is, however, a contrary process at work within both sects and churches. Some people do recover the protest element in Christianity – that is, the inherent protest against social injustice, political oppression, military evils and economic inequality to be found in both the Old and New Testaments. The development of Christian socialism earlier in the twentieth century is one important example; the development of 'liberation theology' in Latin America in the last three decades is another. The critique of communism by Catholics, in countries such as Poland, for instance, is a further development, usually based upon an acceptance of socialism but not in an autocratic form. These are forms of protest within churches and mark a separate phenomenon from sects, in which protest is typically embodied in some supernaturalist form. Sectarian protest usually offers salvation for a chosen elite, but not for everyone, and in this sects are less universalistic than mainstream Christianity is, at least in theological terms.

Finally, it is important to make it explicit that the definition of religion which is used in this article is wider than one based upon religious organisations such as churches and sects. Religion is defined here as those social actions and cultural beliefs which are concerned with the sacred. This provides a wider definition of religion than those which concentrate upon organised groups which hold supernatural beliefs, and enables the sociologist to include other ritual activities such as those of the nation and the state. On the other hand, such a definition avoids including just about all aspects of culture as being religious, a position T. Luckmann approaches in his book, *The Invisible Religion* (1967). This means that a phenomenon such as the Royal Family in Britain is analysed as being a part of the sacred area in the society – although this is not too far removed from organised religion in many situations, in any case. Royalty, in the eyes of many, is assumed to be above party politics. Royalty is 'sacred' and is, therefore, treated as being immune to criticism of the kind which may be made of politicians. This has not always been the case, however, as a number of writers have pointed out – it is a relatively new, post-Victorian phenomenon (see D. Cannadine, 1983).

Religion is also involved in the process of the social regulation of sexuality, the family and marriage through its moral teachings. In some states, under certain historical circumstances, these moral rules form the basis of the laws which regulate these matters. In modern Britain the Royal Family is expected to live by the moral rules of the Church of England, even though some members may lapse from time to time. Such lapses are defined as exactly that – a falling away from maintaining the moral rules they should aim to live by.

In this article there are two areas to be examined – namely the rituals associated with the state and the nation, and the private sphere of the family and the social regulation of sexuality. These are not as unrelated as they may seem to be at first sight. One important link between these two aspects of the social role of religion in modern Britain is the Royal Family. The Royal Family is held up as an example of family life to children and young people, as well as to adults, in numerous ways. For example, the Archbishop of Canterbury wrote in a booklet widely available during the Queen's Silver Jubilee in 1977:

But at this time we specially celebrate, with thanksgiving to Almighty God, the presence, at the heart of our nation and Commonwealth, of a family which has set standards for us all to follow. This has been – and is – a steadying influence in a day when forces are at work which would break up the family as a strong

and loving unit in society; and when that happens, the nation's strength is sapped.
Silver Jubilee, 1977.

One aspect of acquiring an identity and a value system involves the process of being socialised into the ideology of the British nation state and in this the Royal Family and the national ritual events in which it is involved play an important role, especially for children. This is, of course, true in varying degrees for children from a wide variety of cultural and socio-economic class backgrounds, although some may not be socialised in such a manner. In this way it can be seen that there are important links between the two levels and areas of concern here, namely the nation state's ideology and the ideologies to which young people are exposed from the earliest age in their families, and in schools and religious organisations which form a part, therefore, of their sense of individual identity and their views about gender roles, the family and sexual morals. However, it is useful for analytical purposes to try to distinguish the two levels of analysis and to treat them separately. This will be done here.

Civic ritual in Britain

At the level of the nation-state it is important to distinguish two major types of ritual activity which are analytically distinct, though they are often mixed together in empirical cases. The two types are civic ritual on the one hand and religious ritual on the other. In Durkheim's sociology these two were not distinguished analytically and because of this he was unable to distinguish modern nationalism as an ideology, which may have religious overtones or may not, from religious ideologies which cross-cut nation-state borders (see R. Bocock, 1974).

For Durkheim, the sacred was separated off from the profane by 'negative' rituals, and the 'positive' rituals which were then performed in relation to the sacred symbolised the superiority of society over the individual. He wrote in *The Elementary Forms of the Religious Life* about Australian aborigine totemism. Totemism refers to the practice of giving the name of a material thing, often, but not always, an animal, bird or plant, to the different clans which together constitute a tribal group; for example, the eagle-hawk is the totem of a clan in the Mukwara tribe of Australian aborigines. A clan is a group which operates as a network of kin, even though all its members may not be blood relatives. Durkheim argued that the representation of the totem was regarded as sacred because it symbolised the identity of the clan group. 'So if it is at once the symbol of the god and of the society, is that not because god and the society are one?' Durkheim wrote (See A. Giddens, 1971, p. 109).

In more highly differentiated societies, such as modern Britain, the rituals of national identity in which social group identity is created and maintained over time may or may not involve religious organisations. Similarly, religious ritual may be quite distinct from national, civic rituals, and may generate feelings of loyalty to other collectivities than that of the nation-state. This was thought to be the case in the past in Britain with regard to the religious ritual actions of Roman Catholics, for example. There was a suspicion by some that Catholics owed their allegiance to the Roman pontiff rather than to the British monarch and state officials.

The rituals surrounding and involving the members of the British Royal Family are primarily an example of civic ritual in that they symbolically represent the group, the nation state. However, the British monarch is not only the Head of State, but also Head of the Church of England and the Church of Scotland. This complicates the situation somewhat compared with the situation in the United States or France, for example, where the President is purely the Head of State and where, therefore, the civic ritual is closer to a purer type than is the case with the British situation (see R. Bellah, 1970).

In civic ritual the symbolism used refers to, or represents, the collectivity. In this sense, civic ritual is concerned with particular groups, in this case whole nations or even links between several nations such as England, Scotland and Wales. The fact that Northern Ireland does not easily fit in with this list is significant in that it shows that there has not been the same historical linkage between the civic rituals of the nations which make up Britain and those of the two main communities in Northern Ireland, the Catholics and the Protestants. In Northern Ireland the link between what are called here civic and religious rituals is stronger in the two communities than is the case in Britain, where religious ritual is more differentiated from civic, national identity maintaining ritual.

Religious ritual, as a separate analytical type, refers to the ritual which members of churches or sects use to worship their conception of a deity. The membership of these religious organisations may or may not overlap with a particular nation-state. The Church of England, for instance, had been established by the Tudors to contain everyone in the nation-state in one religious organisation, and it still retains a role as an 'ecclesia', or established Church in this respect in England (M. Yinger, 1970, pp. 262–4).

Most modern states in the world contain members of many religious organisations and each of these has its own kind of religious rituals. This can cause trouble if those in power in the major institutions of the state decide that one or more of these religious groups produces some kind of perceived threat to the society. For example, the 'Moonies' and

Scientology became suspect groups by some in Britain during the early 1980s (see Media Project 1, on the Unification Church, i.e. the Moonies, in D207 *An Introduction to Sociology*, an Open University second level course).

It is important to retain this distinction between civic and more specifically religious rituals because unless this is done it is not possible to understand or explain conflicts between church leaders and politicians in key offices of state, for instance. The usual pattern in Britain is for the major civic ritual events, such as Remembrance Day or a Jubilee, to have a significant church figure present, usually the Archbishop of Canterbury, and there is little tension about this from either side. There was some tension and conflict over one event, however, which was meant to be a piece of uncontroversial civic ritual as far as the Prime Minister and other ministers of state were concerned. This was over a service of thanksgiving for victory. The service was meant to express thanks to God for Britain's victory over Argentina at the end of the Falklands/Malvinas fighting in 1982. The church authorities at St Paul's cathedral did not want, and did not allow, a nationalistic victory celebration because they thought that the loss of life on both sides was not something to give thanks for. Rather, church leaders wanted to stress comfort for the bereaved on both sides of the conflict and to attempt to begin to make reconciliation between two supposedly Christian states. This led to a sense of tension and conflict of view between the Church and the government. It illustrated that the state authorities could not always assume that they had a 'tame' church in the Church of England or the other denominations involved. Conflict between the Church and state is possible, and in the case of the Falklands service the conflict was concerned with the type of ritual event to have in a specific situation. The disagreement can be seen in terms of whether the ritual should have been primarily civic, in which the feelings and values of a particular government and of some groups in Britain would be articulated, or whether it should be more in keeping with the feelings and values of the bereaved on both sides in the conflict. This latter focus illustrated that for some church leaders there were wider issues involved concerning the feelings of Christians among the 'enemy', not only those of a triumphant government and of one nation involved in the fighting. Religious ritual quite unexpectedly became significantly different from the civic ritual requirements in this instance (A. Barnett, 1982, p. 90). This example serves to illustrate that the distinction between the two types of ritual is by no means insignificant at the level of practice as well as the theoretical level.

Further back in time there was an interesting controversy about another civic ritual event – the Coronation of Queen Elizabeth II in 1953 – but this time the controversy was among sociologists, not between politicians and church leaders! It is worthwhile re-examining this controversy in sociology for the light it may throw upon some issues which are still important in sociology and social theory more generally. In order to perceive this it is necessary to understand that in the 1950s, in British sociology and in most sociology elsewhere for that matter, there was a general tendency to see rituals as maintaining the society in which they occurred, and to identify the forces and groups for social change as being economic in some unproblematic way. In other words, there was an assumption that rituals were only of interest to conservative sociologists because they served to maintain the status quo, and that radical sociologists should not give much weight to rituals of any kind because they were not the motor of major change, for this was assumed by some to be in the economic sphere. The import of these remarks should become clearer in the next section of this article.

The sociological analysis of the Coronation

One major example of a sociological debate about a major ritual event, namely the Coronation of Queen Elizabeth II in 1953, will be used here to illustrate how the debate between sociologists who used a consensus model and those who used a conflict model affected their respective approaches to the analysis of the Coronation. (The Coronation received some attention from sociologists in the journal, *Sociological Review*, in 1953 in an article by E. Shils and M. Young, and in a critical reply to this by N. Birnbaum which was published in 1955 in the same journal.)

The Coronation took place eight years after the end of World War II, and two years after the end of the 1945–51 Labour government. This historical setting is important to bear in mind because there had been less class conflict during the war years within Britain than before the war. The Labour government had brought in some nationalisation, for example in the coal mining industry and transport, and the welfare state had been developed and established, crucially including the National Health Service. The post-war boom and the coming of affluence still lay in the immediate future for most people, but the effects of the war years and the material problems of the late 1940s were beginning to fade in most people's memories by 1953.

In 1953 television was developing rapidly both geographically and technically, nevertheless many families did not have their own television set and so watched the Coronation with friends or neighbours who did have one. This may or may not have contributed to the way in which the event was perceived by the television audience, in that watching in groups may heighten the impact of what is shared experience. The

Coronation did, no doubt, make some extra impact upon people than might otherwise have been the case by being seen in a group (see D. Chaney, 1983, in this volume). (Also, see the discussion about broadcasting rituals and the state in D209 *The State and Society*.)

One further point worth bearing in mind in this context is that although the Coronation focused specifically upon the monarch as an individual, the Royal Family as a group were involved, too. It is also interesting that the Archbishop of Canterbury mentioned the Royal Family, and not just the Queen, in his article written for the Silver Jubilee in 1977, which I mentioned above. (The celebrations in 1977 were, incidentally, to mark Queen Elizabeth's accession to the throne in 1952 on the death of her father, George VI, the actual coronation being a year later.)

The life-cycle rituals of the central members of the Royal Family also play a major part in the rituals of Britain. Royal weddings are one example of this, for instance the marriage of Prince Charles and Lady Diana in 1981 and of Princess Anne and Captain Mark Phillips in 1973. Royal funerals also evoke the more serious side of Britain's Royal Family life-cycle ritual events, creating important shared collective sentiments.

The Coronation can thus be seen as a major example of a civic ritual event in Britain. The debate which took place about the Coronation in the 1950s still has some important points for a sociological analysis of the place of royal rituals in Britain in the 1980s. I shall return to it following a discussion of the analysis made by Shils and Young mentioned earlier.

Edward Shils and Michael Young (1953) saw the Coronation as a ritual of communion, bringing the whole British nation into a ritualistic dedication to the basic values of its society. The basic values they instanced were: charity, loyalty, justice in the distribution of opportunities and rewards, reasonable respect for authority, and respect for the individual and his freedom. Shils and Young's analysis claimed that many of the population were deeply involved in the ritual, and they saw this involvement as an expression of the people's commitment to the sacred values. The ritual also handled the emotional ambivalence that people have towards moral authority and moral rules. There is no hint, however, of any group whose ambivalence is based on the fact that they disagree with some of the values, or the ways in which these were being interpreted. For example, the value they instance of 'justice in the distribution of opportunities and rewards' is ambiguously worded, but it would seem that even in the euphoria of the Coronation not all were agreed that the actual distribution of rewards was just, although no doubt adhering to the generalised value that justice in the distribution of rewards was desirable. Looking at this analysis later, it seems that Shils and Young were themselves carried away by the seemingly overwhelming consensus about basic British values, and the worth of the society in the early 1950s. The period of high consensus in Britain was short lived. In part it had built up during the Second World War, but was probably not as high as Shils and Young thought even in the Coronation period (see Bocock, 1974).

Shils and Young drew on Emile Durkheim in their analysis of the Coronation, and ignored Max Weber and Karl Marx. They did not see that the Coronation, and other rituals surrounding the Royal Family – such as the giving of honours and decorations and the State Opening of Parliament – serve to legitimate the existing set of families who rule economically, politically (including the new Labour families) and militarily. Yet the nineteenth-century writer William Bagehot, who is quoted by Shils and Young, had argued that this was the case. They failed to draw the conclusion that little has altered since then. According to Bagehot, the monarchy enabled the educated 10,000 to go on governing as before. By commanding their unbounded loyalty, it 'tamed the uncouth labourers of Somersetshire who, in their simplicity, needed a person to symbolize the State'. In this way, 'the English Monarchy strengthens our government with the strength of religion ... It gives now a vast strength to the entire constitution, by enlisting on its behalf the credulous obedience of enormous masses.'

The upsurge in the popularity of the monarchy in England reached its clearest peak in the 1950s, especially at the time of the Coronation. Since then it has been less marked as a phenomenon, but no doubt if there were a national crisis, the monarchy would re-emerge as one of the major symbols of English nationalism. The Church of England can also find that it is itself part of this basic, latent nationalism, and this makes it very difficult for the Church to take clear stands which are critical of the economic and political status quo. The Church of England tends to seek to express a set of core values which overarch the disputes and conflicts in the society, and so to act as a 'reconciler' between disputing parties. The church leaders are most likely to speak out in favour of seeking consensus than in pursuing economic justice through, for example, industrial conflict.

Birnbaum (1955) was critical of Shils and Young's analysis of the Coronation because it accepted a *unitary* view of the values of British society and assumed there was a *consensus* about them, rather than acknowledging that *conflict* about values and distribution of wealth and income were and are present in Britain:

The authors (i.e. Shils and Young) note immediately after remarking on the decline in prestige of the ruling elite, that 'consensus on fundamental values remained'. It is unclear what these fundamental values could have been, since consensus by the authors' own admission did not quite extend to the legitimacy

and efficacy of the society's ruling elite or of its economic institutions. Agreements on 'justice' and 'charity' do not seem to have precluded the social conflicts of the past decades. It is a question whether they alone set the limits, undoubtedly present, which kept Britain from civil war.
(op. cit., p.14)

Later in his critical analysis Birnbaum wrote:

What seems to emerge in the authors' analysis of the Coronation is their own strong feeling of adherence to the official morality of Great Britain – and their preference for conformity to such moralities wherever they appear. In discussing popular response to the Coronation, they tell us that 'antagonism emerged only against the people who did not seem to be joining in the great event or treating with proper respect the important social values – by failing, for instance, to decorate their buildings with proper splendour.' They give no evidence for this assertion, nor any indication of how widespread this aversion might have been. We should also expect them, as social scientists, to show some awareness that such aggression might have been displaced from other spheres. Instead we get what from the language employed seems to be enthusiastic concurrence in it.
(op. cit., p.22)

Norman Birnbaum's critique of the Shils and Young analysis of the Coronation was based upon a sociological theory which did not give any explicit weight to ritual events, and which made no use of the concept of the 'unconscious'. It was based upon a view of human social action as being motivated by a relatively rational pursuit of economic goals by both capitalists and by wage and salary earners. This viewpoint has been a powerful one among many conflict theorists in sociology, but there is no necessary connection, nor historical connection, between the use of a conflict model of capitalist society and rationalistic, economic views of action. There have been social theorists, working in critical theory, and others using more structuralist methods, who have worked with a model of society derived from both Marx and/or Weber, and from Freud. Freud's model makes the *emotional* meanings of religion, ideologies and rituals of importance, just as Marx's model is concerned with the economic and the political (see Bocock, 1983). The two models can be brought together in the analysis of ideology and cultural activities such as rituals without, therefore, assuming that a focus upon rituals and emotions is somehow incompatible with a conflict model of capitalist societies.

In the specific case of the Coronation, and other Royal Family rituals such as weddings, funerals and jubilees, there is no need to deny that many people in the working classes, and in the middle classes, do have positive feelings towards members of the Royal Family and will watch the ritual events on television and in the streets, while still allowing for the point that this does not affect economic and political conflicts in the society.

The precise consequences in terms of the legitimation of the political and economic structure of British society of these royal rituals is then a matter for more empirical investigation. Such rituals help to *construct* a sense of consensus, rather than being seen as simply reflecting a pre-existing agreement as Shils and Young (1953) argued.

There seems to be a plausible case for arguing that there is no major, popularly-based social movement for republicanism in Britain, that the monarchy is accepted as either fairly harmless by some or much more positively by others, and that this has some consequences for the legitimacy of the British political system. The American and French Presidents are both elected political figures and the Heads of State for ceremonial occasions. These two roles are distinct in the British system of a hereditary monarch, who is the ceremonial Head of State, and an elected Prime Minister, who is a politician. Unpopular British Prime Ministers do not produce the problems of conflicting emotions which unpopular Presidents may do. Presidents who are disliked for their policies, or their corruption, are nevertheless treated with the respect due to the Head of State however corrupt they may be. Whether the monarchical system is more stable is difficult to say, but superficially there does seem to be a gain in legitimacy under a monarchy for the constitution as a whole in Britain. Unpopular and corrupt American Presidents helped to enhance the already existing pattern of cynicism, low voting in presidential elections, and a politically apathetic population in the United States during the 1970s.

The comparative stability of the legitimacy of the British constitution is a problem for those who seek radical or revolutionary changes because it makes a radical break very difficult without a major breakdown of economic life, which could lead to a new constitutional settlement based on a republic. Such a legitimation crisis may occur but it seems unlikely, given that Britain has survived worse economic conditions than those of the early 1980s in previous decades of the twentieth century.

New directions

The major issue underlying this ealier debate between sociologists concerned whether Britain was still basically a capitalist society after the Labour government of 1945 or not. Since that time a new issue has developed, raised by feminist writers during the late 1960s and 1970s. This is the issue of patriarchy.

The issues raised about patriarchy by feminists and others have ranged from the fact that men, not women, typically hold the most powerful positions in the major social institutions, including the churches, the armed forces, trade unions, political parties, and industrial companies; to the role of women in the family as mothers and wives. The concept of 'patriarchy' has both a structural aspect – that men hold most of the powerful positions in society, and a cultural or ideological aspect. Juliet Mitchell (1974) defined patriarchy as a culture dominated by the 'Law of the Father' – a term she derived from the French psychoanalyst, Jacques Lacan. In a patriarchal culture dominated by the Law of the Father, gender roles are defined in particular ways such that mothering is seen as work for women, as is most if not all domestic labour (see N. Chodorow, 1978), and fighting in the armed forces is seen as basically a male activity. In a patriarchal culture, women mother; men fight.

A series of institutions can be seen as linked together to make up a major component of British society's patriarchal culture. These are: the nation, the armed forces, the family, the church and the monarchy. Together they could be said to constitute the main part of the archaic heritage of this society, or the central elements of its patriarchal culture. This culture is constituted by certain moral values, beliefs, rituals and symbols which operate within the institutions mentioned. It produces and reproduces the gender roles and definitions of sexuality which most people think of as natural and normal – the heterosexual, monogamous family.

An important component of this ideological structure and set of social practices is the Royal Family. The rituals surrounding not only the monarch but other members of the Royal Family are central events in the 'civil religion' (R. Bellah, 1970) which persists in modern Britain. The recent examples of such royal ritual occasions include the Silver Jubilee in 1977, to celebrate twenty-five years since the Queen came to the throne; the eightieth birthday of the Queen Mother in 1980; and the marriage of Prince Charles and Lady Diana in 1981. There are, in addition to these special events, the regular cycle of royal civic rituals throughout each year, such as the Christmas Day television broadcast by the monarch, the State Opening of Parliament, and the Remembrance Day events.

These rituals are a complicated mix of a number of analytical types of ritual action. The central ones are civic rituals by the Head of State, such as the State Opening of Parliament; life-cycle rituals such as Royal weddings and birthdays; military ritual such as the Trooping of the Colour on the monarch's official birthday; and nationalist communal rituals such as the Remembrance Day ceremonies. These could be said to constitute the civil religion of Britain, to use Bellah's term, rather than being, strictly speaking, religion in the sense of beliefs and rituals which purport to be in contact with the 'holy' or the 'numinous' – as R. Otto (1924) called the special sense of awe which he saw as typifying religious experience and ritual.

'Civil religion' in the United States and Britain is not itself Christianity, according to Bellah, even though it draws upon themes and symbols from Christianity. The 'God' of American civil religion is unitarian, for example, not the complex trinitarian God of Christianity, Bellah argued (Bellah, 1970). A civil religion focuses on a particular nation-state, whereas a major world religion is universalist and does not teach or claim that loyalty to any particular nation-state is a necessary prerequisite for 'salvation'. Civil religions do focus upon generating loyalty to a particular nation state. The Church of England, for example, combines aspects of both types, being a civic religious organisation focused on England, and part of the universal religion of Christianity. Tensions have actually resulted from this dual aspect from time to time, whenever church leaders have stressed universal values and used them to criticise politicians' activities and policies. Politicians have typically expected legitimation from the Church of England, and certainly not criticism. The tension can erupt whenever the church leaders stress universal Christian values of reconciliation, love and the equality of all people in the eyes of God and find fault with particular political actions, for instance, the bombing of civilian targets in the Second World War, which was criticised by Bishop Bell; the criticism of the nuclear deterrent in 'The Church and the Bomb' report in 1982; or the Tory government's handling of unemployment and the 1984 miners' strike criticised by a number of bishops, including the Archbishop of Canterbury. (In this context, it is worth noting that the Church of England still commands attention and retains a latent loyalty among many English people; three out of every five people claimed to be members of the Church of England in a National Opinion Poll carried out for *The Times* in 1978.)

Within sociology there remain different ways of assessing the significance of 'civil religion'. To those who broadly accept the proposition that consensus over fundamental values is central to any identifiable social system, as Bellah tends to do, then a society's civil religion is of great importance in understanding and explaining how societies such as the United States persist and maintain their basic component values over long time periods. If most people are socialised into these values in the rituals of the civil religion in schools and local communities, and in learning about the major events in the history of their society, then it is not so surprising that the state and the economic mode of production in the society become accepted as legitimate, or unchangeable. It is interesting to note in this context that the Soviet Union has developed its own equivalent civil religion and a socialist 'liturgical' year in the ritual occasions it has developed since the revolution in 1917 (see C. Lane, 1981). It is possible to see these rituals as helping to legitimate the Soviet state and mode of production, to make them appear as unchangeable as those in Britain and the United States appear to be.

Some sociologists (R. Bellah, 1970; P. Berger, 1969; E. Shils and M. Young, 1953) have found that it is useful to adopt a view which also sees the role of civil religion in societies, like those of the United States and Britain, as having some importance in trying to explain why there is a lack of a desire for change of the state, and of the main mode of production, among the working classes in these societies. If it is thought that the civil religion of these societies is popularly-based and accepted in a relatively unconscious way by many people in all classes, then the lack of large-scale, popular-based movements for radical social, economic and political change is seen as more easily explained. The people are caught up in the ideology of the civil religion and they do not, therefore, conceive of change as being either desirable or possible. In this double sense, it can be said the existing system is regarded as legitimate. This proposition may be seen as holding more for the United States than in Britain, or the two societies may be regarded as similar in this regard in spite of the existence of a stronger socialist party in Britain than in the United States.

There are other sociologists and some Marxists who have taken a different view, as Birnbaum did. Some have described their position as being 'materialist' (see, for example, B. Turner, 1983). Such writers do not attach much significance to civic or religious rituals and beliefs in societies such as those of modern, industrial, capitalist societies. For example, it has been argued:

Societies are held together not simply or even primarily by common beliefs and ritual practices, but by a multitude of material factors – force, economic coercion, economic dependency, legal compulsion, economic scarcity, habituation and the exigencies of everyday life. Societies can continue to operate with relatively high levels of conflict, disaffection and indifference to norms in combination with pragmatic acceptance of values. The social cement is constantly eroded and swept away by these circumstances without any ultimate descent into anomy and social chaos.
(Turner, 1983, Ch. 2, p. 61; p. 243 in this volume.)

Is it necessary to accept one or other of these positions? Here I wish to argue that there is another position which can be plausibly sustained, and which preserves some of the strengths of both of the analyses which have just been considered above. These were, firstly, that there is a 'civil religion' in modern Britain which plays some part in the ideological sphere in masking the possibility of fundamental change as being either possible or desirable. Secondly, that material factors and class interests are more important than the beliefs, values and rituals associated with civil, or any other kind of religion, in British society. To develop the possibility of a third position, in which ideological factors are *combined with* material ones, rather than *opposed to* one another, with one being treated as more important that the other, it is first of all necessary to clarify the fundamental starting points of the various protagonists involved in the debates.

The most critical point is whether the theory being used in the sociological analysis is one which purports to be materialist or not. If it is not explicitly materialist the chances are that it is implicitly idealist, as in the case of Bellah. This means that ideas, beliefs and values are treated as being more important in analysing social action than material factors such as economic interests and physical force. On a materialist view economic interests are seen as more important than ideas in understanding and explaining social action in a capitalist-based type of society such as that of modern Britain. Physical force is only of marginal significance in such a society in modern conditions. This does not mean that force was not a significant factor in the past in Britain, nor in other societies at present, nor that it may not become important again in the future as a means of maintaining social control in a decaying capitalist Britain on this view.

This difference in starting points has to some extent been overtaken by a new emphasis in philosophy and social theory upon the importance of language. By emphasising language as a central characteristic of the human species, as that which distinguishes humans from all other species which use elementary forms of signal communication rather than the elaborate forms of symbolic communication found in human cultures, recent developments in this area have shifted the ground upon which the debate about materialism and idealism should be conducted. Michel Foucault (1976), for example, emphasised the power relations which are built into various forms of knowledge in what he termed 'discourses'. Words and symbols do not just reflect, or represent, an already established social world. Words, language, or 'discourses' produce and create the social world. Knowledge is a form of power. The creation of organized 'discourses' is part of an expanded notion of the 'political' for Foucault (see also J. Weeks, 1981, chapter 1).

This emphasis upon language entails that both the positions of idealism and materialism need to be changed. Neither can be held in an unmodified form. On the one hand idealism has to be modified to take account of the way in which language is produced in particular discourses within concrete economic and political circumstances, and does not appear outside of the dominant mode of production in any given society. Language, in the form of discourses, is produced, created and maintained in social institutions such as publishing houses; schools, colleges and universities; churches and sects; broadcasting stations, film and television studios and distribution networks. The production of language, or a particular discourse, must be included in the sociology of beliefs and values in ways which has not been done in the past by sociologists inclined towards idealism as their starting point (see R. Williams, 1981).

On the other hand, materialism has to be modified to take account of the new developments about the fundamental role of language in human society. It is not simply one more additional factor to be taken into account in doing sociology. Language use is the key distinguishing feature of the human species. It transforms the relationship between human beings and the natural environment, and this implies that earlier, crudely materialistic views about man as tool-maker, for example, are no longer adequate. This has implications for historical materialism (see A. Giddens, 1981).

The model of the economic, material mode of production, consisting of the social relations of production and the technical means of production, has to be modified to include the means of mental production as being of fundamental importance. That is to say that it is not possible to privilege the position of the production of industrial goods and food beyond the basic means of subsistence, over and above the production of words, symbols and rituals in the means of ideological, or mental, production. For example, the advertising industry in advanced forms of capitalist societies deeply influences the consumption of most material goods from cars and tractors to clothes and food. The world of symbols and language in the broadest sense, including the language of style, fashion and taste, is profoundly intermingled with the world of the production and consumption of material goods. There is no clear dividing line between ideology in the broadest sense and material interests and material desires, for conceptions of what counts as a material interest, or desire, are affected and formed by ideological discourses (see R. Coward and J. Ellis, 1977).

Even physical force and its use, or threatened use, is affected by ideologies. The most potent of the ideologies which affects who kills and maims others, or who gets killed or maimed, in wars are those of nationalism and patriarchal religion. The sense of an ethnic identity is both a political and a religious product. It is perceived competition for material resources between various ethnic communities in the world which lies behind many groups resorting to violence. These perceptions are not given outside any linguistic or symbolic discourse; they are formed and maintained within ideologies about ethnic identity and in the collective rituals of 'civil religions'.

The desirability of fighting, killing, and even of being killed, for a particular ethnic group, or nation, is perpetuated and maintained in civil religion. Patriarchal ideologies socialise males to accept organised violence as a part of the natural order of things. This same discourse maintains that women will 'naturally' stay at home to mother babies and children. These values and beliefs are communicated to people in the civil religion of Britain, with its military ritual occasions, and its rituals of the Royal Family, especially potent in communicating the patriarchal gender divisions – men fight and die for their Queen and country; women mother. The churches are involved in this civil religion too, but they also contain a critical few who argue that warfare, especially nuclear warfare, is evil. Some also think that women should be ordained as priests in the Roman Catholic, Orthodox and Anglican Churches and that the symbolism of 'God' as a father, a male, should be replaced with symbolism which portrays 'God' as female, or as both male and female (P. Nichols, 1981).

Material factors do not exist outside human discourses. Both economic, material, interests of classes and the use of physical force and violence by organised groups, are located within concrete discourses produced in social institutions in a particular historical situation. Religious organisations are involved in the production and reproduction of these discourses in the beliefs, values, symbols and rituals of the particular religious tradition in which they are placed. Civil religion is an important component of these processes in Britain as it is elsewhere in the world. It produces a sense of ethnic identity among each generation and reproduces commitment to the nation for older members of the nations which make up modern Britain. Civil religion is not completely successful in these tasks, but nor is it empty and without efficacy.

The social location of religion

The social location of religion in a society like that of modern Britain has quite specific elements to it. The most important of these elements is that it is clearly differentiated from the economic sphere and that it is located in the private sphere of the family. Religious institutions have become differentiated from the economic sphere. No one could understand how to implement the kind of moral theology that was once developed by the church about a just price or a just wage, nor the sinfulness of taking interest for money loaned to someone else, in a modern capitalist economic system. The economic sphere has become quite separate from the moral control of religious institutions under capitalism (see R.H. Tawney, 1926). This contrasts, incidentally, with some forms of Islam, which do seek to control economic activity by religious precepts.

The arts, technology and sciences have also become differentiated from religious institutions and from control by the hierarchy of the church. There are attempts made to control by law both spheres, however, as can be seen in the attempts by some social organisations to control television, theatre and cinema on the basis of a puritanical interpretation of Christian morality. This surfaces periodically in different guises in Britain, from the finding of the editor of *Gay News* guilty of blasphemy for publishing a poem in 1977, a decision upheld in the House of Lords in 1979 (not 1579, nor 1679, but 1979); to an unsuccessful attempt in 1982 to have a play at the National Theatre banned (*The Romans in Britain*) because it contained a homosexual rape scene; to attempts to control videos of films at home because children may see them and be exposed to sex and violence (see J. Weeks, 1981, in this volume).

In the spheres of science and technology there have been attempts to bring some of the developments here under moral control. For example, there have been groups telling doctors not to perform abortions, and Christian protests over the development of birth control. In the United States there have been a number of skirmishes over the activities of groups which try to prevent Darwin's theory of evolution being taught in schools and colleges, or which try to teach a Biblical version of creation alongside Darwin's version of evolution, as though the two were of equal intellectual and scientific merit. There is also a strong Christian involvement in the Campaign for Nuclear Disarmament – a more significant attempt to control the use of modern technology.

These examples are, however, exceptions. They are newsworthy and strange in the eyes of many people in the societies in which they have occurred because they appear to be left-overs from an earlier historical epoch. Today, many assume religion belongs in the private sphere, not in the public arena. Church leaders should not be political, it is asserted, especially by Conservatives.

Religion is a matter of personal choice, not something which should be imposed upon others in modern consumer orientated societies, such as Britain or the United States. However, in the family, moral values and religious beliefs and practices may be taught to children. On the whole, religion is seen as a matter of adult freedom of choice in modern societies.

As was seen in relation to the role of the Royal Family in Britain, there is still a place for official religion on state ritual occasions. Religious symbolism is used in Britain and the United States as a means of legitimation of the state. In everyday political affairs it is seen as unnecessary for politicians to appeal to religious beliefs and values. Indeed it is an implicit rule that British politicians should not try to claim that they are more 'Christian' than anyone else in the general run of political affairs. Religion is mentioned on certain special occasions only, such as a new Prime Minister taking office. One major difficulty which has faced Christian socialists, for example, is that they appear to be claiming to be more moral, more properly religious, than others, and this appears to reflect badly upon the proponents of that perspective because they appear to have 'a holier than thou' aura about them.

One sociologist of religion, Peter Berger, has argued that there is a tendency towards the institutional separation of state and religion in most societies. He wrote, for example, in *The Social Reality of Religion* (1969):

The global tendency seems to be in all cases the emergence of a state emancipated from the sway of either religious institutions or religious rationales of political action. This is also true in those 'antiquarian' cases in which the same political secularization continues to be decorated with the traditional symbols of religio-political unity, as in England or Sweden. Indeed, the anachronism of the traditional symbols in these cases only serves to underline the actuality of the secularization that has taken place despite them.
(Berger, op. cit., p. 128)

Berger wrote his book before the Iranian revolution of 1979 in which a religious movement did act in politics and provided a religious rationale for their revolution. The point which he made seems mistaken and Berger over-emphasised the split between religion and politics in the modern world. Some powerful ideologies in the modern world do mix religious values and symbols with a more political-economic ideology, as in the various forms of religious socialism, Iranian Islam and in American Republicanism in the 1980s.

As was illustrated by the Coronation and events involving the Royal Family generally, there does seem to be some popular basis to these ritual events in that many people from all socio-economic classes do become involved in these activities even if it is only by watching them on television and reading about them in newspapers and magazines. Berger may perceive these rituals as 'anachronisms' but this is a statement more about his own response than about those of many of the citizens of Britain. For a sociologist who used a phenomenological approach this was a curious lapse in that he failed to pay attention to the meanings of the rituals to the people themselves, but rather imposed his own upon them. Sociologists have not done detailed research on this area in Britain or in the United States.

If these rituals are seen as a means by which a sense of identity is produced among British children and revitalised among adults, then their importance and appeal can be more properly assessed. This sense of national identity is separate from the state as such, although political figures are interested in trying to use any existing means of identity production and reproduction to legitimate their structures and activities. The Royal Family ritual events can be seen as a component of national identity maintenance, and as part of the process of the legitimation of state offices. This is rarely made explicit in the post-war period as it was in the writings of earlier generations, as was illustrated with the quotation from Bagehot earlier in this article.

Religion in a modern capitalist society is pushed increasingly, however, into the private sphere of the family and marriage as its major site of operation, where it can be seen as having a residual role in the morality of sexuality and marital relationships. Even if people reject the sexual and marital morality of the major churches, as there is evidence they do, especially in the case of lay Roman Catholics who reject the Church's teaching on birth control, and many members of the Church of England reject the idea of not remarrying divorced people in churches, for example, there is at the very least some residual acceptance that religious institutions are legitimately involved in this area among some people (see B. Wilson, 1982, chapter 6, especially pp. 161–5).

Religion, therefore, may be said to have a residual role left over from the past at the level of maintaining a sense of national identity and partially legitimating the state. It is at the level of the private sphere of the family, the key social institution concerned with the reproduction of patriarchal ideology, however, that religious institutions have their major social base in a society such as Britain. In other societies, however, such as Poland in the late 1970s and early 1980s, religion's role in carrying a sense of national identity in distinction to the state and communist government of Poland was strong.

Berger analyses the situation of religion in modern capitalist societies as follows:

One of the essential traits is that of 'individualization'. This means that privatized religion is a matter of the 'choice' or 'preference' of the individual or the nuclear family, *ipso facto* lacking in common, binding quality. Such private religiosity, however 'real' it may be to the individuals who adopt it, cannot any longer fulfill the classical task of religion, that of constructing a common world within which all of social life receives ultimate meaning binding on everybody. Instead, this religiosity is limited to specific enclaves of social life that may be effectively segregated from the secularised sections of modern society. The values pertaining to private religiosity are, typically, irrelevant to institutional contexts other than the private sphere.
(Berger, 1969, pp. 132–3)

The plausibility of traditional belief in religions is lost in the minds of millions of people in urban industrial societies, both capitalist and communist, according to Berger. He argued that the rational, bureaucratic forms of work required in any modern and complex society affect people's general consciousness in ways which make it very difficult for moral and ideological directives from the Church to have any impact. In large part this is because appeals pitched at a level of generality common in moral statements of this kind are impossible to apply in most work situations not because the people are immoral, but because no one could apply them in a concrete situation. The everyday routines of bureaucratic organisations and industrial plants do not leave room for either individual initiatives nor deviations from the planned routines. This type of consciousness, Berger seemed to imply, is carried outside the work situation so that religious beliefs, values and symbols lose plausibility in a widespread form in such societies. This is not because people have been converted to some other ideology, Berger would argue, but that no ideology can take root in such a situation. People live in a world deprived of any overall meaning system of any kind. They do, however, continue to search for identity and meaning at a personal level and use the wide variety of religious organisations available in modern pluralist cultures to do so. They may shift from Catholicism to a Buddhist group to an oriental sect and back again in a very short time-span.

In Berger's analysis there is a market place of competing religious roads to salvation from which an individual in a modern city may choose. Or the individual may use secular therapy to try to find some purpose and meaning, some sense of identity, for themselves. The only difference seems to be that religious solutions are usually free of any fees, while those of therapy cost the individual a cash sum for the professional service rendered (see P. Berger, 1969).

The analysis which Peter Berger provided of the process of increasing privatisation of religion in modern societies, that is, the link between religion and the family, highlighted one aspect of the sociological situation of religious institutions, but at the same time it obscured another. At the comparative historical level at which Berger pitched his analysis, it appeared that religious institutions had less and less direct moral influence upon political, military and economic affairs in conditions of advanced capitalism, and that the family, the private sphere, had become the only site where religious-based moral values appeared appropriate and legitimate. However, another aspect of the process was missed in this type of analysis. This additional feature of the social situation of religious morality had been discussed before Berger as 'the social control function of religion'.

Berger was attempting to move away from the teleological aspects of functionalism towards a sociology based upon a phenomenological sensitivity to subjective meaning. This led him to make religions of central importance as providers of meaning in the past, and to provide a sociological account of the loss of plausibility of traditional religious meanings under conditions of advanced consumer capitalism. This type of approach does show why there is a search for meaning outside the traditional denominations and churches of Christianity in the west and a growth of new sects and cults, especially among the generations who have grown up since the end of the Second World War. If someone is searching for a satisfactory meaning system and identity, the old organisations of Christianity appear too certain of themselves to welcome searchers. They are catering for those who have a sense of collective identity which they seek to revitalise in church rituals. They claim to know too much and so thrust it upon people rather than to encourage a personal search. Berger's approach does highlight some of the reasons for the growth of new religious groups in modern capitalist societies such as Britain and the United States in the 1960s and 1970s.

During this same period, however, events moved on. Changes took place in western capitalism which intertwined with changes in social theory and in sociology. For example, at the time Berger was writing, the United States was involved in a war in South-East Asia which it lost. However, a whole generation of young Americans and West Europeans had learned some lessons about the role of the military in the United States and its influence in political circles as a result of their experiences in protesting about that war. In Europe similar lessons were drawn in both West Germany, Britain and France. The main conclusion of all the various events of the late 1960s was that, for the time being, a major change of the system was not possible, and that change had to begin elsewhere – not in the large organisational structures of modern capitalism but in everyday experience.

The main consequence of these perceptions of the political situation in western capitalism was to produce new kinds of social movements outside the orthodox political parties. The prime example of the new type of movement has been the women's movement. This led to an interest in issues concerned with gender and sexuality primarily as these affect women (see, for example, J. Mitchell, 1974). The main impact upon men so far has been through the groups concerned with male homosexuality, although there have been attempts to create a men's movement for all men, heterosexuals included (see A. Tolson, 1978). There have also been groups interested in studying the influence of the media in both conventional political terms, and in less conventional terms, by exploring how common sense is constructed and perpetuated as an ideology. These substantive issues have led to the development of new social theories. These theories are new in the sense that they have involved novel ways of reading, or understanding, earlier theorists, especially Marx and Freud. Berger's phenomenological style of doing sociology of religion was overtaken by these new developments.

The use made of the work of Michel Foucault, on the other hand, has increased – at least in Britain in the late 1970s and early 1980s. Foucault concentrated upon the concept of 'power' as a generalised capacity in a society, not as a concept whose central focus is upon the state and its repressive apparatuses of control and violence, as in Weberian sociology, for instance. As mentioned earlier, Foucault's approach emphasises 'discourses' and the social construction of categories which create the worlds in which people live. In the private sphere, which was of concern to Berger, various discourses penetrate to regulate sexuality. This is something omitted by Berger, but is the central focus for Foucault. The discourse created by the Catholic Church, and other religious organisations, especially since the reformation and the counter-reformation, spoke endlessly about sexuality in order to regulate it. This detailed control of sexuality applied mainly to elites, educated people, rather than to the great majority of the faithful who went to confessions very infrequently. Foucault, however, went on to argue that, nevertheless, an ideal was created of the ideal the good Christian should aim to achieve. He said:

An imperative was established: not only will you confess to acts contravening the law, but you will seek to transform your desire, your every desire, into discourse. Insofar as possible, nothing was meant to elude this dictum, even if the words it employed had to be carefully neutralised. The Christian pastoral prescribed as a fundamental duty the task of passing everything having to do with sex through the endless mill of speech.
(Foucault, 1979, p. 21)

Foucault quotes one of the confessors: 'Tell everything, not only consummated acts, but sensual touchings, all impure gazes, all obscene remarks ... all consenting thoughts' (ibid.).

This Christian tradition of speaking about sexuality frequently as a major area of sin, while forbidding certain words to be used and cloaking everything in decent expressions, has been continued in the 1970s both by the Catholic Church and by lay Protestants and Catholics alike, especially in both Britain and the United States (see J. Weeks, 1981, in this volume).

The Christian churches have become split over the issues raised by the women's movement, by gays and by sexual liberationists. Some, both among the ordained elites in the churches and among the laity, are on the side of maintaining the traditional archaic heritage of Christianity, as is especially true of those who produce the Vatican documents about sexuality, and of the National Viewers' and Listeners' Association whose secretary is Mrs Mary Whitehouse as the standard bearer of decency (J. Weeks, 1981, in this volume). Others, again both among ordained and lay people, take a more liberationist view on matters concerning birth control, divorce and re-marriage, abortion, pre-marital sexual intercourse, homosexuality, lesbianism and the ordination of women. These people are also, but not necessarily, involved in the peace movement against nuclear weapons. The peace movement in Britain has had Christians involved in it since the late 1950s, from Canon Collins to Mgr Bruce Kent (see F. Parkin, 1968, on the earlier phase).

The focus upon 'discourses' has produced a new way of conceptualising the importance of religious organisations' texts, whether these are sermons, articles in magazines and church newspapers, prayers, or explicit moral rules and guidelines. Such texts can be seen not as a left-over from some earlier, supposedly more religious period of history, but as one way in which social regulation takes place in modern societies. Religious organisations still have power in the sense that they can generate discourse which is real in its social effects upon members, and maybe others less directly, especially in the sphere of sexuality, gender roles and, to some extent, in the area of the organised preparation for war. The consequence of churches' discourse about sexuality has been to make what had, to a large extent, been a private matter into a public one. The churches were involved in turning private troubles into public issues long before the more recent social movements among women and gay people tried to do so.

Conclusion

Religion in modern Britain has been analysed here at the level of the nation-state as a complex mixture of a civil religion and as part of a universal world religion. The Royal Family is a central component of British civil religion and forms a focus for ritual activity and the revitalisation of loyalty to the nation-state. In this sense it is a major component of the ideological practices which help to legitimate the state, the constitution, governments, law and the armed forces by bringing them into contact with the 'sacred'.

The social location of religion was discussed using the concept of privatisation. Religion is seen by most people as being especially relevant to the family, sexual behaviour and gender issues. The Royal Family is involved in this aspect, too, by supposedly epitomising how family life ought to be conducted. The concept of patriarchy, which has been developed by feminists and others, was used as one way of providing a theoretical link between the ideology of the nation-state and that of the private sphere. Britain's civil religion can be seen as expressing in its teachings, in its values, in its social practices and in its organisations such as the Churches of England and Scotland, a form of patriarchal ideology. This ideology fundamentally centres upon two main themes: men should be willing and able to fight, kill and die; women should desire to be wives and mothers.

Britain's civil religion, therefore, legitimates the state and patriarchal ideology by symbolically representing and expressing in its social practices these themes which perpetuate traditional definitions of gender. The universal religion of Christianity has historically been involved in doing this work of legitimation in other societies, too, but Christians are increasingly challenging this role. Tensions between church leaders and politicians result from this dual aspect of the churches in Britain – namely that they are both part of the civil religion of the nation-state, and part of a wider, more universalistic, world religion which contains the values of love, reconciliation, justice, equality, peace and joy for all.

References

Althusser, L. (1971) *Lenin and Philosophy and Other Essays*, London, New Left Books.

Archbishop of Canterbury (1977) *Silver Jubilee*, London, The Queen's Silver Jubilee Trust.

Badcock, C. (1980) *The Psychoanalysis of Culture*, Oxford, Basil Blackwell.

Barnett, A. (1982) *Iron Britannia*, London, Allison and Busby.

Bellah, R. (1970) 'Civil religion in America', in *Beyond Belief*, New York and London, Harper and Row.

Berger, P.L. (1969) *The Social Reality of Religion*, London, Faber and Faber.

Birnbaum, N. (1955) 'Monarchs and sociologists', in *Sociological Review*, Vol. 3.

Bocock, R. (1974) *Ritual in Industrial Society*, London, George Allen and Unwin.

Bocock, R. (1983) *Sigmund Freud*, London and New York, Tavistock and Ellis Horwood.

Cannadine, D. (1983) 'The context, performance and meaning of ritual: the British monarchy and the invention of tradition, c. 1820–1977', in E. Hobsbawm et al., *The Invention of Tradition*, Cambridge University Press.

Chaney, D. (1983) 'A symbolic mirror of ourselves: civic ritual in mass society', *Media, Culture and Society*, Vol. 5, pp. 119–35.

Chodorow, N. (1978) *The Reproduction of Mothering: Psychoanalysis and the Sociology of Gender*, Berkeley, California, Berkeley University Press.

Coward, R. and Ellis, J. (1977) *Language and Materialism*, London, Routledge and Kegan Paul.

Durkheim, E. (1912) *The Elementary Forms of the Religious Life*, translated by J. Ward Swain, New York, Collier Books, first published in paperback by Collier in 1961.

Erikson, E. (1974) *Identity: Youth and Crisis*, London, Faber and Faber, first published in England in 1968.

Foucault, M. (1978) *The History of Sexuality*. Volume 1: *An Introduction*, London, Allen Lane; translation copyright Random House Inc., New York, 1978.

Freud, S. (1908) 'Civilized sexual morality and modern nervous illness', in *Collected Papers*, and reprinted in *An Introduction to Sociology*, edited by Bocock, R. et al., 1980, London, Fontana.

Freud, S. (1912) *Totem and Taboo*, Standard Edition, Vol. 13, London, Hogarth Press.

Freud, S. (1923) *The Ego and the Id*, Standard Edition, Vol. 19, London, Hogarth Press.

Giddens, A. (1971) *Capitalism and Modern Social Theory*, Cambridge University Press.

Giddens, A. (1981) *A Contemporary Critique of Historical Materialism*, London, Macmillan.

Goffman, E. (1963) *Stigma: the Management of Spoiled Identity*, Englewood Cliffs, N.J., Prentice Hall.

Klapp, O. (1969) *Collective Search for Identity*, New York and London, Holt, Rinehart and Winston Inc.

Lacan, J. (1977) *Ecrits: a Selection*, London, Tavistock Publications.

Lane, C. (1981) *The Rites of Rulers: Ritual in Industrial Society: the Soviet Case*, Cambridge University Press.

Lane, C. (1983) 'Women in socialist society with special reference to the German Democratic Republic', in *Sociology*, Vol. 17, No. 4, pp. 489–505.

Luckmann, T. (1967) *The Invisible Religion: the Problem of Religion in Modern Society*, London and New York, Macmillan.

MacIntyre, A. (1967) *Secularization and Moral Change*, Oxford University Press.

Martin, D. (1978) *The Dilemmas of Contemporary Religion*, Oxford, Basil Blackwell.

Marx, K. (1845) 'Theses on Feuerbach', in *On Religion*, London, Lawrence and Wishart.

Mitchell, J. (1974) *Psychoanalysis and Feminism*, Harmondsworth, Penguin Books.

Nichols, P. (1981) *The Pope's Divisions*, Harmondsworth, Penguin Books.

Otto, R. (1924) *The Idea of the Holy*, Harmondsworth, Penguin Books edition, 1959.

Parkin F. (1968) *Middle Class Radicalism*, Manchester University Press.

Robertson, R. (1970) *The Sociological Interpretation of Religion*, Oxford, Basil Blackwell.

Shils, E. and Young, M. (1953) 'The meaning of the coronation', *Sociological Review*, Vol. 1, pp. 63–82.

Tawney, R. H. (1926) *Religion and the Rise of Capitalism*, Harmondsworth, Penguin Books.

Troelstch, E. (1931) *The Social Teachings of the Christian Churches*, translated by O. Wyon, London, George Allen and Unwin.

Tolson, A. (1978) *The Limits of Masculinity*, London, Tavistock.

Turner, B. S. (1983) *Religion and Social Theory*, London, Heinemann Educational Books.

Weeks, J. (1981) *Sex, Politics and Society*, London, Longmans.

Williams, R. (1981) *Culture*, London, Fontana.

Wilson, B. (1982) *Religion in Sociological Perspective*, Oxford University Press.

Yinger, M. (1970) *The Scientific Study of Religion*, London and New York, Collier-Macmillan Limited.

16 B.S. TURNER

Social cement

From *Religion and Social Theory* by B.S. Turner, 1983. Reproduced by permission of the publishers, Heinemann Educational Books, now available from Gower.

Civil religion

In the treatise on the social contract Rousseau had argued that Christian spirituality rendered it unfit to serve as a civil religion; Alexis de Tocqueville, however, in the two volumes of *Democracy in America* (1946) which appeared in 1835 and 1840, claimed that Christianity was the vital basis of democratic politics in America. Having shaken off absolutism and religious intolerance in Europe, the religion of the settlers and migrants in American society could be accurately described as 'a democratic and republican religion' (de Tocqueville, 1946, p. 229). For historically contingent reasons, Christian religion in America had come to be modelled around the structure of secular politics. The separation of state and church, the absence of an established religion, the emphasis on freedom of conscience and the institutionalisation of religious freedoms meant that the organisation of the innumerable sects and denominations was paralleled to the democratic competition of parties within the political sphere. Withdrawn from overt political conflicts, religion provided a base-line of beliefs and manners so that 'by regulating domestic life it regulates the State' (de Tocqueville, 1946, p. 233). Religious organisation was not only homologous with politics, religion provided much of the ritualism and symbolism of the turning-points in American history. In short, Christianity functioned as the unrivalled civil religion of the new republic and 'religious zeal is perpetually stimulated in the United States by the duties of patriotism' (de Tocqueville, 1946, pp. 236-7).

The Tocquevillian thesis that the structural differentiation of American society and its democratic politics were directly matched by religious belief and thought became the basis of most subsequent commentaries on America's civil religion in the sociology of religion. It formed the principal theme of Parsons's view of the evolutionary development of

Christianity towards American denominationalism (Parsons, 1963) [...] However, the *locus classicus* for the whole debate on the civil religion in America remains Will Herberg's *Protestant, Catholic, Jew* (1960), which first appeared in 1955.

In providing an explanation for the 60 per cent increase in church membership between 1926 and 1950, Herberg presented his argument within the context of the differential response of immigrant generations to their own and host cultures. The central concepts for understanding these cultural responses were formulated in terms of self-identification and social location. Emigration to the United States jettisoned the majority of migrants out of traditional village life into a society which was mobile, individualistic and culturally plural. In some respects they had experienced the transition from mechanical to organic solidarity and the loss of a localised *conscience collective*. Although the economic problems of mere survival were dominant issues for the first-generation migrants, there was the additional problem of transplanting and conserving their traditional, ethnic culture in the New World. It was the regressive attempt to establish village and ethnic links within the new community that marked the first stage of Americanisation. Given the paramount problem of communication in a migrant, multilingual society, immigrants inevitably converged into language groups. The migrant church no longer functioned as the focus of village culture, but rather became the main vehicle for the maintenance of language and ethnic culture in a defensive capacity. The church as the principal articulator of 'old country' interests provided the new migrant with familiar institutions of self-identification and social location.

The response of second-generation migrants to host and ethnic cultures was far more ambivalent. The second generation was American-born, yet still migrant and partially assimilated. At home they followed the interests and spoke the language of their immigrant culture; at school and at work, their interests were American and their language English. A number of solutions for this cultural schizophrenia were adopted by these marginal communities. Some sectors of the second-generation communities were able to exploit their marginality by acting as mediators between the host and immigrant communities. The great majority of the second-generation immigrants, however, found their cultural strangeness an obstacle to social mobility and successful assimilation. A necessary condition of social advancement and acceptance was Americanisation. This segment of the second-generation community, therefore, responded to their social marginality by rejecting their ethnic culture and, since the ethnic church was a bastion of immigrant traditional, country culture, this also required a rejection of the religion of their parents.

With the emergence of a third generation, the situation of assimilation and social location was once more fundamentally transformed. The third generation felt American, spoke its language and had no sense of foreignness. Yet they still had an acute problem of self-identification and social location in an impersonal, mobile society. They possessed neither the community and religious links of their grandparents nor the politico-ethnic interests of their fathers. For the third generation, religious identification became an optimal choice, largely because American society expected the immigrant to modify all aspects of his ethnic culture without necessarily abandoning his church. Yet the continuity of religion into the third generation is deceptive. Just as the immigrant was assimilated into society by a process of Americanisation, so religion underwent a similar cultural accommodation. One facet of religious transmutation was that the multifarious sects and denominations became socially defined as Protestant, Catholic or Jewish. There was thus a process of cultural standardisation, since these three labels were regarded as socially and religiously equivalent. The religious definitions were thus regarded not so much as theological as social. The church had become a social community in which people married, raised their children and discovered their leisure pursuits. The three great communities of American life did not represent three institutionalised forms of a basic Judaeo-Christian faith so much as three divisions of the 'American Way of Life'.

The American Way of Life is not an epiphenomenon of Christianity, but a separate and independent religion with its own beliefs, rituals and saints. There is, however, some degree of cultural diffusion between the two religions:

It should be clear that what is designated under the American Way of Life is not the so-called 'common denominator' religion; it is not a synthetic system composed of beliefs to be found in all or in a group of religions. It is an organic structure of ideas, values and beliefs that constitutes a faith common to Americans and genuinely operative in their lives, a faith that markedly influences, and is influenced by the 'official' religions of American society.
(Herberg, 1960, p. 77)

In its political guise, the American Way of Life stands for the Constitution, democracy and individual freedom: on the economic side, it represents *laissez-faire*. Above all, the civic religion espouses individualism, pragmatism and personal activism. In brief, the American Way of Life may be aptly described as a secularised Protestant Ethic:

as a kind of secularised Puritanism, a Puritanism without transcendence, without a sense of sin or judgment.
(Herberg, 1960, p. 81)

The sense of optimism and emphasis on this-worldly activity and discipline in the civil religion can thus be regarded as 'the derivatives of a religious regulation of life' (Weber, 1961, p.313) which had originated in the asceticism of the American sects.

The social dominance of religion in American culture and its salience in the political sphere appear to challenge the assumption which was widely shared by nineteenth-century social scientists that the advance of urban industrial society would necessarily bring about increasing secularisation. As a number of contemporary writers have observed (MacIntyre, 1967), the Herberg thesis does provide a means of reconciling the expectation of increasing secularisation with the facts of public adherence to religious institutions and beliefs in the United States. The theoretical reconciliation takes the form of asserting that in America Christianity has survived industrialisation at the cost of its traditional theological content. The appearance of public support for Christian institutions – baptism, marriage, Sunday school and worship – masks a profound diminution and transformation of the content of religion. The churches come to fill the role of social clubs and communal gatherings for mobile, alienated, urban middle classes (Whyte, 1956); at the national level, Christianity could play an important part in the American stance against atheist communism in the cold war. There is evidence of a trend away from orthodox Christian belief (Stark and Glock, 1968), but this situation is combined with adherence to religious practice and institutions which operate alongside loyalty to the flag, attachment to Independence Day rituals and emotional commitment to such sacred places as the Arlington National Cemetery. The system of beliefs which lies behind these national practices becomes relatively unimportant in relation to the social functions and effects of the quasi-religious rituals of the civil religion. The Christian religion survives in the context of a secular society because it continues to produce that crucial social element without which the pluralistic and conflictual society of North America could not survive.

There have been many criticisms of the Herberg thesis and major objections to the data on which the argument ultimately rests [...] the implication in this debate that American Christianity is a defective, surrogate religion has, however, received its main challenge from Robert Bellah's article 'Civil religion in America' (1970) and, as a result, the whole problem of religion in a Godless society has been kept to the forefront of sociological inquiry into the nature of industrial society [...]

Bellah's argument has been that the American civil religion is separate and distinct from official Christianity, but also that it possesses 'its own seriousness and integrity' (Bellah, 1970). Although there is also an overlap between Christianity and the civil religion, the symbols, beliefs and rituals of the American Way of Life have emerged and evolved as responses to crises and turning-points in American history. These major events were primarily the Revolution, the Civil War and the entry of

America in the twentieth century into global power-politics, especially in Vietnam. The civil religion is also overlaid with the themes of sacrifice, martyrdom and restoration in the deaths of Abraham Lincoln and John F. Kennedy. Its sacred scriptures include the Declaration of Independence, the Constitution and the Gettysburg address. In Bellah's terms, therefore, the civil religion is not just a vague or general veneer which religion has cast over the shoulders of nationalism – it is a religion with content, substance and particularity which provides a moral challenge rather than a comforting sop to national feeling.

Bellah's defence of the validity of civil religion has to be understood alongside his epistemological position, which he developed in an article on 'Christianity and symbolic realism' (1970). Whereas Durkheim had argued that there are no religions which are false, Bellah more strongly asserts against reductionism that: 'religion is a reality *sui generis*. To put it bluntly, religion is true'. (1970, p. 93)

Symbolic realism

Symbolic realism invites us to take religion seriously and, in particular, to recognise the ineradicable importance of symbols and practices in human life. Symbolic realism is thus a contemporary solution to the nineteenth-century catastrophe of the death of God, in which religion was seen to be simultaneously necessary and false. By shifting attention towards symbols and practices as essential to the human condition, Bellah can embrace religious institutions as genuine (as a reality *sui generis*) without faltering intellectually over the stumbling-block of religious truth-claims. We might thus summarise Bellah's perspective under the slogan: God is dead; long live religion!

On closer inspection, it turns out that symbolic realism fails to answer the perennial problem of reason in relation to revelation; it fails to tell us what religious symbols symbolise and therefore avoids the issue of who or what it is that forms the subject of religious practice. For the symbolic realist, it is the fact of worship itself, the practice of religion, which constitutes religious phenomena in spite of the absence of theistic beliefs. The notion that *homo religiosus* is one who takes practices rather than beliefs seriously is provided by Peter Berger's assertion: 'It is in worship that the prototypical gesture of religion is realized again and again.' (Berger, 1969, p. 109).

In this context, it is useful to make a distinction between two functions of symbolism. Religious symbols may embody or condense moods, feelings and values, but symbols may also refer to specific places, persons or events in history. The sign of the Cross in Christianity condenses moods of sacrifice and passion, but it also refers to the specific crucifixion of Jesus of Nazareth. The implication of the arguments of sociologists like Bellah and Berger is that religious symbols can be regarded as almost exclusively condensational rather than referential. By treating Christianity and the civil religion as primarily sets of condensational symbols, symbolic realism offers a method of avoiding the fact that at least traditionally Christians have understood their own symbolism as both expressions of mood and summaries of religious and historical facts. By directing attention away from the truth-claims of religion as to the eternal significance of historical events, symbolic realism conjoins rational man with religious society.

An appreciation of the social value of religion and its therapeutic importance for the individual brings the rational actor to opt for religious practice without commitment to the truth or falsity of religious beliefs. Symbolic realism, which offers a defence of Christian commitment, may paradoxically turn out to be a powerful restatement of American secularity. The symbolist argument against reductionism may be a natural counterpart to the American emphasis on religious practice as essentially beneficial, with or without the traditional beliefs which ultimately explain those practices. It has been frequently argued that Americans believe in religious practice rather than in traditional Christian orthodoxy: 'The faith is not in God but in faith: we worship not God but our own worshipping' (Herberg, 1960, p.84). This commitment is an ironic reformulation of Durkheim's reductionism in which the object of religious symbols and practice was society itself. Furthermore, the notion that religion is 'a good thing' has become basic to American popular piety, which has slowly come adrift from the traditional Christian bases of belief and practice. Symbolic realism can operate as a justification for religion *per se*, regardless of content, in the same way that President Eisenhower's much-quoted observation:

Our government makes no sense unless it is founded in a deeply felt religious faith, and I don't care what it is

served as a legitimation for theological indifference to the cognitive content of religion. Practice makes perfect, even where the beliefs themselves may be rather remote or dubious. The argument here is that Bellah's symbolic realism is ironically the intellectual counterpart to the situation where Protestant, Catholic and Jew become equivalent labels, not for religious communities, but of social identification with the American polity.

Public rituals

In British sociology and anthropology, similar theoretical developments were taking place in contemporary debates over the importance of collective rituals in public life. For example, in the article by Shils and Young (1953) on 'The meaning of the coronation', it was argued that the coronation affirmed the nation's moral values; the ceremony was a 'national communion' which united British society around the symbols and rituals of monarchy. The national communion did, of course, assume the successful integration of the British working class within the political system. Similar arguments were advanced in favour of the investiture of the Prince of Wales (Blumler *et al.*, 1971), which was seen as an act of strengthening and legitimating family solidarity and national awareness. In a more comprehensive fashion, it has been suggested that industrial society is pulled together by a diverse ensemble of secular rituals such as the football cup final, cricket test matches, Guy Fawkes' Night and miners' gala parades (Bocock, 1974).

Although Durkheim's analysis of totemic practices in simple societies was an impressive contribution to our knowledge of the social mechanisms of religious practice, belief and experience, it is difficult to see how the analysis of religion as social cement can be fully satisfactory with respect to modern society. Even in its amended form as a 'civil religion', the notion of a sacred canopy embracing contemporary society is not wholly convincing. In the absence of conventional, overtly religious beliefs common to all sections of society, sociologists have focused on rituals, ceremonies and national practices as the binding force in industrial society. One problem with these Durkheimian perspectives on rituals as elements of social integration is that the vagueness of the concept 'ritual' permits a facile transition from the religious to the secular plane.

The concept of 'ritual' as any regular, repetitive, standardised activity of a non-utilitarian character is thus broad enough to embrace the most diverse collection of activities from changing the guard at Buckingham Palace to Memorial Day, from the opening of Parliament to saluting the flag. There is, in principle, no method of restricting the list of rituals which could count as part of the civil religion; unfortunately the diversity of the examples does not appear to carry any theoretical embarrassment for advocates of the efficacy of civil religions. Given the vagueness of the concept, it would indeed be difficult to know what to exclude (Goody, 1977).

The civil-religion argument does suffer from a common methodological difficulty which it shares with all arguments relating to the notion of a dominant culture. It equates social prevalence with cultural dominance, confusing frequency with social effects. A strong thesis about a dominant culture or civil religion would have to show that the beliefs and practices in question played a necessary part in the maintenance and continuity of a social system. It cannot be assumed that beliefs and practices which are publicly available necessarily have significant effects in the upkeep of crucial social processes and social arrangements. Most civil-religion arguments or arguments concerning nationalism are weak theories which point to the presence of certain allegedly common practices and suggest that these have integrative consequences. With respect to such ceremonies as the Royal Wedding, Independence Day celebrations or the coronation, one can show that these have social effects in the trivial sense that people are involved in them at various levels, but one has to go further to demonstrate that these rituals have specific effects on the stability of capitalist society. From the existence of communal rituals, one cannot make the assumption that these are functionally necessary or that they perform the functions ascribed to them. On existing evidence, the civil religion is at best loosely and only periodically connected with the re-activation of a problematic *conscience collective*, but the precise connection between these common sentiments and the structural arrangements of industrial society is inadequately specified.

Nationalism and the 'conscience collective'

The sociological treatment of civil religions from Durkheim onwards provides ample illustration of the problems that also attend those theories which attempt to discover in national sentiment a parallel to religious enthusiasm. Both Marxists and sociologists have seen nationalism as a form of *conscience collective* over-riding the divisions of capitalist society, an ideology masking the naked conflicts of economic interest (Bottomore, 1979). Despite the apparent prevalence of nationalist beliefs in the political life of capitalist societies, the exact nature of the link between nationalism and capitalism has remained a matter of dispute.

There exist a number of general arguments about the significance of the nation-state and nationalist ideology in the development of capitalist economies (Poggi, 1978) and about the role of nationalist movements as responses to imperialism (Smith, 1971). The nationalist sentiment which concerned Durkheim does, however, often appear to be a short-term consequence of rather specific, historically contingent events; it is often difficult to produce any important general statements about the importance of nationalist rituals and emotions with respect to the necessary conditions of an industrial society. Disenchantment and disillusion with the First World War as marked in the poetry of the period, for example, would have to be set alongside the initial enthusiasm of patriotic commitment.

There is thus ample room for methodological dispute, but there are equally important theoretical issues at stake. The debates about the civil religion, the Herberg thesis, the *conscience collective* and so forth are ultimately directed at a basic issue in social philosophy, namely, the relationship between consent and coercion, consensus and conflict in social life. Parsonian sociology and American structural functionalism have, in various ways, been criticised for exaggerating both the extent and importance of value consensus in society (Dahrendorf, 1968). However, Marxist theories of capitalist society are confronted by the mirror-image problem of explaining the absence of revolutionary, proletarian politics in the core regions of the western world. The presence of nationalist beliefs and sentiments among the working class is often thought, at least in part, to explain this peculiar state of affairs. There is an assumed parallel between the religious, particularly millenarian, movements of the feudal Middle Ages and the irrational upsurges of fascism and nationalism in the twentieth century (Cohen, 1957).

The issue of nationalism as a surrogate religion is instructive in this context. Nationalism may appear to fulfil functions of social integration in certain crisis periods, such as that which obtained in France between the Franco-Prussian War and the end of the First World War, but nationalism may also be socially divisive within an ethnically or culturally diverse political collectivity. For example, European politics in the 1970s were dominated by political threats to the unity of centralised nation-states under the impact of regional and separatist movements. Nationalist and cultural politics in Ireland, Wales, Scotland, Brittany and the Basque regions threatened to cripple conventional politics (Nairn, 1975). Within a longer time-scale, British politics have always been fragmented along religio-nationalist lines, separating the Catholic and Celtic fringe from the Protestant centre (Hechter, 1975). When nationalist sentiment serves to define a political boundary against an external enemy in a war situation, it may have the intra-social effects noted by Durkheim; but when nationalist feeling sets off a reactive wave of separatist politics within an existing political system, then nationalism is socially corrosive. Since nationalist movements are often closely related to religious differences, as in Scotland or Canada, religion can have a role in consolidating social and economic divisions. Religious rituals may not so much preserve the social fabric as embody its internal conflicts (Lukes, 1975).

Conclusion

There are three major objections to be raised against the assumption that religion – either in the form of a civil religion or in an amalgamation with nationalism – can act as the social cement of modern society in the same way that it supposedly bound traditional societies together. First, it does not provide a genuinely satisfactory solution to the problem of class and class conflict in industrial society. The whole Durkheimian tradition in the sociology of religion can be criticised because it:

nowhere confronts the possibility that religious beliefs are ideologies, which help legitimate the domination of some groups over others.
(Giddens, 1978, pp. 103–4)

The empirical evidence points to significant religious differences between social classes in terms of religious affiliation, style and practice. Denominational differences follow the fractures within the national class structure and at the local level provide the cultural contour of class politics within the city.

Secondly, as with any theory of common culture, there is a tendency for sociologists to neglect alternative conditions of social cohesion, as they exaggerate the effects of religious decline on social stability. Societies are held together not simply or even primarily by common beliefs and ritual practices, but by a multitude of 'material' factors – force, economic coercion, economic dependency, legal compulsion, economic scarcity, habituation and the exigencies of everyday life. Societies can continue to operate with relatively high levels of conflict, disaffection and indifference to norms in combination with pragmatic acceptance of values. The social cement is constantly eroded and swept away by these circumstances without any ultimate descent into *anomy* and social chaos.

Finally, although sociologists of religion have emphasised the social functions of religious and secular practices – coronations, national ceremonies, historic festivals – in modern society, they have failed to pay attention to that range of disciplinary practices of which Michel Foucault, Nicos Poulantzas and Louis Althusser have written so eloquently.

References

Bellah, R. (1970) 'Civil religion in America' in *Beyond Belief*, New York and London, Harper and Row.
Berger, P. L. (1969) *The Social Reality of Religion*, Faber and Faber, London.
Blumler, J. G., Brown, J., Ewbank, A. J. and Nossiter, T. (1971), 'Attitudes to the monarchy: their structure and development during a ceremonial occasion', *Political Studies*, Vol. 19, No. 2, pp. 149–71.

Bocock, R. (1974) *Ritual in Industrial Society: A Sociological Analysis of Ritualism in Modern England*, London, George Allen and Unwin.

Bottomore, T. (1979) *Political Sociology*, London, Hutchinson.

Cohen, W. (1957) *The Pursuit of the Millennium*, London, Mercury Books, Heinemann.

Dahrendorf, R. (1968) 'Out of Utopia', in R. Dahrendorf, *Essays in the Theory of Society*, London, pp. 107–28.

Giddens, A. (1978), *Durkheim*, London, Fontana, Collins.

Goody, J. (1977) 'Against "ritual" – loosely structured thoughts on a loosely defined topic', in S. F. Moore and B. G. Myerhoff (eds.), *Secular Ritual*, Amsterdam, Van Goreum, pp. 25–35.

Hechter, M. (1975) *Internal Colonialism, the Celtic Fringe in British National Development 1536–1966*, London, Routledge and Kegan Paul.

Herberg, W. (1960) *Protestant, Catholic, Jew*, New York, Anchor Books.

Lukes, S. (1975) 'Political ritual and social integration', *Sociology*, Vol. 9, No. 2, pp. 289–308.

MacIntyre, A. (1967) *Secularization and Moral Change*, Oxford University Press.

Nairn, T. (1975) 'Old nationalism and new nationalism', in G. Brown (ed.) *The Red Paper on Scotland*, Edinburgh, pp. 22–57.

Parsons, T. (1963), 'Christianity and modern industrial society', in E. A. Tiryakian (ed.), *Sociological Theory, Values and Social Cultural Change, Essays in Honour of Pitrim Sorokin*, New York, The Free Press, pp. 33–70.

Poggi, G. (1978), *The Development of the Modern State, a Sociological Introduction*, London, Hutchinson Educational.

Shils, E. and Young, M. (1953) 'The meaning of the coronation', *Sociological Review*, Vol. 1, pp. 63–82.

Smith, A. D. (1971) *Theories of Nationalism*, London, Duckworth.

Stark, R. and Glock, C. Y. (1968) *American Piety, the Nature of Religious Commitment*, Berkeley and Los Angeles, University of California Press.

Weber, M. (1961) From *Max Weber, Essays in Sociology*, edited by H. Gerth and C. Wright Mills, London, Routledge.

Whyte, W. H. (1956), *The Organization Man*, New York, Touchstone Books.

Currents and counter-currents

From *Sex, Politics and Society* by J. Weeks, 1981. Reproduced by permission of the publishers, Longman Group Ltd.

The limits of permissiveness

At this stage we need to step back, to reflect on the achievements and failures of this 'liberal hour'. For in its contradictory course it revealed all the strengths and weaknesses of the liberal approach to sexuality. On its positive side were a series of important gains. Reform was achieved, through the pragmatic manoeuvres of the Parliamentary liberals and their extra-Parliamentary auxiliaries. There was an important shift towards privatisation of decision making, towards a legal acceptance of moral pluralism. But its weaknesses flowed from its strengths. Reforms were gained through a programme of necessary compromises; frequently they were piecemeal and often unsatisfactory in nature and implied no positive endorsement of radically different moral stances. Indeed, as Professor Richards has written, 'A feature of the Parliamentary debates on this subject is that the fundamental moral issue was consistently avoided.'[1] As a result they neither satisfied radicals nor appeased moral conservatives, and not surprisingly, morality became more than ever a battleground in the succeeding decade. Sexual liberals did not retreat from the front; on the contrary they produced an important series of documents advocating further reform – particularly on the 'age of consent' for women and male homosexuals, and on obscenity and film censorship.[2] But increasingly as the 1960s faded into oblivion and the harsher 1970s blew their cold winds, liberals lost their purchase on parliamentary reformers – and remember, the parliamentary moment is always the decisive one for the liberal approach to reform – and the initiative passed to more radical forces, relying to a much greater degree on the principles of self-help and popular mobilisation. On the left, the revival of the women's movement and the emergence of a gay liberation movement fundamentally challenged some of the sexual assumptions that were common to both liberalism and moral traditionalism; while on the right, the 1960s and

1970s saw a revival of an evangelical moralism, fired by an apprehension of basic changes, but made despairing by the legislative reforms. An anxious correspondent of Mary Whitehouse noted of the 1967 reforms: 'The last session of Parliament has subjected us to the progressive moral disarmament of the nation BY LAW and there's worse to come.'[3] There was not – but the fear was real enough. The contradictory effects of some of the reforms provided fuel enough to the controversy, as a brief examination of three major reforms will underline: on divorce, on homosexuality and on abortion.

The 1969 Divorce Reform Act firmly asserted the institutional basis of marriage – its declared aim was to 'buttress the stability of marriage'. But by embracing a second aim – 'to enable the empty shell to be destroyed' – it effectively dismantled the apparatus of moral blame which attached to the concept of a 'matrimonial offence'. Once the partners had agreed that a marriage had broken down, a divorce was generally assured. The institutional framework of permanent monogamy was to that extent undermined. In a climate where the family appeared to be weakening as a unit as a result of long-term changes, economic and social, the rising divorce figures were inevitably seen by radicals as a sign of the family's instability and by conservatives as a sign of its breakdown. Both views were probably premature, though the increase in resort to divorce was dramatic. In 1911 the proportion of married who divorced was 0.2 per cent; by the mid-1950s it was 7 per cent; by the early 1970s it was 10 per cent and rising. Between 1970 and 1979 the divorce rate trebled for those under 25, and doubled for those over 25. In Britain, at the end of the 1970s, there was one divorce for every three marriages.[4] Marriage was obviously no longer the sacred and permanent bond it was intended to be. But simultaneously, marriage remained as popular as ever, and nearly half of those who got divorced remarried within five years.[5] Marriage, or at least coupledom, remained the social norm, though it was an alliance built increasingly along the lines of sexual attraction and emotional compatibility rather than an open-ended commitment for life.[6]

The tensions within the dominant ideology – between compulsory monogamy and pleasure, between enhanced individualism and familial responsibility – were thus transforming the nineteenth-century ideal. But what they implied for the future remained unclear. What they did not imply, however, was any collapse of the heterosexual norm. Reforms in other areas of sexual life were contained within this dominance, as the development of attitudes to homosexuality revealed. The Sexual Offences Act which liberalised the law on male homosexuality was never intended as a clarion call to sexual liberation. As Lord Arran, who piloted reform through the House of Lords, put it, 'I ask those who have, as it were, been in bondage and for whom the prison doors are now open to show their thanks by comporting themselves quietly and with dignity.'[7] That appeal to discretion was echoed among many other erstwhile reformers, alarmed at what they saw as a rush towards openness. But even more than this cold shower, the new law itself imposed a series of drastic limitations. In the first place, homosexuality was never fully legalised, as a series of court decisions underlined. In June 1972 the House of Lords upheld the verdict against *IT* (*International Times*), which declared it unlawful to publish contact advertisements in which homosexuals indicated their wish to meet others. Their lordships opined that the 1967 Act 'merely exempted from criminal penalties' but did not make it 'lawful in the full sense'.[8] This had important effects in the decisions of the police and the courts, but it was compounded by a second factor deriving from the private acts/public decency dichotomy of moral reformism. For one effect of this was to define more clearly which activities (largely in the sphere of 'public decency', such as importuning in public lavatories and cruising grounds) still remained offences, and the police in effect put this clarification into practice. Between 1967 and 1976 the recorded incidence of indecency between males doubled, the number of prosecutions trebled and the number of convictions quadrupled.[9] The prosecutions caused less of a stir and perhaps had a less drastic impact on most individual's lives, as the stigma against homosexuality gradually changed;[10] but the controlling effect of the law accentuated in certain areas, particularly as some crusading police chiefs sought to increase the 'privatisation' and moral 'segregation' of homosexuals.[11] But by an inevitable reflex, the inadequacy of the law reform, and the continuing moral oppression, in turn provided some of the preconditions for the birth of the gay liberation movement, concerned not with apologetics or liberal tolerance but with questioning the hegemony of the heterosexual norm. Neither effect could have been intended by the reformers of the 1960s.

Similar contradictory results emerged from the Abortion Act, which remained a much more controversial reform than any other. The number of recorded abortions went up significantly after 1968, rising from 35,000 per annum to 141,000 in 1975; or moving from a rate of 4 per 100 live births in 1968 to 17.6 in 1975.[12] By 1980 over a million legal abortions had been carried out. Several factors accounted for this rise, the major one being the move from 'backstreet abortions' to ones provided legally in the Health Service. But another important factor was a probable increase in the resort to abortion, as publicity over it increased, as techniques improved, and as there was a growing acceptance by women of abortion as an adjunct to birth control when that failed. In other words, many women were seizing the opportunity provided by the 1967 Act to deliberately control their own fertility. It was this area of 'choice' which disturbed some former supporters of reform, and during the 1970s they combined with the traditionalist opponents of reform to try to amend the law in a more restrictive manner. There was abundant evidence that the so-called 'abuse' of the law was minimal,[13] and the actual elements of 'abortion on demand' in the 1967 Act were limited, dependent as they were on the attitude of the medical profession. But by 1980 it was possible almost to succeed in amending the law drastically in a restrictive manner, against a substantial mass of medical and popular opinion.[14] What is striking about this is that though the resolution necessarily came in Parliament, the battle had been in large part fought out through propaganda and mass mobilisation on the terrain of public opinion. The Society for the Protection of the Unborn Child (SPUC) and similar bodies had been able to mobilise considerable conservative, cross-class support from the late 1960s, building largely on the organisational strength of the Roman Catholic and evangelical churches. In response, the reforming initiative passed from the Abortion Law Reform Society to the more militant groupings within the Women's Movement, led by the National Abortion Campaign, which was able to mobilise mass feminist, libertarian and socialist support (culminating in a massive march sponsored by the Trades Union Congress in October 1979) on a slogan of 'A Woman's Right to Choose'. In arguing the positive merits of abortion, as a necessary aspect of a woman's freedom to control her own body, the terms of the debate were being altered. This was only one aspect of an important shift in the debates on sexuality; the liberal moment was passing.

If we seek a single moment when the tide changed, we need look no further than 1968. Towards the end of that year the Wootton Report on Drug Dependency was published, advocating a more liberal attitude towards 'soft' drugs.[15] The report was a classic exposition of liberal reformist principles, which Baroness Wootton had long advocated, and relied on the distinction between morality and law which was central to the 1960s reforms. Its proposals were modest. But the social and political climate had changed drastically. Symbolically, Roy Jenkins had left the Home Office, to preside over the massive defensive actions to shore up the British economy. He was replaced by James Callaghan, the embodiment of labourist traditionalism. He rejected the Wootton Report; and in so doing proclaimed that he was pleased to have contributed to 'a halt in the advancing tide of so called permissiveness'.[16]

But this was only one response to the more elusive undercurrents of social life which were undermining the old liberal, social-democratic consensus. For 1968 was the year of revolt and reaction through the world, from the United States to Czechoslovakia, from Tokyo to Paris. And the May Events in Paris above all demonstrated the fragility of the post-war belief in effortless progress and prosperity, revealing sharply the contradictions at the very heart of modernised capitalism, as one of its major products – 'youth' – began to reject its values. The student revolt, and the spark it provided for the French general strike, suggested for the first time since the war that the old order could be overturned, that 'anything was possible'.[17] The revolt was short-lived; the immediate effect a deeper political conservatism. But the intellectual and moral ferment unlocked by the Paris events, and its echoes throughout the world, posed fresh questions of both left and right. The deeply unsettling problems left unresolved in 1968 set the agenda for social and moral debates in the ensuing decade: the choice seemed to be between a radical rupture or a deepening conservatism and a retreat to more authoritarian positions. As Hall *et al.* have put it, 'The general social and political polarisation which characterises the next decade began from this point.'[18]

The effects, as ever, were more muted and fragmented in Britain than elsewhere, whether in terms of student radicalism or political conservatism. But as the Callaghan position indicates, it was still enough of a divide to take it as a symbolic point. For the eddies of the great events abroad deeply affected both the British counter-culture and the respectable, and one fed on the other.

The new moralism

Let us take, for a start, the 'respectable'. The student revolts, the first mass open-air pop concert, the continuing economic crisis, the panic over black immigration and the massive anti-Vietnam War demonstrations in Grosvenor Square: all apparently random events, but all connected in 1968 as signs of breakdown or transformation in the old order. What we can see, in response, from the late 1960s, is a growing sense of social crisis, which demanded general solutions. The series of moral panics over morality and manners which punctuate the 1950s and 1960s were giving way to a generalised social panic, and in this new climate, moral authoritarianism again came to the centre of the stage.[19]

Its archetypal exponent was a deeply religious, respectably middle-class lady, a former teacher whose ire had been stirred by the social changes of the 1950s and 1960s, and in particular their effects on children, and who from being a hesitant and reluctant campaigner in 1963 had by the late 1970s blossomed into an international figure, listened to by statesmen, commanding instant media attention, the model of a moral entrepreneur – Mrs Mary Whitehouse.[20] It will not do simply to personalise Mrs Whitehouse's campaigns. Far from being a crank, a latter day Mrs Grundy, she commanded wide, often cross-class support. And while she herself was rooted in a tradition of anticommunist Moral Re-armament, she was supported in her campaigns by old Roman Catholic social

democrats like Lord Longford and by evangelical and Lawrentian human-
ists like David Holbrook, as well as by the more obviously disorientated
'respectable' middle class. But despite all provisos there was something
deeply representative about Mrs Whitehouse and the campaigns she
fostered. For in her profound religious conviction, in her desire for a new
Christian-based moral order, in her yearning for a past that had gone (and
perhaps had never been), in her sense of the damaging penetration of the
privacy of the home and sacredness of sex by modern media, with its
explicitness, agnosticism and ever-absorbing nature, she evoked that
sense of collapse that underlay the move to the right in the 1970s, but
had its origins in the changes of the 1950s and early 1960s. 'Significant
social groups in society felt abandoned by the scramble of some for the
affluent "progressive" middle ground and threatened by rising materialism below; amidst the "never had it so good society", they yearned for
a firmer moral purpose. They provided the backbone for the entrepreneurs
of moral indignation.'[21] A general sense of anxiety, generated by real
(though often exaggerated) changes tended to find expression in resistance
to changes which were actually marginal to the main thrust of social
development, in morals and style. So Mrs Whitehouse's step in 1963,
with one friend, and while still a teacher, to 'do something' about television explicitness, which led to the establishment of the Clean Up TV
Campaign, immediately evoked a surprising but representative mass
response. By the turn of the decade Mrs Whitehouse and the National
Viewers and Listeners' Association (NVALA, successor to CUTVC) had
become an influential social force, precisely because they expressed
inchoate but basic fears.

Some attempt has been made by sociologists to explain the effectivity
of the campaign (and similar ones with which it was closely associated,
such as the evangelical Festival of Light) in terms of status loss amongst
the threatened groups of the population. As Roy Wallis has put it, 'Economic and social changes have eroded the supports for formerly dominant
values borne by a class of individualistic entrepreneurs ... some social
groups have proven resistant to new norms and values and their members are therefore mobilisable in the defence of the earlier standards of
morality to which they adhere.'[22]

The problem with this approach is the rather mechanistic relationship
it suggests between class position and moral values. It would no doubt
be easy for an empiricist sociologist, exploring the membership of
NVALA, to prove that it neither consisted entirely of threatened petit
bourgeois, nor had any consistent class goals. As Tracey and Morrison
have pointed out, a much more unifying factor for the new moral crusade
was its opposition to the forms that 'secularisation' had taken and the
general religious basis of its ideology.[23] What was sought after was a

moral regeneration as a response to perceived moral decline and lack of moral leadership. But this in turn cannot be divorced from wider social and political currents. For just as the moral reforms of the 1960s were closely associated with a particular political approach, so the moral conservatism represented by Mrs Whitehouse, while eschewing overt political commitment, was fully complicit with a political approach which by the end of the 1970s had achieved a precarious hegemony. Sir Keith Joseph, representing the new conservatism, could, without any sense of incongruity, advise his supporters to 'take inspiration from that remarkable woman',[24] though in practice the new economic conservatism remained separate from moral conservatism (restrictions on abortion were not endorsed by the 1979 Conservative government). Nevertheless, the new moralism was indeed part of a general reaction against the social democratic ('Butskellite') consensus that had dominated the post-war world. As its underpinnings in post-war prosperity were undermined, and with a developing reaction to the 'socialism' and 'welfarism' that were seen as the roots of social decay, the restoration of moral standards and the stability of the family became one of the catchwords of the conservative repertoire, alongside law and order, and self-help. The religious absolutism of Mrs Whitehouse and her supporters was merely one aspect of that wider social move. Its social bases *were* often the disgruntled middle class, the threatened professional, the small business ethos represented by Mrs Margaret Thatcher. But in the symbols it raised and the anxieties it articulated it was able to extend beyond to other, and perhaps unlikely, social supports.

For the liberal, throughout the twentieth century, sex has been seen, in the phrase endorsed by Havelock Ellis (almost the patron saint of 1960s reform) as the last refuge of individuality, the core of private life, the focus of social being. But just as, for the liberal, it was this area of life that most needed to be freed from religious constraints, for the moral conservative it was this area of privacy that had been most invaded, and desecrated by the post-war world. Sexual change therefore became the symbol of all the changes that had destroyed the stability of the pre-war moral order. As Mr Ernest Whitehouse (Mary's husband) put it, 'that has been the area in which the biggest breakdown in moral standards has occurred'.[25]

For Mary Whitehouse, as she said in a submission to the Annan Committee on Broadcasting, 'The essence of sex is that it is a private personal experience between two people'. She and her supporters were therefore gravely offended by the attempt to treat sex as something secular. 'To accept the biological imperative, to acknowledge the importance within human behaviour of gratification, to indulge in practices long forbidden, is to rid sex of its sacred connotations.'[26] Sex was clearly intended to be heterosexual and monogamous, the cement of marriage, not the focus for hedonism. And the shrine embodying this holy essence was the family. The strongest theme of the conservative moral ideology was now, as it had been for two hundred years, its familialism. It was the family that had been most undermined by the secularisation and demystification of sex. From this central commitment to the centrality and holiness of the family all the common concerns of the moral conservatives really flowed: with television, which penetrated the heart of this domestic setting, worming in its secular noises and visions; with pornography, making explicit and profane what should be privatised and sacred; and with blasphemy, which took in vain the name of the Father and Son, who gave meaning to the moral world, embodied in the family unit. The image and the word: these were the major foci for ardent moral endeavour. The elevation of Sir Hugh Greene, Director General of the BBC from 1960, to the pinnacle of the moralists' demonology (above even South Bank theologians and trendy sociologists) was no accident, for he embodied extremely well, and at its sharpest, the break with the Reithian moral principles that had guided British broadcasting – and indeed British life. As Director General of the BBC in 1948, Sir William Haley (later editor of The Times, itself equally moral) had affirmed the BBC's commitment to a Christian ethic. Greene, on the other hand, explicitly wanted to encourage, as he put it, the variety of British life, all that was new and adventurous – to express its pluralism of values. For his pains he, more than anyone else, was blamed by Mrs Whitehouse for the decline of standards and the insidious weakening of morality.[27] Herein we see the epitome of the conspiracy theory of moral decay. It was not a result of social change but of the infiltration of godlessness that had entered into the heart of the body politic. If there is one characteristic that unifies the new conservatism it is the search for a single causative factor that would account for decay. It could be found in liberalism, permissiveness, social-ism, spies within, or blacks. Mrs Whitehouse in addition found at least one seed of decay in the liberal figure of Sir Hugh Carleton Greene.

If broadcasting corrupted, pornography represented the final desecra-tion and commercialisation of sex. Pornography (which had become more openly sold and explicit in the 1960s) became for the moralists of the 1960s and 1970s what prostitution had been for the social puritans of the 1880s and 1890s: a manifestation of decay,[28] a canker at the heart of respectability. But now the disease was terminal, unless a return to firm moral standards was orchestrated. For Mrs Whitehouse and most of her co-thinkers it was only religion which could provide the source for this renewed moral inspiration. Hence the growing concern with blasphemy. The most spectacular achievement of Mrs Whitehouse during the 1970s was the successful revival of the archaic blasphemy laws, which had long been thought to be in decent desuetude, in the case brought against *Gay News*. The publication by *Gay News* of a poem, 'The Love that dares to speak its name', in which a centurion expressed his homosexual fantasies about the crucified Christ, brought together all her major concerns, and determined her to make a once-and-for-all stand. For the lines of the poem were, in the words of Tracey and Morrison, 'not just offensive but constituted within themselves a radically different set of values and perspectives to those which the traditional Christian would accept as legitimate.'[29] Homosexuality was a potent symbol of this. Mrs Whitehouse might claim, as she did, that she loved the sinner while hating the sin, but the public and unashamed articulation of a homosexual consciousness perhaps as much as anything reflected the changes that had taken place. The success of her prosecution polarised opinion. For the liberal and radical it was a triumph of religious authoritarianism. For the conservative it was a victory for faith, a significant gain for the sanctity of Christian religion; and perhaps a protection that might be extended to all religions.

Though there is a consistency in the vision of the moralist as represented by Mrs Whitehouse, there is nevertheless a significant shift in tactics during the course of the 1960s which underlines the wider changes we have noted. Although there were various cross-currents, the purity organisations generally advocated a moral revival rather than a simple imposition of moral standards. NVALA as such rejected attempts to endorse a widespread moral censorship; what was necessary was a restored sense of 'responsibility'. The early emphasis was therefore on persuasion, especially of those in positions of power in broadcasting, to improve 'standards', particularly by removing 'corrupting influences'. Giving force to this attempt was a belief that public opinion was fundamentally behind the moralists. Over and over again the campaigners had recourse to the supposed weight of public support, as expressed in letters and petitions, as if the weight of signatures itself could move mountains. This populism reached its climax in 1972 with the launching of a Nationwide Petition for Public Decency following the quashing of the conviction against *Oz* magazine. There was a continuing appeal to the inarticulate to weigh in behind the moralists, to give them legitimacy. Inevitably this populism went with a sense of moral leadership. 'All history has been shaped by a tiny minority. The "misty millions" go where they are led.'[30]

But increasingly by the early 1970s, as the weight of the pen failed to move the establishment sufficiently, Mrs Whitehouse and her colleagues had recourse to the law – first, in the use of existing law, by the bringing of private prosecutions for obscenity (and blasphemy); second, by actually pressing for changes in the law. In the early 1970s there was a spate of prosecutions for obscenity, in many of which Mrs Whitehouse or her co-thinkers intervened; against *The Little Red Schoolbook*; against the School Kids' edition of *Oz* magazine; against the *International Times* for its contact advertisements, against the Swedish film, 'More About the Language of Love' and others, reversing the general official drift of the 1960s against prosecution. Not all were successful; the release of the *Oz* editors led to the launching of the National Petition. But it represented a new pursuit of the obscene through legal harassment, one sharpened by the emergence of well-placed police chiefs committed to evangelism and moral purity, as well as more traditional areas of 'law and order' within their purview; James Anderton of Manchester became the most representative figure of this type, but he was not alone.

This moral endeavour was supplemented as the 1970s wore on by ardent attempts in Parliament to change the law in a more restrictive fashion. The abortion law suffered a series of onslaughts, as we know. Less significant but equally indicative were the efforts to promote an Indecent Display Bill, which would have limited the opportunities of shops to display any dubious published wares; and the panic passing of a Protection of Children Bill in 1978 which by seeking to control the use of children in pornography looked fair set to cause more problems than it resolved, because of its loose formulation and adoption of moralistic rather than utilitarian criteria.[31]

It was quite apparent that the morality campaigners tapped a vein of real unease, and the search for a new moral absolutism became the more ardent as the 1970s faded into the 1980s. Nor was this a localised phenomenon. Within the Christian world it was widely noted that Pope John Paul II was seeking to give a firmer moral leadership than his predecessors had found possible, a leadership based on very traditional standards with regard to birth control, abortion, marriage, divorce and homosexuality. While in the world of Islam a new fundamentalism burst over Iran and other nations, challenging the bitter fruits of inadequate 'modernisation' in the name of received truths – truths which led to the stoning or execution of adulterers and sodomites. In their search for moral revival, the British purity organisations were on a less fundamentalist and extreme plain. But many professed to see in Mrs Whitehouse and her colleagues a more domesticated but no less dangerous breed of *ayatollahs*. She and her co-thinkers had demarcated an important divide [...]

By the 1980s the most striking feature is the absence of an agreed moral framework.[33] On the most basic level individuals cleaved to fundamental values, of love, honesty, faithfulness. But what these values meant in the real social world was far from clear. Did adherence to these values mean, for instance, that one had to adhere to the traditional values of family life? Or could they be realised in less formal, less binding, even less monogamous, frameworks? Did the new emphasis on sexual pleasure involve a commercialisation of sex, as the moralist believed? Or did it imply a healthy demystification of the sacredness of sex? Was sex being debased and trivialised, or was it being freed from the shackles of tradition and prejudice? For the historian the very posing of the questions is of major significance. It implies above all that the importance given to sexuality, and the individual and social meanings constructed from this process, are not eternal givens, are not simple products of objective forces outside human control, but are products of human endeavour in the context of given historical circumstances. It is this which in the end explains the great changes that have taken place in sexual definitions over the past two hundred years. It is this which will account for the changes that will surely take place in the future.

Notes

1 Peter G. Richards, *Parliament and Conscience*, p. 82.

2 See for example: Sexual Law Reform Society, *Report of Working Party on the Law in Relation to Sexual Behaviour*, duplicated 1974; Policy Advisory Committee on Sexual Offences, *Working Paper on the Age of Consent in Relation to Sexual Offences*, HMSO, London, 1979; Joint Working Party on Pregnant School-girls and Schoolgirl Mothers, *Pregnant at School*, National Council for One Parent Families, London, 1979. All these documents were concerned with the age of consent or minimum age for sexual activity; the first and third advocating a reduction of the 'age of consent' to 14, for homosexuals and females. The second was less liberal, suggesting, as a logical continuation of Wolfenden, a minimum age of 18, with a minority recommendation of 16. (It is worth noting that no male member of the Policy Advisory Committee signed the minority report.)

3 Tracey and Morrison, *Whitehouse*, p. 67.

4 Ryder and Silver, *Modern English Society*, p. 253; Office of Population Censuses and Surveys figures; *Guardian*, 19 December 1979; 24 September 1979.

5 Which is not to say that signs of strain were not apparent. Between 1971 and 1976 the proportion of one-parent families rose from 8 to 11 per cent.

6 In some countries the logic of the development led to a decrease of legal marriage. In Sweden and Denmark during the 1970s the marriage rate halved, and cohabitation became common. One estimate suggested that only about 50 per cent of couples under the age of 30 who were living together were married. So between 65 and 75 per cent of all children born technically outside wedlock were born into marriage-like situations. Marriage might be declining but the ideal of the nuclear family was not. *New Society*, 6 December 1979. See also Jan Trost, 'The Choice not to Marry', in Marie Corbin (ed.), *The Couple*.

7 Quoted in Hyde, *The Other Love*, p. 303. For further details of the general exhortations to discretion see Weeks, *Coming Out*, pp. 176ff.

8 15 June 1972.

9 See Roy Walmsley and Karen White, *Sexual Offences, Consent and Sentencing*, Home Office Research Study No. 54, London, HMSO, 1979, and the commentary on it in *New Society*, 15 November 1979. For this reason many

opposed reducing the age of consent to the new age of majority, 18, because it would only introduce a new threshold. For the working of this logic amongst gay activists in New Zealand, see Lindsay Taylor, 'Gay Politics in New Zealand', *Gay Left*, No. 9, 1979.

10   But see Bob Cant, 'Living with Indecency', *Gay Left*, No. 8, Summer 1979.

11   This was particularly true in Manchester under Chief Constable James Anderton; and also in certain police districts of London, e.g., around Earls Court.

12   See table in Greenwood and Young, *Abortion in Demand*, p. 70.

13   As was made clear in the *Report of the Lane Committee on the Working of the Abortion Act*, Vol. 1, Cmnd 5579; Vol. 2, Cmnd 5579–I; Vol. 3, Cmnd 5579–II, HMSO, London, 1974. The Committee was set up under pressure from backbench MPs.

14   See opinion-poll findings in *The Sunday Times*, 3 Feb. 1980, p. 3, in which only one-third of those questioned thought the law should be tightened up.

15   Advisory Committee on Drug Dependence, *Cannabis*, HMSO, London, 1968. For a discussion of the Report see Jock Young, *The Drug Takers: The Social Meaning of Drug Use*, Paladin, London, 1971.

16   Quoted in Hall *et al.*, *Policing the Crisis*, p. 250.

17   For documents on 1968, see Vladimir Fisera (ed.), *Writing on the Wall: May 1968: A Documentary Anthology*, Allison & Busby, London, 1978.

18   Hall *et al.*, *Policing the Crisis*, p. 242.

19   *Ibid.*, Ch. 8.

20   For Mary Whitehouse, see her own *Who does she think she is?*, New English Library, London, 1972; Tracey and Morrison, *Whitehouse*, which is based on papers and interviews with her and her colleagues in NVALA; and David E. Morrison and Michael Tracey, 'American Theory and British Practice: The Case of Mary Whitehouse and the National Viewers and Listeners Association', in Dhavan and Davies (eds), *Censorship and Obscenity*.

21   Hall *et al.*, *Policing the Crisis*, p. 234.

22   R. Wallis, 'Moral Indignation and the Media: An Analysis of N.V.A.L.A.', *Sociology*, Vol. 10, No. 2, May 1976.

23   In *Whitehouse* and in their article, *op. cit.*

24   Quoted in Hall *et al.*, *Policing the Crisis*, p. 314.

25   Quoted in Tracey and Morrison, *Whitehouse*, p. 177.

26   *Ibid.*, pp. 91, 185.

27   William Haley, *Moral Values in Broadcasting*, Address to the British Council of Churches, 1948; Hugh Greene, 'The Conscience of the Programme Director', Address to the International Catholic Association for Radio and Television, cited in Tracey and Morrison, 'American Theory and British Practice'.

28   The classic statement is *The Longford Report*, 1972; see Tracey and Morrison, *Whitehouse*, p. 181.

29   *Ibid.*, p. 91.

30   *Ibid.*, p. 142. There is a useful summary of the prosecution in *Uncensored: Journal of the Defence of Literature and the Arts Society*, No. 4, Winter 1979/ 1980.

31   The Protection of Children Act (July 1978) was designed, in the words of its preamble, 'to prevent the exploitation of children by making indecent photographs of them; and to penalise the distribution, showing and advertisement of such indecent photographs'.

32   Herbert Marcuse, *One Dimensional Man*, Routledge and Kegan Paul, 1964. On Marcuse, see Paul Robinson, *The Sexual Radicals*; and Martin Jay, *The Dialectical Imagination*. See also Reimut Reiche, *Sexuality and Class Struggle*, New Left Books, London, 1970.

33   For evidence of a general liberalism in public opinion on sexual issues, despite a general drift to the economic right, see David Lipsey, 'Reforms People Want', *New Society*, 4 Oct. 1979. See also the critique of the conflation of moral and economic conservatism by E. Wilson in *New Left Review*, No. 122, July–Aug. 1980, p. 85.

A symbolic mirror of ourselves: civic ritual in mass society

From *Media, Culture and Society*, Vol. 5, Issue 2, 1983. Reproduced by permission of the publishers, Sage Publications Ltd, London.

Introduction

In this paper I shall be concerned with the significance for ritual of its being performed in a mass culture. I take the interaction between the actual events in the ritual forms of ceremonial festivals and their presentation in the mass media to be an opportunity to study the terms in which the public, at least in part, are able to participate in the collective life of their nation. The bulk of the paper will be taken up, therefore, with planning decisions in the BBC about how to cover (represent) three major festivals between 1946 and 1953 – the Victory Parade of 1946, the Festival of Britain in 1951 and the Coronation of 1953.[1] They are arguably the major events in the years following the Second World War which brought together the Monarchy, religious leaders, other members of the traditional British Establishment and political leaders. In a *Times* editorial the Victory Parade was described as an occasion when the British: 'were enabled to see in a symbolic mirror the image of themselves' (10 June 1946, p. 5).

The period of these State occasions is particularly interesting because the ending of the War, which had itself forced the State into many new kinds of political mobilization, was followed by the first social democratic government with a large and unimpeachable mandate for radical social change. As a contribution to social change one might assume that the imagery and symbolism of the State and Nation would be altered in ways that were consistent with new structural arrangements. The radical government lasted six years, in a sense culminating in the Festival of Britain, to be followed by the first of a series of consumer-oriented new prosperity conservative governments. It was felt at the time that much of the style of this new conservatism was expressed by euphoria generated at the Coronation of a young Queen two years after the change of government. The three State occasions then span a period of marked differences in social and political climate in which the symbolism of the nation as community should be a barometer of expectations about the political community.

Ritual and the nation state

The difficulties that arise with the use of a concept of ritual are that the term has been used so often in so many different contexts that it would not be difficult to become bogged down in justification and explanation. I shall therefore describe some reasons for my use of ritual fairly arbitrarily and not attempt to consider all the implications. The first point is that ritual collects a class of occasions which are felt to be peculiarly significant for the collectivity. The process of imbuing the occasion with formal significance is frequently accomplished through the use of distinctive forms of dress, ceremonial settings and a formal, often archaic, form of speech. As these marking devices, dress, settings and speech are among the most important ways of marking drama from reality it is unsurprising that ritual ceremonies are frequently described in very theatrical terms. Ritual occasions therefore seem to be highly self-conscious, in the way that we say that actors are necessarily conscious of playing with rôle and identity, but they are stagings which purport to be natural in that they are not put on for commercial benefit or political advantage.

The dramatic core to ritual alerts our attention to a second important feature. This is that drama works through structural categories. The idiosyncrasies of a particular narrative are dependent upon shared categories of relationship, identity, time and orderliness for comprehensibility and meaning. In a ritual ceremony which is not usually organized about the telling of particular narrative the forms of presentation are more clearly about themselves. The meanings being enacted are those of a necessity of structure and what is being celebrated is the ability to impose order: 'collective ritual can be seen as an especially dramatic attempt to bring some particular part of life firmly and definitely into orderly control' (Moore and Myerhoff, 1977, p. 3).

Part of the meaning of a ritual is that collectivity is shown to be possible and that doubts and tensions are formally proscribed. The essence of a ritual is that a collectivity is postulated or affirmed which might otherwise only have an ambiguous social existence. This does not mean that all participants in the ritual will be equally convinced of its truth nor that when there is an unequal division of power within a collectivity the more powerful will not use their access to staging rituals as ways of legitimating their authority and precluding alternative political arrangements. Thus, for example, traditional celebrations within an institution such as a school will, at least in part, work to affirm the unbridgeable status divisions between teachers and pupils. The political character of ritual is therefore always present, particularly in civic rituals, but these political aspects are usually expressed paradoxically through being denied in favour of an integrated community.

Bocock (1974) has suggested four types of ritual in industrial society which vary by the nature of the sponsoring authority. These are religious, civic, life-cycle and aesthetic rituals although Bocock recognizes that these are analytic distinctions and any particular ritual may contain elements from more than one type. Civic rituals, for example, have a tendency to spread and take over other types of ritual such as secular marriages and funerals, and there is an increasing subordination of religious concerns to State pomp on the occasions of life-cycle rituals of members of the Royal Family. The flowering of civic ritual has been closely interdependent upon the development of national, secular publics and means of communication between such publics. Public life is interrelated with civic ritual in two ways: first, an increasing proportion of media space is devoted to both the rituals and the activities front and backstage of ritual performers to the extent that, as I shall argue, civic ritual has become a distinctive genre of mass communication; second, the spectacular character of civic ritual in mass society has come increasingly to consist of the degree of media attention so that ever larger audiences can be ever more intimately present although their participation remains vicarious.

A nation is an abstract collectivity because it is too big a social entity to be experienced by any individual. Therefore the 'we-feeling' of the community has to be continually engendered by opportunities for identification as the nation is being manufactured: 'A nation becomes "one and indivisible" through a continual process of communalization ... The most effective symbols of implementing the process are those of common historical fate, of common triumphs of the past: national history bespeaking of grandeur; a national mission; assurance of the nation's worth for mankind' (Gerth and Mills, 1954, pp. 296–7). The use of manufacture in relation to communalization is not meant to imply that it is done cynically, but rather that specific people have to be employed in the management, staging and publicity which is part of ceremonial festivals. The interdependence of mass media and civic ritual only extends the army of presenters. The stock of national images and the rhetoric of their presentation have continually to be reconsidered, developed and extended in terms of what presenters perceive the public mood and expectations to be. The mystical significance of master symbols of the nation does not preclude the inclusion of elements of mundane experience. As Kingsley Martin (1962, p. 116) has pointed out of the Queen's father: 'the importance of his reign is that he restored the ideal conception of the domestically correct and conventional monarch ... In so doing he laid the foundation on which the new TV Monarch was built.' The marriage of the mass media and the most traditional institutional symbol of the nation was actively being consummated during the years 1945–1953, which span these festivals.

Media and civic rituals

I have stressed the interdependence of civic ritual with mass media of communication in the urban industrial state, to the point of claiming that such rituals are a distinctive genre of media programming. There seem to be several reasons for this interdependence and they can be organized into those relating to civic ritual and those relating to features of mass communication. The first point is that if such rituals are dramatizations of the nation as a symbolic community then the infinite reproducibility of media performance makes audiences possible on a scale previously unimaginable. Indeed it is the number and complexity of the publics which the audience constitutes that ensures they are essentially abstract for ritual sponsors. Thus, it is not just that ritual makes the abstract nation tangible. Media organizations supposedly acting as the voice of public opinion necessarily usurp the public on whose behalf they speak. It must be so because the pressures of performance production preclude any adequate process of consultation; public opinion is those attitudes available to producers. The sponsors of civic ritual in seeking to democratize the appeal of that which they are staging are forced to adapt to the expectations and presuppositions of the communications forms which make their audience accessible. In doing so the dramatic impact of the ritual is transformed. Of course, for those present at the procession, service or whatever, the primary emotional impact is still present; but they must be aware that for the vicariously listening or viewing mass audience they as onlookers are as essential for the success of the spectacle as more starring performers. There can be no single response then but for performers through onlookers and spectators a series of more or less self-conscious involvement with ritual as programme material. The initial aura of the occasion cannot be retrieved only the potential of the new level of performance can be pursued.

For media producers the attractiveness of civic ritual as a programming resource closely parallels the points made above. The concept of a dramatic spectacle is of a highly formalized parade of social types in an elaborate setting organized by a narrative in which moral certitudes are affirmed in ways which often combine inducing awe in the audience with sentimental involvement. As such civic rituals are spectacular displays for which the framework of audience interest can be presumed. There is an easy combination of news as happening with dramatic sequencing so that the twin criteria of immediacy and significance are self-evidently satisfied. It is relevant in this respect to note that programme producers are likely to feel themselves faced mainly with technical problems of ensuring access, continuity and exhaustiveness rather than more complex issues such as the point of view of whose side should be represented. Technical problems can be solved with ingenuity and enthusiasm leading to the sort of uncritical praise found in contemporary newspaper reports; a process that is doubly reassuring for producers who lack any deep familiarity with the public on whose behalf they are staging the presentation. Finally, it is because civic ritual is about the nation as symbolic community that a nation-wide appeal can be presumed. There is none of the competitiveness between genres associated with conventional programming, the ritual speaks for itself and indeed seems to offer a distillation of what national broadcasting should do best.

The further implication of this argument is that the dramatic dimension to collective experience will not just be retained in mass society but will be importantly extended and transformed in the cultural forms of mass communication. It may well be that there are laws or institutional forms to public drama which help to determine structural change (cf. Klapp, 1964, chap. 9). If this is so it takes us some way towards explaining a paradox in the politics of mass society – that the majority of men and women are able to endorse the commonsense, middle-of-the-road rhetoric of institutionalized normality while at the same time being intermittently willing to pursue sectional interests. The political constituencies of mass society are not consistently based on lines of economic cleavage such as class but are an imprecise mixture of quasi-ritualized rhetoric of concensualism and shifting more localised concerns based on occupation, leisure interests, generation, race and sex etc [...]

The Victory Parade 1946

The Victory Parade had to be more hurriedly prepared for than the other two festivals for although the Corporation had been planning for Victory in Europe for two years, the decision to hold a celebratory procession on 8 June 1946 was only formally announced by Atlee in the House of Commons in February.

At the first meeting to discuss how the BBC should cover it the Director General decided that programmes for that day 'should be generally gay and cheerful' (BBC Written Archives Centre, subsequently referred to as WAC, R34/920, 1 February 1946). Another early choice determining the character of the occasion turned on style of reporting. In the run-up to VE night the decision had been made to present the celebration through the responses of common people as far as possible. This had led to an emphasis upon 'vox pop' broadcasting which had been extensively and favourably commented upon at the time.[2] But the plans for coverage of the Victory Parade suggest a Corporate attitude of sympathetic obser- vation rather than popular identification. Of the five commentary positions selected to cover the event only one was provided with a hand- grip microphone with extension suitable for crowd interviews. There were in addition commentators in the procession itself and in an aircraft circling above, but while these may be said to have added to the breadth of coverage they did not speak from the viewpoint of the man in the street. Similarly the coverage of the evening celebrations had a mix of fixed commentary positions with mobile transmitters in a launch and an air- craft, only the commentary position in Piccadilly Circus had a possibility of direct crowd participation [...]

The issues raised by a study of the representation of a civic ritual such as the Victory Parade in 1946 concern ritual in social democratic societies. There is some evidence that the victory being celebrated was conceived by those who planned it in interestingly unusual ways and that public broadcasting had an opportunity to act as a medium for popular partici- pation in ways that were correspondingly challenging. The opportunity was not taken up and there was instead a repetitive stress on predictable features such as military function, bravery, technical complexity and occasional colourful features such as the severally repeated note that the Commander of the West African Contingent in the Parade was an exceptional 'Big Game Hunter'. The character of the occasion was in general presented as uncomplicated national integration, formality and celebration of military virtues. This is not to imply a lack of popularity. The contemporary press was united in praising Corporation coverage and listeners' appreciation indices were consistently high. This should be unsurprising as, of course, the public at large had no more idea of what ritual in a changing society might be like than did Corporation executives – the familiar might therefore be especially welcome.

Festival of Britain

The Festival of Britain posed the nature of collective celebration in a social democracy even more forcefully. The suggestion was resented in certain quarters because it was closely identified with a Labour Govern- ment and 'the idea it expressed most, that of the post-war Welfare State' (Strong, 1976, p. 9); and as Asa Briggs (1979, p. 19) has commented: 'for the more conservative (with a small c) its predominant styles; "anti-commercial" in tone, already grated.' It was a Festival that celebrated social change, without being particularly partisan, from the viewpoint of the common, anonymous, man and woman. In this respect one para-doxical aspect gradually became apparent – for a Festival so identified with post-war Labourism it seemed to celebrate a mood of change which 'marked the climax of the age of austerity and the shift to a new era of affluence' (Briggs, 1979, p. 392), an era soon to be identified with Conservative governments.

This meant that the Festival was intrinsically political in that it was about what British society could and should be like even if this was to be articulated through versions of previous achievements: 'The Festival tried to regain the national identity of Britain which people had felt during the war: in the South Bank Exhibition, and various local events throughout the country the nation's achievements and goals for the future were to be displayed. The ideal motives about influencing civilisation filled the air again' (Brown, 1978, p. 245). The political basis to the Festival did not mean, however, that the rituals which constituted the opening of the Festival were significantly different – there were the conventional elements of monarchy, processions, religious services and formalized rhetoric of endorsement. It was rather that these elements were set in a significantly changed political context and the BBC's rôle in articulating the meaning of ritual for this context became particularly problematic [...]

Coronation

The third festival, the Coronation, was the most traditional in many ways but coming early in a period of social stability and affluence, it also presaged the ideology of post-war Conservatism. To the extent that the BBC saw itself as looking and commentating on behalf of the nation conservatively (with a small c) then the Coronation should have posed fewer problems in terms of attitude and stance etc., than the previous festivals. In practice new problems were raised by the previous successes of the Corporation. In that it had become generally accepted that civic rituals were public occasions staged and accessible to the media, and thereby mass audiences, it was hard to devise criteria for restricting public access. It was because previously mysterious parts of traditional ritual became literally visible that this Coronation, more than any other royal ceremonial, marked a turning point between symbolism articulat-ing constitutional relationships and ritual as dramatic spectacle. This was realized at the time and was controversial, although the spectacular implications of monarchy as superstar were not fully appreciated. What is particularly interesting is that debates over media participation in civic ritual were not so much raised for the BBC by the wider political society but were initiated by the Corporation in pursuit of what they felt to be the public's rights [...]

Among the general principles which were laid down to govern the televising of the ceremony in the Abbey were 'There will be no close-ups of any person. There will be no picture of any person during (i) the Anointing, (ii) the Communion prayers, (iii) there will be no picture of any individual kneeling in worship' (WAC, T16/169, n.d.). In addition the same document formulated a distinction, originally made by the Head of Outside Broadcasts for Television, between ordinary shots and sym-bolic shots. The latter would focus on inanimate features of the Abbey such as 'the altar cross, the Coronation Plate or some Abbey stone work' (ibid.). As there were to be no close-ups the Service would be filmed in a mixture of midshot, longshot and symbolic shot, the latter planned to amount to at least a third of the total footage of the Service. Given this reverential approach, almost pretending not to look, it is perhaps less surprising that the transmission of the pictures on American networks intermingled with advertisements caused such consternation (Briggs, 1979, pp. 457–73) [...]

Notes

1   The substantive research reported in this paper was undertaken at the BBC Written Archives Centre, Caversham, Reading. The staff there were consistently helpful and co-operative and the author gratefully acknowledges their generous assistance.

2   The report of the Listener Research Department on the Victory Broadcasts of May 1945 stressed how much the naturalness and social geographical breadth, had been appreciated: 'If there was a criticism, it was that there had been too much commentary' (WAC, LR/3470/24.5.45).

References

Banham, M. and Hillier, B. (eds) (1976). *A Tonic to the Nation: The Festival of Britain 1951*, London, Thames and Hudson.

Birnbaum, N. (1955). Monarchs and Sociologists, *Sociological Review*, vol. 3, no. 1.

Blumler, J. G., Brown, J., Newbank, A. J. and Nossiter, T. J. (1971). Attitudes to the Monarchy: Their Structure and Development During a Ceremonial Occasion, *Political Studies*, vol. 19, no. 2.

Bocock, R. (1974). *Ritual in Industrial Society*, London, George Allen and Unwin.

Briggs, A. (1979). *The History of Broadcasting*, vol. IV, London, Oxford University Press.

BBC (1951). *The BBC's Contribution to the Festival*, London, BBC Publications.

Brown, G. (1978). Which Way to the Way Ahead? Britain's Years of Reconstruction, *Sight and Sound*, vol. 47, no. 4.

Dyer, R., Geraghty, C., Jordan, M., Lovell, T., Paterson, R. and Stewart, J. (1981). *Coronation Street*, BFI Television Monograph 13, London, British Film Institute.

Elliott, P. (1980). Press Performance and Political Ritual, in Christian H. (ed.), *The Sociology of Journalism and the Press*, Sociological Review Monograph 29, Keele, University of Keele.

Festival Council (1952). *The Story of the Festival of Britain 1951*, London, HMSO.

Gerth, H. and Wright, Mills, C. (1954). *Character and Social Structure*, London, Routledge and Kegan Paul.

Klapp, O. (1964). *Symbolic Leaders: Public Drama and the Public Men*, Chicago, Aldine.

Martin, K. (1962). *The Crown and the Establishment*, London, Hutchinson.

Moore, S. G. and Myerhoff, B. G. (eds) (1977). *Secular Ritual*, Amsterdam, Van Gorcum.

Shils, E. and Young, M. (1953). The Meaning of the Coronation, *Sociological Review*, vol. 1, no. 2.

Strong, R. (1976). Prologue: Utopia Limited in Banham, M. and Hillier, B. (eds).

Williams, R. (1981). *Culture*, London, Fontana.

IV   RELIGION AND RESISTANCE

Since the Protestant Reformation, modern capitalist societies have established a rupture between religion and the political and economic spheres.
In other types of society religion and politics, for example, were not
so highly differentiated as in capitalism, as can be seen in the Jewish
prophets such as Isaiah, and in early Christianity, as in the Song of Mary
– 'He has cast down the mighty from their thrones: and has lifted up
the lowly' – this is revolution. The mixture of religion and the political
can also be found in many situations which were subject to colonial rule
by Europeans such that religious and political protests were often blended
together among the indigenous people. The ending of colonial rule in
most parts of the non-industrial world did not entail that those peoples
once subject to alien political powers also ceased to be subject to economic and cultural power from the post Second World War imperial powers,
including the United States. This has meant that since political independence, as in Jamaica for instance, cultural and politico-economic
protest against the economic dependency situation has continued to find
some expression in what we might call 'religious' terms, that is in terms
of the verbal and non-verbal symbols, rituals, and social groups which
originally developed under different political circumstances.

The article by Stuart Hall examines the historical development of
religious-style resistance in Jamaica, in the sect known as Ras Tafari in
particular, and points out how these same symbols have been used by
some young blacks in Britain in the 1970s and 1980s to articulate a form
of resistance to the dominant culture of that society.

Not all religious protest or resistance takes the same form as that of
the Rastafarians. In the typology of religious sects developed by Bryan
Wilson, in the piece included here, the Rastafarians would be seen as
predominantly a 'revolutionary' sect; that is, the response to the world
among this group is eschatological, and the revolutionary change will be
made by a supernatural figure. Other religious groups offer a different

response to the world, such as 'conversionist' sects which seek to re-make the fallen world through changes to individuals achieved by having conversion experiences, as in the early stages of the development of the Salvation Army for example. 'Utopian' sects partly withdraw from the world, often living communally, but with a view to re-making the world later on. There are some aspects of Rastafarianism which also fit this type, in that many Rastafarians live communally. The difference from a fully utopian sect is that they expect supernatural leadership in re-making their situation, whereas utopian sect members would do most of the work themselves, albeit with supernatural aid. Such typologies as this one developed by Bryan Wilson are heuristic devices – no more, no less.

In many ways, the sociology of religion has been at its most powerful in offering explanations and typologies of sectarian development in historical and modern conditions. What appear at first sight, and within the 'common sense' framework of the western middle classes, as puzzling religious phenomena in a supposedly secular age, appear more understandable to the same groups after reading a sociological account of one or more of these sectarian movements. The sociology of sects is also important for the sociology of the world religions in that they bear the marks of their birth, often as sectarian movements, even when established as major cultural formations in some part of the world. This is true of early Christianity, which can be seen as a sectarian protest movement, among Jews in the first instance, against Roman colonial and imperial power.

19 S. Hall

Religious ideologies and social movements in Jamaica

Introduction

This article is a study of religion as an ideological domain in which I attempt to show how religious ideologies function in a specific social and historical context. The 'case' examined is that of religious culture in Jamaica, from the period of slavery to the present, with a special focus on popular religions and their relation to social movements. I analyse how Jamaican popular religion became the 'bearer' of a set of rich 'systems' of ideological meaning; how those meanings function by being linked with certain social positions; how they create new collective actors or 'subjects' and become articulated with a series of social and political movements.

In this introductory section, I sketch out the theoretical framework within which the particular historical 'case' is treated. This framework is then used to structure the main body of the article, where I analyse how popular religion has developed in Jamaica over the past three centuries. I have used the case study to establish some general theoretical points about how to conceptualise the modes of operation of religious ideologies.

Religious beliefs and practices can be conceptualised theologically, as revealing certain sacred 'truths' about the nature of the universe. They can be analysed sociologically, in terms of the social structure and the different types of religious institutions and their social function. They can be viewed anthropologically – as part of the customs, belief systems, culture or 'folkways' characteristic of particular peoples and societies. In this article, essentially, I treat religion as an ideological field. That is, I examine how the variety of religious systems and practices which one finds among the Jamaican people throughout their history function 'ideo-logically'. By this I mean that religion has profoundly shaped Jamaican culture and left its imprint on the major forms of social consciousness. I therefore treat religion as one of the many kinds of discourse (languages, practices) through which social groups or classes represent relationships between the secular and spiritual world and which provide systems of meaning, frameworks of interpretation or intelligibility, through which they 'make sense of' or 'give meaning to' their social existence and justify or legitimate particular interests and actions.

This approach can be briefly located within the classic sociological traditions. (See the extracts from 'classic' authors in this volume.) I closely follow Marx, who regarded religion as an ideological belief system, articulating real social interests, though I question how far religion is *simply* a form of 'false consciousness' produced by an alienated social reality. I agree with Weber in the crucial link between religion and 'meaning', but do not follow him in relating its study to the subjective experiences of individuals alone. I agree with Durkheim's emphasis on the fact that social solidarity underpins all religious experiences, though I do not follow him in treating religion in terms of function without reference to meaning. I stand quite close to Berger and Luckmann's argument that religion is an attempt to construct around the social world a meaningful symbolic order − a 'sacred canopy' − but cannot follow them in defining all religions as merely a shield against the threat of chaos and anomie. Religion also seems to me to have a more positive and critical function in many social settings.

On the other hand, I place primary emphasis on religion as a domain of ideological meaning. Religion is not a unitary domain but includes both the established institutional churches and the various sects and ecstatic movements, often on the margin of society, which appeal to the dispossessed sections of society − the religions of the oppressed. One point of interest is the complex transactions and relations between these different religious discourses.

I use the term 'meaning system' in a special sense. I do not mean that these frameworks are systematic, internally logical, coherent, consistent or, indeed, true. We are dealing with meaningful, but not necessarily factually or empirically correct, statements. Also, we are analysing chains or sets of meanings, not isolated ideological elements. These chains of meaning exhibit a 'logic' of their own. Once you locate yourself inside them a recognisable chain of inference seems to connect one proposition to another. (This idea is not wholly dissimilar from Foucault's notion of a 'regime of truth'. See the extract in the *Politics and Ideology* Course Reader.) There are many different 'logics' within any one society − though there are also relations of power and dominance between them. Different groups in the society make use of different ideologies to make their social existence, interests and practice intelligible. There is a constant struggle as to which 'regime' forms the main source of social conceptions. What distinguishes *religious* ideology from other ideological domains (e.g. political or social belief-systems) is that, in religious discourses, meaning about the practical and historical world is constructed within a symbolic or metaphorical language based on some chain of equivalences or imaginary 'correspondences' between this secular world and the world of the spirit or spiritual life.

Many different typologies of religious behaviour have been offered in the sociological literature. One useful schema is that provided by Bryan Wilson (extracted in this volume) based on the sect's or church's response to the world. Wilson reminds us that sects change their character over time; that the revolutionist type often appears in 'mission territories' where native religion has fused or syncretised with messianic strands in Christianity. In societies of any complexity, the religious domain, like that of any other ideological field, will be composed of interconnected chains of discourses, or overlapping religious formations. This is especially true of the religious life of the popular classes where religion often plays a directly political or quasi-nationalistic role. Religious ideology is therefore dealt with here, not so much as 'a language', but more as a semantic field in which the 'struggle for social meanings' occurs.

Our emphasis on the 'struggle to articulate meanings' derives from a particular view of language which underpins the conception of ideology being advanced. The conventional view of language is that things (objects, events) in the world carry within themselves a clear and unambiguous meaning. The role of language is to give a name to a meaning which already exists. The view of language advanced here is that things have no unambiguous meaning 'in themselves' and language is the system which, by *representing* the world, imposes meaning on the world. The emphasis thus falls on the *productive* role of discourse – i.e. producing forms of intelligibility (see Foucault, op. cit.). Thus what concerns us is the articulation between the social relationships and institutions in which social collectivities exist, on the one hand, and on the other hand, the variety of ways in which their positions and experiences can be signified or represented. Of course, though we separate these two aspects analytically, they cannot in the end be totally distinct, since how we act and what relationships we sustain depend in part on how we understand and define them. In the end, ideology does not reflect on already constituted reality – it helps to constitute it. It is because ideology *does* have real effects that Marxists say that ideas can become social forces in their own right: because they alter our practice they therefore have material results. However, this tells us little or nothing about the empirical validity or truth content of ideology. Ideologies may be false, partially correct, or full of explanatory value. Myths can be as powerful in their ideological consequences as scientific truths.

Religious discourses which may appear fixed in a dogmatic mould, may, in fact, be able to express novel truths, new insights, emergent possibilities. Meaning is never fixed, once and for all. This open-endedness of religious and other types of ideological discourse means that we cannot explain how religions function *now* simply by tracing them back to their origins, since they have been subject to constant modification and transformation through history. A central focus in our analysis will be this process of historical transformation. Nevertheless, there is something critically important about the moment of the *formation* of a particular field of meaning. The first part of the article therefore traces this process. 'Formation' covers the historical moment when the various elements or 'core' of an ideology first coalesce and form a definite discursive formation or repertoire on which subsequent periods draw. I assume this formative moment to have occurred with the foundation of slave society in Jamaica, and the forcible synthesis, under the 'peculiar' conditions of slavery and colonisation, of the diametrically opposed 'worlds' of African religion and western Christianity. Jamaican religion since then has developed through the dialectical relationship between these contradictory worlds.

However, far from treating the ideological field as having been fixed or frozen by that moment of formation, the main emphasis of my treatment is on the almost continuous process of rupture and transformation which occurs, historically, in the wake of this fusion of the 'elementary forms' of Afro-Jamaican religion. I view this as a constant process of breaks, interruptions and reorganisation, in which the religious formation is reordered, rearranged, dislocated and repositioned, so as to provide new religious languages and practices within which to articulate new historical realities. This occupies the second half of the article. As Gramsci has remarked, more generally, concerning ideological formations:

What must be explained is how it happens that in these periods there coexist many mysteries and currents of philosophical thoughts, how these currents are born, how they are diffused and why in the process of diffusion they fracture along certain lines and in certain directions ... It is this history which shows how thought has been elaborated over the centuries and what a collective effort has gone into the creation of all present methods of thought which has subsumed and absorbed all this past history, including all its follies and mistakes. (Gramsci, 1971, p.327)

Ideological conflict and change is therefore not conceived in terms of the self-sufficient 'religious world view' of one group wholly replacing or being substituted for that of another; but rather in terms of a constant process of formation and re-formation through which emphases are shifted, elements borrowed, abandoned or transformed, rituals reinterpreted and reshaped, doctrines elided, symbols fused, so as to constitute new systems of meaning out of old ones, new religious logics and practices through which new social forces and new historical realities can be 'spoken'. Adaptation, negotiation, internal transformation, ironic inversion, resistance, rupture, elision, reconstitution – these are only *some* of the many modes in which ideological contestation and resistance is sustained. (On this point see the further development by Colin Mercer in *Politics and Ideology*.)

The classic approach to religion has often consisted essentially of asking which social group or class is the source of this or that ideology. This suggests that social collectivities are fully formed *before* they 'express themselves' through a particular ideology. In fact, in the very process by which individuals become members of a social collectivity, they also *become* the bearers or 'subjects' of particular belief systems. More often we find a double movement in which new collective subjects are formed in the same process by which the group articulates itself or 'speaks its truth' through a particular discourse. The two processes mutually sustain and determine one another. (This is more fully discussed in Laclau, 1977.)

Religious ideologies, however 'other worldly' they appear, inform social practices and have a mobilising 'practical' impact on society. They organise men and women into action, win 'hearts and minds'. They form the 'common sense' in which the everyday practicalities of life are calculated and expressed. Ideologies draw groupings together; they help to constitute and unify congregations, supporters, participants; they cement social alliances. (On this point see the extract from Gramsci (1971) in the Course Reader on *Politics and Ideology*.) They also serve to divide: for ideological practices have a critical function in marking out and separating – 'drawing the distinction' – between those who are legitimate, who belong – 'the faithful', brothers and sisters – and those who do not – the enemy, Satan, the demon king, Babylon. Religious ideologies are *both* the medium in which collective social solidarities are constructed *and* the means through which ideological conflict and difference is pursued.

Ideology has its own way of operating and is not simply 'the economy' or some other such 'reality' merely assuming the false disguise of religious ideas. We must assume that the fact that ideas take a particular religious form, does have certain real effects. Thus the rise of the bourgeoisie in the seventeenth century was shaped by the fact that, in the Civil War, it took the form of a struggle around Puritanism; just as the class struggles in Northern Ireland are profoundly shaped by the fact that they are cross-cut by the sectarian division between Catholic and Protestant. It is not, therefore, possible to 'read off' the meaning of an ideology simply from an analysis of the mode of production or from the economic facts or even from the class position of those who hold particular ideas. On the other hand, ideology is not autonomous of the socio-economic and political contexts in which it operates. Ideologies do express and advance certain interests; they are used to legitimate particular structures of power, to defend a particular order of society (or to oppose it); they do become linked with certain groups and classes and, as such, either help to preserve their position of privilege and domination or are used by others to contest that position. In this sense, most conflicts, whether they arise from economic exploitation, political oppression or social inequality, will also be articulated in the domain of ideology because it is the domain in which, as Marx said, 'men [and women] become conscious of their contradictions and fight them out'.

I

Let us turn, now, to the Jamaican 'case'. The indigenous culture of the original Carib and Arawak peoples (the original inhabitants of the Caribbean islands) was almost totally destroyed during the Spanish occupation, long before the British captured Jamaica. From the early 1700s until the abolition of slavery, the slave plantation economy provided the historical conditions in which the different elements of Jamaican culture coalesced. Essentially, two cultural forces were yoked together: the dominant 'culture' of the white English colonisers – plantation owners, overseers, estate mechanics, merchants, lawyers and the colonial administrators; and, on the other hand, the 'cultures' of the enslaved and colonized blacks – initially, those transported into slavery from West Africa, subsequently, the 'creole' slave populations born and bred in the New World. 'Europe' and 'Africa' thus always connoted two internally differentiated, mutually distinct, but interdependent cultural 'castes' – what Curtin (1955) later called the 'Two Jamaicas'. Gradually, from the liaisons between blacks and whites emerged the 'coloured' population, ranked as an intermediary group on a social ladder carefully graded by colour, ethnic and racial characteristics. On rough estimates, the Jamaican slave population stabilised at around 300,000/340,000 between 1800 and 1830; with about 59,000 'coloureds' of whom about 15,000 were still slaves (Patterson, 1967; Braithwaite, 1971). Gradually, the 'free coloureds' became the basis of Jamaican 'creole' culture and the backbone of the modern Jamaican middle class. Lower-class Jamaicans were the descendants of black slaves.

The vast majority of Jamaican slaves came from the 'nations' of West Africa (the Ashanti, Ibos, the Mandingo and captives from Dahomey) (Patterson, 1967). Transportation across the Atlantic – the 'middle passage' – was full of indescribable horrors. Those who survived bore a distinctly African cultural heritage with them into slavery in the New World. This included African religious beliefs and magical practices, forms of folklore, languages and art; child rearing, marital and funeral customs; cooperative and tribal forms of property and labour; a traditional agriculture, distinctive forms of diet, cuisine, etiquette and modes of social intercourse.

How much of this African culture survived the conditions of enslavement? This is the subject of a protracted, bitter and unfinished controversy, the classic confrontation which occurred between the anthropologist, Melville Herskovits (1941), who painstakingly attempted to unearth and identify 'African survivals' in the culture of the New World and the sociologist, E. Franklin Frazier (1966), who argued that slavery effectively destroyed the social basis of African culture and traditional life forever. This issue has never been finally resolved: Frazier was too extreme but probably had the better of the argument.

Cultural practices cannot exist in a void. Clearly the conditions were not favourable under slavery for the survival of African cultures intact, as relatively coherent entities. Slaves were dispersed in a deliberate effort to break up kinship, linguistic and religious groupings. They were bought and sold on the basis of physical stamina alone, though a racist 'folklore' did arise among slaveowners to distinguish between them on the basis of stereotyped characteristics. Thus the Ashanti were reputed physically strong but rebellious; the Ibo 'docile' but cunning and deceitful, etc. (Curtin, op. cit). Many contemporary racist stereotypes originated in this earlier 'folk' taxonomy. Once purchased, slaves were 'seasoned' into forced plantation labour and the slave quarters – conditions utterly different from those which had previously sustained their distinctive ways of life. The new division of labour imposed its own differentiations on earlier tribal distinctions, dividing male from female field hands and drivers from skilled slaves and 'house niggers'. Later importation introduced a further differentiation between newly-arrived 'Africans' and 'creoles'. In these different ways the old African worlds were fragmented and destroyed. Slavery presented the slaveholding class with a never-ending problem of controlling the slave population, enforcing discipline by whip and force as well as by deference and paternalism of slave discipline. Slave owners quickly recognised the 'African' element as a key factor in this matter (Lewis, 1834). The more slaves preserved something of their past heritage, or renewed it through contact with recent arrivals and, the stronger their memory of Africa, the greater was their hunger for freedom, the more recalcitrant to hard labour they became, and the more prone to disobedience, rebellion, suicide or escape.

The French anthropologist, Roger Bastide, has nevertheless observed how tenacious the popular memory of Africa was:

While the slaves' minds might remain African, their actions were gradually being Americanised ... in the long run, and especially after the abolition of the slave trade, such memories were bound to lose their original clarity. They were out of place in this new environment; slowly but inevitably they became blurred, and at last faded into total oblivion ... If these memories were to survive, they had to attach themselves to some existing custom, establish a foothold in the here-and-now, find some sort of niche or hiding-place. Of the conflict between tradition (which is determined to preserve the past at all costs) and society (which remains in constant flux) Halbwachs writes: 'From this it emerges that social thought is, in essence, a matter of memory, and that its entire content consists of accumulated recollections; but of such recollections only a limited number survive, and these not in their entirety. In both cases the criterion for survival is the ability of a society, at any given time, to reconstruct their content within the framework of contemporary custom'. Since Negroes could no longer find, in the New World, anything like the old African context of their traditional beliefs, they had to discover – or invent – a brand-new social framework which would contain them.

(Bastide, 1971)

Language provides us with one excellent illustration of this process. The four hundred slave languages mapped by Dalby (1977) used different vocabularies but had considerable similarities in grammar, syntax and meaning and had been influenced by contact with European languages. These evolved into a native creole speech under the conditions of slavery. Commands and instructions in English from the master class had to be quickly learned. But slaves also drew on their own forms of intercourse, 'learning from each other in countless verbal interactions: grumbling, retelling anecdotes and old stories, joking, moralizing, plotting and planning'. They adopted many of the basic forms of the speech of the dominant class, but they persistently *inflected* them through African forms, word order and grammatical structures (Jahn, 1968; Cassidy, 1961; LePage, 1960; Sutcliffe, 1982). The contours of what today is a distinct dialect – Jamaican creole – were therefore already in evidence in Jamaica by the mid-eighteenth century (Sutcliffe, 1982). Braithwaite (1971) wryly observes that 'It was in language that the slave was perhaps most successfully imprisoned by his master, and it was in his (mis-)use of it that he perhaps most effectively rebelled'.

This process is worth commenting on as an example of ideological negotiation and resistance. Thus slave dialect speakers adapted to the dominant language for the sake of sheer survival, yet retained certain African forms and terms. They exploited the resources of language to win themselves a little cultural space, a degree of autonomy, from absolute domination by the master language. They learned to flatter and to deceive, to *negotiate* the system of paternalism and obedience on which the unequal reciprocities of slave society depended. Creole speech was a synthesis built up, briccolage-fashion, out of the elements to hand.

Another example can be taken from music, singing and dancing. Some dancing and singing the Europeans considered harmless – even quaint, 'picturesque'. But much of it seemed to them too enthusiastic, too openly sensuous and erotic. They were also aware that some singing and dancing had religious meaning, but they could not clearly distinguish the religious from the secular, and after a time neither could many slaves. So both persisted, the one form frequently hidden within the other. The 'Jonkunnu' procession performed at Christmas with masqueraded dancers was tolerantly observed as a suspension of 'real time', a carnival or festival. Most Europeans were unaware of its deep African religious significance. The singing, drumming and dancing which accompanied funerals and burial wakes had roots in African rituals of burial, and the summoning of ancestral gods. *Kumina*, the dance form most closely connected to African religious ceremonies, was less easily assimilated and driven underground. So was *Buru*, a more secular and satirical tradition on which reggae later drew. Alongside these slaves imitated their masters in an elegant quadrille. Some songs were African chants, half-remembered from the past, interlarded with English words and contemporary slave references. Some were work songs, built on African chant-and-response choruses, but adapted in musical form and content to slave work conditions and employed to lighten heavy fieldwork, and raise the depressed spirit. Some were imitated European songs. Many were used as covert communication between groups permitted no other form of intercourse during work hours. These enunciated secret messages of hope – whether real ones, about escape routes, or spiritual ones, about 'escape' from 'bondage' to a 'promised land' was never altogether clear (Levine, 1977). (In North America a similar musical synthesis constituted the roots of the gospel and secular 'blues', and of jazz.)

Interpreting these cultural practices depended on which code was used to de-code what the practices meant, since they were designed to mean different things to different audiences. Missionaries often declared the dancing 'most licentious', the music 'rude and monotone': 'the singers and dancers observing the exactest precision as to time and measure with stamping of the feet, accompanied by various contortions of the body ... strange and indecent attitudes'. 'Making the head and limbs fixed points, they writhed and turned the body upon its own axis, slowly advancing toward each other, or retreating to the outer parts of the circumferences. Their approaches to each other ... were highly indecent ...' This grim misreading arises from imposing one system of culture decoding over another one. What was being described was in fact a highly formalised pattern of traditional African dancing. However, because its precise connection to ritual and ceremonial had been lost or suppressed, it appeared more mysterious and threatening, because decontextualised, to western eyes. Genovese records that in North American churches, slaves 'kept awake and looked very much edified while the singing was going on but ... slept through the sermon' (Genovese, 1975, p. 204). But to the music, one Reverend complained 'the blacks *vibrated*, charged as with electric influence that quickened not deadened'. Genovese comments that 'he could not understand that the black response to tone and gesture implied its own content'.

II

We have considered how the different elements of Africa and Europe fused or coalesced together, under the domination of plantation slavery, to form a new matrix or cultural formation (Rubin, 1959). We turn next to examine Jamaican religious culture specifically and its historical development, especially the fusion of African and Christian traditions. Religion had always pervaded traditional West African life — 'not just one complex of African culture but the catalyst of the other complexes' according to G. A. Ojo (*Yoruba Culture*, cf. Genovese, 1975, p. 717). Belief in a supreme being, remote from daily life, was supplemented by worship of a more 'available' pantheon of local gods, good and bad spirits, associated with natural forces, whose worship was organised into cult groups. Religious practice was ceremonial, accompanied by dancing, feasting, drumming and procession. Witchcraft and magic were the principal means whereby these spiritual powers were recruited into the control of everyday life.

None of these African religious practices or cosmologies survived the impact of slavery intact. Witchcraft and magic were formally outlawed on the plantations, though they continued to flourish unseen. The *obeah* man or woman, a recurrent figure on the Jamaican plantation, was a magical practitioner, able to summon up good and bad spirits on behalf of clients: priest, magician, conjurer and healer. These sorcerers came to play a key role as go-between amongst the plantations' slave populations, and some emerged as political leaders of an informal kind. More influential in collective worship and ceremony were the priests of the Kromanti religious cults, the *myal-men*, who kept alive as far as possible the rituals and ceremonies surrounding worship, birth and death. Important aspects of African religious practice were preserved to a degree in *myalism* and *obeah*.

Curtin argues that the strongest African survivals in Jamaica are, in fact, to be found in religion. Until the growth of Methodism in the nineteenth century, *myalism* was widespread amongst the slaves; and *myal-men*, ostracised and suppressed as anti-witchdoctors, became in reaction associated with the leadership of slave revolts and were deeply implicated in some of the major Jamaican slave uprisings.

Gradually, however, there ceased to be a coherent set of African beliefs and practices; instead, its elements persisted, hidden in the more dispersed form of a black 'folk religion' including superstition, the wearing of charms, and a variety of magical practices and beliefs which survived emancipation and the colonial period in this 'folk' form into the twentieth century and independence (Beckworth, 1929). This 'folk religion' still exists today as a substratum of belief, especially in the more remote parts of rural Jamaica (Barrett, 1976).

When the Christian missions to the slaves were introduced in the nineteenth century, it was with this 'folk religious' base that it fused to form a distinctive Afro-Christianity. From the 1840s onwards we see Christian revivalism beginning to advance in Jamaica but at the price of being 'rethought in African terms'. Common features were the use of the ecstatic trance, nocturnal meetings, processions led by a 'captain' to the accompaniment of muffled drum beats, and baptism (Christian) in sacred rivers (African 'cult of the waters') (Bastide, 1971, p. 166). These forms persist in twentieth-century Jamaica, in the ceremonies of Pocomania – a direct fusion or synthesis of African religion and revivalist Protestantism – and in other unorthodox churches of Revival Zion led by 'shepherds' and a band of 'governesses'. In the more extreme forms of Pocomania, Protestant prayers and hymns coexist side by side with animal sacrifice and incantations to the dead.

The official Christian religion of the slave-owning class was Anglicanism but the Anglican clergy never seriously undertook the task of christianising the slave population. During the first half of the nineteenth century, the Dissenting sects began to make a serious impact but it was not until the second half that the Christian sects became a major fact of life amongst the whole population. The Baptists made many converts in the 1780s and 1790s with the help of George Leile, an ex-slave black preacher on a mission from Georgia: their advance amongst the slaves was facilitated by their extensive use of black preachers. Black Baptism was increasingly charged by the planter class with fomenting slave revolt. George Leile, who had founded his own Baptist church, was imprisoned for 'uttering dangerous and seditious words'.

A variety of Christian sect churches was established in Leile's wake, and these formed the basis of the black Baptist movement, a distinct, indigenous Afro-Christianity. Afro-Christianity was *unorthodox* from the beginning and syncretic (i.e. fusing different traditions of practice and belief). Native Baptists borrowed the traditional form of congregational organisation from England, including the class-leader system – but transformed it into a system of collective contact and mobilisation among the slaves. Typically, the class-leaders became 'real spiritual guides, taking a position equivalent to leadership of a myal cult group, and their power over their classes was authoritarian to the point of tyranny' (Curtin, *op. cit.*).

The outer forms of religious christianisation may have been distinctly European. But the underlying rhythm of practical observance, the hidden content, the ethos and tonality of practice was 'native', if not positively 'African'. When the European missionaries arrived, they were often obliged to graft their work and teaching on to 'native roots'. They succeeded in spreading a spirit of intense religious fervour in the black population, a fact evident from the depth and intensity of religious practice in the Jamaican population to this day. But who was grafting what on to what remains considerably more ambiguous to this day (Barrett, 1976).

The Methodists began, like other dissenting groups, with a strong anti-slavery bias but quickly accommodated to the pressures of the plantation class. They opposed African 'superstition' and preached a message of industry and social peace. Yet Methodism was never fully accepted by the plantocracy because of its ambivalent stand towards the institution of slavery. Certainly, the agitation for abolition not only intensified slave rebelliousness but increasingly acquired a Methodist religious note.

In this extensive encounter between the folk religion and Christianity many slaves and free men were genuinely converted. Many others, in Braithwaite's words, 'found the missionaries a convenience' (Braithwaite, 1971). This 'conveniencing' was itself complex. Since Christianity was official and thus tolerated, though not positively encouraged by the slave owning society, it provided a public and officially sanctioned *space* in which slaves could meet together, learn new things, including how to write and read – if only to read more intensely and in a peculiarly native way, the Bible. Opinion was divided in plantation society as to the advantages and disadvantages of teaching slaves to read and write. Rightly, since certain Biblical passages acquired a seminal significance. The most important were those which reminded slaves of their condition or could be used to speak of and refer to it: especially the story of the driving of the Israelites, God's chosen people, into servitude in Egypt, the suffering of the lost tribes, slavery, darkness and their subsequent liberation by Moses, together with the account of the captivity in Babylon and the prophecies of salvation. Blacks throughout the New World sang and spoke incessantly of Moses and the Promised Land. Here Christian eschatological and messianic ideas fused with African religion and the slave experience.

Afro-Christianity survived and flourished so to speak, in Dissent's 'official' shadow. It provided a powerful and sanctioned religious framework and language within which black men began to develop accounts and explanations in quasi-Christian religious terms of their 'peculiar' situation, to enunciate their experience of slavery as well as to mobilise, politically, around the growing movement for slave emancipation.

III

In the period after emancipation – the period in which Jamaica became a 'crown colony', the slave population was transformed into a 'free' labour force of small peasants and rural proletariat. The plantocracy regarded black religion, white missionaries, the Haitian revolt and pressure from England for the abolition of slavery as a single conspiracy. Their fears were confirmed in 1831 by the rebellion led by Samuel Sharpe, a slave and class-leader in a Native Baptist congregation.

With the failure of the Morant Bay rebellion, in 1865, when the local planters made their last bid to throw off Westminster and become an independent Commonwealth – a sort of UDI by the Jamaican settler class – Jamaica became instead a fully dependent crown colony. This uprising was preceded by an intense religious revival, which in Curtin's words, 'turned African'. The fusion of 'African', native and Christian elements was driven to a new point, as the Day when God would come to Jamaica approached. The two leading figures in the rebellion were both 'religious'. Gordon, a wealthy coloured lawyer, fierce nationalist and opponent of the ruling planter class, was 'an evangelical religious fanatic', whom Governor Eyre hanged for his pains. Paul Bogle, who raised the cry of a popular rebellion, was an ex-slave and a Native Baptist preacher, who was hanged off the yard-arm of HMS *Wolverine*.

Between emancipation and the 1920s, Jamaica was transformed from a slave society into a dependent 'colony' (D. Hall, 1959). The old slave populations formed the basis of an independent small peasantry and the landless plantation proletariat of the sugar estates. The coloured middle strata evolved roughly into the professional administrative classes. The declining plantocracy (Ragatz, 1963) was replaced at the apex of society by a more complex ruling class, composed principally of settler whites and Jamaicans of 'high colour', with money, education and 'breeding' (i.e. imitating English cultural standards) and the growing number of white expatriates in commerce and business, representing the penetration of new foreign capital into the colonial economy. The society remained rigidly divided, with the legal castes of slavery being replaced by the more complicated divisions of a class-race-colour system of stratification (S. Hall, 1975).

One cultural *pole* of this society became fully 'creolised': coloureds or

blacks but with Anglicised social attitudes and *mores*. This was respectable middle-class and lower middle-class 'creole' Jamaica. To some degree
all Jamaicans, rich, poor and middling, white, black and brown, were
assimilated within this 'creolised' culture and way of life. When respectable middle-class Jamaican society came, in the 1930s, to dream of
'national independence', it was to the legitimation of *this* 'creole culture'
(with its intrinsic, though frequently invisible, 'white bias' – a cultural
system with its real apex *somewhere else*, over the ocean) which they
imagined would be permanently installed, once colonial rule had disappeared. At the other cultural pole was 'lower-class Jamaica', the
lumpen poor of the cities and towns, the hill-top cultivators, the landless
rural proletariat and the 'country people' who remained largely within
an indigenous culture derived from the 'folk culture' of slavery, which
had taken root in 'the Other Jamaica', and which thrived and prospered
largely unpenetrated (though not untouched) by the culture of 'respectable' colonial society.

In this 'Other Jamaica' an enormously varied religious life and practice
flourished. The obeah-man survived in the tenement yards. At night, the
sleep of respectable middle-class Jamaica would be disturbed by drumming, singing, burial 'wakes' and 'nine night' celebrations. In the shanty
settlements around Kingston, male and female domestics on their way
home, the hustlers of streets, and the great mass of the black unemployed,
would be attracted into 'yard' religious services: each the home of a rival
revivalist sect, each with its own 'preacher' and attendants, celebrating
some black deity of infinitely mixed lineage in a medley of practices and
observances. The complex forms of Christian, 'native' and African rituals
most characteristically produced an intense *millenarianism*. The preaching and the harangue was of sin, hell-fire and punishment; but the
testimonies were of the 'suffering' people. The hymns were 'Moody and
Sankey', but elongated by darker and deeper rhythms, accompanied by
tambourines, hand-clapping and drums. The 'service' often verged on the
ecstatic, exalted and transporting – lifting men and women, whose eyes
were dazed with hard work and the sheer struggle for survival, into a
temporary spiritual 'other world'. But the prophesying and 'tongues' were
of the fulfilment to come, the *redemption*, the *deliverance*. These are the
classic forms of the religions of the oppressed, and they assumed a
common form in many missionary colonial settings as can be seen from
Bryan Wilson's extract (in this volume).

In the 1920s there was another surge of revivalism leading to the
founding of a diverse set of black Christian *sect* churches (each then,
almost at once, splitting into further sectarian fractions), many of them
Pentecostalist branches of the 'Churches of God'. (Cf. *inter alia*: Calley,
1965; Simpson, 1954.) In the fifteen sections of West Kingston – the

urban heartland of this culture – which Simpson studied, eleven had no established churches, but contained over sixty revivalist churches, in addition to the Churches of God, City and Pentecostal missions, Jehovah's Witnesses and the Churches of Christ the Redeemer, and not including the less visible 'cult' practices of Pocomania and the extensive congregations of Revival Zion. Revival Zion was less influenced by African ritual than Pocomania but retained an unorthodox synthesis of the Christian Trinity and a pantheon of spirits, spirit possession, drumming, clapping and 'speaking in tongues'.

This intensified revivalism was also distinguished by the appearance of forms of an explicitly black quasi-political movement, based on the dream of returning the children of the enslaved 'Back to Africa'. It is around this metaphor that a widespread convergence between popular religion and socio-political movements was forged.

IV

We turn now to the emergence of the Rastafarian movement and the development, out of the complex syncretic culture whose formation we have been tracing, of a new fusion between religious, political and nationalist elements. One of the great messianic figures of this period was Alexander Bedward, an uneducated worker, mesmeric preacher, healer and baptiser, who finally declared himself the Son of God, promised he would ascend to Heaven in a chariot of fire, bearing up the elect with him, after which he would destroy the 'unheathen' remnants below. He was obliged to postpone his ascension, and his prophesied 'flight' in 1921 took him only as far as the Kingston asylum, where he was committed for lunacy. But we can parallel in many other colonial religious movements his 'promise' to lift 'the oppressed' out of struggle and 'suffering' directly into the Promised Land (cf. Hodgkin, 1962; Burridge, 1971; Worsley, 1957). By the time of Bedward's appearance, slaves and the sons and daughters of slaves had been singing, praying and hoping for years about *some* kind of deliverance from a lifetime of suffering.

'Bedwardism' was only one of a spectrum of religious millenarian forms in which this secular dream of the 'deliverance from oppression' crystalised. Better known was the Jamaican evangelical preacher Marcus Garvey who, in 1914, founded the Universal Negro Improvement Association, emigrated to North America where he began to preach a heady mixture of black nationalism and evangelical revivalism, attracting, by the 1920s, two million members in what was certainly the largest mass black movement ever seen in the United States until the 1960s. Garvey was a formidable orator, a skilful opportunist, a demagogue, often suspected of being a con-man. His doctrine was deeply confused, being both anti-imperialist and anti-communist. His actual schemes for repatriation to Africa by the Black Star Line came to nought. Yet, undoubtedly, in his confused way, he forged the first, modern black nationalist movement in the New World, whose force ultimately rested on the fact that it connected with the powerhouse of native religious ideas and culture.

Blacks, he said, were born free but were everywhere in chains. They had been forcibly abducted into bondage. They must return to their 'homeland' – Africa. His slogan was 'Back to Africa'. He believed black people would not be free until there was a strong African nation, which could extend its protective arm to them everywhere (cf. Cronon, 1964). Where, precisely, in Africa, and how this 'nation' was to be established, were not spelled out. 'Look to Africa where a black king shall be crowned ...', he said.

Garvey was deported from the United States to Jamaica in 1927. He did not win as many followers there but his message found an echo in that 'Other Jamaica'; and from this relative failure arose yet another religious development: the foundation of the Ras Tafari brethren.

Ideology is not simply a set of ideas or beliefs: rather, it is a discursive *practice* which is informed by or structured around a 'core' set of conceptions, images or ideas. However, essential to any ideological practice is its capacity to rearticulate elements so as to generate *new* accounts of experience or explanations of the world – to maintain different 'cosmologies'. But for this purpose, there must be an identifiable 'core' of elements, concepts or ideas which, differently combined in different historical periods, and using different rules of construction, may be (a) sufficiently distinct so as to differentiate one ideological formation from another; and yet (b) be capable, in different combinations, of generating new definitions and discourses. Here, we consider not only what the 'core conceptions' of Rastafarian ideology are but also the diverse ideological sources out of which its highly distinctive cosmology was elaborated.

Garvey sent his black brothers back to the Bible: and out of this intensified search in the Sacred Book, which has justified so many different interpretations in its time, there emerged the doctrine and movement of the Ras Tafari. The *Book of Revelations* spoke of 'the Lion of Judah' who loosed the seven spirits of God. Those inspired by Garvey discovered him in the real world in the person of the first modern black King of an independent African nation – Emperor Haile Selassie I of Ethiopia, whom they at once declared the reincarnation of Jesus, the Living God, King of Kings, Black Messiah, Redeemer: Jah. His mission was to 'deliver' black men from Babylon. Men like Howell, Hibbert, Dunkley and Rickets were among the first to preach the Lion of Judah's divinity (Cashmore, 1979; Nettleford, 1970; Smith *et al.*, 1960). In the early days, Rastafarians were continually harassed by the police, despised by respectable Jamaicans, and their community at Pinnacle was broken up and dispersed. Garvey, who was regarded as a latter-day Moses sent to lead the exiled back, had indeed looked to Ethiopia, though not specifically to Haile Selassie (Cashmore, 1979, p. 22). But the ideological discourses which make such 'equivalences' possible were already richly available in the metaphorical structure of Jamaican religious culture (on 'equivalences' see Colin Mercer's discussion in *Politics and Ideology*).

Rastafarianism is distinguished from other other-worldly sects by its Garveyite emphasis on the internal self-disciplining of the brethren, on the injustices of and need to reform social conditions, its militant hostility to the forces which oppress them in 'Babylon', its pride in its black African lineage, its millenarian hope of salvation, and its dream of 'going back home to the Promised Land' (now Ethiopia rather than West Africa). The invasion of Ethiopia by Mussolini in the 1930s fulfilled another prophecy of the *Book of Revelations* – that 'the Beast and the kings of the earth and their armies' would gather together 'to make war against him'. (For the early history of the movement, cf. Smith *et al.*, 1960; Barrett, 1968; Nettleford, 1970; Cashmore, 1979.)

The doctrines of the Ras Tafari are based on a detailed exegetic decoding of the Sacred Book. Rastafarian brethren place considerable emphasis on 'reasoning', which is a form of exegetical argument, largely directed towards proving by ingenious derivation the 'truths' of Rastafarian doctrine by a complex chain of metaphorical inferences. Each Rastafarian can 'reason' for himself. He is not bound or tied by the received dogma maintained by the institutions of his sect, for it is a highly individualised, decentralised movement, with strikingly little hierarchy or authority structure compared with most religious denominations. Hence the doctrine, though clear in its broad framework, is as a meaning-system or a conceptual schema open to constant modification and reinterpretation. Its function as a practical guide to conduct and attitudes outweighs any aspiration it may have to doctrinal coherence or logical consistency in the western rationalist sense. Students of Rastafarianism often point to this open-weave, loose-texturing quality of Rastafarian discourse (cf. Hebdige, 1979; Owens, 1977; Garrison, 1979, 1976; Dalrymple, 1976; Cashmore, 1979).

At the conceptual core, we find two key ideas. First, the identification with Africa: the belief that the Rastas are the lost ancient tribe of Israel, enslaved by white Babylon; and the equivalence made between 'redemption from slavery' and return to the Promised Land. The ideology here works in the narrative mode. History is a millenarian sequence or cycle: enslavement/exile – awakening/brotherhood – redemption/return. The cosmology is sharply polarised: black/white, good/bad, Zion/Babylon.

This 'story' makes sense of the whole slave and post-slave experience of blacks in the American diaspora. The divinity of Haile Selassie, the second core concept, is not so important, in my view, as 'Africa'. Though Rastafarians invoke 'Jah' (an early form of 'Jehovah'), he is not always literally identified with Haile Selassie. Significantly, Selassie's deposition and death has not fundamentally weakened the cohesion of Rastafarian doctrine – especially since it can be 'reasoned away'. As one old Rastafarian figure said sceptically to the present author, when asked to explain Selassie's death: 'When last you hear the truth about the Son of God from the mass media?'.

'Babylon' is articulated in Rastafarianism in terms of the experience of 'suffering', 'oppression', 'endless pressure' in the here and now by the chosen people. Its composition differs with the context: the brown middle classes who dominate 'the system' in Jamaica, the white power structure in Britain. Babylon overtly uses repression to keep the Rastas down, but – being subtle and clever – also draws out or steals the Rastaman's energy and creative power. The promised destruction of Babylon, the release into Zion and the dawning of a new age gives Rastafarianism the classic millenarian structure of many religious sects – especially, it should be remarked, Judaeo-Christian ones developed in a colonial or imperial context – while at the same time being a deliberate reversal or inversion of white Christianity. Rastas are committed to a life of simplicity and poverty and must live in peace and love within the brotherhood. Rastafarianism believes that the spirit of Jah inheres equally in *each* individual. 'The supreme authority is within yourself because Jah is living within I and I' (Plummer, 1978). Hence none should be the object of another's subjugation or domination. This fundamental equality of the spirit is reflected in the refusal to use the third person pronoun. Linguistically, Rastafarians always refer to 'you and me', as 'I and I'.

'I and I' is no simple linguistic device. Garvey always insisted that the movement of black emancipation required a new subject – the 'New Negro', the product of a 'second emancipation' (Cashmore, 1979, p. 21). This could only come about if there was a parallel inner transformation, with blacks throwing off the sense of inferiority they had deeply internalised and spiritually renovating themselves from within. Much of the language of Rastafarian doctrine seems directed towards achieving this inner discipline. It is therefore designed to produce a new collective 'subject', a new type of subjectivity, as the 'bearer' of Rastafarian practices and culture (see Laclau (1977) in the *Politics and Ideology* reader). This new subjectivity involves the positive identification of oneself as black, the investment of pride in that self-identification, coupled with a reorientation of consciousness around the awareness of Africa. The construction of this subjectivity has led to a significant release of creative energy – Rastafarian culture places a high emphasis on creative self-expression and has been enormously productive in the arts, music, painting, sculpture, design and handicrafts, etc. There is a powerful sense of 'them' and 'us' – and of the 'true self'. What is most important, however, is the new conceptual map the doctrine makes available to explain a long historical oppression.

In practice, attitudes towards women among Rastafarians are highly traditional. They are regarded as second in status to men, and with the duty to look after and support them. They are treated with courtesy, enjoined to dress and behave modestly and with dignity; though respected as the Rastaman's 'Queen' they are also taught to accept the rightfulness of male superiority. In this respect, Rastafarianism does not significantly diverge from the male patriarchalism of traditional Jamaican society.

Rastafarians follow what they interpret as the injunction of the Bible not to cut their hair ('locks'). They adopt the green, yellow, red and black colours of Ethiopia. They are usually vegetarians. If employed, they prefer to be self-employed – as small cultivators, carpenters, craftsmen. The majority scrape a living communally in permanent unemployment. To limit contact with and dependence on 'Babylon', they try to do without money, which they consider a token of their wider withdrawal from involvement with an alien society which oppresses them. They preach a gospel of brotherhood, of 'peace and love' though one strand within Rastafarianism is more aggressive in its stance towards white society. In general, Rastas are bound to one another by strong ties of loyalty, solidarity and support. Many use *ganja* (marijuana) to facilitate withdrawal into the world of the spirit; respectable Jamaican society – against all the pharmacological evidence – steadfastly persisted in the belief that smoking 'the weed' drove Rastas to frenzy, crime and violence.

Lantenari (1965), in his survey of the religions of the oppressed, makes the mistaken judgement that Rastafarianism is 'typically an escapist movement rather than a revolutionary force'. Though there is a strong element of other-worldly withdrawal in Rastafarian ideology and practice, there have always been powerful factors inflecting the movement in a more activist and radical direction, as Wilson more correctly observes (Wilson, 1963, in this volume). In part this is due to its social composition and territorial basis. Rastafarianism has always appealed to the most oppressed, most disadvantaged, sections of the Jamaican populace – the urban underclass. Second, there is its consistent orientation to Africa and the cry of repatriation. This put a question mark over their commitment to the emerging, independent Jamaican state and awakened one of the deepest of subversive themes amongst the black poor – the African connection. The subversive impact of the enunciation of these long-repressed themes (Africa and slavery) and the challenge it threw out to the dominant classes of repectable Jamaica can hardly be over-estimated.

Third is the analysis of social conditions in Jamaica which Rastafarian-ism posed. Rastas insisted that black men had not only been oppressed under slavery, but were *continuing to be oppressed* in 'modern' Jamaica. In the context of the move towards political independence this was a scandalous proposition. Jamaicans were now supposed to be a united peo-ple, 'one for all and all for one'. In fact, not only was the country deeply divided in political allegiance and outlook between the two political par-ties and philosophies – the business-orientated Jamaica Labour Party, and the social-democratic People's National Party, but more serious-ly, independence had brought to completion the social and economic hegemony of the brown middle classes, the inheritors of the nationalist movement, in dependent partnership with white metropolitan interests. It was this post-independence power structure which Rastafarianism challenged.

Rastafarianism thus came to be the 'language' in which the rising aspirations of the popular black masses of the society were expressed. It succeeded in shifting the index of cultural hegemony in Jamaican society and began to substitute for the dominant cultural system of white bias an alternative regime 'grounded' on the African connection, black-ness and the vernacular culture. In the course of this reversal or 'cultural revolution' the society pivoted on its axis, and where previous assimi-lation to white models had provided the 'touchstone' of cultural authority, now the 'black roots', from which Rastafarianism itself arose, became the authenticating reference-point. This 'reversal' was cultural and ideo-logical rather than political or economic. But its consequences were nevertheless profound. Jamaica became, for the first time in its history, *culturally* 'black', and in the course of this, Rastafarianism was itself transformed from the position of the esoteric doctrine of a small, excluded and oppressed religious sect into something more closely akin to a mass cultural ideology.

The general social unrest, excessive rates of unemployment, extensive economic poverty and distress, the high rates of crime and the daily, sporadic violence which characterised the 1960s and 1970s was given a cultural articulation by the emergence of the 'movement of Jah people'. The widespread adoption of Rasta attitudes to the smoking of ganja un-doubtedly attracted to the cult a fringe of what can be called Rasta 'fellow travelling', counter-cultural youth, including black students and some politicised members of the middle-class intelligensia. But its impact was most profound on lower-class youth and the urban masses, and this could be seen in the gradual adoption of Rasta insignia, slogans and beliefs as cultural symbols by Kingston's 'rude boys' – the young 'hard men' of the street who made a style out of their defiance of established authority (cf. Hebdige, 1974). Garrison (1979) describing the loose and eclectic structure of the movement, differentiated between the 'religious' (organised around societies like the Ethiopian Orthodox Church); the 'secularists', working for some goals but not fully identified members (e.g. the Rastafarian Movement Association); and 'sympathisers' who deployed Rastafarian symbols and motifs as a counter-cultural idiom of protest.

This diffusion of Rastafarianism within Jamaican lower-class culture coincided with the great awakening of the civil rights, black nationalist and black power movements in North America. It closely followed the period of decolonisation and the nationalist independence struggles of the Third World, especially Africa. Rastafarianism as a popular social movement was the *form* in which an indigenous *black cultural nationalism* took root as a popular ideology among the Jamaican masses. Rastafarianism had no organised political programme as such. But it functioned as a revolutionising ideological force.

It is something of a paradox that, in the very moment when the Rasta movement and doctrine asserted that blacks were 'strangers' in an 'alien' land, and could only be released from 'suffering' when repatriated to the African homeland, Rastas were not simply finding roots in Jamaica, but were becoming, ideologically, the *essence of Jamaican-ness*. The alienation, which doctrinal Rastas thought of in terms of the 'lost tribes' Israelites, and more secular interpreters referred to slavery, was once more re-appropriated as the statement of a radical but fundamental truth about twentieth-century post-independence Jamaican society. It was *here*, day-to-day, in the concrete experience of everyday life as well as in the concrete structures of 'modern' Jamaican society that the people were 'suffering'. It was to a 'Promised Land' *in Kingston* that those who responded to the Rasta call wanted, in the long run, to be 'repatriated'. It was from their very present material, social, cultural and spiritual expropriation that they looked for 'redemption'. The links established here between the 'other-worldliness' of the doctrine and the 'here-and-now' of its practical and ideological references is critical in understanding how religious systems come to refer to real historical conditions. To sustain the metaphorical nature of this discourse, what Rasta posed for Jamaican society as a whole was *how Africa could be liberated* – not the spiritual Africa over the ocean, but *the concrete 'Africa' here at home*: the 'African' of the diaspora, so long a symbol in a hidden, repressed and forgotten discourse.

This cultural discourse mobilised, for the first time since formal independence, the radical energies of the lowest sections of the mass of the people, who – without being converted *en masse* to Rastafarian doctrine and practice – became in large measure 'cultural Rastafarians'. In the 1970s, as unemployment and poverty deepened, the political leadership of Jamaican society set about trying to harness and articulate to itself this newly-created cultural energy-source. Both the rival political parties were unable fully to harness and realise its cultural potential, for that would have involved a massive upheaval of the social order from end to end. Rastafarianism, in this sense, remained a marginal social movement, though ideologically central. It never 'seized power', or became the leading organised political force or was established as the dominant social ideology. Its deep suspicion of traditional politicians and its religious and millenarian structure – both as doctrine and as social movement – had the real effect of establishing certain limits, beyond which it could not move as a mobilising, political force. It therefore deeply informed and infused political and national-cultural life, assisting into existence the first authentically black national-popular Jamaican culture, and mediating the relationship between the political elite and the ghetto, while remaining somewhat distanced from the actual interplay of power and politics in everyday Jamaican society. Its quasi-religious character simultaneously inhibited its becoming a fully secularised political force, and yet guaranteed its connections with the popular ideological roots of the society.

In the critical election in the 1960s, Edward Seaga (now Prime Minister of Jamaica, leader of the Jamaican Labour Party, and Washington's closest ally in the Caribbean; then a vigorous young politician with an organised following among Kingston's youth gangs) tried to appropriate a new form of African-based music which had appeared in the shanty-towns and which had strong links with Revival-Pocomania – the *ska* – and erect it into a national music. In the parallel critical election in the 1970s, which initiated Jamaica's most radical political phase, the rival leader, Michael Manley (later, Washington's sternest critic and friend of Fidel Castro) appeared on political platforms, clasping an African headman's staff (referred to in Rasta-talk as a 'Rod of Correction'), and claimed the sponsorship of the leading Rastafarian reggae musician, Bob Marley. His campaign was spearheaded by Delroy Wilson's reggae song with the full Rastafarian promise, 'Betta Must Come'. In this radical period, although formally the Rastafarian movement maintained its distance from full identification with the Manley government, Rasta terminology suffused the political language. The music, painting, drumming and crafts of the Rasta brethren acquired the informal status of 'Jamaican art'; the symbols and rituals of the sect flourished.

V

How does a new mobilising quasi-religious ideology of this type come to pervade a whole society or culture? Curiously enough, not by the 'normal' route of founding a 'church' and enlarging a congregation but by far more secular means. One answer lies in the exploration of new media – the musical explosion which occurred in the 1970s. This period witnessed the creation of a native music industry, local recording studios, the flowering of small 'dub' groups, the heroic battles for popularity between rival disc-jockeys (DJs) and 'sound systems' and a rich vein of musical creation everywhere.

Already, in the early 1950s, a renaissance of Jamaican music had begun, drawing on African rhythms and black North American 'soul', jazz and 'gospel' influences, but with a characteristic native inflection, leading to a succession of new musical forms – from ska and bluebeat to rocksteady. The trend has been steadily back towards a slower, more bodily rooted, more rhythmically 'basic' and less 'harmonic' music and orchestration – a music overtly and authentically 'Afro-Jamaican' in form and inspiration (Johnson and Pines, 1982). In the 1960s and 1970s much of this new music was extensively recorded in the small recording studios which sprang up and exported. The social basis of its development lay deep in the infrastructure of black shanty-town life: in the parties, the dances, the bands, the competitions between DJs and their 'sound systems', the record shops and street music characteristic of lower-class life and entertainment (cf. Hebdige, 1979; Kallyndyr and Dalrymple, undated; Dalrymple, 1976). By far the most popular of the new indigenous musical forms to emerge was the music called reggae. But the music, lyrics and performances of reggae bands, were suffused with the emblems and the doctrines of Rastafarianism. The best known, and now internationally recorded and recognised, of these performers – Bob Marley and the Wailers – combined direct social comment on the life and conditions of the dispossessed classes in the Kingston ghettoes and political commentary on Jamaican society with invocations of Rasta philosophy. It is a throbbing, steadily-driving, rhythmically sinuous yet militant music. Its themes are the themes of pressure, suffering, struggle, redemption and release. The lyrics were littered with Biblical and Rasta references but were firmly entrenched in events and situations drawn from the black ghetto experience. The titles of Marley's early songs are significant in themselves. They included *Soul Rebel, African Herbsman, Rasta Revolution, Rude Boy, Simmer Down, Duppy Conqueror, Trenchtown Rock, Keep on Moving, No Woman No Cry, Rebel Music, Positive Vibration, Rastaman Vibration, Get Up, Stand Up* … Bob Marley was a committed Rastafarian, a man from Trenchtown in lower Kingston: a rebel, quietly militant figure with a capacity to articulate in the new language of 'suffering and rebellion' what his audience was thinking, feeling and hoping for. He had remarkable musical gifts, both as performer and songwriter. But he was only one of hundreds of small 'roots' groups (including, in the early phase, Prince Buster, Desmond Dekker, Jimmy Cliff, Toots and the Maytals) playing new and modified versions of reggae, which reverberated across the land out from the urban depths, in the 1970s. Despite its subsequent commercialisation, reggae's success continues to depend fundamentally on its capacity to articulate the experiences of the oppressed masses (Boot and Thomas, 1976).

That music, and the wider message which it bears, has nowhere taken such profound roots as amongst the alienated black youth in English cities – the children of those thousands of Jamaican unemployed who came to Britain as immigrant labour in the 1950s and 1960s, who have become in their turn alienated from white society and from the racism of the 'home country'. In *their* search for authentic cultural roots and an alternative social identity, young black people in Britain in the 1970s adopted not only reggae music but the whole 'rude boy' style and later the full panoply of the emblems and language of the Rastafarian sect (see the richly interpretative analysis of this transition by Hebdige, 1979).

The development of a specifically black British variant of Rastafarianism, the diffusion of Rasta ideas, symbols and motifs in the ghetto culture of British cities and the emergence of a specifically British reggae and Afro-Caribbean musical culture – startling a cultural development as it is – is nevertheless itself part of a wider process: the formation of a black counter-culture of resistance among second and third generation blacks in Britain. This 'resistance' culture has come – as Rastafarianism did in Jamaica in the 1970s – to provide the basis of new modes of self-discovery and self-identity for blacks, as well as ethnic pride, a sense of history and culture, ways of articulating the experience of oppression and forms in which to imagine an alternative future. Life in the black communities and 'colony' areas of British cities increasingly has come to draw on and depend on this cultural/ideological resource in the struggle for survival. An additional irony is the degree to which this specifically black counter-culture has influenced and interpenetrated the sub-cultures of white youth.

This most recent appropriation of Rastafarianism in Britain is perhaps the most surprising and unexpected of the movement's many transformations – pointing up the extraordinary flexibility, the multi-accentuality, of ideological systems, their capacity to be adapted to ever new circumstances, to articulate new experiences, to become the vehicle of new aspirations in new historical contexts. The great migration of Afro-Caribbean peoples to Britain from the 1950s onwards was, in essence, a movement of a black rural, colonial people into a highly urban, secular, industrialised white culture. The experience has been deeply 'dispossess- ing' especially for young blacks in the second and third generations, whose routes 'back' to their homeland are firmly closed, but who are often treated as an 'alien wedge' within the majority white culture of the 'host' English society, and who continue to be excluded and oppressed by their secondary status in white society. It is therefore not surprising that, in the 1970s and 1980s, a significant proportion of these young people have rediscovered themselves and their own black culture, and learned to 'speak' of their experience of oppression, racial harassment and discrimination in the language, imagery and symbolism of Rasta- farianism (Pryce, 1979).

In this latest twist it is Britain – the white social system and the police – which is signified as 'Babylon': the period of migration which is 'exile'. It is the ending of this new kind of oppression which is regarded as the promise of Zion and of freedom to come. The language and ter- minology of Rasta reasoning remains basically the same – complexly articulated around borrowings from the Bible and the Prophetic Books. But what is now enunciated within this apparently limited discourse is the ever-present troubles of black Afro-Caribbeans, still – after 400 years – wandering the diaspora in search of redemption.

VI

The Rastafarian 'case' allows us some concluding reflections on the nature of religious ideology. Ideologies are not fixed doctrines or belief systems. They can be adapted to express different meanings in different historical circumstances. A second point is the *multi-accentual* character of ideology. The same repertoire of concepts, symbols, imagery and doctrine can articulate a variety of meanings and positions, depending on how the elements are combined and accented. Symbols – like 'The Promised Land' – do not carry a single, unilateral meaning. They belong to rich connotational chains of meaning, which can be differently in- flected or positioned. Rastafarianism, for example, imposes its own set of connotations on many well-established signifiers (e.g. Moses, Babylon, Israelites, Zion) which it has 'stolen' from other discourses (e.g. that of white Biblical interpretation), dissociated from their original meaning and position, imported as elements into a different, signifying chain, deflecting the terms to a new meaning in the process. Each signifier is really a condensation of many meanings. 'The Promised Land' signifies, at one and the same time, the return of the lost tribes of Israel from enslavement in Egypt (from the original Bible story), the more symbolic

Christian prophetic promise of heaven, salvation and redemption to come; overlaid with the promise of the return of the enslaved peoples to their African homeland, the slave's actual hope of freedom and escape, and the general social and practical belief that the fate of an oppressed people will ultimately be rewarded by a transformation of their social and historical conditions here on earth. *All* these meanings are present, condensed into a single term; but one aspect – the return to Africa – is the one which is foregrounded by its insertion into the logic of Rastafarian discourse. The differences between different ideological systems arise, not because each term or concept belongs exclusively to one doctrine or system but precisely through this work of multi-accentuality (Volosinov, 1973) which ideology performs across language.

Another aspect concerns the forms of consciousness which are generated by religious ideologies. We think of consciousness as the forms of awareness which lead groups to think and act in certain ways. But the case study suggests that it is ideological discourse and practice which produce particular forms of 'consciousness'. Rastafarianism, as doctrine and practice, had tended to produce a particular Afro-Caribbean type of religio-political consciousness, grounded in the historical experience of the black masses, infused by particular traditions of African and Christian thinking, reasoning and practice. Many who were already, literally, black 'became black', culturally, only within the discourse of Rastafarianism. Consciousness, in this sense, is not so much the product of the ideological attitudes we consciously adopt, as the result of the largely unconscious process of locating ourselves within a particular structure of discourse or 'reasoning'.

To what extent are the mass religious ideologies we have been discussing 'true'? In one sense, not at all: their metaphorical status is obvious. Whatever else Haile Selassie, the deposed King of Ethiopia, was, he was unlikely to have been Jah, the Great Redeemer. And yet, within another 'logic', Rastafarianism may be 'truer' to the real historical experiences of new world blacks than many more literally accurate accounts and explanations. In a language literally inaccurate and untrue, many black people have been empowered to define for themselves, make sense of and interpret a historical experience of which their everyday 'language' did not, for many years, enable them to speak at all or which imposed on them alien categories. The question of truth is of only indirect relevance in the study of ideological discourses. Their value lies rather in their capacity to generate meanings around which action and struggle can become socially organised.

Finally where did these 'ideas' come from? One view is that each class or substratum has its own 'thoughts' and that its ideologies will be simply the expression of the thoughts appropriate to them, given their class position in society. But this account does not fit our case. Of course, there are tendencies of strong and weak affinity between particular bodies of discourse and particular social groups: the white plantocracy was highly unlikely to think about conditions of existence in a discourse generated by Rastafarianism. Yet in more general terms, the universe of religious languages has never been parcelled up and ascribed to the different classes in Jamaica. What we find instead is social classes at different historical moments, operating selectively across the rich universe of religious discourse, and beginning to articulate their position and experience *through* combinations of different ideological terms and constructions, or within a particular ideological logic. Religion and its subdivisions in Jamaica in this sense has no absolutely fixed class or social 'belonging- ness' (Laclau, 1977 in *Politics and Ideology*): Moses belonged to them *all* – to slaveholding Anglicanism, dissenting Methodism, Pentecostal Revivalism, black folk religion and Rastafarianism alike. What is more striking is how certain ideological religious 'logics' came to be articulated, in specific historical moments, to specific social and class positions: how, for example, the particular syncretic background of Jamaican religious culture provided the terrain on which the articulations were made bet- ween the urban dispossessed and the discourse of cultural Rastafarianism in the historical conjuncture of post-political independence. These links between class and discourses are not fixed or determined for ever: the same groups can and may well develop alternative modes of conscious- ness. On the other hand, ideologies cannot have real historical effects unless links *can* be forged between ideas and a social group or movement. When these articulations 'work' it enables new political or cultural sub- jects to emerge and new symbols to become the unifying points in the organisation of the collective struggles of the masses.

References

Barrett, L. (1968) *The Rastafarians: A Study in Messianic Cultism*, Puerto Rico.
Barrett, L. (1976) *The Sun and the Drum: African Roots in Jamaican Folk Tradi- tion*, London, Heinemann Educational Books.
Bastide, R. (1971) *African Civilizations in the New World*, London, Hurst and Co.
Beckworth, M. (1929) *Black Roadways: Jamaican Folk Life*, Chapel Hill.
Beltran, C. (1959) 'African influences in the development of Negro culture in the New World', in Rubin (ed.).
Boot, A. and Thomas, M. (1976) *Jamaica: Babylon on a Thin Wire*, London, Thames and Hudson.
Braithwaite, E. (1971) *Creole Society in Jamaica 1770–1820*, Oxford, Clarendon Press.
Burridge, K. (1971) *New Heaven, New Earth*, Oxford, Blackwells.
Calley, M. (1965) *God's People*, Oxford, Oxford University Press.

Cashmore, E. (1979) *Rastaman*, London, Allen and Unwin.

Cassidy, F. (1961) *Jamaica Talk*, London, Macmillan.

Cronon, J. (1964) *Black Moses: The Story of Marcus Garvey*, Wisconsin, Madison.

Curtin, P. (1955) *The Two Jamaicas*, Cambridge, Mass., Harvard University Press.

Dalby, D. (1977) *Language Map of Africa*, London, International African Institute.

Dalrymple, H. (1976) *Marley: Music, Myth and the Rastas*, Middlesex, Carib-Arawak.

Frazier, E.F. (1966) *The Negro Church: The Negro in America*, New York.

Garrison, L. (1975) *Rastafarians, Protest Movement of Jamaica, Afras Review*, Sussex University.

Garrison, L. (1979) *Black Youth, Rastafarianism and the Identity Crisis*, London, ACER.

Genovese, E. (1971) *The World the Slaveholders Made*, New York, Vintage Books.

Genovese, E. (1975) *Roll, Jordan, Roll*, London, Andre Deutsch.

Gramsci, A. (1971) *Selections from the Prison Notebooks*, London, Lawrence and Wishart.

Hall, D. (1959) *Free Jamaica, 1835–65*, New Haven, Yale University Press.

Hall, S. (1975) 'Pluralism, race and class in Caribbean society', in *Race and Class in Post-Colonial Society*, Paris, UNESCO.

Hebdige, D. (1979) *Subcultures: The Meaning of Style*, London, Methuen.

Herskovits, M. (1941) *The Myth of the Negro Past*, New York.

Hodgkin, T. (1962) *Mahdism, Messianism and Marxism in an African Setting*, Khartoum University.

Jahn, J. (1968) *A History of Negro African Literature*, London.

Johnson, H. and Pines, J. (1982) *Reggae: Deep Roots Music*, London, Proteus and Channel 4.

Kallyndr, R. and Dalrymple, H. (1974) *Reggae: A People's Music*, London, Carib-Arawak.

Laclau, E. (1977) *Politics and Ideology in Marxist Theory*, London, Verso.

Lantenari, V. (1965) *Religions of the Oppressed*, London, MacGibbon and Kee.

Lepage, R. (1960) *Jamaican Creole*, London, Macmillan.

Levine, L. (1977) *Black Culture and Black Consciousness*, New York, Oxford University Press.

Lewis, M. (1834) *Journal of a West Indian Proprietor*, London History of Jamaica (3 volumes), London.

Nettleford, R. (1970) *Mirror, Mirror*, London/Kingston, Collins-Sangsters.

Owens, J. (1977) *Dread*, Kingston, Sangsters.

Patterson, O. (1967) *The Sociology of Slavery*, London, MacGibbon and Kee.

Plummer, J. (1978) *Movement of Jah People*, Nottingham, Russell Press.

Pryce, K. (1979) *Endless Pressure*, Harmondsworth, Penguin.

Ragatz, L. (1963) *The Fall of the Planter Class in the British Caribbean*, New York, Octagon.

Rubin, V. (1959) *Plantation Systems of the New World*, Washington.

Simpson, G.M. (1955) *Jamaican Revivalist Cults*, in *Social and Economic Studies*, vol. 5. Kingston, University of the West Indies.

Smith, M., Augier, R. and Nettleford, R. (1960) *The Rastafarian Movement in Kingston Jamaica*, Kingston, University of the West Indies.

Sutcliffe, D. (1982) *British Black English*, Oxford, Blackwell.

Worsley, P. (1957) *The Trumpet shall Sound*, London, MacGibbon and Kee.

Volosinov, V.N. (1973) *Marxism and the Philosophy of Language*, New York, Seminar Press.

A typology of sects

First published in 1963 in *Archives des Sciences Sociales des Religions*, 16. Translated by J.M. Robertson. Reproduced by permission of the publishers, CNRS.

... Sects are ideological movements having as their explicit and declared aim the maintenance, and perhaps even the propagation of certain ideological positions [...] But sociological distinctions are not simply based on the distinctions of theological belief and practice, and certainly not on the *odium theologicum* which tries to characterize sects as extremist. In a valuable contribution to our conception of the denomination as a type, D.A. Martin places the denomination in opposition to the sect, without always giving enough attention to the diversity among sects. He describes them as if they were always revolutionary or introversionist [...] Martin writes: 'While the denomination is characterized by moderation, the sect is either communist or anarchist, revolutionary or quietest, nudist or uniformed, ascetic or licentious, completely sacramental or non-sacramental, worshipping in a wild communal rant, or, like the Seekers, utter silence' (Martin, 1962). Martin thus characterizes sectarian eschatology as adventist and sects as revolutionary, except in the case where too great a disillusionment has made them quietist. It is always easy to criticize a typology by underlining the case which does not correspond to the proposed classifications; but Martin's is too gross. Sects are not easily marshalled into a few dichotomies. The Brethren, Quakers and Christadelphians are neither communist nor anarchist; the different Darbyist groups, Jehovah's Witnesses, Church of God in British Isles and Overseas, the holiness movements do not worship in a wild rant nor in total silence; the Assemblies of God are neither ascetic nor licentious. But who would deny that these are sects? In fact, this kind of analysis takes the part as the whole; it overlooks the way in which separate elements combine together, and almost completely ignores the various possibilities for the transformation of sects.

From the sociologist's point of view, there are three sorts of drawback to the theological or doctrinal classification of sects. First of all, such a classification limits the possibilities for the comparative study of sects within different religious traditions. In the second place, it prevents recognition of other significant aspects of the character of sects, for the doctrine may persist when the social organization and the orientation of the movement have changed. Thus, classification which grows from doctrinal description does not sufficiently take into account the organizational and dynamic aspects of sects. Thirdly, because it is theological, this kind of classification runs the risk of stigmatizing the sect and characterizing it in terms which are essentially normative [...]

I wish here to develop a classification I used in a previous study of the transformation of sects (Wilson, 1959), in the hope that this typology can be shown to be of use in the analysis of sectarian movements in non-Christian and non-Western environments. I also wish to attempt a first, tentative step, and only by way of experiment, in applying this typology to religious movements at the fringes of Christianity. This classification takes as its central criterion the sect's *response to the world*. It is hoped that we shall find there an adequate principle of classification, capable of advancing the comparative study of sects and also of sect development.

One clearly sees that our criterion of response to the outside world constitutes a variable influenced by doctrinal thought, although it is not perhaps determined by that alone. It recognizes the ideological character of sects, without nevertheless neglecting the way of life of the sect's members, which also necessarily affects the manner in which they accept, reject, neglect or attempt to transcend, to improve or to transvaluate the opportunities which worldly society may offer. Here we have a factor which can effect change without producing specific doctrinal changes, in response simply to the social changes affecting the members of the sect. Of course, a certain specific type of response is more likely to be seen in certain age groups, in certain social classes, among people with particular educational backgrounds or in certain ecological contexts. It might also be more attractive to one sex than another; it will suit better a rural situation, or an urban or a suburban one. And it may arise and develop at one stage rather than at another of the social and cultural history of the sect under review. In this article we shall not be able to examine all these variables individually. But we shall intimate certain relationships between different types of sects and different stages of cultural development.

I should now like to propose a seven-fold classification of sects [...] I define each type in terms of its response to the world, of the kind of reaction which dominates the customary practices and its members' beliefs. For each of these types is suggested the typical theological position in Christian sects, by giving a few specific examples of these movements. We define also the activities to which they typically devote themselves

and refer to the biblical texts which they favour. The reader will understand that I do not claim that all these texts hold the same importance
in Christian tradition, but that I seek simply to illustrate the way in
which sects attempt to integrate with this tradition. I have not tried,
except very tentatively and where the evidence is perfectly clear, to
suggest from which social groups these sects recruit.

The *conversionist* sect is the typical sect of 'evangelical', fundamentalist Christianity. Its reaction towards the outside world is to suggest that
the latter is corrupted because man is corrupted. If men can be changed
then the world will be changed. This type of sect takes no interest in
programmes of social reform or in the political solution of social problems
and may even be actively hostile towards them.

Its judgement on man and events tends to be moralizing, because it
is believed that man is entirely responsible for his actions. It rejects all
causal explanations which take into account the influence of environment on behaviour, or any other determinist explanation. Typical
activities of this type of sect are revivalism and public preaching at mass
meetings rather than door to door. The leaders of the sect mobilize the
group and use techniques of mass persuasion in order to convert individuals. The dominant note in the atmosphere of the group is of an
emotional, but not ecstatic, nature. Among Christian sects, the texts
regarded highly are those which encourage the preaching of the Gospel
throughout the world. They attach great significance to the relationship
between the individual and a personal saviour, a relationship expressed
in direct emotional terms rather than in a symbolic or ritualistic manner.
They hold the total understanding of the doctrine to be less important
than the profound feeling of the essential personal relationship. In the
same way as they interpret the Scripture literally, the sect's members
tend to take this relationship literally. For them the Saviour is a person,
a sort of benevolent and suffering Superman. The Salvation Army, in the
first stages of its existence, the Assemblies of God and other pentecostal
movements, as well as independent evangelical sects, are examples of
this type of sect.

One recognizes the *revolutionary* type in the eschatological
movements of the Christian tradition. Its attitude towards the outside
world is summed up in a desire to be rid of the present social order when
the time is ripe – if necessary by force and violence. Its members are
awaiting a new order under God's direction. They will then become the
holders of power as the friends and representatives of God. This type of
sect is hostile at one and the same time to social reform and instantaneous
conversion. It is not opposed to causal explanations, in so far as one
accepts its own assumptions of causal categories. It tends to explain
the world in determinist terms, just as it tends to consider the fate of

individuals as pre-determined. In the Christian tradition, we have therefore a position which is more Calvinist than Arminian. One meets here less tendency to moralize than among the *conversionists*, for reproaches are out of place when one likes to consider all events as the accomplishment of a divine plan. The members of these sects occupy themselves actively in prophetic exegesis, in comparisons of inspired texts and between the predictions of the sect and contemporary events. They often have long-drawn-out internal debates elaborating prospects of the future. Conversion is considered to be an occasional and gradual occurrence, and comes about only when the stranger to the sect has familiarized himself completely with the complexity of sect belief and is convinced of its truth. Permission to belong is not given freely, and the revolutionary sect, when it is fully institutionalized, seeks to maintain itself in a state of vigilance and doctrinal purity. Its meetings are matter-of-fact, unemotional occasions. These are occasions to praise God decently and without emotional excess, for speaking of one's calm certainty that the promises will be fulfilled. The biblical texts in favour in these circles are directly eschatological or else obscure visions from prophetic books which can be interpreted as relevant predictions for the present period. They see God as a divine autocrat, as a leader, a dictator whose impenetrable will imposes itself on the progress of the universe. One finds in these sects little feeling of a direct relationship with divinity. On the contrary, their members have the feeling that they are God's instruments, waiting for the decreed moment, agents of His work and will. Jehovah's Witnesses, Christadelphians and the Fifth Monarchy Men (England, seventeenth century) are typical representatives of these ideas.

The pietist sects represent the *introversionist* type whose response to the world is neither to convert the population nor to expect the world's overturn, but simply in retiring from it to enjoy the security gained by personal holiness. This type is completely indifferent to social reforms, to individual conversion and to social revolutions. None of these elements seems significant to these sects in their view of their position and task on this earth. The introversionist sect may accept, especially in its early stages, some particular inspirational experiences and retain them for objective phenomena significant for the entire group, or consider them as purely individual revelations which might help the growth of personal piety. These groups are concerned more with deepening than widening spiritual experience. One finds among them a certain disdain for those 'without holiness' and with little or no desire to introduce them to it. These movements' meetings are 'assemblies of the saved' (gathered remnant). The community will support the individual and hold him in its bosom, rather than push him to seek his mission in the outside world. These groups, if Christian, put great weight on biblical texts which exhort the faithful to be a law unto themselves and to live apart from the world. They conceive of a divinity of the type of the Holy Spirit rather than in a more personalized way. The real relationship in this case is less than between sinner and saviour, rather than between outpouring vial and rerceiving vessel. Typical examples of this category of sects can be seen in certain 'holiness movements', as well as in European pietist movements of the eighteenth century.

Manipulationist sects, which I previously called gnostic, are those which insist especially on a particular and distinctive knowledge. They define themselves *vis-à-vis* the outside world essentially by accepting its goals. They frequently proclaim a more spiritualized and ethereal version of the cultural ends of global society but do not reject them. These sects instead try to change the methods appropriate to attaining these ends. They sometimes claim that the only way of achieving this is to use the special knowledge taught by the movement. That is the only true and worthwhile way of acquiring health, wealth, happiness and social prestige. Although reinterpreting 'worldly' activities, these sects offer special techniques and verbal modes of assurance which justify the pursuit and attainment of cultural goals. These movements are thus of the type sometimes called 'cults', and which Marty (1960) depicts as positively oriented towards the outside world. They offer, by means of publicity, facilities for learning their systems but do not provoke conversions since the important thing is for them to acquire spiritual attitudes rather than to offer specific activities or relationships. The group life of these movements is often reduced to an absolute minimum, their gnosis being impersonal. Anyone may accept it and use it for his personal ends since its efficacy is not dependent on any relationship or on any mystical process. When the members of these movements come together, the chief function of their assembly seems to be not so much for worship or devotion as to claim prestige and social status for successes achieved using the special teachings of the sect. These movements are often syncretist, even within the Christian tradition. But they use evangelical texts such as those where Christ affirmed that he had many other things to say, but that men could not bear to hear them. Divinity is understood, implicitly or explicitly, as a source of laws or principles to apply in one's daily life. The idea of a personal saviour is reduced here to a minimum and one notices the absence of any emotional relationship with God, or a relationship of authority. Provided he can take the trouble, anyone can learn the doctrine, which can be applied universally. These sects take little interest in eschatology. They are interested in results in this world, and the hereafter seems to them simply an enhancement of present joys. Typical groups of this type in Christian countries are Christian Scientists, Unitarians, Psychiana, Scientology and Rosicrucians [...]

Thaumaturgical sects are movements which insist that it is possible for men to experience the extraordinary effect of the supernatural on their lives. Within Christianity, their principal representatives are spiritualist groups whose main activity lies in seeking personal messages from the spirits, obtaining cures, effecting transformations and performing miracles. These sects define themselves in relation to the wider society by affirming that normal reality and causation can be suspended for the benefit of special and personal dispensations. They resist acceptance of the physical process of ageing and death and come together to affirm a special exception from everyday realities which assures each individual and his loved ones of perpetual well-being in the next world. For the present, they procure immediate advantages by accomplishing miracles. In several ways these groups differ little from manipulationist sects, except that their response to the world is less universalist and more personal. Moreover, they do not claim a special gnosis, but tend rather to call upon spirits and other powers to perform oracles and miracles. The ends they seek can be defined in terms of compensation for personal losses rather than the specific quest for cultural goals. Here religious activity is not far removed from magic. When these groups assemble, they form an audience in which the majority hope for personal benefits or watch others obtain them. If they are Christian, these groups put great weight on the various miraculous happenings in the Scriptures. The Gospel according to St Mark especially appeals to them. Their most characteristic activity is the 'seance' or public demonstration. The relationships they seek tend to be more with lost relatives than with God or a saviour and their conception of a saviour is seldom elaborated. We find among these groups the national Spiritualist Church and the Progressive Spiritualist Church.

The *reformist* sects seem to constitute a case apart. But the dynamic analytic approach to religious movements demands a category corresponding to those groups which, though sectarian in more than one respect, have affected transformations in their early response towards the outside world. Originally revolutionary, this attitude may have become introverted later. The history of the Quakers is a typical example of this. Revolutionary at the start and becoming introvertionist during the eighteenth century they have gradually adopted a reformist position. This type of sect, possessing a very strong sense of identity, studies the world in order to involve itself in it by good deeds. It takes unto itself the role of social conscience. The sect also accepts a place in the world without being of the world or touched by its impurity. It associates with the world but keeps apart from it. The favourite texts of these sects, even if they do not hold fast to them, are those according to which faith without deeds is in vain and which support the view that the sect is itself the leavening of the lump. Their doctrinal position is mitigated, subsumed by their humanitarian orientation and their reformist tendencies towards the outside world. The Christadelphians may at some time in the future end up by being transformed into this kind of sect, even though their doctrinal position is much more extensive and could not be easily abandoned. The interest in this category lies in the importance it would seem to have for the study of the transformations of sects when the structure persists although the response to the outside world is modified.

The *Utopian* sect is perhaps the most complex type. Its response to the outside world consists partly in withdrawing from it and partly in wishing to remake it to a better specification. It is more radical than the reformist sect, potentially less violent than the revolutionary sect and more constructive on a social level than the conversionist sect. It sets out through its activities to construct the world on a communitarian basis. It does not seek only to establish colonies but also proposes a programme for the reorganization of the world along community lines. Thus it aims at a sort of social reconstruction, but of a kind essentially different from that of such groups as the Quakers. It does in fact propose measures for social reorganization, and not only improvements and reforms within the existing framework of society. In the case of a Christian movement, the favourite biblical texts may be those of the Acts recounting the establishment of the primitive Christian community in Jerusalem. But sects of this sort are unlikely to have a clear conception of divinity. They may be conversionist in some measure but the converts they want are of a distinctive kind. As a consequence of the demands made of their members, they are likely to be rather suspicious of the candidates for conversion, rather like the monastic Orders. Among Christian groups (or more or less Christian) of this type, one might name the Tolstoyans, the Community of Oneida, the Brüderhof and perhaps also certain sections among the Christian Socialists.

In the case of Utopian sects, it seems necessary to distinguish between those which consider the founding of 'colonies' as their essential religious mission, as the specific means of attaining grace, and those for whom this represents but one reasonable means. Thus groups such as certain Mennonites, the Amana Society and the Shakers, communal in practice, have become so in response to particular circumstances, rather than as part of their original vision. Their practice of communal living does not constitute their response to the outside world, but their defence against it. This was in particular the appropriate way in which to adapt to the colonial (American) society into which they had immigrated, and which threatened to disperse them and assimilate them in piecemeal fashion into the irreligion of the 'frontier' situation. The practice of communal life, sometimes assisted by linguistic distinctiveness, became for these groups an important means of protecting their way of life from that of the wider society; and in a society where land was cheap and awaited only clearing, vicinal segregation by means of communal living became an almost natural means of defence. Of course, it could have happened that communal living assumed a very great significance for a movement and one should not neglect its importance as a decisive factor in the creation of a specific kind of change in introversionist movements. Gradually, as the original inspiration becomes less active – as was the case with the Shakers and the Amana society, introverted groups which at their inceptions claimed special spiritual gifts – communal living may then become an end in itself.

It would seem that, when sects do persist, they always undergo processes of mutation; some of the reasons for this have already been studied. Because sects cannot cut themselves off completely from the world they are influenced by external factors. But the internal causes are perhaps even more significant: the response of the founders towards the outside world becomes difficult to maintain for successive generations. The latter may equally re-evaluate and reinstate the devices of isolation set up by the founders, and what were in the beginning only institutional defence mechanisms may gradually become intrinsically important and no longer just as a means. Communitarianism, first adopted as protection, or the ideology and practices of the sect can thus be transformed from defence to response. It may in turn become the object of new mechanisms of defence and rationalization, and doctrinal or spiritual legitimation may, consequently, take the place of something which originally was purely circumstantial. Thus one can observe the internal consequences and even the *systematic ideological consequences* of what was at the beginning simply defensive action and an institutional adaptation is brought about [...]

Any typology of sects must point up, and not hide, the fact that sects pass through processes of change. It is not only a question of the process of denominalization, which is the typical change within conversionist sects (see Wilson, 1959). All organizations are prone to suffer an attenuation in commitment to their original values and this is especially true among protest movements. The sect manifests this tendency most particularly in its response to the world. Indeed, the structures, duties and official doctrine are much more resistant to change. But the attitude towards the outside world, which constitutes the major issue of debate between the sect and the wider society, may itself shift imperceptibly. An extremely clear illustration of this type of change can be found in the case of the revolutionary sect which, while remaining essentially a sect, may gradually change its attitude towards the outside world. An intense revolutionary spirit is difficult to maintain, especially when it depends upon the expectation of a supernatural sign, the date of which is of necessity frequently postponed. The revolutionary sect appears to be susceptible to two kinds of development. In the first case, the sect may bind its fate so tightly to the idea of active revolution that it does actually stage a rebellion: in that case it seems impossible to preserve the original religious position in its primitive form, even approximately. Sudanese Mahdi-ism, the Marching Rule Movement of the Solomon Islands, the Taiping rebellion (see Wallace, 1956) and perhaps the case of the Fifth Monarch Men (England, seventeenth century) seem to furnish examples of this type of transformation. The change into a military force tends to lead to the suppression of the sect by state authorities or to turn it into a secret party, precarious in its existence, and henceforward more political than religious. The second possible mutation may be harder to trace. It is difficult to maintain over a long period the hope of a divine appearance or a cataclysm, and it may perhaps be easier to keep it up by recruiting new adherents, enthusiastic for what to them is a new perspective, than to recruit a second generation or successive generations of members from among the children of members. But if the sect is well protected and has a good chance of maintaining its internal recruitment, then its response to the world will probably take on new aspects in spite of the persistence of doctrinal declarations, interpretations of the Scriptures or ritual. It seems that the revolutionary sect which persists, in these circumstances, becomes more passive, more withdrawn and that it then grows nearer in fact to the position of the introversionist sects. The change wrought among the Quakers would seem to be of this order [...]

Of course one can best study the typical changes of sects in terms of internal factors (disappointment of eschatological hopes, recruitment of a second generation). But the influence of the wider society must not be omitted in studying the birth and transformation of sects. It is obvious that sects of the manipulationist and introversionist type can only come about at certain stages of social and cultural development. A manipulationist sect can come into being only when metaphysical thought has extended into the religious and philosophical traditions of a society. Sects of this type tend to succeed among semi-intellectuals who have some knowledge of scientific or philosophical reasoning and imitate it up to a point. Manipulationist sects are universalist and this also is a cultural variable found only at relatively advanced stages of cultural development. These sects comprise more 'educated' people; they are unlikely to originate from the working classes. They tend to offer visions of prestige and power, as well as the short cuts for achieving them. They attract groups who have some ambition in this direction. The special means offered by the sects to attain these goals are defined in terms of verbal techniques and metaphysical theories. They use a language which

attracts confidence and creates assurance, and their pre-occupation with
the explanation of their theories tends to exclude all other activity. Well-
being in this world, perceived in terms of health, wealth, comfort and
social status, constitutes the practical sanction for these sects' teaching.
The achievement-oriented society offers its rewards through extremely
competitive processes. In response, these sects offer new methods which
allow an escape from tensions and the achievement of cultural goals,
especially for those who are sensitive to social status, and struggle to
attain it. Sects of this type were particularly significant during the
nineteenth and twentieth centuries in industrial societies (see Griswold,
1954; England, 1954; Wilson, 1961).

For quite different reasons, the introverted attitude also tends to be
manifest only in certain kinds of social circumstances. The retreat from
the wider society and the rejection of its dominant religious teachings
and practices are only possible when the social institutions have reached
a certain degree of autonomy from each other, and in circumstances
where religious expression and practices have ceased to constitute a
necessary public performance. The idea of private life must be established
before an introversionist religion can originate, especially in its non-
communitarian forms. In monasticism the retreat from the world was
practised under the auspices of the dominant social ideology and led to
a style of life separated from the world outside, but one could also say
that it was undertaken in the name of that world. In the case of the
introversionist sect, the retreat constitutes a more radical 'contracting
out', even though it does not renounce all social contacts, but essentially
only the customary and dominant religious and moral consensus. It can
thus only originate in a society already partly secularized, or in a society
where military conquest, for example, has put in doubt the traditional
religion and made possible some differentiation. Participation in secular
activities can continue, but if this leads to difficulties in the field of
religious practice then communitarian tendencies and segregation might,
in favourable circumstances, occur. But introversionist sects have not
always been able or wished to become communitarian; their method of
retreat seeks to establish a personal religious privacy, not vicinal segregation. They do not consider that this isolation is necessarily endangered
by secular activities if these are deemed 'necessary'. Thus certain holiness
movements and strict Darbyists admit that their members need to expose
themselves to the affairs of the world while keeping their private lives
pure of the contamination of that world. While conversionist and revolutionist sects insist on a doctrine of witness and its public expression,
the introversionist sects deny the value of such activity and reject its
theoretical implications. Introversionism seems to have constituted an
attitude which was tenable in seventeenth-century Europe, but it is clear

that the social climate is today less favourable to this kind of religious attitude. Compulsory education, sanitary and social regulations, increased
economic control of individual activity on the part of the State, the
extension of taxes, obligatory military service or the use of certain
procedures approved by nations to secure exemption from it – all these
factors bring the sectarian into closer involvement with the wider society.
The development of mass communications and the reliance which
governments have upon them, the extension of the division of labour,
the development of large scale man-power recruitment, the disappearance
of the small business – all this makes effective isolation more and more
difficult. The diffuse dependence of the individual on society makes his
withdrawal harder all the time and the individual's widening social
experience, his access to a great variety of cultural, social and leisure
activities probably reduce the relative attractions of a life of retreat.
Organic solidarity does not necessarily lead to increased allegiance to
society and its goals, but it does make complete independence more
difficult to attain or even to contemplate. These circumstances may, at
least for some time, produce among the sects responses which facilitate
the persistence of those already 'established', but at the same time make
less likely the growth of new sects, at least of the introversionist type,
and perhaps also of the revolutionist type.

If we now leave the Christian world for what one might call the
mission territories, we can quickly see that manipulationist sects and
introversionist sects are not likely to develop there. Indigenous sects,
which abound in these societies, are either revolutionist or
thaumaturgical. These two kinds of responses are primitive and simple.
Thaumaturgical practice characterizes primitive religion and magic, and
when societies reach the degree of complexity where religious deviation
becomes possible, thaumaturgy becomes an almost inevitable part of it.
Nevertheless, healing sects often owe much to the thaumaturgical
tradition of Christianity itself. Sects of this kind are born in primitive
societies in reply to social change and to deterioration in the traditional
culture. One of the aspects of this phenomenon is the introduction of new
ideologies which become in turn a source of religious ideas and practices
accessible to purely native religious movements. The 'Zionist' sects of
South Africa (see Sundkler, 1948; Dougall, 1956; Hunter, 1936) illustrate
this syncretization of pagan and Christian thaumaturgical practices, as
do the so-called Pocomania sects of Jamaica (Simpson, 1956). But it is
quite unlikely that manipulationist or introversionist sects will come into
being among the indigenous populations of these two territories, of which
one is more or less detribalized and the other is an under-developed non-
tribal society.

We frequently find the revolutionist type of religious movements in these mission territories, and it has been called, or called itself 'Ethiopian' (Cook, 1933; Westermann, 1937; Roux, 1945; Sundkler, 1948; Shepperson, 1952; Schlösser, 1949; Thwaite, 1936). The Ras Tafari movements of Jamaica are movements similar in their salient features. They insist in the typical manner, but in varying degrees, on the adventist or chiliastic expectation, on the coming reversal of roles between the adherents and their enemies, and all share the same awaiting of the millennium (Simpson, 1955). In certain contexts these movements have been identified with a type of incipient nationalism, or, where the term 'nationalism' is anachronistic, they are at least taken for semi-political movements. One may well consider some of them in these terms but in other cases to call them such is to go beyond the evidence. Many of them are nearer to those revolutionist sects which are not completely institutionalized. They do not necessarily lead to revolutionary activity but look forward to a revolutionary transformation of their society, or at least of their own circumstances. In general, they believe that a supernatural intervention in their favour will bring about the revolution.

Researchers accept the consideration that revolutionist sectarianism is a response to a situation of cultural strain. There seems some reason to suppose that this is a spontaneous response of oppressed or colonized peoples who make their wish-world into their response to the real world. But we cannot always be sure that this type of movement constitutes a spontaneous response and if we wish to draw a clear picture of the circumstances and cultural conditions to which revolutionary sects respond, we need to be able to dissociate the effects of cultural contact from those of cultural diffusion. Even very slight cultural contact seems capable of producing recognizable effects at the level of religious interpretation. But the responses of revolutionary sects as such may be provoked and stimulated by missionary activity, even by that of a more or less orthodox kind. We must also consider another factor: the fact that the Christian Scriptures carry a very clear revolutionist element which forms the doctrinal core of European and American revolutionist sects. These have often actively proselytized in under-developed countries and have disseminated their teaching far and wide. Paradoxically they are not alone in having communicated ideas of the return of Christ and the millennium, since these teachings are also after all part of the message of the many fundamentalist groups we can call conversionist. Nevertheless, in the context of mission territories, it could be that doctrines relatively less significant in the European or American situation may be just those most easily accepted by native peoples.

Thus several pentecostal sects, some of which call themselves holiness movements, and other fundamentalist groups, among them the Darbyists, have been working in Jamaica since 1919; the Seventh Day

Baptists (in Nyasaland), the Brethren Church (in Nigeria), the so-called Open Bible Standard Church Group (French West Africa) and many other groups were at work in Africa around 1955. The Seventh Day Adventists were reported to have about two thousand missionaries in the missionary lands at this time, and the American Assemblies of God had about seven hundred and fifty. These two groups have made a considerable number of converts in different parts of Africa and in other territories (see Thiessey, 1955, pp. 411 ff.; Pierce Beaver, 1954; Price and Mayer, 1956; Price, 1957). Already in the period around 1930, the penetration of the Seventh Day Adventists into the mission fields of more orthodox groups provoked complaints (Burton, 1936; Keesing, 1941, pp. 225 ff.). The Mormons and Jehovah's Witnesses maintain a substantial but secret number of lay missionaries in these countries, and the latter try to transform all their converts into as many 'publishers' of their particular form of adventism [...]

It remains for us to establish in which of their aspects the native revolutionist movements constitute simply a response to cultural contacts without borrowing the eschatological and messianic ideas of Christianity. The nativist movement, the promise of the return of ancestors and their customs, seems to constitute a response of this type. The cargo cults seem also to arise without ideological borrowing. These two movements are of the revolutionist type, but perhaps we have less proof in the case of the returning Messiah as an indigenous myth giving birth to religious activity, although this has been suggested regarding the case of the Manseren cult of Biak in New Guinea. If some revolutionist sects originate outside all Christian influence we have evidence of the wider usefulness of our categories, which are no longer culture-bound. In order to study this question, and some other connected problems, we must analyse the indigenous sects and make sure of distinguishing between their different elements. We could then link the latter to the conditions of cultural contact and to levels of social development. Köbben (1960) has begun an analysis of this type. It seems probable that in less advanced societies the possibilities of response to the outside world are limited, and that only two of them (revolutionist or thaumaturgical) constitute possibilities of original response in pre-literate societies. These two responses, it will be noted, permit considerable elements of fantasy. Both clearly existed in the history of Christianity; although the thaumaturgical response has given rise to fewer sectarian organizations as such, it has existed within the Christian tradition in cult movements of one kind or another, or as residual paganism. As a primitive position and as a transformation of the revolutionist position the introversionist sect seems only to manifest itself in certain conditions of social development. For manipulationist sects, conditions favouring their appearance seem to be those in which the religious, intellectual and educational monopoly of traditional religious functionaries has been broken, and in circumstances which make status insecurity common and social mobility possible, at least for a certain number.

References

Anon (1951), 'A visit to the Apostles and town of Aiyetoro', *Nigeria*, vol. 36.

Allen, C.H. (1951), 'Marching rule: a nativistic cult of the British Solomon Islands', *South Pacific*, vol. 5.

Balandier, G. (1955), *Sociologie actuelle de l'Afrique noire*, Presses Universitaires.

Berger, P.L. (1954), 'Sociological study of sectarianism', *Soc. Res.*, vol. 21, pp. 467–85.

Berndt, R.M. (1952), 'A cargo movement in the Eastern Central Highlands of New Guinea', *Oceania*, vol. 23, pp. 40–65 and 137–58.

Berndt, R.M. (1954), 'Reaction to contact in the Eastern Highlands of New Guinea', *Oceania*, vol. 24, pp. 190–228.

Boardman, E.P. (1951), 'Christian influence on the ideology of the Taiping rebellion', *Far Eastern Quart.*, vol. 10, pp. 115–24.

Bodrogi, T. (1951), 'Colonization and religious movements in Melanesia', *Acta Ethnograph. Acad. Scient. Hungar.*, vol. 2, pp. 259–90.

Brewster, A.B. (1922), *The Hill Tribes of Fiji*, Lippincott.

Burton, J.W. (1936), *Missionary Survey of the Pacific Islands*, World Dominion Press.

Cato, A.C. (1947), 'A new religious cult in Fiji', *Oceania*, vol. 18, pp. 146–56.

Chinnery, E.W.P., and Haddon, A.C. (1917), 'Five new religious cults in British New Guinea', *Hibbert J.*, vol. 15, pp. 448–63.

Clark, E.T. (1937), *The Small Sects in America*, Abingdon.

Comhaire, J.L. (1953), 'Religious trends in African and Afro-American urban societies', *Anthrop. Quart.*, vol. 26, pp. 95–108.

Comhaire, J.L. (1955), 'Sociétés secrètes et mouvements prophétiques au Congo belge', *Africa*, vol. 25, pp. 54–8.

Cook, L.A. (1933), 'Revolt in Africa', *J. Negro Hist.*, vol. 18, pp. 396–413.

Cunnison, I. (1951), 'A Watchtower assembly in Central Africa', *Int. Rev. Miss.*, vol. 40, pp. 456–69.

De Bruyn, J.V. (1951), 'The Manseren cult of Biak', *South Pacific*, vol. 5, pp. 1–11.

Dougall, J.W.C. (1956), 'African separatist churches', *Int. Rev. Miss.*, vol. 25, pp. 257–66.

England, R.W. (1954), 'Some aspects of Christian Science', *Amer. J. Sociol.*, vol. 59.

Firth, R. (1935), 'The theory of "cargo" cults: A note on Tikopia', *Man*, vol. 55, pp. 130–32.

Fletcher, A.C. (1891), 'The Indian Messiah', *J. Amer. Folk-Lore*, vol. 4, pp. 57–60.

Griswold, A.W. (1954), 'New thought: a cult of success', *Amer. J. Sociol.*, vol. 59.

Hunter, M. (1936), *Reaction to Conquest*, Oxford University Press.

Keesing, F.M. (1941), *The South Seas in the Modern World*, Allen and Unwin.

Köbben, A.J.F. (1960), 'Prophetic movements as an expression of social protest', *Int. Arch. Ethnograph.*, vol. 49, pp. 117–64.

Koskinen, A. (1953), 'Missionary influence as a political factor in the Pacific Islands', *Suomalaisen Tiedeakatemian Tolmituksia, Annales Academiae Scientiarum Fennicae*, Sarja Ser. B, vol. 78 (Helsinki).

Krader, L. (1956), 'A nativistic movement in Western Siberia', *Amer. Anthrop.*, vol. 58, pp. 282–92.

Lane, G.H. (1927), *Fox Pitt Rivers, The Clash of Cultures and the Contact of Race*, Routledge.

Lerrigo, P.H.J. (1922), 'The prophet movement in the Congo', *Int. Rev. Miss.*, vol. 11, pp. 270–1.

Martin, D.A. (1962), 'The denomination', *Brit. J. Sociol.*, vol. 13, pp. 1–14.

Marty, M.E. (1960), 'Sects and cults', *Ann. Amer. Acad. Polit. Soc. Scien.*, vol. 332, pp. 125–34.

Pierce Beaver, R. (1954), 'Expansion of American Foreign Missionary activity since 1945', *Miss. Res. Lib. Occas. Bull.*, vol. 5, no. 7.

Pos. H. (1950), 'The revolt of "Manseren"', *Amer. Anthrop.*, vol. 52.

Price, F.W. (1957), 'The younger churches: some facts and observations', *Miss. Res. Lib. Occas. Bull.*, vol. 8, no. 7.

Price, F.W. and Mayer, K.E. (1956), 'A study of American Protestant Missions in 1956', *Miss. Res. Lib. Occas. Bull.*, vol. 7, no. 9.

Quick, G. (1940), 'Some aspects of the African Watch Tower Movements in Northern Rhodesia', *Int. Rev. Miss.*, vol. 29, pp. 216–26.

Roux, E. (1945), *Time Longer than Rope*, Gollancz.

Schlösser, K. (1949), *Propheten in Afrika*, Limbach, Brunswick.

Shepperson, G. (1952), 'Ethiopanism and African nationalism', *Phylon*, vol. 14, pp. 9–18.

Schepperson, G. (1954), 'The politics of African Separatist Movements in British Central Africa, 1892–1916', *Africa*, vol. 24, pp. 233–46.

Simpson, G.M. (1955), 'Political cultism in West Kingston, Jamaica', *Soc. econ. Stud.*, vol. 4, pp. 133–49.

Simpson, G.M. (1956), 'Jamaican revivalist cults', *Soc. econ. Stud.*, vol. 5, pp. 321–42.

Sundkler, B.G.T. (1948), *Bantu Prophets in South Africa*, Butterworth.

Thiessey, J.C. (1955), *A Survey of World Missions*, Inter-Varsity Press.

Thompson, B. (1908), *The Fijians: A Study of the Decay of Custom*, Heinemann.

Thwaite, T. (1936), *The Seething African Pot*, Constable.

Troeltsch, E. (1931), *The Social Teaching of the Christian Churches*, Macmillan.

Wallace, A.F.C. (1956), 'Revitalization movements', *Amer. Anthropol.*, vol. 58, pp. 264–81.

Westermann, D. (1937), *Africa and Christianity*, Oxford University Press.

Williams, F.E. (1934), 'The Vailala madness in retrospect', in E.E. Evans-Pritchard *et al.*, *Essays Presented to C.G. Selleman*, Kegan Paul, pp. 36–79.

Wilson, B.R. (1958), 'The appearance and survival of sects in an evolutionary social milieu', *Arch. soc. Relig.*, vol. 5, pp. 140–50.

Wilson, B.R. (1959), 'An analysis of sect development', *Amer. soc. Rev.*, vol. 24, pp. 3–15.

Wilson, B.R. (1961), *Sects and Society*, Heinemann and California University Press.

Winks, R.W. (1953), 'The doctrine Han-Hanism', *J. Polynes. Soc.*, vol. 62, pp. 199–236.

Worsley, P. (1957), *The Trumpet Shall Sound*, McGibbon & Kee.

Yinger, J.M. (1946), *Religion in the Struggle for Power*, Duke University Press.

Yinger, J.M. (1957), *Religion, Society and the Individual*, Macmillan.

Index

Compiled by Tom Hunter